LLMs for Modern Software Delivery and DevOps

Applying Large Language Models to Software Delivery and SRE

Gu Huangliang, Zheng Qingzheng, Niu Xiaoling, Che Xin

<packt>

LLMs for Modern Software Delivery and DevOps

Portfolio Director: Kartikey Pandey
Contracting PPM: Lucy Wan
Relationship Lead: Aaron Tanna
Project Manager: Sonam Pandey
Content Engineer: Apramit Bhattacharya
Technical Editor: Simran Ali
Production Designer: Ajay Patule

First published: July 2026

Production reference: 1190626

Published by Packt Publishing Ltd.
Grosvenor House
11 St Paul's Square
Birmingham
B3 1RB, UK.

ISBN 978-1-80760-919-1

www.packtpub.com

Contributors

About the authors

Gu Huangliang is a Senior DevOps and R&D Efficiency Specialist with extensive experience in operations and development. His work focuses on enterprise IT digital transformation and implementation, and he is dedicated to building intelligent operations systems for businesses. He is currently employed at a licensed financial institution.

He is included in the China Commerce Association Expert Think Tank and serves as Deputy Director of the Think Tank Expert Committee of the National Internet Data Center Industry Technology Innovation Strategic Alliance. He is a Candidate Expert for the Jiangsu Banking and Insurance Industry Fintech Expert Committee, a Specially Appointed Expert for the Ministry of Industry and Information Technology's Enterprise Digital Transformation IOMM Committee, a Specially Appointed Expert for the China Academy of Information and Communications Technology's Trusted Cloud Standard, and a Specially Appointed Expert for the China Academy of Information and Communications Technology's Low-Code/No-Code Promotion Center. He is also a Tencent Cloud Most Valuable Professional (TVP) and an Alibaba Cloud Most Valuable Professional (MVP). He is the author of the best-selling books DevOps Authoritative Guide and Enterprise-Level DevOps Practical Cases: Continuous Delivery Edition, and a core author of the DevOps Capability Maturity Model and Enterprise IT Operations Development White Paper. He is a frequent speaker at technology summits.

Zheng Qingzheng is a Senior Researcher at the FinTech Research Center. He holds a Ph.D. in Computer Science from Durham University, UK, and an M.Sc. in Computer Software Engineering from Swansea University, UK.

He formerly served as a Technical Planning Engineer and Image Research Engineer at Huawei. His work focuses on financial big data risk control and machine vision. He has participated in the development of facial recognition, telecom CRM, and in-memory database systems. He has published three papers and holds three authorized patents.

Niu Xiaoling is Chair of the DevOps Standards Working Group and Editor of DevOps International Standards. She is a long-term researcher in DevOps, including cloud service operations management system reviews.

She has contributed to more than 20 domestic and international standards, including the Cloud Computing Service Agreement Reference Framework, Object Storage, Cloud Database, DevOps Capability Maturity Model, Y.3525 Cloud Computing, Requirements for Cloud Service Development and Operation Management, and the General Evaluation Method for Intelligent Cloud Computing Operations. She has conducted DevOps maturity assessments for more than 50 projects and has extensive experience in standards development and evaluation testing.

Che Xin is Deputy Director of the Government and Enterprise Digital Transformation Department at the China Academy of Information and Communications Technology (CAICT) Cloud Computing and Big Data Research Institute.

They are primarily engaged in technical research and transformation consulting planning in areas including the Enterprise Digital Transformation Maturity Model (IOMM), Trusted Digital Services, Integrated Cloud Platforms for Digital Infrastructure, Middleware Series, Low/No-Code, Modularization, Safe Production, and Smart Operations. Xin is responsible for developing relevant standards, conducting evaluation and testing, and organizing technical practice exchanges.

About the reviewer

Krishna Mohan Akurathi is Director of Data Science at CVS Health. Across 16 years — from consulting in retail, insurance, and healthcare to a decade at CVS spanning forecasting, personalization, and customer decision science — his work has delivered $100M+ in documented impact at $22B+ revenue scale. He has architected production ML systems (TFT, gradient boosting, autoencoders on Azure), RAG pipelines, a Snowflake MCP server, and promo/pricing agents — delivering self-service analytics against live warehouse data using Claude Enterprise. Krishna holds a Master's in Operations Research from NIT India, and serves on the HBR Advisory Council and the AI Xecutive Council, and mentors data science and ML practitioners through Boston University.

I would like to thank the editorial team at Packt for the opportunity to contribute to this project. The questions this book raises — how LLMs hold up under real production conditions — are ones I encounter every day. I hope the perspective I brought to each chapter is useful to practitioners building these systems for the first time. I want to acknowledge my team at CVS Health — their work in production AI gave me the grounding for this review.

Table of Contents

Part 2: Enterprise Readiness and Software Delivery Foundations 135

Chapter 5: Building Enterprise AI Applications with RAG and Multi-Agent Systems 137

Chapter 9: Applying Code LLMs in Software Development 305

Chapter 10: Applying LLMs in Project Management 345

Preface

Large Language Models (LLMs) have transformed natural language processing and accelerated the rise of domain-specific foundation models. Yet inside software delivery organizations, the practical story is more complex. Many enterprises are still looking for convincing, repeatable ways to make LLMs useful in production, not just in demonstrations or isolated experiments.

Over the last decade, software delivery itself has evolved significantly. DevOps improved build, deployment, and collaboration practices. DevSecOps, DataOps, NoOps, MLOps, and related practices extended this delivery ecosystem. Site Reliability Engineering renewed the focus on reliability, stability, operational rigor, and business continuity. Platform Engineering then emerged as a broader organizational approach, aiming to connect tools, workflows, and teams through a more unified, business-aware internal platform.

However, as organizations scale, the software delivery chain has also become more complex. Delivery engineers, operations teams, testers, developers, security engineers, and project managers are often required to work across an expanding range of tools, frameworks, processes, and specialized workflows. This creates a growing cognitive load. The problem is no longer only a lack of tools or features; it is the burden of learning, connecting, and operating too many fragmented systems while still being expected to deliver reliable software and business value.

LLMs do not automatically solve this problem. Adding another chatbot or standalone model interface will not, by itself, reduce tool sprawl or simplify delivery work. What is needed is an integrating platform approach: one that centralizes delivery data, curates software-delivery-specific corpora and telemetry, grounds models through retrieval and guardrails, and embeds AI assistance into the delivery platform itself. In this view, AI support must become part of real delivery work, including coding, testing, releasing, operating, securing, and coordinating projects, with measurable outcomes, governance, and safe rollback.

This book is an attempt to close the gap between model capability and delivery reality. It moves from model mechanics to enterprise readiness, and then to practical software delivery scenarios that can be evaluated and adapted.

The goal is to help you understand not only how LLMs work, but also where they can create measurable value inside software delivery organizations, and how they can be introduced without increasing complexity or risk.

Who this book is for

This book is for engineers, technical leads, and practitioners working in or around DevOps, SRE, and Platform Engineering who want to understand where LLMs fit in modern software delivery without making existing workflows heavier or harder to manage.

It is also for anyone operating along the software delivery chain, including developers, testers, security engineers, project managers, requirements and product roles, SRE and operations engineers, and delivery coordinators. If your work involves pipelines, repositories, reviews, incidents, tickets, requirements, releases, testing, security, or operational workflows, this book is intended to help you separate durable LLM-enabled practices from hype.

The book is also relevant for LLM practitioners who understand models but need to make them work within change-management, delivery, reliability, and governance constraints. It can also support academic programs and training courses focused on AI-assisted software engineering, AI-assisted delivery, or modern platform organizations.

What this book covers

Chapter 1, Understanding the Foundations of Large Language Models, traces the development of language models from early theoretical and statistical approaches to neural sequence models and LLMs. You will learn how N-gram models, HMMs, RNNs, LSTMs, and attention shaped the path toward modern large language models.

Chapter 2, Understanding the Transformer Architecture Behind Large Language Models, explains why the Transformer became the foundation of modern LLMs. You will learn how embeddings, positional encoding, self-attention, multi-head attention, feed-forward layers, residual connections, and layer normalization work together inside the Transformer architecture.

Chapter 3, Tracing the Path from Bigram Models to GPT and ChatGPT, connects the Transformer architecture to GPT-style language generation. You will learn how a simple bigram model illustrates next-token prediction, how GPT models generate text, and how training and generation techniques can be improved.

Chapter 4, Applying Efficient Fine-Tuning Techniques to LLMs, introduces the main ways pre-trained LLMs can be adapted to specific tasks and domains. You will learn about full-parameter fine-tuning, parameter-efficient fine-tuning, PEFT, LoRA, QLoRA, and practical fine-tuning workflows.

Chapter 5, Building Enterprise AI Applications with RAG and Multi-Agent Systems, Building Enterprise AI Applications with RAG and Multi-Agent Systems, shows how LLMs can be grounded in enterprise knowledge and connected to business workflows. You will learn how RAG works, how it addresses enterprise constraints such as accuracy and domain knowledge, and how multi-agent systems can coordinate more complex tasks.

Chapter 6, Building a Modern Software Delivery Foundation, Building a Modern Software Delivery Foundation, explains the delivery environment in which enterprise LLM capabilities must operate. You will learn how DevOps, Platform Engineering, and SRE support collaboration, automation, reliability, observability, and value delivery across modern software organizations.

Chapter 7, Applying LLMs in Intelligent Operations and Maintenance, Applying LLMs in Intelligent Operations and Maintenance, explores how LLMs can support operations and maintenance work. You will learn how LLMs can improve log analysis, intelligent O&M knowledge bases, ticket handling, capability evaluation, and multi-agent root cause analysis.

Chapter 8, Applying LLMs in Software Testing, examines the role of LLMs in dynamic and static software testing. You will learn how LLMs can support test generation, static analysis, vulnerability repair, deployment challenges, and the evaluation of AI-assisted testing workflows.

Chapter 9, Applying Code LLMs in Software Development, focuses on code-focused LLMs and their use in development workflows. You will learn about large code models, representative code LLMs, downstream coding tasks, code generation and completion, and agent-based approaches to project-level code generation.

Chapter 10, Applying LLMs in Project Management, shows how LLMs can support project delivery and coordination. You will learn how LLMs can assist with requirements analysis, task planning, communication, collaboration, risk management, decision support, intelligent workflows, and project management case studies.

Chapter 11, Applying LLMs in Cybersecurity, explores how LLMs can be applied to security workflows while also introducing new risks. You will learn how LLMs can support threat detection, security operations, alert triage, vulnerability repair, and the management of security risks introduced by LLM adoption.

To get the most out of this book

You do not need a research lab to use this book. You should, however, have a working intuition for how software delivery teams operate. Familiarity with delivery pipelines, code repositories, code reviews, incidents, tickets, testing workflows, operations, and security practices will help you connect the book's concepts to real organizational settings.

The book was originally developed from Chinese-language material and has been translated and adapted for a global audience, with examples and explanations adjusted where needed to make the concepts more accessible across different software delivery contexts.

The book assumes that you want to understand both the model side and the delivery side of LLM adoption. You will benefit from a basic awareness of LLM concepts such as Transformers, token budgets, fine-tuning, and Retrieval-Augmented Generation, but the early chapters introduce the necessary foundation before moving into applied delivery scenarios. If these concepts are already familiar, you may move more quickly through the foundation chapters and focus on the practice chapters.

Code examples and implementation patterns are presented so they can be adapted to mainstream software delivery stacks. When a concept depends on an infrastructure assumption, that assumption is called out. The emphasis is not on one fixed toolchain, but on helping you understand the principles, constraints, workflows, and evaluation points needed to apply LLMs responsibly in software delivery contexts.

Download the example code files

The code bundle for the book is hosted on GitHub at `https://github.com/PacktPublishing/LLMs-for-Modern-Software-Delivery-and-DevOps`. We also have other code bundles from our rich catalog of books and videos available at `https://github.com/PacktPublishing`. Check them out!

Download the color images

We also provide a PDF file that has color images of the screenshots/diagrams used in this book. You can download it here: `https://packt.link/gbp/9781807609191`.

Conventions used

There are a number of text conventions used throughout this book.

`CodeInText`: Indicates code words in text, database table names, folder names, filenames, file extensions, pathnames, dummy URLs, user input, and Twitter handles. For example: "For real applications, libraries such as `tiktoken` or `sentencepiece` can be used to implement more practical tokenization workflows."

A block of code is set as follows:

```
# Set random seed
def set_seed(seed_value=42):
```

```
    torch.manual_seed(seed_value)
    torch.cuda.manual_seed(seed_value)
    torch.cuda.manual_seed_all(seed_value)  # If using multiple GPUs
    torch.backends.cudnn.deterministic = True
    torch.backends.cudnn.benchmark = False
    np.random.seed(seed_value)
    random.seed(seed_value
```

Any command-line input or output is written as follows:

```
[2024-07-10 22:57:04][DEBUG]: == Working Agent: Researcher
[2024-07-10 22:57:04][INFO]: == Starting Task: Research the latest
technical trends related to DevOps and write
A report
```

Bold: Indicates a new term, an important word, or words that you see on the screen. For instance, words in menus or dialog boxes appear in the text like this. For example: "**GPT** stands for **Generative Pre-trained Transformer**"

> Warnings or important notes appear like this.

Get in touch

Feedback from our readers is always welcome.

General feedback: If you have questions about any aspect of this book or have any general feedback, please email us at customercare@packt.com and mention the book's title in the subject of your message.

Errata: Although we have taken every care to ensure the accuracy of our content, mistakes do happen. If you have found a mistake in this book, we would be grateful if you reported this to us. Please visit http://www.packt.com/submit-errata, click **Submit Errata**, and fill in the form.

Piracy: If you come across any illegal copies of our works in any form on the internet, we would be grateful if you would provide us with the location address or website name. Please contact us at copyright@packt.com with a link to the material.

If you are interested in becoming an author: If there is a topic that you have expertise in and you are interested in either writing or contributing to a book, please visit http://authors.packt.com/.

Share your thoughts

Once you've read *LLMs for Modern Software Delivery and DevOps*, we'd love to hear your thoughts! Scan the QR code below to go straight to the Amazon review page for this book and share your feedback.

`https://packt.link/r/1807609197`

Your review is important to us and the tech community and will help us make sure we're delivering excellent quality content.

Part 1

Foundations of Large Language Models

In this first part, you will build the technical foundation needed to understand how large language models work and how they are adapted for practical use. You will begin by tracing the evolution of language modeling from early statistical and sequence-based approaches to modern LLMs. You will then examine the Transformer architecture, including embeddings, positional encoding, attention, self-attention, and multi-head attention, before moving into GPT-style generation and ChatGPT.

This foundation also includes fine-tuning, because understanding LLMs is not complete without understanding how pre-trained models are adapted to specific tasks and domains. You will learn how techniques such as PEFT, LoRA, and QLoRA make adaptation more efficient and practical.

This part of the book includes the following chapters:

1

Understanding the Foundations of Large Language Models

Large language models (**LLMs**) did not appear suddenly. They are the result of decades of progress in natural language processing, from early theoretical models of information and probability to statistical language models, neural networks, and large-scale pre-trained systems such as BERT and GPT. Understanding this development path is important because it shows what problems earlier models tried to solve, where they were limited, and why modern LLMs represent such a major shift in how machines process language.

This chapter introduces the foundations of LLMs by tracing the evolution of language modeling techniques. You will first examine the major stages in the development of natural language processing, then explore important pre-LLM models such as N-gram models, Hidden Markov Models, RNNs, and LSTMs. Finally, you will compare HMMs and N-gram models to understand how different modeling assumptions shape the way language systems process sequences.

In this chapter, we will be covering the following main topics:

- Tracing the development of LLMs
- Exploring foundational NLP models before LLMs
- Introducing neural networks for sequence modeling
- Addressing long-sequence challenges with LSTMs

Tracing the development of LLMs

In 1775, James Watt improved the steam engine, successfully solving a core problem in the process of industrialization and ushering in a new chapter in the Industrial Revolution. In 1879, Thomas Edison invented the light bulb, bringing light to the darkness. In 1882, the world's first commercial power plant was built, laying the foundation for the modern electrical system. In 1887, Nikola Tesla developed the alternating current system. These great inventions not only changed the way people lived but also propelled societal progress.

Entering the 20th century, technology embarked on an entirely new phase. In 1946, the advent of **Electronic Numerical Integrator and Computer** (**ENIAC**) marked the beginning of the electronic computer era, thus ushering humanity into the computer age. In 1975, the appearance of the Altair 8800 brought computer technology into the personal domain for the first time, kicking off the era of the personal computer. A series of subsequent technological advancements greatly accelerated the arrival of the Information Age. In 1989, the birth of the World Wide Web made information exchange unprecedentedly convenient; in 1998, the founding of Google further fueled the rapid development of the Internet era.

After entering the 21st century, Apple released the first iPhone in 2007, swiftly heralding the era of mobile internet. This once again led to a dramatic transformation in the way people lived and how they accessed information, until 2020, when OpenAI released GPT-3 — an event that marked the full arrival of the era of artificial intelligence. The cycle has compressed from centuries to decades.

The arrival of the AI era is an important turning point in the development of human society. In this new era, whether as individuals or organizations, practitioners slow to engage will find the gap harder to close. AI models are the core element of the new era, and technology practitioners need to be thorough with their background knowledge of this technology in order to better adapt to and drive the development of the new age.

To understand how LLMs became possible, it is useful to look at the major stages of **natural language processing** (**NLP**) that came before them. Each stage introduced a different way of modeling language, moving from theoretical foundations to statistical methods, neural networks, and finally large-scale pre-trained language models.

Mapping the evolution of NLP models

Before LLMs emerged, NLP models experienced several stages of development. The following are some crucial stages.

Establishing theoretical foundations for language models

Theoretical models, represented by **Shannon's information theory**, study the information quantity and entropy of natural language. In 1948, Shannon applied **Markov process models** to natural language modeling and proposed extending the concept of entropy from thermodynamics to the field of natural language modeling.

These early theoretical ideas provided a foundation for treating language as information that could be measured and modeled. As computing resources became available, researchers began applying statistical methods to model word sequences and speech patterns more directly.

Applying statistical models to natural language processing

The representative models of this stage are the **N-gram model** and the **Hidden Markov Model (HMM)**. The N-gram model is a relatively simple statistical language model, which assumes that the probability of a word occurring depends only on the previous *N-1* words. It is used for text prediction. HMM is a statistical model for handling sequential data and is suitable for tasks such as speech recognition and machine translation.

Statistical models made language processing more practical, but they still relied heavily on fixed assumptions and manually designed probabilities. As machine learning advanced, neural network models offered a way to learn richer representations from data.

Introducing neural networks for sequence modeling

The representative models of this stage are the **Recurrent Neural Network** (**RNN**) and the **Convolutional Neural Network** (**CNN**). RNNs can handle sequential data and are suitable for tasks such as machine translation and speech recognition. CNNs can process image data and are suitable for text classification, sentiment analysis, and other tasks.

Neural network models improved the ability to process sequences and learn patterns from language, but larger datasets and greater computing power enabled a further shift. This led to the development of pre-trained language models and eventually LLMs, which could learn broad language representations from massive corpora.

Scaling toward LLMs

Representative models of this stage include **BERT** and **GPT-3**, among others. BERT is a pre-trained language model released by Google AI in 2018, and it has attracted widespread attention due to its outstanding language understanding capabilities. The advent of BERT marks the transition of the natural language processing field from traditional manual feature engineering to the deep learning era.

According to the implementation sequence of key algorithmic models, the development trajectory of natural language models is shown in *Figure 1.1*. The graph shows the history of NLP models and the required computing power from 1950 to 2020. The computational power data in *Figure 1.1* come from Wikipedia.

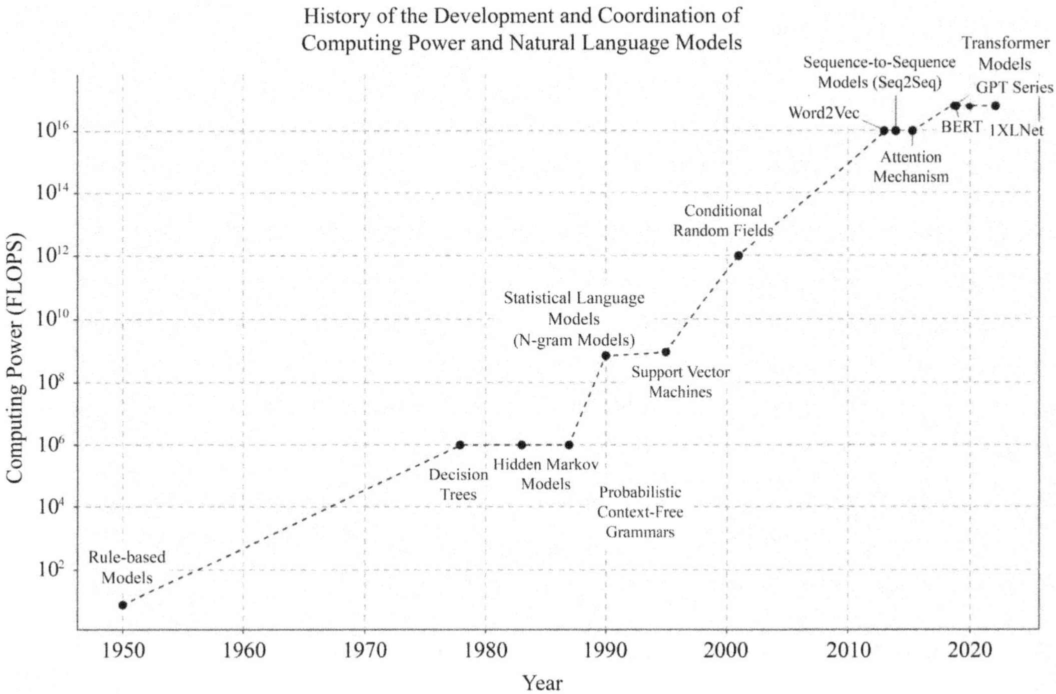

Figure 1.1: The development trajectory of natural language models

As explained above, NLP is founded on theory. With limited computing power, statistical methods were employed to model natural language. As computing power increased, neural network models were gradually applied to the field of natural language processing. With the realization of even greater computational power, LLMs emerged, marking the entrance of natural language processing into the AI era.

Although we have entered the era of LLMs, traditional natural language processing models still possess unique advantages, such as low computational resource consumption and fast response speed. In practical applications, the appropriate model should be selected based on the specific task requirements.

With this historical progression in mind, the next section looks more closely at the foundational models that shaped NLP before the rise of modern LLMs. Understanding models such as N-grams, HMMs, RNNs, and LSTMs will make it easier to see what problems LLMs were designed to overcome and why earlier approaches still matter in some practical scenarios.

Exploring foundational NLP models before LLMs

Before modern LLMs, NLP relied on simpler statistical and sequence-based models to represent language, predict words, and infer hidden patterns from observed data. This section introduces two important foundational approaches: **N-gram models**, which predict language based on observed word frequencies, and **Hidden Markov Models** (**HMM**), which use hidden states and transition probabilities to model sequences. Understanding these models helps clarify what earlier NLP systems could do well, where they were limited, and why later neural models became necessary.

Understanding N-gram models

In the field of natural language processing, the N-gram model is a relatively simple statistical language model. It is based on the **Markov assumption**, which means the probability of a word appearing depends only on the previous *N-1* words. The formula for the N-gram model is as follows:

$$P(w_n \mid w_1, w_2, \dots, w_{n-1}) = C(w_1, w_2, \dots, w_n) \,/\, C(w_1, w_2, \dots, w_{n-1})$$

In this equation, $w_1, w_2, \dots, w_n$ is a word sequence of length n, $C(w_1, w_2, \dots, w_n)$ is the number of occurrences of this sequence in the corpus, and $C(w_1, w_2, \dots, w_{n-1})$ is the number of occurrences of the previous $n-1$ words of this sequence in the corpus. The number of parameters in the N-gram model increases exponentially with N, so in practice, 2-gram or 3-gram models are usually used.

From the perspective of understanding the basic concepts, we can temporarily ignore the complex principles behind the formula and directly discuss how the N-gram model is used in practice. Suppose there is a chain composed of multiple words; the N-gram algorithm observes units made up of every N consecutive words in that chain to predict which word may appear in the next group of words. This is where the name "N-gram" comes from, with "gram" referring to a word.

For example, when you say the phrase "I like to eat," and there is previously a phrase like "I like to eat apples," the N-gram model may predict the next word to be "apples" because in previous data, "apples" often appears after "I like to eat." This is why the N-gram model is used for text prediction.

The design of the N-gram model is quite straightforward: it is similar to a large table that records the frequency of different word combinations. For a 2-gram (i.e., **Bigram**), the table records the probability of every pair of words; for a 3-gram (i.e., **Trigram**), it records the probability for every three-word combination, and so on. When designing this model, you only need to determine the value of *N*, that is, how many words to consider as a group to predict the next word, then collect data and fill in the probability table.

Although the N-gram model is somewhat outdated, it still performs well in certain specific scenarios. For example, in some vertical domains, the N-gram model can achieve good results through training on large amounts of data. In resource-limited situations, the N-gram model can achieve satisfactory results with less training data. In scenarios that require a fast response time, the N-gram model can deliver good results with relatively little computation.

Applying N-gram models in practical scenarios

Because N-gram models are simple, fast, and based on frequency statistics, they remain useful in tasks where lightweight prediction is more important than deep contextual understanding. The following examples show where this type of model can still be applied effectively.

Spelling check and error correction

The N-gram model can be used to predict the probability of word sequences, thereby supporting tasks such as speech recognition and machine translation. By comparing the probabilities of different word sequences, it is possible to infer which sequence is more likely to be the user's intended input. For example, if a user types "spel checker", the N-gram model can determine that the sequence "spell checker" is more common than "spel checker", thus suggesting the correct spelling.

So, in spelling correction, the model compares the likelihood of different word sequences and selects the one that appears more probable based on previous data. A similar principle can also be applied to simple text generation, where the model predicts likely next words from recent input.

Text generation

Although deep learning models have made significant progress in text generation, the N-gram model still has practical applications in certain simple scenarios or resource-constrained situations. For instance, in predictive text functions for keyboard applications or auto-reply for simple chatbots, the N-gram model can quickly generate text suggestions based on previous inputs.

Beyond these examples, the main strengths and limitations of N-gram models can be summarized through their key characteristics.

Characteristics of N-gram models

The above examples show how N-gram models use frequency patterns for lightweight prediction. Their main strengths and limitations can be summarized through the following characteristics:

- **Prediction based on frequency statistics**: The N-gram model predicts the next word according to the occurrence probability of lexical sequences. The model assumes that the appearance of the current word depends only on the previous *N-1* words.
- **The N-gram model is stateless**: In the N-gram model, there is no explicit definition of "state"; the model directly operates on the observed sequences (such as words in text). Each part of the sequence is considered independently.
- **Simplicity and computational efficiency**: The design and implementation of the N-gram model are relatively simple, and computational efficiency is high, but as *N* increases, the model's size and complexity grow dramatically.

N-gram models work directly with observed word sequences and use frequency statistics to predict what may come next. Hidden Markov Models take a different approach: they assume that an observed sequence is generated by an underlying sequence of hidden states. This makes HMMs useful for tasks where the system must infer something not directly visible from the data that can be observed.

Understanding Hidden Markov Models

Apart from the N-gram model based on statistical thinking, the **Hidden Markov Model** (**HMM**) is also an important model in natural language processing. The basic idea of HMM is to assume that the observed sequence is generated by an unobservable state sequence, and the transitions of the state sequence follow a Markov chain. The formula of HMM is as follows:

$$P(O \mid I) = \sum_{Q} P(O|Q)P(Q|I)$$

In this equation, $P(Q/I)$ is the probability of the **state sequence** Q under condition *I*, and $P(O/Q)$ is the probability of the **observed sequence** *O* given the state sequence Q. The purpose of the summation is to compute the probability of the observed sequence *O* under all possible state sequences Q. The parameters of HMM include the state transition probability matrix, observation probability matrix, and initial state probability vector. The training process of HMM usually uses the Baum-Welch algorithm, and the decoding process generally uses the Viterbi algorithm.

The above formulas and algorithms may seem rather abstract, but you can better understand the usage of HMM from practical application perspectives.

Applying HMMs in practical scenarios

The idea of hidden states becomes easier to understand through practical examples. In each case, the model observes available evidence and uses it to infer an underlying condition or intention that cannot be seen directly.

Weather forecasting

Imagine you are an ancient meteorologist who cannot directly know whether tomorrow's weather will be sunny, cloudy, or rainy. However, you can infer tomorrow's weather by observing natural phenomena, such as bird behavior, wind direction, and the shape of clouds. In this scenario, tomorrow's weather (sunny, cloudy, rainy) belongs to the hidden states, as you cannot directly access it; whereas the behaviors of birds, wind direction, and cloud formations are observable states, as these can be directly observed. HMM can help you predict tomorrow's weather (hidden state) based on the observed natural phenomena (observable states). By learning from historical data, HMM understands the transition probabilities between different weather states (for example, the probability that a sunny day turns into a cloudy day) as well as the probability of observing certain natural phenomena under specific weather conditions (such as the probability of seeing specific bird behaviors on a Sunny day). Therefore, even if you cannot directly observe tomorrow's weather, you can still make the most likely prediction based on today's observations.

Weather forecasting illustrates the general idea of hidden-state inference: the model uses visible clues to estimate an unseen condition. A similar idea can be applied to text input, where the system observes what the user has typed and infers the most likely intended continuation.

Intelligent recommendations

When using the keyboard app on a smartphone and you start typing "I want to eat," the keyboard automatically suggests possible words for you, such as "apple," "pizza," or "ice cream." In this context, the keyboard app uses HMM to predict which word you are most likely to type next. In this example, the sequence of words you actually intend to enter (like "I want to eat pizza") belongs to the hidden states, because the keyboard app cannot directly access your thoughts, while the words you have actually typed ("I want to eat") are the observable states, which the app can directly obtain. By analyzing large amounts of text data, HMM learns the transition probabilities between words (for example, the probability that "I want to eat" is followed by "pizza") as well as the probability that the next word appears given a sequence. Therefore, even though the app does not know your exact intention, it can use your input and the learned language model to recommend the most suitable word for you.

N-gram models and HMMs are both effective tools for processing sequence data, widely used in NLP and other fields. Although there are certain similarities between them, they have significant differences in theoretical foundations and applications. HMMs focus on state transition probabilities and the probability of observations given a state. By analyzing observed data, HMMs infer the sequence of hidden states that cannot be directly observed and are commonly used in application scenarios such as weather prediction and text input.

Characteristics of HMMs

From these examples, we can identify the features that distinguish HMMs from simpler sequence models:

- **State-based and transitions:** HMM is a state-based probabilistic model, where the sequence of states is hidden and cannot be directly observed. The model infers these hidden states from the observed sequence (such as words or phonemes).
- **HMMs have states:** HMMs define hidden states and the transition probabilities between these states. Each state is associated with a set of possible observations, which are defined by an observation probability distribution.
- **Complexity and powerful modeling capability:** HMMs can model the complex processes underlying observed sequences. Although their training and inference are more complex than N-gram models, they are able to capture deeper sequential dependencies.

N-gram models and HMMs both process sequential data, but they differ in how they represent that data. N-gram models work directly with observed word sequences, while HMMs separate observed signals from hidden states. The next section compares these two approaches in terms of observations, states, dependencies, and typical application areas.

Comparing HMMs and N-gram models

The main theoretical differences between HMM and N-gram models are as follows:

- **Observations and states:** N-gram models act directly on the observed sequence, whereas HMMs distinguish between the observed sequence and the hidden state sequence.
- **Dependencies:** The dependencies in N-gram models are relatively simple and limited to a fixed length (*N-1*), while the state transitions in HMMs can capture longer-term dependencies, and the model structure allows for more flexible sequential dependency modeling.

- **Range of application:** Due to these differences, HMMs are generally used for more complex tasks, such as speech recognition or sequence alignment in bioinformatics, where the model needs to infer underlying structures behind observed data. N-gram models, on the other hand, are more suitable for tasks that directly predict based on sequential data, such as text generation or simpler language models.

N-gram models and HMMs show how earlier NLP systems handled sequences through frequency statistics, hidden states, and transition probabilities. However, these approaches relied on fixed assumptions and could not learn flexible contextual representations directly from large amounts of data. Neural network models introduced a new direction by learning sequence patterns from data, which is the focus of the next section.

Introducing neural networks for sequence modeling

Early developments of statistical models only considered frequency statistics and did not fully take into account the temporal relationships in sequence data. HMMs introduced the concept of state transition probabilities, thereby gaining a preliminary ability to predict based on state changes. However, the state transition probabilities in HMMs are fixed and cannot be dynamically adjusted based on the temporal dependencies in sequence data. For time series processing tasks, such as language modeling, speech recognition, or any form of time series analysis, the stateless nature of HMMs limits their effectiveness, as processing sequence data often relies on contextual information. The design inspiration for **Recurrent Neural Networks (RNNs)** comes from the way the human brain processes sequential information, especially its ability to maintain information states through time. By introducing recurrence, RNNs are able to retain information in their internal states, enabling them to dynamically process varying sequence lengths and capture temporal dependencies in time series data. This structure allows RNNs to pass information from the past to the current task, resulting in more effective learning and prediction. The basic structure of an RNN is shown in *Figure 1.2*.

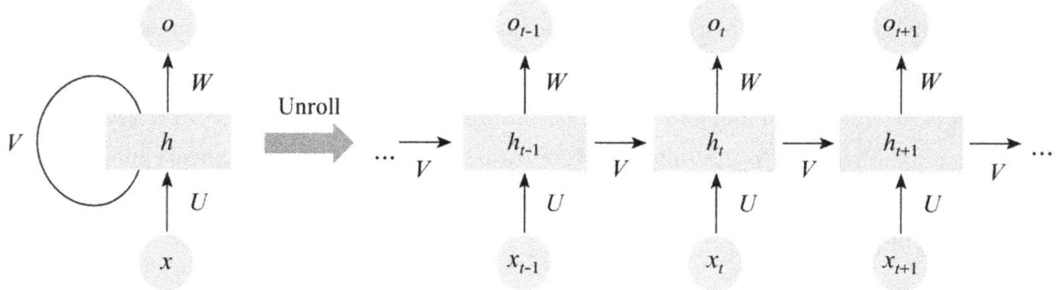

Figure 1.2: Basic structure of an RNN

Figure 1.2 shows a simple RNN structure, illustrating three consecutive time steps as an RNN processes sequence data.

- x_t denotes the input at time step *t*. This is the current element of the sequence received by the network.
- *h* represents the hidden layer of the network, which is the core of the RNN. The hidden layer can transmit information between different time steps, thereby retaining information from previous inputs.
- h_{t-1}, h_t, h_{t+1} respectively represent the hidden states at time steps *t-1*, *t*, and *t+1*. Each hidden state h_t is calculated based on the previous step's hidden state h_{t-1} and the current input x_t.
- *o* denotes the output layer, which generates output at each time step.
- o_{t-1}, o_t, o_{t+1} denote the outputs at time steps *t-1*, *t*, and *t+1*, respectively. The output is usually computed based on the current time step's hidden state h_t.

The function of an RNN is to process sequence data, making it particularly suitable for tasks such as time series analysis, speech recognition, and language modeling. By maintaining hidden states, RNNs can capture the temporal dependencies in sequences, thereby generating or predicting the next element in the sequence. This structure enables RNNs to take previous contextual information into account for more accurate predictions in sequential tasks.

Although RNNs improved on earlier statistical models by maintaining information across time steps, their recurrent structure also introduced training difficulties. These limitations become especially clear when RNNs process long sequences, where gradients must pass through many repeated time steps during training.

Identifying the limitations of RNNs

RNNs have two major architectural limitations:

- **Vanishing gradient:** RNNs are prone to the vanishing gradient problem during training. This occurs because the gradients of RNNs are computed through **BackPropagation Through Time (BPTT)**, and during backpropagation, the gradient is repeatedly multiplied by a value less than 1, causing the gradient to gradually disappear.
- **Exploding Gradient:** RNNs are also susceptible to the exploding gradient problem during training. This happens because the gradients are calculated through backpropagation through time, and in this process, the gradients are continually multiplied by a value greater than 1, causing the gradients to rapidly explode.

These problems are mainly caused by the recurrent connections in the RNN structure and the use of saturated activation functions such as `tanh` or `sigmoid`. In long sequences, as gradients are backpropagated to earlier layers, the chain rule is applied multiple times, causing the gradients to be multiplied by a series of weight matrices and accumulated over multiple time steps. If the values in these weight matrices are less than 1, the gradients will gradually decay, leading to vanishing gradients; if the values are greater than 1, the gradients will grow rapidly, resulting in exploding gradients.

These training challenges made it difficult for standard RNNs to retain useful information over long sequences. LSTMs were introduced to address this problem by adding a memory cell and gating mechanisms that control how information is stored, updated, and passed forward through time.

Addressing long-sequence challenges with LSTMs

LSTM (**Long Short-Term Memory**) networks are a special type of **RNN**, specifically designed to solve the problems of **gradient vanishing** and **gradient explosion** that occur when RNNs process long sequence data. LSTM addresses these issues by introducing key structures. *Figure 1.3* shows a simple internal structure of an LSTM.

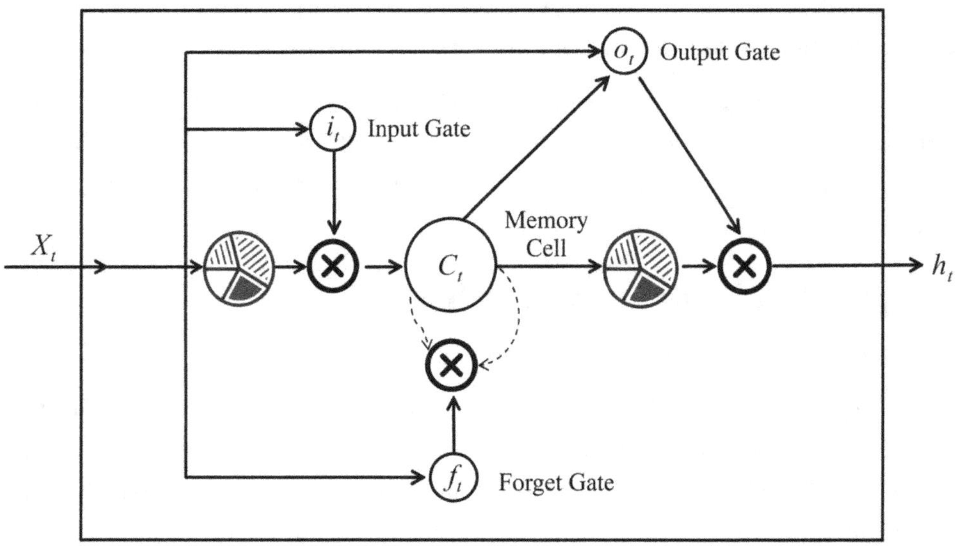

Figure 1.3: Internal structure of LSTM

To understand how LSTMs address the limitations of standard RNNs, it is useful to examine the internal components that control memory over time. The memory cell and its gates determine what information is retained, updated, forgotten, and passed forward through the sequence.

Explaining the LSTM memory cell and gates

The core of LSTM is a structure called the **memory cell**, which can retain information over long sequence data. The memory cell consists of an internal state called the **cell state** and an external state called the **hidden state**. The cell state can transmit information between time steps, thus maintaining memory of previous inputs. The hidden state is calculated based on the current input and the hidden state from the previous time step. The memory cell of the LSTM also includes three gates: **forget gate**, **input gate**, and **output gate**. These gates control the updating of the cell state and the output of the hidden state, allowing LSTMs to capture temporal dependencies in long sequence data:

- **Forget gate**: Applies a sigmoid function to a linear transformation of the cell state from the previous time step and the current time step's input to compute the forget probability. This is then multiplied element-wise to decide which information to forget from the cell state.
- **Input gate**: Uses sigmoid and tanh functions to control which information to update and how to update it, combining the previous time step's cell state and the current time step's input to form a new cell state.
- **Output gate**: Uses a sigmoid function to perform a linear transformation of the current time step's cell state to determine the output probability, which is then multiplied element-wise to decide which information to output.

The roles of the forget gate, input gate, and output gate are not just to "decide" what operations to perform on certain information, but rather to control the flow of information via learned weights.

In addition to introducing the gating mechanism, LSTM also implements other improvements such as **peephole connections** and **coupled forget gates**:

- **Peephole connections:** Through peephole connections, the forget gate can directly access the memory cell state C_t at the current time step to decide how much information to forget, thereby controlling the information flow more precisely.
- **Coupled forget gates** allow for more effective handling of noise in the input sequence. A typical application scenario is the "machine translation task." LSTM can remember the semantics and structure of sentences in the source language and retain this information during translation, thus generating more accurate translation results.

These mechanisms improved the ability of recurrent models to preserve information over longer sequences, but they did not remove all practical limitations. Researchers therefore proposed related architectures and extensions that made recurrent sequence models more efficient, more context-aware, and better suited to complex language tasks.

Connecting LSTM variants to attention

LSTM also has some issues in practical applications, for which researchers have proposed several improved models. *Figure 1.4* shows three branch models of LSTM:

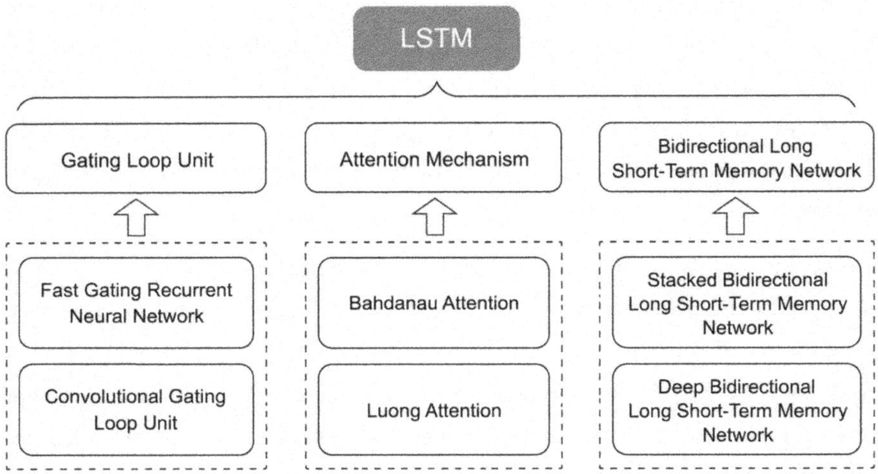

Figure 1.4: Three branch models of LSTM

The three important branches of LSTM are described as follows:

- **Gated Recurrent Unit**: A simplified version of LSTM with fewer parameters and faster training speed, suitable for scenarios that require higher speed and efficiency, such as speech recognition.
- **Attention Mechanism**: Enables the model to focus on the parts of the input sequence most relevant to the current output, suitable for tasks like text summarization and machine translation.
- **Bidirectional Long Short-Term Memory Network**: Able to process sequence data by simultaneously utilizing both past and future information, suitable for scenarios that require modeling global dependencies in the input sequence, such as sentiment analysis and text classification.

Among these branches, the attention mechanism became especially important. It allowed sequence models to focus on the parts of the input that were most relevant to the current output, improving performance on tasks such as summarization and machine translation. This idea was later developed further in the Transformer architecture, where attention became the central mechanism for processing language.

Summary

You now have a foundational understanding of how LLMs evolved and how earlier NLP techniques led to modern AI systems.

LLMs are the result of a long technological progression—from early theoretical models and statistical approaches like N-gram and Hidden Markov Models, to neural network architectures such as RNNs and LSTMs, and eventually to modern deep-learning-based language models like BERT and GPT.

You have learned the core principles, characteristics, and applications of key language modeling techniques, as well as the theoretical differences between statistical and neural approaches. By understanding these foundations, you are better prepared to grasp how modern LLMs work and how they fit into the broader evolution of artificial intelligence and natural language processing.

With this foundational understanding of how natural language processing evolved, you are now ready to explore the architecture that powers today's most advanced AI systems. In the next chapter, we will examine the Transformer model, the cornerstone of modern LLMs, and learn how mechanisms such as attention, word embeddings, and positional encoding enable machines to process and understand language effectively.

2

Understanding the Transformer Architecture Behind Large Language Models

In the field of modern **natural language processing**, with the rapid development of **deep learning** technology, traditional sequence models such as **RNN** and **LSTM** have gradually exposed efficiency and performance bottlenecks, especially when dealing with long-distance dependencies. The serial computation characteristic of these models leads to inefficiency in both training and inference processes. To address this issue, the Google AI team proposed the **Transformer** model in 2017. This groundbreaking innovation has completely changed the way sequential data is processed. By introducing the **self-attention mechanism**, the Transformer model not only overcomes the limitations of traditional models but also lays the foundation for the future of natural language processing. Today, the latest **large language models** are all built on this architecture. An in-depth study of the principles and applications of the Transformer model is not only key to understanding contemporary natural language processing technology but also an important step for the future development of **artificial intelligence**.

We will be covering the following main topics:

- Tracing the origins of the transformer model
- Understanding the core principles of the transformer architecture
- Representing text with word embeddings
- Encoding word order with positional information
- Explaining the attention mechanism

- Implementing transformer self-attention
- Exploring the design of multi-head attention
- Assembling the transformer architecture

Tracing the origins of the transformer model

Models represented by **RNNs** and **LSTMs** perform excellently in handling sequential data. However, due to their serial computing characteristics, they are inefficient during training and inference. The fundamental reason lies in the processing logic of **RNN** and **LSTM** models, where the output at each time step depends not only on the current input but also on the output of the previous time step. This means that the output for all previous time steps must be computed before calculating the output at the current time step.

Moreover, **RNN** models struggle with **long-distance dependencies**, as issues such as vanishing or exploding gradients make it difficult for the model to learn such dependencies. **LSTM** models alleviate the problems of vanishing or exploding gradients by introducing **memory gate mechanisms**, enabling them to handle long-distance dependencies more effectively.

To address this issue, the Google AI team proposed the **Transformer model** in 2017, a deep learning model designed for processing sequential data. The introduction of the **Transformer** marked a shift in the field of **natural language processing** from traditional models such as **RNN**, **LSTM**, and **GRU** to a new era of deep learning models capable of parallel training. Currently, the most popular large language models are all built based on the **Transformer model**. Therefore, understanding the basic principles of the **Transformer model** is crucial for mastering the working mechanisms and application scenarios of large language models. To understand why the Transformer became the foundation of modern large language models, it is useful to look next at the core principles of its architecture: how it represents input sequences, how attention captures relationships between tokens, and how the encoder and decoder work together to process language.

Understanding the core principles of the transformer architecture

The paper *Attention is All You Need* is the pioneering work of the Transformer model, proposing a brand-new sequence modeling method—the **Self-Attention Mechanism. Self-attention** is a technique used to capture dependencies within input sequences, allowing the establishment of long-range dependencies between different positions. Its core lies in calculating a weight for each position in the input sequence, reflecting the dependency of that position with other positions.

This mechanism enables the model to capture long-range dependencies between different positions, thereby better handling dependencies in sequential data. The architecture of the model is shown in *Figure 2.1*.

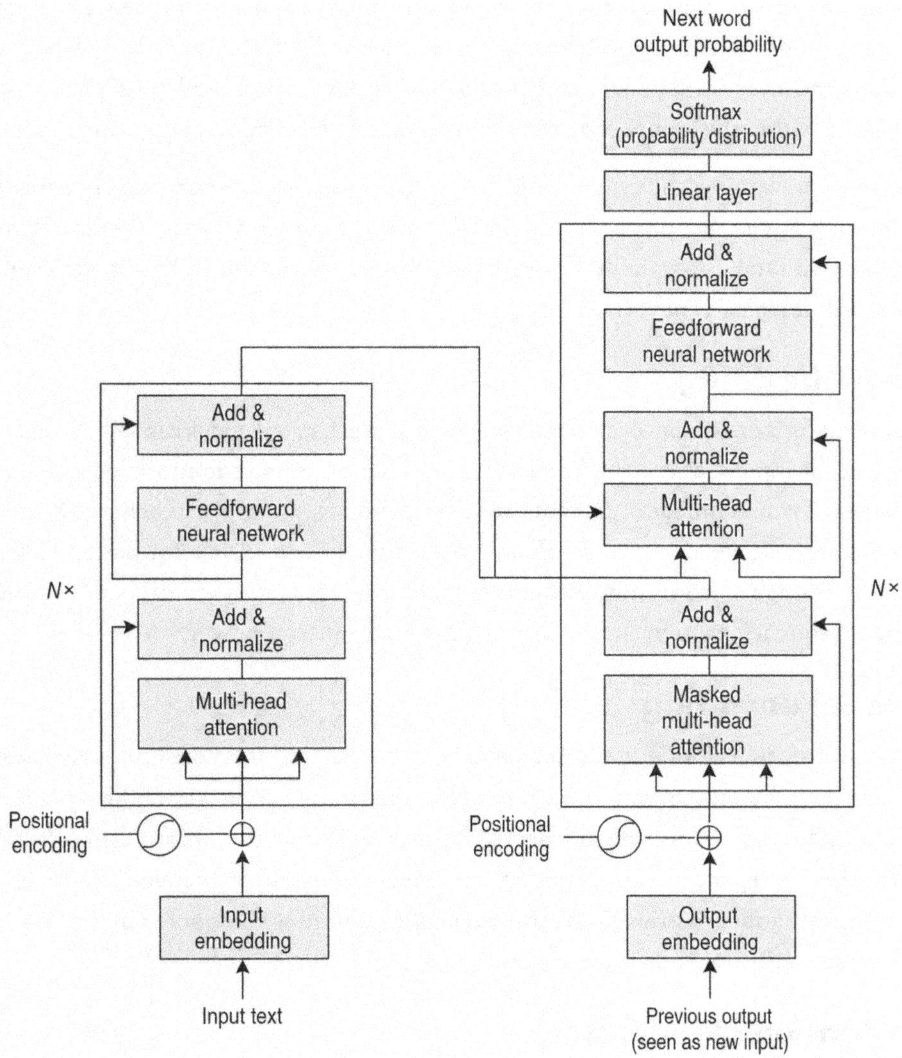

Figure 2.1: Architecture of the Transformer model

The **Transformer model** consists of an **encoder** and a **decoder**. The encoder is made up of multiple stacked identical layers, each including a **Multi-Head Attention Mechanism** and a **Feed-Forward Neural Network**. The decoder is also composed of multiple stacked identical layers, each comprising a multi-head attention mechanism, a feed-forward neural network, and an encoder-decoder attention mechanism. The encoder and decoder are connected via residual connections and layer normalization. This structural design of the model can effectively capture dependencies within the input sequence, thus enhancing the expressive power of the model.

To understand how this architecture works in practice, it is useful to break the Transformer into the main components that process input tokens, preserve sequence order, calculate contextual relationships, and stabilize training. The success of the Transformer model relies on the following seven key technological innovations.

Word embedding

Word embedding is one of the core technologies of the Transformer model, capable of transforming each word in the input sequence into a vector to represent the semantic information of that word. The core idea of **word embedding** is that the model generates a vector for each word in the input sequence, and these vectors are combined to represent the semantic information of the input sequence. The design of **word embedding** allows the model to better capture the semantic features in the input sequence, thereby improving the model's expressive power.

Positional encoding

Since the Transformer model does not contain any recurrent relationships associated with position, it requires a method to represent the positional information within the input sequence. **Positional Encoding** is a technique used to represent the position information in the input sequence, capable of generating a position vector for each position in the sequence to express its positional information. **Positional encoding** is an indispensable component of the Transformer model, compensating for its lack of a recursive structure.

Self-attention mechanism

The **self-attention mechanism** is the core of the Transformer model. Its core idea is that for each position in the input sequence, the model calculates a weight to represent the dependency relationship between this position and other positions. This mechanism enables the model to capture long-range dependencies between different positions, thus better understanding the dependency structure in sequential data.

Multi-head attention mechanism

The **multi-head attention mechanism** is an extension of the self-attention mechanism, capable of capturing dependencies in the input sequence more effectively. Its core idea is that the model computes multiple different self-attention scores and merges these scores to represent the dependencies between different positions in the input sequence. The robustness and scalability of the multi-head attention mechanism enhance the stability of the model and make it extensible to other types of attention mechanisms.

Feedforward neural network

The **feedforward neural network** is another core component of the Transformer model, capable of performing nonlinear transformations on each position of the input sequence. The core idea of the feedforward neural network is to perform nonlinear transformations on each position of the input sequence and integrate these transformation results to represent the feature information of the input sequence. The flexibility of the feedforward neural network allows it to be combined with other types of network layers to achieve more complex functions.

Residual connection

Residual connection is one of the core designs in the Transformer model and can improve the training efficiency of the model. Its core idea is that the model adds the input and output of each position in the input sequence, and uses the result as the input to the next layer. This design enables the model to better capture the feature information in the input sequence, thereby enhancing training efficiency.

Layer normalization

Layer normalization is one of the core techniques in the Transformer model and can improve the training efficiency of the model. Its core idea is that the model normalizes each position in the input sequence and uses the normalized result as the input to the next layer. This design is widely used in various sub-layers of both the encoder and decoder to enhance the model's capability of handling sequences of different lengths and its generalization performance.

To understand how this architecture works in practice, it is useful to break the Transformer into the main components that process input tokens, preserve sequence order, calculate contextual relationships, and stabilize training.

Representing text with word embeddings

Neural networks cannot process raw text directly, so text must first be converted into numerical representations. Word embeddings provide a way to represent words as dense vectors that can capture semantic relationships between them. This section first explains why simple encoding methods such as one-hot encoding are limited, then shows how word embeddings can be learned through a small neural network example and visualized in a two-dimensional space.

Before examining how word embeddings learn semantic relationships, it is useful to begin with the simplest question: how can words be represented as numbers at all?

Converting text into numerical representations

One simple method is to use **One-Hot encoding.** One-Hot encoding is a technique that converts text data into numerical data, enabling each word in the input sequence to be transformed into a vector to represent its semantics. The core idea of One-Hot encoding is that the model generates a vector for each word in the input sequence and then combines these vectors to represent the semantics of the input sequence.

We can explain the principle of **One-Hot encoding** with an example. Suppose we have a vocabulary where each word has a number, and each word can be represented by a vector in which each dimension corresponds to a word, as shown in *Figure 2.2*.

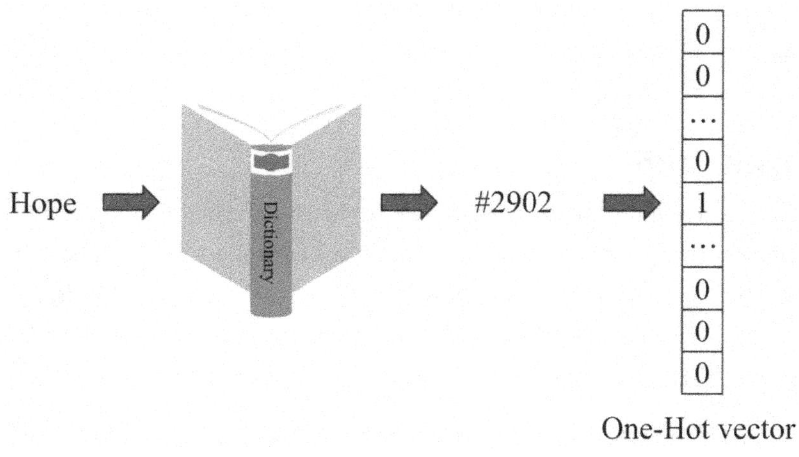

Figure 2.2: Example of the concept of converting text to an encoded representation

This method has some limitations in that it cannot effectively capture the semantic relationships between words, as it only processes words independently and does not consider similarities between words.

To address this problem, we can use **word embedding** techniques. Words with similar meanings are closer in the word embedding space, while words with different meanings are farther apart.

Word embedding technology maps each word into a continuous vector space so that the semantic relationships between words can be captured more accurately. For example, words with similar meanings are closer together in the word embedding space, while words with dissimilar meanings are farther apart. Suppose we have a simple text corpus containing only the following content:

I like raising dogs.

He likes raising cats.

He likes planting trees.

After preprocessing the text, the vocabulary obtained is: "I" "like" "raising" "dogs" "he" "cats" "planting" "trees." We can use word embedding techniques to convert these words into vectors and visualize these vectors in a two-dimensional space, as shown in *Figure 2.3*.

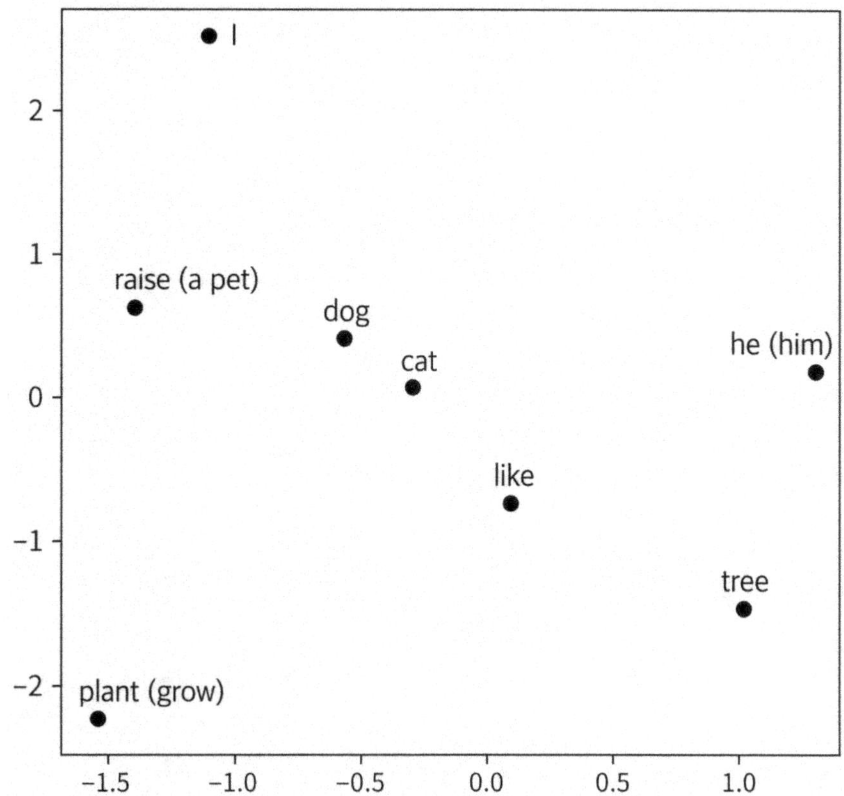

Figure 2.3: Schematic diagram of word embedding mapped to 2D space

Although one-hot encoding can represent words numerically, it treats each word as independent and cannot capture similarity between words. Word embeddings address this limitation by learning dense vector representations in which related words can appear closer together in vector space.

How do word embeddings achieve this effect

We can regard word embedding as a learning task, constructing a probabilistic prediction model for words using neural network models. To see how this works in practice, the following example builds a small word embedding model from a simple English corpus. The first step is to prepare the environment, create the sample dataset, build the vocabulary, and convert word pairs into training examples.

Environment preparation and data initialization

The following code demonstrates the basic data processing flow for word embeddings:

```
import torch
import torch.nn as nn
import torch.optim as optim
import matplotlib.pyplot as plt
import random
import numpy as np

# Set random seed
def set_seed(seed_value=42):
    torch.manual_seed(seed_value)
    torch.cuda.manual_seed(seed_value)
    torch.cuda.manual_seed_all(seed_value)  # If using multiple GPUs
    torch.backends.cudnn.deterministic = True
    torch.backends.cudnn.benchmark = False
    np.random.seed(seed_value)
    random.seed(seed_value)

set_seed(42)  # Call the function and set the seed

# Create a dataset from sentences
raw_text_list = [
    'I like cats',
    'he likes dogs',
```

```
    'he plants trees'
]

# Split sentences into word groups
word_list = [sentence.split() for sentence in raw_text_list]

# Flatten the word list into one large list
raw_text = [word for sentence in word_list for word in sentence]

vocab = set(raw_text)
vocab_size = len(vocab)

word_to_ix = {word: i for i, word in enumerate(vocab)}
ix_to_word = {i: word for i, word in enumerate(vocab)}

# Create data pairs, each containing the current word and the next word
data = []
for sentence in word_list:
    for i in range(len(sentence) - 1):
        context = sentence[i]
        target = sentence[i + 1]
        data.append((context, target))
```

The above code covers the following aspects:

- **Data Processing**: The raw text is split into words and converted into a series of (current word, next word) pairs. These pairs serve as the model's input and output (target), and are used to analyze the probability distribution of each word and the next word during model training.
- **Vocabulary**: All unique words form a **vocabulary**; each word is assigned a unique index.
- **Random Seed**: Set the random seed to ensure reproducibility of the results. This is important because in deep learning, setting the **random seed** guarantees that the model's training results are reproducible. However, since our dataset is too simple and may be affected by different programming system environments, you may get different results during actual testing.

After the dataset and vocabulary have been prepared, the next step is to define the neural network that will learn the word embeddings. The model begins with an embedding layer, then uses linear layers and an activation function to predict the next word from the current word.

Model definition

- **Embedding Layer:** The first layer of the model converts word indices into dense vectors of fixed size. These vectors are learnable and will be updated during training to better capture the semantic relationships between words.
- **Linear Layers and Activation Function:** The embedding vectors pass through two linear layers and a **ReLU activation function** in sequence, forming the model's hidden layers to enhance the model's nonlinear expressive capability.
- **Output Layer:** The final linear layer maps the output of the hidden layers to a vector with the same size as the vocabulary. This vector is transformed into a probability distribution using the `log_softmax` function, representing the probability of each word in the vocabulary being the next word, given the current word.

```
class Model(nn.Module):
    def __init__(self, vocab_size, embed_size):
        super(Model, self).__init__()
        self.embeddings = nn.Embedding(vocab_size, embed_size)
        self.linear1 = nn.Linear(embed_size, 128)
        self.linear2 = nn.Linear(128, 64)
        self.linear3 = nn.Linear(64, vocab_size)
        self.activation = nn.ReLU()

    def forward(self, inputs):
        embeds = self.embeddings(inputs)
        out = self.activation(self.linear1(embeds))
        out = self.activation(self.linear2(out))
        out = self.linear3(out)
        log_probs = nn.functional.log_softmax(out, dim=1)
        return log_probs

# Parameters
EMBEDDING_DIM = 2
```

Once the model structure has been defined, it can be trained on the word-pair data. During training, the model compares its predicted next-word distribution with the actual next word, calculates the loss, and updates the embedding vectors through backpropagation.

Training process

For each (current word, next word) pair, the current word's index is used as input, and the model's forward pass generates the probability distribution of the next word. Using the negative log likelihood loss function (`NLLLoss`), the model's predictions are compared with the actual next word to calculate the loss value. Through backpropagation and gradient descent (using the **SGD optimizer**), model parameters (including embedding vectors) are adjusted to reduce the loss.

```
# Create model
model = Model(vocab_size, EMBEDDING_DIM)
loss_function = nn.NLLLoss()
optimizer = optim.SGD(model.parameters(), lr=0.05)

# Train model
for epoch in range(3000):
    total_loss = 0
    for context, target in data:
        context_idx = torch.tensor([word_to_ix[context]], dtype=torch.
long)
        model.zero_grad()
log_probs = model(context_idx)
loss = loss_function(log_probs, torch.tensor([word_to_ix[target]],
                                          dtype=torch.long))
loss.backward()
optimizer.step()
total_loss += loss.item()

if epoch % 50 == 0:  # Print the loss value once every 50 epochs
    print(f'Epoch {epoch}, Loss: {total_loss}')
```

After training, the learned embedding vectors can be inspected visually. Plotting the vectors in two-dimensional space helps show whether the model has learned useful relationships between words in the small training corpus.

Visualization of word embeddings

After training is completed, extract the **embedding vector** for each word and visualize them in a two-dimensional space. The positions of these embedding vectors in space should reflect the **semantic relationships** between words, such as similar words being mapped to locations close to each other.

```
# Get word embeddings and plot
embeddings = model.embeddings.weight.data.numpy()
plt.figure(figsize=(8, 8))

for i, word in ix_to_word.items():
    plt.scatter(embeddings[i][0], embeddings[i][1])
    plt.annotate(
        word,
        xy=(embeddings[i][0], embeddings[i][1]),
        xytext=(5, 2),
        textcoords='offset points',
        ha='right',
        va='bottom'
    )

plt.show()
```

The above code is primarily used to illustrate the main workflow of designing and training a **word embedding model**. It demonstrates the fundamental principles and training process of word embedding models from an experimental perspective. In practical applications, the training process for word embedding models is more complex. For example, there are multiple details in this example that can be further optimized:

- **Data Preprocessing Stage**: The data preprocessing stage ignores issues such as how to handle **stop words** and **punctuation**. **Tokenization** for large blocks of text is not demonstrated.
- **Model Training Process**: In the **model training process**, this example passes the index of a single word (via `context_idx`). However, when dealing with **natural language processing** tasks, especially when using embedding layers, it is common to process a batch of data rather than a single data point. This approach can improve training efficiency and is also the data processing method expected by most deep learning frameworks. For demonstration purposes, the example handles a single data point, but this is not best practice in real-world scenarios.

  The model training process uses a simple **SGD optimizer**. In practical applications, more sophisticated optimizers such as **Adam** or **RMSprop** may be used. These optimizers typically converge faster and can more effectively handle issues such as **vanishing or exploding gradients**.

> Typically, the training process also includes a **validation step** for evaluating the model's performance on unseen data, thereby monitoring and preventing **overfitting**. This part is not covered in this example.

Word embeddings allow the Transformer model to represent the meaning of tokens as numerical vectors, but they do not by themselves tell the model where each token appears in a sequence. Since word order is essential for understanding language, the next section introduces positional encoding, which adds sequence-position information to the token representations.

Encoding word order with positional information

Positional encoding is a key design in the Transformer model that allows it to process sequence order without relying on recurrence or convolution. Without positional information, the Transformer would treat the input as a set of tokens and would not be able to distinguish where each token appears in a sentence. This could cause the model to misunderstand sentences where word order changes the meaning, such as "He fights the tiger" and "The tiger fights him."

Positional encoding addresses this problem by adding position information to the token embeddings before they are processed by the self-attention mechanism. As a result, the model can use both the meaning of each token and its position in the sequence when learning sentence structure and context.

The original Transformer paper, *Attention Is All You Need*, used sinusoidal positional encoding. In this approach, the encoding for each position is generated using sine and cosine functions. For each position in the sequence, the positional encoding is defined as follows:

```
For even dimensions 2i:
PE(pos, 2i) = sin(wi × pos)
For odd dimensions 2i + 1:
PE(pos, 2i + 1) = cos(wi × pos)
```

Here, w_i is a frequency parameter related to dimension i, usually set as $w_i = 1/10000^{2i/d_{\text{model}}}$, where d_{model} represents the model dimension.

The main advantage of sinusoidal positional encoding is that it can represent relative position relationships through linear transformations. Because the encoding is generated from fixed mathematical functions rather than learned for a fixed maximum sequence length, it can be applied to sequences of different lengths. However, for very long sequences, the periodic nature of sine and cosine functions may make distant positions harder to distinguish, which can affect the model's ability to capture subtle long-range positional relationships.

Later models, such as BERT and GPT-2, used learned absolute positional embeddings. In this approach, each position has a learned vector that is added to the token embedding. For example, BERT uses the sum of token embeddings, segment embeddings, and positional embeddings as its input representation, as shown in *Figure 2.4*.

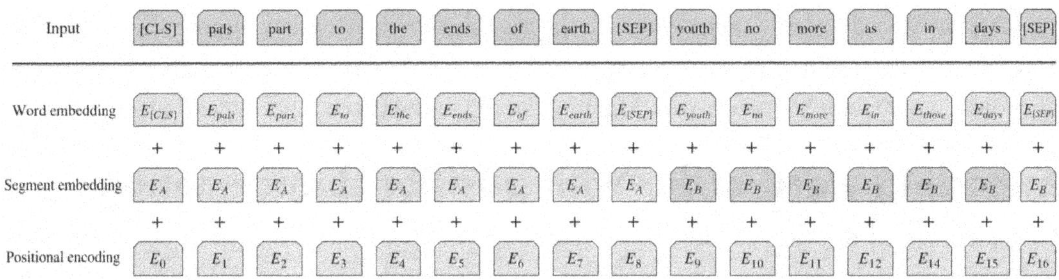

Figure 2.4: The concept of absolute positional encoding in the BERT model

Learned absolute positional embeddings are straightforward to implement because each position is assigned a trainable vector. However, they are usually tied to a predefined maximum sequence length. For example, BERT is commonly configured with a maximum input length of 512 tokens. If a sequence exceeds the supported length, the model cannot directly use learned positional embeddings for the additional positions unless the architecture or embedding table is extended.

To address the limitations of fixed or absolute position representations, researchers have proposed relative positional encoding methods. Instead of representing only the absolute position of each token, these methods model the relative distance between tokens. One influential approach is relation-aware self-attention, where relative position representations are incorporated into the attention calculation so that the model can account for how far apart tokens are from one another.

The core advantage of **relative position encoding** lies in its ability to capture the relative positional relationships between elements in a sequence through learned positional representations. This allows the model to better understand and distinguish the relative distances and directions between different positions. A major drawback of **relative position encoding** is that it depends on specific task data, so it may not generalize well to other tasks. In addition, the computational cost of relative position encoding can be high, as it requires calculating the relative position between every pair of elements. This may decrease the efficiency of model training and inference.

Building on the idea of relative position information, newer techniques such as Rotary Position Embedding (RoPE) and Attention with Linear Biases (ALiBi) have been introduced. RoPE incorporates relative position information through rotation operations applied during attention computation, making it effective for handling longer sequences without adding many extra parameters. Models in the Llama family and Falcon use RoPE.

ALiBi introduces a linear bias into the attention scores so that the model can account for relative distance during attention calculation. Instead of adding a separate positional embedding to the token representation, ALiBi modifies the attention scores directly. This helps the model handle longer contexts more efficiently and allows positional information to influence attention behavior.

Because RoPE and ALiBi modify how positional information is incorporated into attention, they will be revisited in the next section when the self-attention mechanism is introduced.

Overall, positional encoding methods have evolved from fixed sinusoidal encodings to learned absolute embeddings and relative-position techniques such as RoPE and ALiBi. These developments have improved Transformer models in several ways:

- **Generalization**: Positional encoding methods help models handle sequences of different lengths more effectively
- **Flexibility**: Learned or relative position representations allow models to adapt positional information to specific tasks and architectures
- **Efficiency**: Relative-position methods such as RoPE and ALiBi can improve long-sequence processing by incorporating position information directly into attention computation
- **Performance**: Better positional representations help models capture long-distance dependencies and improve performance across NLP tasks

Positional information tells the Transformer where each token appears in a sequence, but position alone is not enough for understanding language. The model must also determine which tokens are most relevant to one another in a given context. The next section introduces the attention mechanism, which allows the Transformer to calculate these relationships and assign greater importance to the parts of the sequence that matter most for the current prediction.

Explaining the attention mechanism

The **attention mechanism** is an extremely sophisticated data processing technique. It enables the model, when dealing with a sequence, to not only focus on different positions within the sequence but also on the relationships between elements inside the sequence. **Self-attention** is an extension of the attention mechanism; it provides a more flexible and powerful way to handle sequential data, allowing the model to establish direct dependencies between any positions in a sequence. The introduction of the self-attention mechanism, especially in the **Transformer** model, has become a milestone in the NLP field, greatly advancing the development of pretrained language models.

Below, we will explain the core elements of the self-attention mechanism through a simple example and then briefly introduce its implementation in the Transformer model.

Suppose you encounter the following fill-in-the-blank question, as shown in *Figure 2.5*, which is a typical conceptual diagram of the **attention mechanism**.

Buy apples or buy ____

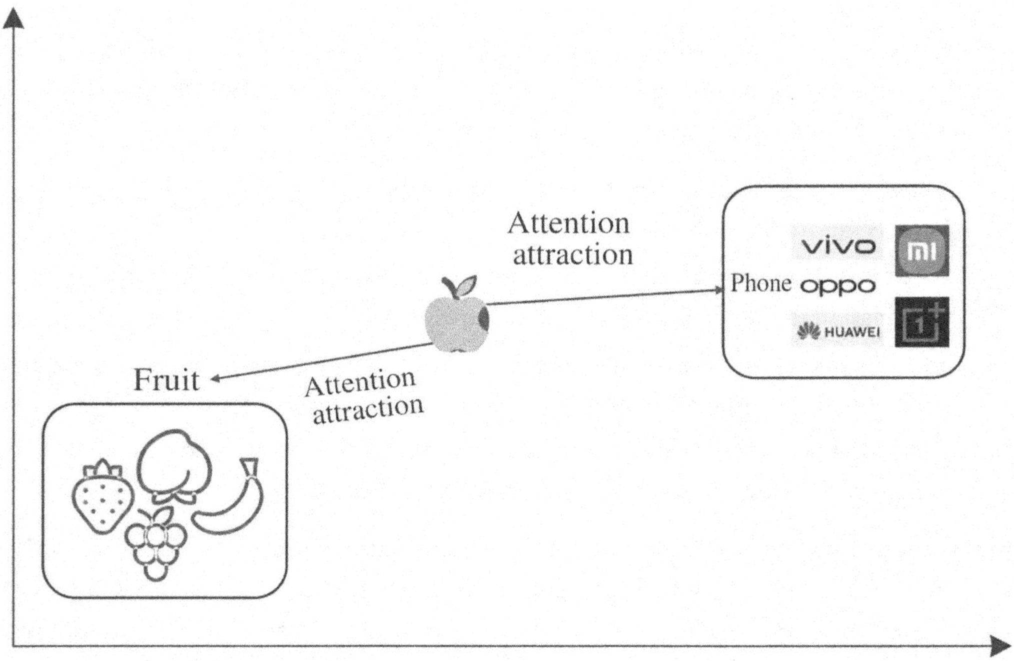

Figure 2.5: Conceptual diagram of the attention mechanism for "apples"

If there is no further context, it is difficult to determine what should be filled in the blank. However, if the context is that the fruit at home has been eaten up, you can infer that the blank should be filled with another kind of fruit, such as "oranges." If the context is that your wife's phone is broken, then you can infer that the blank should be filled with **Samsung** or **Xiaomi**, because in this case, **"apple"** refers to a **phone**.

Through the demonstration in *Figure 2.5*, we can understand **attention** as the association relationship between keywords and context. Suppose the attention mechanism connects the blank with **mobile phones**, then the content to fill in becomes a matter of choosing between different phone brands. If the attention mechanism links the blank with **fruits**, then the filled content is a matter of choosing between different fruits. The probabilities of different brands or fruits appearing are related to the sample data provided during **training**.

The **attention mechanism** first appeared in the paper *Neural Machine Translation by Jointly Learning to Align and Translate*. This paper proposed a new neural machine translation model that combines the **encoder-decoder architecture** with the attention mechanism, enabling the model to focus on the parts of the input sequence most relevant to the current output. The initially introduced attention mechanism was mainly used to weight the outputs of the encoder so that the decoder could focus on the parts of the input sequence most relevant to the current generated word. This mechanism is generally used as a component of the encoder-decoder architecture.

The attention mechanism in the paper *Neural Machine Translation by Jointly Learning to Align and Translate* is divided into two parts: **learning global correspondences** and **learning local correspondences**.

Learning global correspondences

The model uses a single attention mechanism to learn the global correspondences between the source and target languages. Specifically, the model first encodes each word in the source and target languages using **word embeddings** to obtain word vectors. Then, the **attention mechanism** is used to compute the similarity between each target word and all source words. Finally, a weighted sum based on attention weights is performed on the source words to obtain a **context vector** relevant to the target word.

Learning local correspondences

The model first uses the context vector from the first stage as a **query vector**, then uses the source language word vectors as **key vectors** and **value vectors**, and finally calculates the local correspondences between each target word and all source words through the attention mechanism.

The attention mechanism was first used to help a decoder focus on relevant parts of an encoded source sequence. In the Transformer model, this idea is extended through self-attention, where the words within the same sequence compare with one another to determine which tokens are most relevant in context.

Showing how self-attention captures sentence context

The basic principle of the **self-attention mechanism** is the comparison of similarity between words. In the attention mechanism, every word is compared for similarity with other words, and the degree of similarity determines the importance of each word within the sentence. This similarity comparison helps the model better understand semantic relationships in the sentence, and thus more accurately capture the semantic information of the sentence.

Its specific principle can be explained in three parts: **word embedding transformation**, **similarity calculation**, and **spatial transformation**.

Word embedding transformation

Converting textual information into vector representations is necessary for computers to understand text, since computers can only process numeric information. A good **word embedding** model enables computers to better comprehend the text and thus capture its semantic information more effectively.

Similarity calculation

Calculate the similarity between each word in a sentence and every other word. This step is aimed at finding the correlation between each word and every other word in the sentence.

Spatial transformation

Apply different transformations to the word embedding vector data to find the most suitable transformation method, so as to better capture the semantic relationships between words.

Next, let's use a simple example to illustrate this process. Suppose the following sentence is input:

```
My wife's phone is broken, should I buy an Apple or Android?
```

First, the computer will extract the words from the text and convert them into vector representations. High-quality **word embedding models** can help computers better understand text and thus capture semantic information more accurately. We use the pre-trained model `bert-base-uncased` and reduce the word embeddings to two dimensions using **PCA**, thereby visualizing the words in these two sentences. *Figure 2.6* shows the visualization effect of the word embedding vectors.

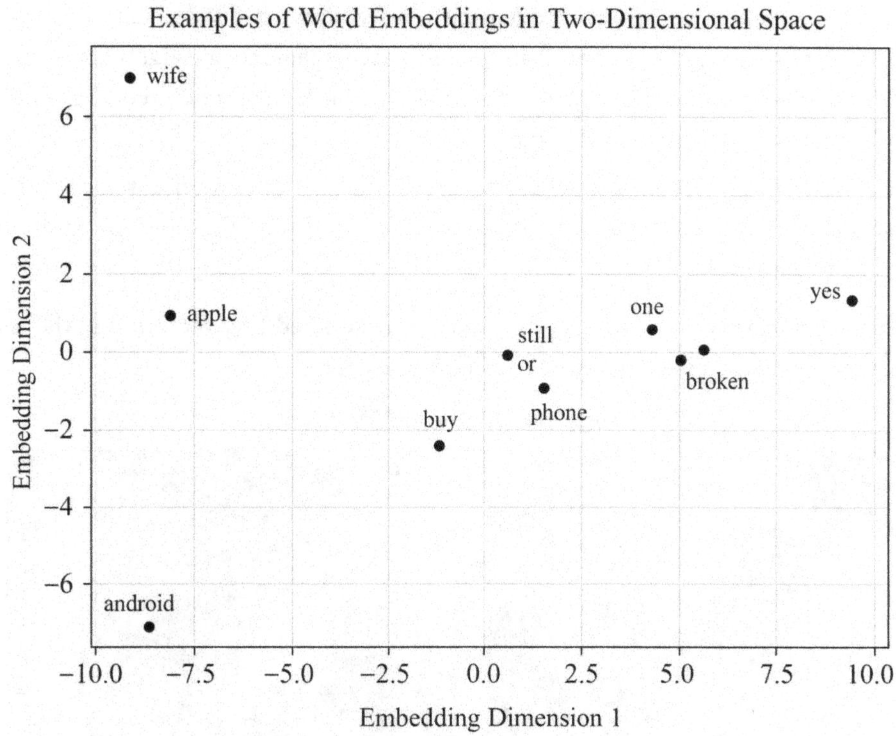

Figure 2.6: Visualization of word embedding vectors in 2D space

When processing sequences (such as text), the **attention mechanism** allows the model to dynamically focus on certain parts of the sequence. This mechanism enables the model to identify and assign higher weights to **keywords** in a sentence, thereby improving the efficiency and effectiveness of information processing. The processing flow is roughly divided into the following four steps:

1. **Similarity calculation.** The model calculates the similarity between each word in the sentence (called the **"query"**) and all other words (called the **"keys"**), usually achieved via dot product or other correlation measures.
2. **Normalization.** Next, the **softmax function** is used to normalize these similarity scores, so that the sum of all scores corresponding to each word equals 1. The purpose of this step is to convert the raw similarity scores into a probability distribution, highlighting the words in the sentence that are most relevant to the current word.

3. **Weighted sum.** After normalized scoring for each word, the model computes a weighted sum of the **"values"** of all words in the sentence to generate a weighted representation. This step focuses on the parts most relevant to the current word, reducing or ignoring the influence of less relevant parts.
4. **Output.** Finally, the model generates a weighted representation for each word in the sentence, capturing the interrelations between words and their relative importance to the current word.

We performed similarity calculation on the above **word embedding vectors**, and the results of the similarity calculation between words are shown in *Figure 2.7*.

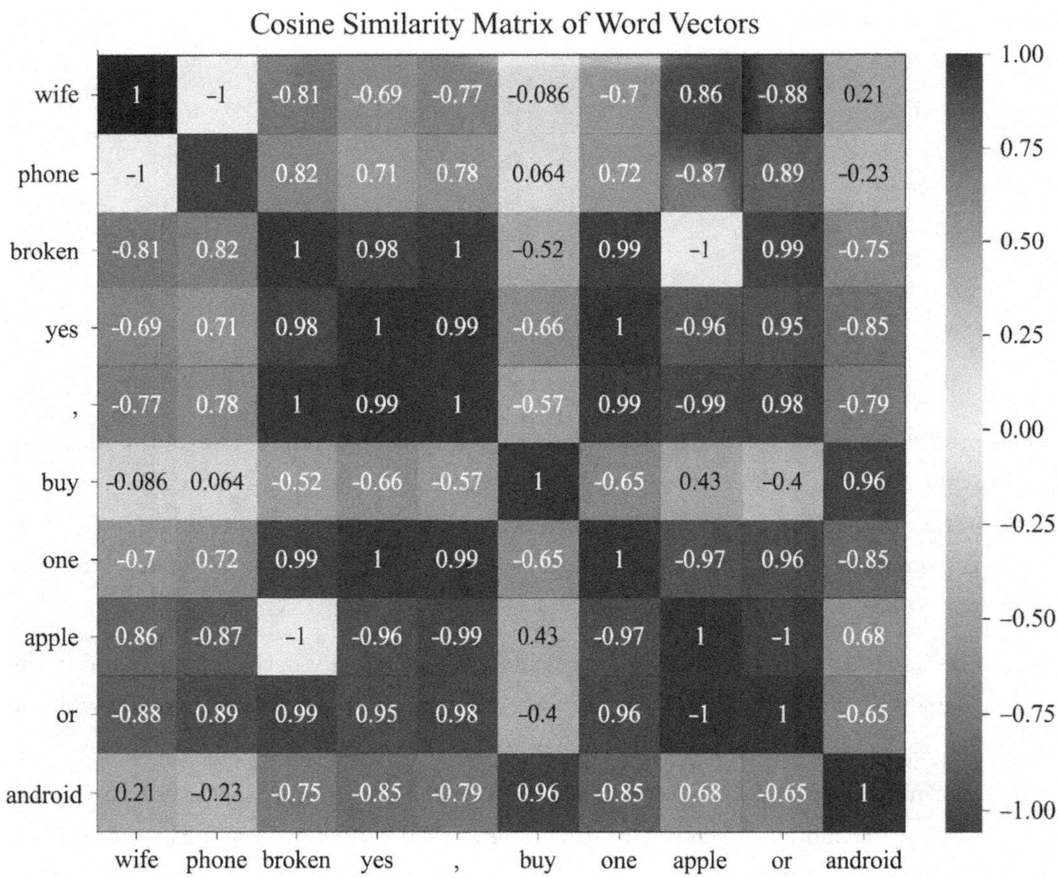

Figure 2.7: Similarity calculation results

Through **softmax normalization**, we can obtain the weights of each word relative to other words. By computing the **"weighted sum,"**, we realize an attention-based update of word correlations. A comparison between **word embedding** and **attention weight embedding** is shown in *Figure 2.8*.

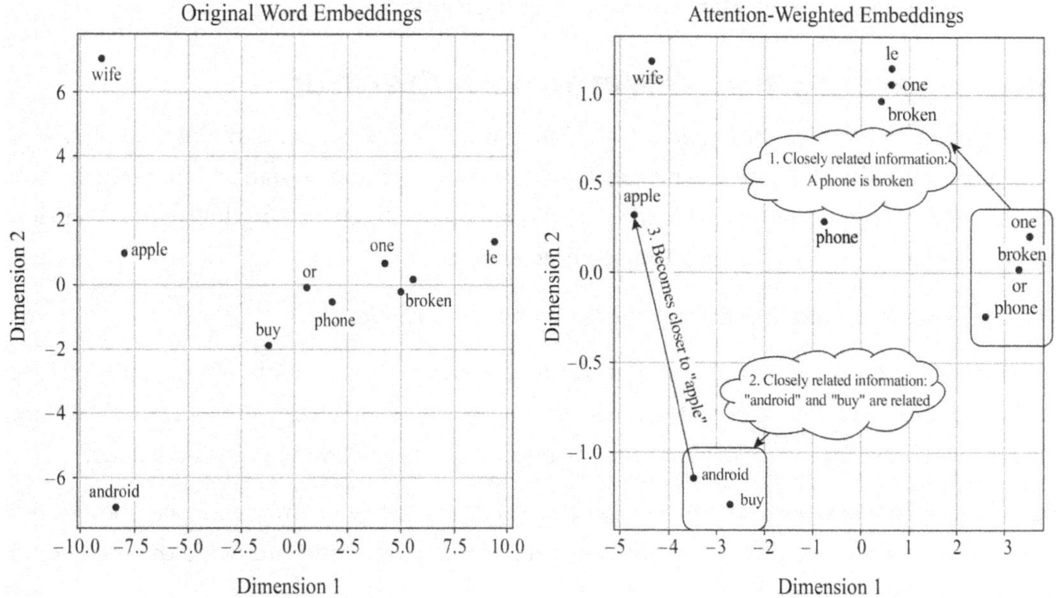

Figure 2.8: Comparison of word embeddings and attention weight embeddings

The left side of *Figure 2.8* shows the output of the original **word embedding model**, while the right side presents the weights computed through the **attention mechanism**. By comparison, we can observe three changes after adding attention weights:

- The position of "one phone broke" is tighter, making the grouping with other phrases more distinct
- The relationship between the words "buy" and "Android" is closer
- The positional relationship between "Android" and "Apple" is closer, which can be judged by the value changes on the vertical axis

The above case is merely a simple simulation of **attention weight calculation.** In fact, within the **Transformer model**, the **attention mechanism** is implemented through **Multi-Head Attention. Multi-head attention** allows the model to focus on different parts of the input sequence simultaneously, thereby improving the model's **expressiveness** and **generalization ability**.

This conceptual example shows why attention is useful: it allows the model to assign different levels of importance to different tokens based on context. The next section moves from this intuition to implementation by explaining how Transformer self-attention uses query, key, and value representations to calculate attention weights in practice.

Implementing transformer self-attention

In the previous sections, the **attention mechanism** of the **Transformer model** was explained from a conceptual and theoretical perspective. However, the actual design and implementation of the model are more complex. This section will explain the practical workflow of the **attention mechanism** and the **multi-head attention mechanism**.

The **attention mechanism** addresses the following two problems.

It enables dynamic focus on the information most relevant to the current task, regardless of the position of that information in the sequence. This is not limited to relationships within a sentence but also includes long-range dependencies across sentences and even entire documents.

The **attention mechanism** dynamically assigns weights to each word in a sequence, allowing for more effective use of long-distance contextual information and thus improving the accuracy of the next word prediction.

The data processing workflow of the **Transformer model** includes the following four steps:

1. At the input stage, the **Transformer model** converts text sequences into word embedding vectors, and supplements positional encoding information in the word embedding vectors (using sine and cosine encoding, respectively, for odd and even positions)
2. Using word embeddings containing positional encoding information, the model generates corresponding query (Q), key (K), and value (V) representations through the Q, K, and V weight matrices in the model. These representations are used to calculate attention weights, which reflect the correlation among different parts of the input sequence. By combining the computed attention weights with the values, the final attention output is generated. This output captures the contextual information of the sequence and can be used for the next layer of the model.
3. After the processing of each **Transformer layer**, the result calculated by the **attention mechanism** is directly added into the residual network. The data then passes through the feed-forward network, goes through the residual connection and layer normalization, and is finally normalized to yield the probability distribution for the next word prediction result.

4. The predicted result is used as new input, and together with previous inputs, positional encoding is updated for further prediction processing. In this process, **multi-head masked processing** is involved. To ensure that the model does not "see" words that have not yet been predicted during training, a mask is used to cover these words, simulating the generation process during inference and ensuring that each prediction is made based only on preceding words.

The implementation of **positional encoding** has been explained earlier. This section focuses on how to train and learn with word embedding vectors containing positional encoding information. First, we start with the calculation of word similarity. The core of the **attention mechanism** is to identify important information in a sentence, with these important associations obtained through word similarity calculations. The result of the similarity calculation is highly dependent on the **word embedding model**. In **natural language processing**, the same word may have completely different meanings in different contexts. To enable the model to accurately judge the similarity of words based on context and determine their meanings in specific scenarios, we need to train auxiliary model parameters to dynamically adjust weights according to the context, construct updated word embedding vectors, allow the model to capture subtle differences in context, and assign different interpretations to the same words while preserving the original semantic information.

Let's illustrate this process with a simple example.

Suppose during training, the **Transformer** is given the input sentence: "one **Apple** phone." The **attention mechanism** of the Transformer model will compare the similarity of each word in the sentence with other words and determine the importance of each word in the sentence based on the similarity scores. Taking the similarity calculation between "Apple" and "phone" as an example, we can show the necessity of training the Q and K weight matrices.

As mentioned earlier, in the simulated two-dimensional word vector space, "Apple" could be related both to "fruit" and to "phone." The raw **word embedding vectors** cannot dynamically adjust similarity results, so for **polysemous** words, a single embedding model struggles to adapt to similarity judgments in different contexts.

Therefore, given an **embedding model**, we need to find a way to dynamically adjust its vector space so that the similarity calculation results for the same word can differ under different contexts. *Figure 2.9* well demonstrates the practical effect of the **word embedding transformation matrix**: by training via machine learning, more suitable transformation matrices are found to achieve better word embedding performance.

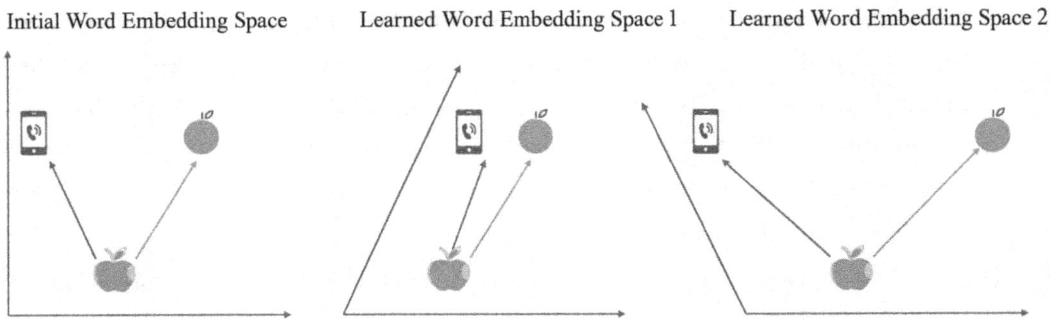

Figure 2.9: Demonstration of the effect of the word embedding transformation matrix

The example above shows why the model needs a way to adjust word representations according to context. The next question is how the Transformer model learns these transformations. This is where the query and key weight matrices become important.

Learning the query and key transformation matrices

We can achieve this by training the Q and K weight matrices. The core concept is shown in *Figure 2.10*.

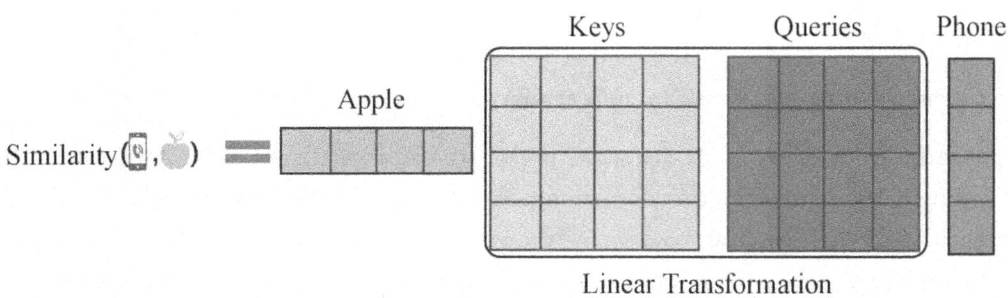

Figure 2.10: Source of the definition of the linear transformation matrix for word embeddings

In *Figure 2.10*, some terms are explained as follows:

- **Keys:** Refers to the Key vectors of the input sequence; each Key vector represents the semantic information of a word
- **Queries:** Refers to the Query vectors of the input sequence; each Query vector represents the semantic information of the word for which the attention weight is currently being calculated
- **Similarity:** Refers to the similarity between the Key vector and the Query vector
- **Linear Transformation:** Refers to applying a linear transformation to the Key and Query vectors

After the query and key transformations have been introduced, the next step is to see how they are used inside self-attention. The self-attention mechanism combines queries, keys, and values to calculate attention weights and produce a context-aware representation of each token.

Explaining the self-attention calculation

During the training process of the **self-attention mechanism**, the **Scaled Dot-Product Attention** mechanism is a very core component. In this mechanism, the model first computes the similarity between the Q vector and the K vector, then converts the similarity into attention weights via the **Softmax** function, and finally multiplies the attention weights by the V vector to obtain the final output.

Because the attention output depends on the Q, K, and V transformations, these matrices must be learned during model training. The following subsection explains how the Q and K matrices are initialized, updated through forward and backward propagation, and optimized to capture context-specific relationships between tokens.

Training the Q and K weight matrices

Let's first take a look at the calculation formula for **scaled dot-product attention:**

$$Attention(Q,K,V) = Softmax\left(\frac{QK^T}{\sqrt{d_k}}\right)V$$

The computation of scaled dot-product attention is shown in *Figure 2.11.*

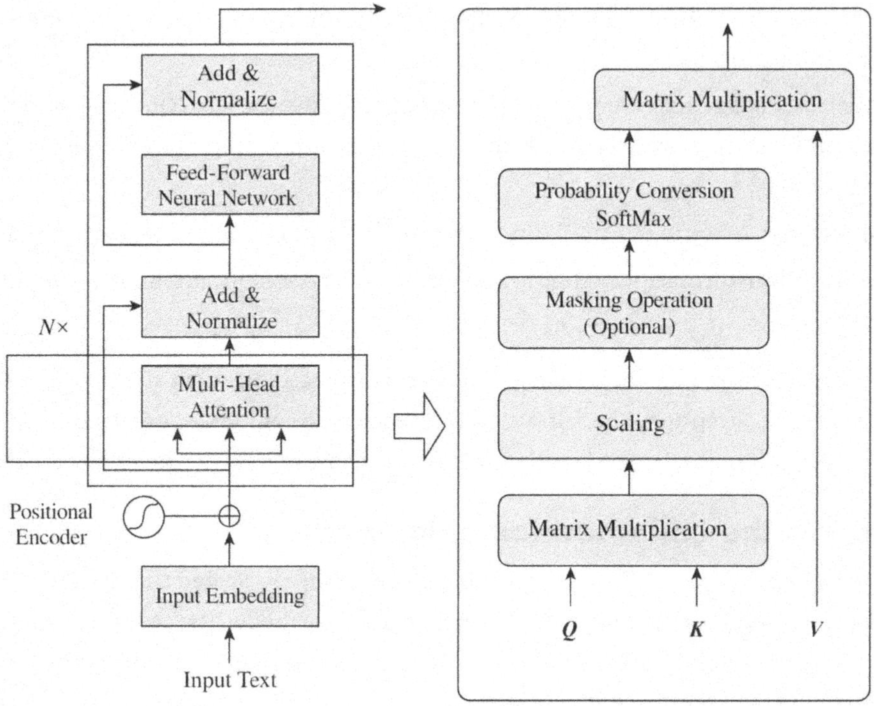

Figure 2.11: Calculation of scaled dot-product attention

As seen in *Figure 2.11*, the process includes four steps:

1. **Word embedding vectors**. First, the input words are converted into word embedding vectors, and then position encoding is added.
2. *Q*, *K*, *V* weight matrices. The word embedding vectors are multiplied by the weight matrices *Q*, *K*, and *V*, respectively, to obtain the **Query** (*Q*), **Key** (*K*), and **Value** (*V*).
3. **Calculation of attention weights.** The similarity between the **Query** (*Q*) and the **Key** (*K*) is calculated, and then the attention weights are obtained by applying the **Softmax** function.
4. **Weighted sum**. The attention weights are multiplied by the **Value** (*V*), then summed to get the attention output.

In the transformer model, the transformation matrices are acquired by training the weight matrices of *Q* and *K*. Specifically, the training process is as follows:

1. **Initialization.** Randomly initialize the weight matrices for *Q* and *K*.
2. **Forward propagation**
    - Map the words in the input sequence to word embedding vectors
    - Perform linear transformations on the *K* and *Q* vectors to obtain new *K* and *Q* vectors
    - Compute the similarity between the *K* and *Q* vectors
    - Apply Softmax normalization to the similarity scores to obtain the attention weights
    - Perform a weighted sum of the *V* vectors based on the attention weights to obtain the final output
3. **Backpropagation**
    - Calculate the **loss function**
    - Update the **weight matrices** of *Q* and *K* based on the loss function
4. Repeat steps *2* and *3* until training is complete

The goal of this training is to enable the transformer model to learn the similarity relationships between words in different contexts. For example, in the sentence "Apple phone", the Transformer model should be able to learn that there is a higher similarity between "Apple" and "phone." In the computation process of the attention mechanism, both the *Q* vector and the *K* vector need to undergo a linear transformation. The weight matrix of the linear transformation is shared, meaning all words share the same weight matrix. The number of rows in the shared weight matrix is equal to the size of the vocabulary; for however many words are in the vocabulary, that's how many rows are in the shared weight matrix. The number of columns in the shared weight matrix equals the dimension of the word embedding vectors. The dimension of the word embedding vectors determines the model's capacity to express the semantic information of words. In practical applications, the size of the shared weight matrix may be limited by computational resources. Some techniques can be used to reduce the size of the shared weight matrix, such as **parameter pruning** and **knowledge distillation**.

Once the training process for the attention weight matrices is clear, the next step is to examine the actual calculation performed during attention. Scaled dot-product attention explains how similarity scores are computed, normalized, masked when needed, and then used to produce the final weighted output.

Understanding scaled dot-product attention

The core principle of the **scaled dot-product attention mechanism** can be explained in the following scenarios:

1. Compare the similarity of each word in a sentence with other words. This process is achieved by computing the dot product between the Q vector of each word and the K vectors of other words. The result of the dot product represents the similarity between the two vectors; the higher the value, the greater the similarity. This process can be seen as building a similarity matrix between words within a sentence.

   The effect of similarity computation is shown in *Figure 2.12*.

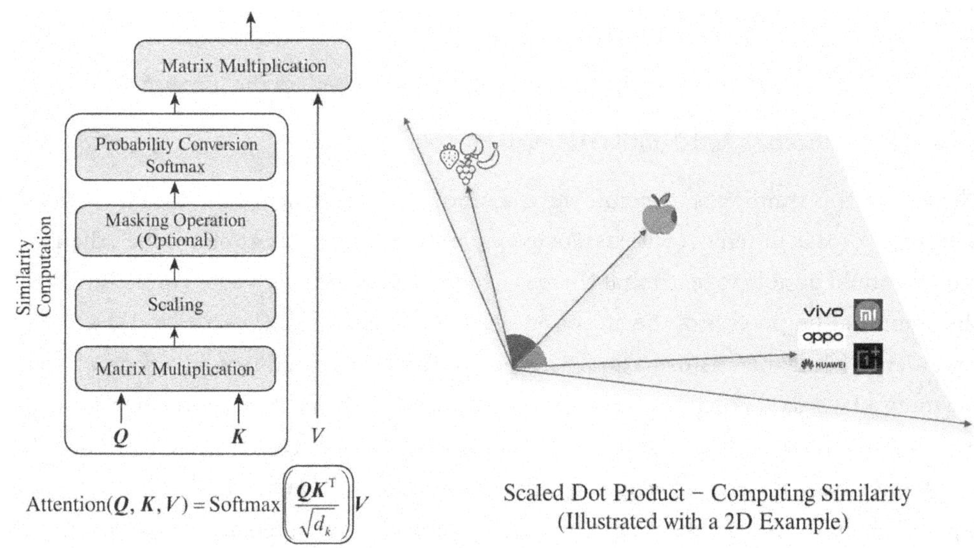

Figure 2.12: Example of similarity calculation based on scaled dot-product attention (1)

The left gray box area of *Figure 2.12* describes the calculation process of the scaled dot-product in the formula. The right side of the figure uses the angle between vectors in a two-dimensional space to represent the similarity between two words. The two-dimensional vector space undergoes different spatial transformations during the training process through deep learning.

2. After scaling, masking, and Softmax processing, attention weights are obtained. After calculating similarity, the model performs scaling processing on the similarity to prevent values from being too large or too small. Next, the model applies **masking** to the attention weights to ensure that the model does not "see" words that have not yet been predicted. Finally, the model applies **Softmax** to the scaled similarities to obtain the **attention weights.** This process can be viewed as building a matrix of attention weights between words within the sentence, identifying the key directions of similarity within the sentence to better capture its semantic information. The effect is shown in *Figure 2.13*.

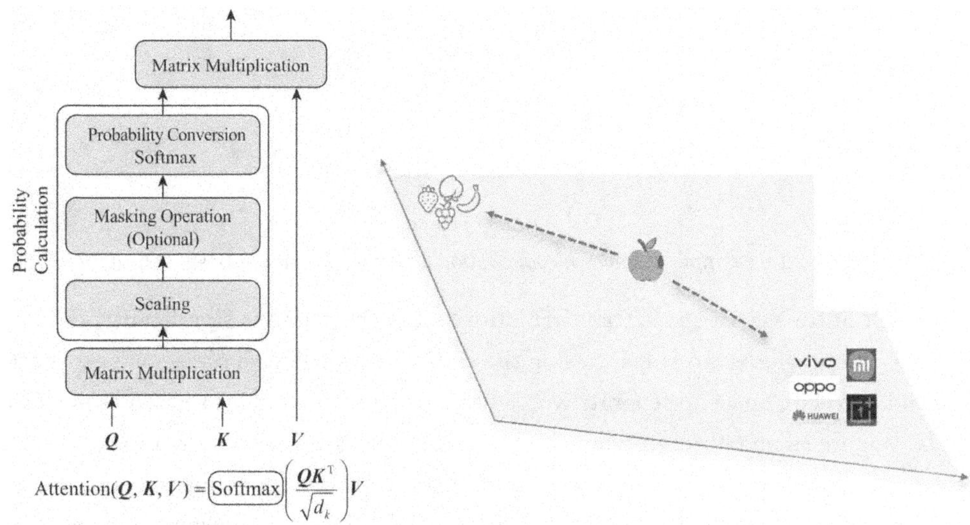

Figure 2.13: Example of similarity calculation based on scaled dot-product attention (2)

3. Calculate the weighted sum to obtain the final output. After calculating the attention weights, the model multiplies the attention weights by the value (**V**) vectors and sums them to get the final output. This process weights the **word embedding vectors**, making their grouping with other phrases more distinct, as shown in *Figure 2.14*.

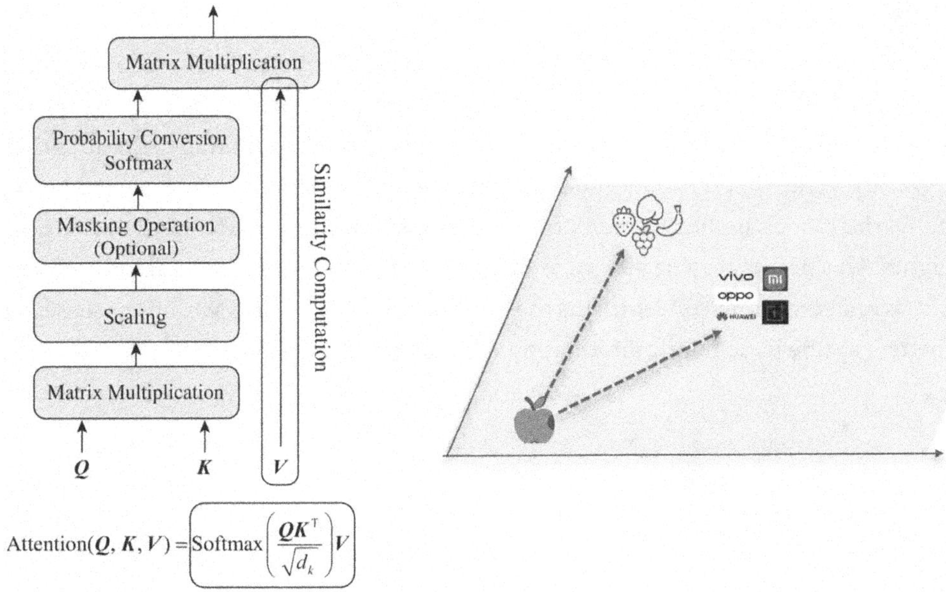

Figure 2.14: Example of similarity calculation based on scaled dot-product attention (3)

The result of the vector space transformation in the third step is significantly different from those in the previous two steps. During the similarity calculation phase, we expect the word embedding vector space to separate words with different meanings as much as possible, while in the weighted sum phase, we want similar words to be clustered together to better predict the probability of the next word. Why is it designed this way? Do you still remember the original intent of the Transformer model? Its goal is to predict the probability of the next word, which aligns with the goal of the large language models we use today. The model continuously tries to predict the next word and adjusts its parameters based on the prediction to better anticipate the next word.

The output of the self-attention mechanism (i.e., the weighted values) is typically used as intermediate representations in sequence processing tasks, and these representations are further processed by subsequent network layers to predict the next word or perform other tasks. Thus, the self-attention mechanism provides a flexible internal representation, offering each element in the sequence a contextual representation that synthesizes information from the entire sequence. The design of the Transformer model nests multiple identical processing layers. Through multi-level data processing, the self-attention mechanism can capture representations at different levels, for example, from individual words or characters to more complex semantic concepts and relationships. Each layer is able to learn more abstract representations of information from the previous layer's output. This hierarchical processing helps the model understand the complex structure of language, including syntactic and semantic information. With multilevel data processing, the model not only distills information but also integrates and re-encodes it to generate richer and more complex representations. This process involves capturing and integrating information from different parts of the sequence to support complex reasoning and comprehension tasks.

The discussion so far has explained how Transformer self-attention uses learned transformations, similarity scores, normalization, masking, and weighted sums to build contextual token representations. The next section extends this idea by showing how the Transformer uses multiple attention heads in parallel, allowing the model to capture different types of relationships within the same sequence.

Exploring the design of multi-head attention

In the Transformer model, the **multi-head attention mechanism** is implemented by combining multiple attention mechanisms. Each attention mechanism is called a **head**, and multiple heads work in parallel, with each head learning different representations. This mechanism enables the model to focus on different parts of the sequence simultaneously when processing sequences. For example, some heads may focus on the **syntactic structure** of the sentence, others may focus on the **semantic information**, while others might focus on **sentiment information**. Through the multi-head attention mechanism, the model can model sequences from different perspectives, thereby enhancing its expressive and generalization capabilities.

In the final layer of the model, the outputs of multiple heads are concatenated and then passed through a **linear transformation** to obtain the final output. During this process, the model learns the weights among the different heads in a deep learning manner, as well as how to combine the outputs from multiple heads. Building upon what was learned earlier, the following will introduce the design details of the multi-head attention mechanism.

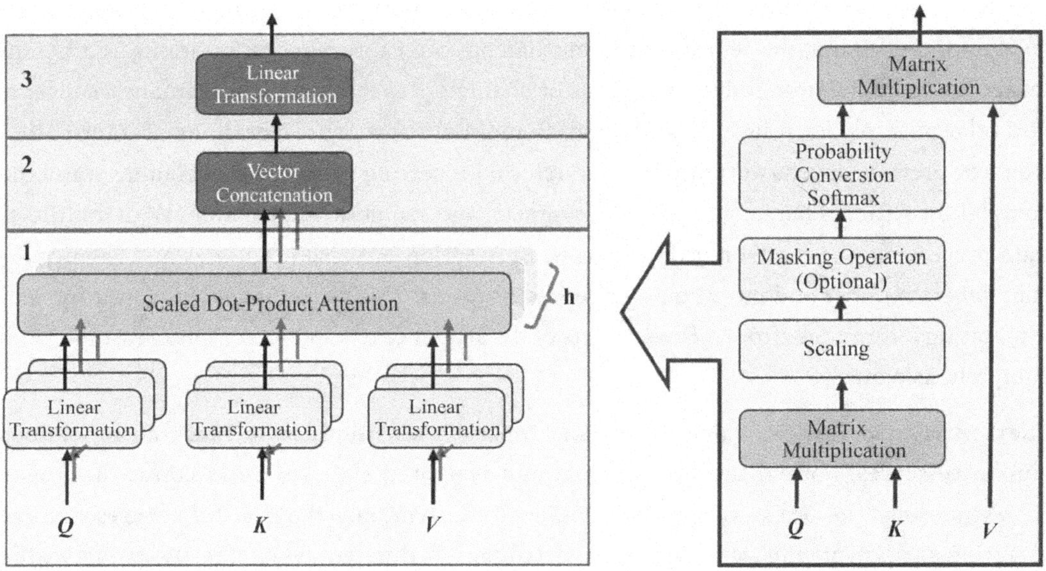

Figure 2.15: Structure of the multi-head attention mechanism

As shown in *Figure 2.15*, the **multi-head attention mechanism** actually consists of the following three parts:

- **Structure of the multi-head attention mechanism.** The model is designed with a fixed number of heads, and each **head** performs a linear transformation on the input ***Q***, ***K***, and ***V***. The linear transformations for each head may differ; these are actually implemented by training weights. Linear transformations allow the model to capture key information in different embedding spaces. For example, some transformations capture long-range structural information while others capture short-range dependencies. This design enables the **Transformer model** to consider multiple types of dependencies simultaneously when processing sequential data.

- **Concatenating the attention outputs calculated by each head.** The output of each head is an independent **attention vector**, which are concatenated to form a long vector. The reason for concatenating the attention outputs from each head is to merge the different information captured by each head into a comprehensive representation. Since each head may focus on different aspects of the input sequence, the concatenation operation allows the model to utilize this diverse information in subsequent processing. The concatenated vector contains information from all different heads, which is further integrated by a **linear layer** to provide a unified output for downstream tasks. In the original **Transformer model**, the number of heads is set to 8, and each head has a dimensionality of 64.
- Integrate information from **multi-head attention** through linear transformations, ultimately outputting the attention representation. In the **multi-head attention mechanism**, each head can independently learn features regarding the relationships within the input. The **linear layer** is responsible for integrating these features, allowing downstream network layers to utilize information from all heads for decision-making. The linear layer not only performs weight scaling, but also incorporates non-linear activation functions (such as **ReLU**) to enhance the model's representational power.

Multi-head attention allows the Transformer to examine a sequence from several representational perspectives at the same time. However, attention is only one part of the full architecture. The next section brings the components together by showing how embeddings, positional information, attention layers, feed-forward networks, residual connections, layer normalization, the encoder, and the decoder form the complete Transformer model.

Assembling the transformer architecture

After examining word embeddings, positional encoding, self-attention, scaled dot-product attention, and multi-head attention separately, we can now bring these components together to understand the full Transformer architecture. At a high level, the original Transformer was designed as an encoder-decoder model for sequence-to-sequence tasks such as machine translation.

The initial goal of the Transformer model was to build a "language translation" system. The translation process can be represented as: **Input ⟶ Encoder module ⟶ Decoder module ⟶ Output**. The abstract structure of the Transformer is shown in *Figure 2.16*.

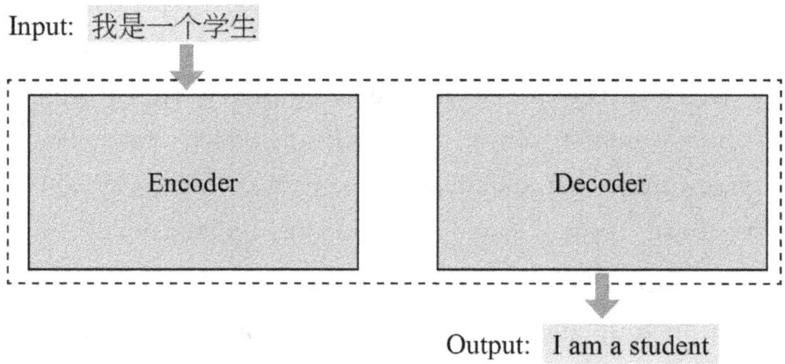

Figure 2.16: Abstract structure of the Transformer

The encoder and decoder are neural network modules that work together to transform an input sequence into an output sequence. Each module contains multiple encoder and decoder components. These components are connected in series and can be regarded as a multi-layer homogeneous network. In the earliest papers, this structure consisted of a 6-layer encoder-decoder architecture. The structures of the Transformer encoder and decoder are shown in *Figure 2.17*.

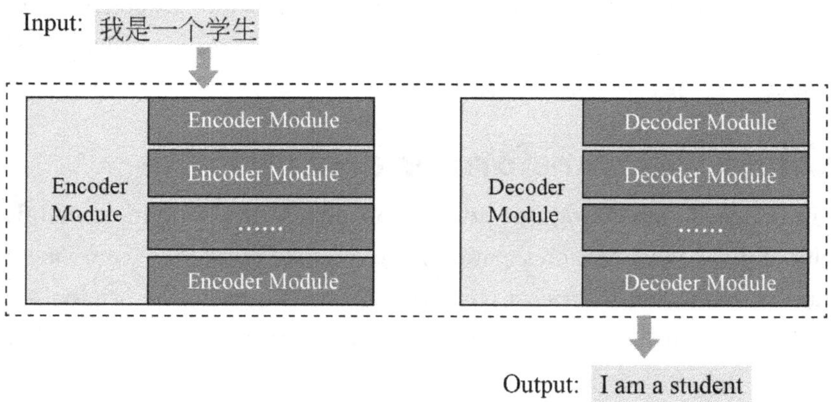

Figure 2.17: Transformer encoder and decoder structure

Different Transformer-based models use different parts of this architecture: encoder-only models such as BERT use the encoder stack, decoder-only models such as GPT use the decoder stack, and encoder-decoder models use both.

Each encoder contains multiple submodules, among which the core components are the self-attention mechanism and the feed-forward neural network. The self-attention mechanism is used to capture long-range dependencies within the sequence, while the feed-forward neural network performs non-linear transformations on the information in the sequence. The internal structure of the Transformer encoder is illustrated in *Figure 2.18*.

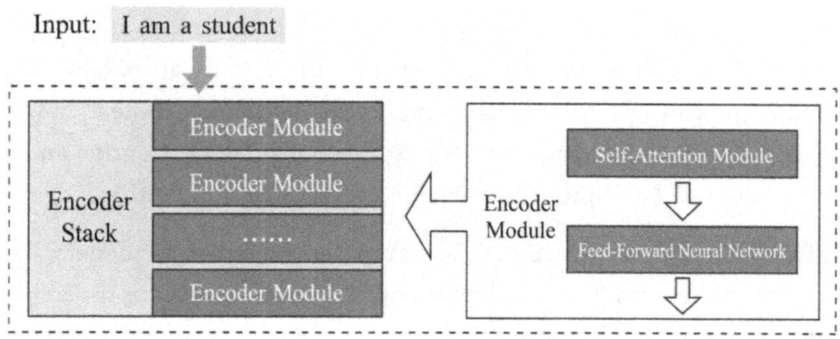

Figure 2.18: Internal structure of the Transformer encoder

The self-attention mechanism enables the model to consider all elements of the entire sequence when processing each element within the sequence. This allows the model to capture dependencies between any two elements in the sequence, regardless of their distance from each other. After the self-attention mechanism captures the dependencies within the sequence, a feedforward neural network (usually composed of two fully connected layers) independently applies nonlinear transformations to the representation at each position. The feedforward neural network uses the same parameters at all positions in the encoder layer, but these parameters are applied independently to each position. This means that even if the inputs at different positions are the same, the outputs after passing through the feedforward neural network may still be different. Additionally, the self-attention layer and the feedforward neural network layer are integrated through residual connections, which are typically followed by layer normalization to stabilize training and accelerate convergence.

Summary

In this chapter, you learned why the Transformer model became the foundation of modern large language models and how it improved on earlier approaches such as RNNs and LSTMs. You saw that Transformers address major limitations of older sequence models—especially inefficient sequential processing and difficulty handling long-range dependencies—by using self-attention and parallel computation.

You were introduced to the core structure of the Transformer, including its encoder-decoder architecture, and to the major components that make it effective: word embeddings, positional encoding, self-attention, multi-head attention, feed-forward networks, residual connections, and layer normalization. You also learned why text must first be converted into numerical form, how word embeddings capture semantic meaning, and how positional encoding helps preserve word order.

A major part of the chapter focused on the attention mechanism. You learned how attention helps the model determine which parts of a sequence are most relevant in context, how Q, K, and V vectors are used to compute attention, and how scaled dot-product attention and multi-head attention enable the model to capture different kinds of relationships within language.

By the end of the chapter, you gained both a conceptual and structural understanding of the Transformer—not only as a model originally designed for translation, but as the architecture that powers today's most important language models. This chapter prepared you to better understand how modern AI systems process language through contextual understanding, efficient training, and layered representation learning.

Building on this understanding of the Transformer architecture and its key mechanisms, you are now ready to explore how this model evolved into modern generative systems. In the next chapter, you will trace the path from the Transformer to GPT and ChatGPT, beginning with simple language models such as the bigram model and gradually examining how autoregressive training and large-scale pretraining enabled today's conversational AI systems.

3

Tracing the Path from Bigram Models to GPT and ChatGPT

In the evolution of natural language processing, the birth of the **Transformer model** marked a significant turning point for deep learning technology. However, the original Transformer model was not sufficient to support the generative demands of complex LLMs like **ChatGPT**. The emergence of ChatGPT is the result of a gradual evolution based on the Transformer model. By introducing innovations such as **autoregressive pre-training**, OpenAI expanded the Transformer model—originally designed for machine translation—to a broader range of language generation tasks. In this process, the GPT model, with its unique paradigm of **pre-training** followed by **fine-tuning** and a design specifically aimed at **text generation**, opened a new chapter for **LLMs**. This chapter will guide readers from the basics of **bigram models**, gradually exploring the core principles of GPT, and revealing how it evolved step by step into ChatGPT.

We will be covering the following main topics in this chapter:

- Tracing the evolution from transformer to ChatGPT
- Building a basic bigram language model
- Understanding how GPT models generate text
- Improving GPT model training and generation

Tracing the evolution from transformer to ChatGPT

The original Transformer model was not designed for the kind of multi-turn conversation that ChatGPT supports today. So how did one evolve into the other? This chapter will start from the basic principles of the Transformer model, gradually introduce the fundamental concepts of ChatGPT, and finally explain how to use the ChatGPT model for dialog generation tasks.

The Transformer model was first proposed by Google to solve the problem of machine translation. This model is based on large-scale parallel corpora (such as English-French sentence pairs) and learns by minimizing the cross-entropy loss between the model's predicted next-token probabilities and the true next tokens. Based on this, OpenAI proposed the GPT model, extending the Transformer architecture to a broader range of natural language processing tasks. **GPT** stands for **Generative Pre-trained Transformer**. Like the Transformer, GPT is based on the Transformer architecture, but its core idea is to use **unsupervised pre-training** on large-scale corpora to learn deep language representations, followed by **fine-tuning** with a small amount of adaptive training to complete specific downstream tasks. GPT differs structurally from Transformer in that GPT only uses the decoder part of the Transformer, mainly for generative tasks such as text generation and dialog generation.

The initial version of the Transformer model was trained on **one-to-one parallel corpora**, had limited data, and could only be applied to machine translation tasks. To break through this limitation, OpenAI proposed a new **pre-training method**, which trains the model in an **autoregressive manner** and combines both **masked prediction** and **next sentence prediction** strategies to enable the model to learn the structure of language directly from large amounts of unlabeled text. The core idea of **autoregressive pre-training** is to give a sequence and generate its elements step by step. This method makes use of large-scale text data and can be applied to a variety of natural language processing tasks.

Masked prediction means randomly masking some words in the text sequence and requiring the model to predict the masked words to learn the contextual relationships between words. **Next sentence prediction** means that given a text sequence, the model judges whether the next sentence is related to the given text, helping the model learn logical relationships between sentences. GPT was the first model to adopt the autoregressive pre-training method and achieved excellent results. Subsequently, improved models such as **BERT** and **RoBERTa** also adopted similar pre-training methods.

This chapter focuses on the GPT and ChatGPT models and analyzes them from the following aspects.

Fine-tuning pre-trained models is a common approach in current LLM applications. The GPT model adopts a pre-training plus fine-tuning paradigm, which was subsequently widely applied to various **natural language processing (NLP)** tasks. Pre-trained models learn general language characteristics from large-scale corpora and are then fine-tuned on specific tasks, significantly improving the model's performance and efficiency.

LLMs have a wide range of applications. GPT and its subsequent versions have demonstrated outstanding performance on various natural language processing tasks, including text generation, translation, summarization, question answering, and more. This shows that a single pre-trained model, through fine-tuning, can be adapted to multiple tasks, significantly enhancing the model's versatility and flexibility.

The consensus is that the larger the number of parameters, the more powerful the capability. The latest GPT model, with its enormous scale, has showcased the potential of LLMs in understanding and generating natural language, driving the development of large-scale language model research and sparking widespread discussions about the possible impacts of LLMs.

Next, a **bigram model** will be introduced as the starting point for language model training. Then, the basic principles of the GPT model will be described, including the structure of GPT, pre-training methods, and so on.

Building a basic bigram language model

The **Bigram Model** is one of the simplest language models. Based on the **Markov assumption**, it assumes that the occurrence of a word is only related to the previous word. The core of the **Bigram Model** is that, given a text sequence, the model needs to predict the next word.

When training the model, how can text be converted into numbers that can be computed? A common method is to construct a dictionary that maps characters or words to numerical indexes. In this way, the text sequence can be transformed into a sequence of numbers and input into the model for training. During model prediction, numeric indexes can be converted back to characters or words to obtain the model's output.

This method is widely used in natural language processing and is fundamental to building text datasets. This example uses character-level tokenization for simplicity. In this approach, each character is treated as a token and mapped to a numerical index. This works reasonably well for demonstrating the basic mechanics of language-model training, especially with Chinese text, where individual characters can carry meaningful information. However, production GPT-style models usually do not rely on simple character-level tokenization. Instead, they typically use subword tokenization methods such as **Byte Pair Encoding** (**BPE**), WordPiece, or SentencePiece, which split text into reusable word pieces and handle large vocabularies more efficiently. For real applications, libraries such as `tiktoken` or `sentencepiece` can be used to implement more practical tokenization workflows.

The following sample demonstrates how to convert text into numerical indexes. Collect the file "Three Hundred Tang Poems", which contains multiple poems from the Tang Dynasty. The goal is to train a model so that it can automatically generate Tang poetry.

> This chapter uses *Three Hundred Tang Poems* as a small character-level text corpus to demonstrate the mechanics of language-model training. To make the example easier for readers to follow, the Tang poetry referenced in the explanation and generated examples has been translated into English. The same workflow can be applied to other text corpora as well; for example, readers may use an English public-domain corpus such as Shakespeare's works or WikiText-2 by changing the dataset path, tokenization choices, and generated text examples.

The training data is as follows: each Tang poem is treated as a sentence, and these sentences are concatenated to form a long text. The input to the model is this long text, and the objective is to predict the next word. Issues to be solved in the process include how to convert text to numbers, how to design the model, and how to train the model.

The first step in this workflow is data representation. Before the model can learn from text, the text must be converted into numerical form so that it can be processed by the neural network. The following subsection shows how the corpus is read, how the character vocabulary is created, and how characters are mapped to numerical indices.

How text is converted to numbers

First, let's explore the data of *300 Tang Poems*. The relevant code is as follows:

```
txt_file='tang_300_new.txt'

with open(txt_file, 'r', encoding='utf-8') as f:
    text = f.read()
print('the length of the text is: ', len(text))
chars =list(set(text))
print('len of characters', len(chars), ' , characters:', chars)
```

Next, establish a **mapping table** from characters to numbers to convert text into numbers. At the same time, in order to convert the predicted numbers back to characters, a **mapping table** from numbers to characters is also required. The mapping table is shown below:

```
# Build the mapping from characters to numbers and from numbers to
characters
char_indices = dict((c, i) for i, c in enumerate(chars))
indices_char = dict((i, c) for i, c in enumerate(chars))

# Basic function for converting text into numbers
def text_to_indices(text):
    return [char_indices[c] for c in text]

def indices_to_text(indices):
    return ''.join(indices_char[i] for i in indices)
```

After the text has been converted into numerical indexes, the next step is to define a model that can learn from those indexes. In a bigram language model, the design is intentionally simple: the model receives the current token, converts it into an embedding, and predicts the next token. This simple structure makes it easier to understand the basic prediction loop before moving on to GPT-style models.

How to design the model

How can an LLM automatically generate a piece of poetry? Similar to ChatGPT, generating a paragraph of text according to instructions is relatively complex, so the goal can be simplified to: "Give a random word as input, and let the LLM automatically generate a new poem." Recalling the *text generation* effect of the LLM used, does it output word by word? The process of gradually generating the same sentence is actually a continuous prediction process.

Suppose the LLM generates a sentence: "Thirty deeds turned to dust and earth, eight thousand miles of clouds and moon."

```
Three (ten), # 'ten' is the predicted result
Thirty (merit), # 'merit' is the predicted result
Thirty merits (fame), # 'fame' is the predicted result
Thirty merits and fame (dust), # 'dust' is the predicted result
Thirty merits and fame are dust (and), # 'and' is the predicted result
Thirty merits and fame are dust and (earth), # 'earth' is the predicted
result
Thirty merits and fame are dust and earth (,), # ',' is the predicted
result
Thirty merits and fame are dust and earth, (eight), # 'eight' is the
predicted result
Thirty merits and fame are dust and earth, eight (thousand), # 'thousand'
is the predicted result
Thirty merits and fame are dust and earth, eight thousand (li), # 'li' is
the predicted result
Thirty merits and fame are dust and earth, eight thousand li (road), #
'road' is the predicted result
Thirty merits and fame are dust and earth, eight thousand li road (cloud),
# 'cloud' is the predicted result
Thirty merits and fame are dust and earth, eight thousand li road cloud
(and), # 'and' is the predicted result
Thirty merits and fame are dust and earth, eight thousand li road cloud
and (moon). # 'moon' is the predicted result
```

The result after each prediction is used as input and added to the next prediction, forming a **loop**. Thus, the text generation process of a LLM is essentially a continuous prediction process. This prediction process can be abstracted as a model whose input is a word and whose output is the next word. The structure of this model is a neural network: the input of the neural network is a word, and its output is the next word.

> In this example, the model is implemented at the character level for simplicity: each character is treated as a token, and the model predicts the next character rather than the next full word. This is convenient for demonstrating the mechanics of token mapping, embedding, training, and generation. In production LLMs, however, text is usually processed with subword tokenizers such as BPE, WordPiece, or SentencePiece, which split text into reusable word pieces rather than individual characters.

Starting from a simple bigram model, the input is one token, and the output is the next token. The statistical formula involved in the traditional bigram model is as follows:

$$P(w_{t+1} \mid w_t) = \{P(w_t, w_{t+1})/P(w_t)\}$$

Here, w_t is the input word, and w_{t+1} is the output word. This formula means that given a word w_t, we need to predict the **probability** that the next word w_{t+1} appears. This **probability** consists of two parts: the numerator is the probability that w_t and w_{t+1} occur together, and the denominator is the probability that w_t appears.

From the neural network implementation perspective, a **bigram model** usually uses an **embedding layer** to convert vocabulary into dense vector representations, followed by one or more **linear layers** (possibly including **activation functions**) to predict the probability distribution of the next word. The model may also include a **Softmax layer** to convert outputs into a **probability distribution.** This process is mathematically represented as follows:

$$z_{t+1} = NN(v_t)\ Pw_{t+1}|w_t = Softmax(z_{t+1})$$

Among them, v_t is the **embedding vector** of the input word w_t, **NN** is the **neural network**, z_{t+1} is the output of the neural network, $Pw_{t+1}|w_t$ is the **probability distribution** for the next word w_{t+1}. This formula indicates that given a word w_t, it predicts the probability distribution of the next word w_{t+1}. This probability distribution is computed by the neural network **NN** and transformed into a probability distribution via the **Softmax function.**

A **bigram model** predicts the next token using only the immediately previous token. Although this is much simpler than GPT, it is a useful starting point because it has the same basic input-output pattern: the model receives token IDs, converts them into embeddings, and predicts the next token. Training this simple model helps build intuition for tokenization, embedding layers, cross-entropy loss, and the repeated prediction loop that GPT later extends with attention and deeper Transformer blocks.

Below is a code implementation of a simple **bigram model.** The code consists of four parts: **model preparation, parameter initialization, training process,** and **generation process.**

```
import torch
import torch.nn as nn
from torch.nn import functional as F

# Set hyperparameters
batch_size = 64
max_iters = 3000
```

```
eval_interval = 500
learning_rate = 0.02
device = 'cuda' if torch.cuda.is_available() else 'cpu'
# These values are chosen for a small character-level vocabulary on a
single GPU
# For larger corpora or models, batch size and learning rate are typically
tuned together.
# Manually set the random seed to keep results reproducible
torch.manual_seed(42)

# Load text data
with open('tang_300_new.txt', 'r', encoding='utf-8') as f:
    text = f.read()

# Build the character-to-index mapping
chars = sorted(list(set(text)))
vocab_size = len(chars)
stoi = {ch: i for i, ch in enumerate(chars)}
itos = {i: ch for i, ch in enumerate(chars)}
# Encode the entire text
data = torch.tensor([stoi[c] for c in text], dtype=torch.long)
n = int(0.8*len(data))  # Use 90% as training data
train_data = data[:n]
val_data = data[n:]

# Define the model
class BigramLanguageModel(nn.Module):
    def __init__(self, vocab_size, embedding_dim):
        super().__init__()
        self.token_embedding = nn.Embedding(vocab_size, embedding_dim)
        self.fc_out = nn.Linear(embedding_dim, vocab_size)

    def forward(self, current_idx):
        x = self.token_embedding(current_idx).squeeze(1)
        logits = self.fc_out(x)
        return logits

# Data loading function
```

```
def get_batch(data, batch_size):
    indices = torch.randint(0, data.size(0) -1, (batch_size,))
    current_idx = data[indices]
    next_idx = data[indices + 1]
    return current_idx.to(device), next_idx.to(device)

# Instantiate the model and optimizer
model = BigramLanguageModel(vocab_size, embedding_dim=512).to(device)
optimizer = torch.optim.Adam(model.parameters(), lr=learning_rate)

# Training loop
model.train()
for iter in range(max_iters):
    optimizer.zero_grad()
    current_words, next_words = get_batch(train_data, batch_size)
    logits = model(current_words.unsqueeze(1))
    loss = F.cross_entropy(logits, next_words)
    loss.backward()
    optimizer.step()

    if iter % eval_interval == 0:
        print(f"Step {iter}: Training Loss = {loss.item()}")

# Model evaluation (simple example)
model.eval()
with torch.no_grad():
    current_words, next_words = get_batch(val_data, batch_size)
    logits = model(current_words.unsqueeze(1))
    val_loss = F.cross_entropy(logits, next_words)
    print(f"Validation Loss: {val_loss.item()}")
# Prediction / generation function
def generate(model, start_char, num_chars):
    model.eval()
    current_idx = torch.tensor([stoi[start_char]], dtype=torch.long,
device=
                                         device)
    generated_text = start_char
```

```
    for _ in range(num_chars):
        logits = model(current_idx.unsqueeze(0).unsqueeze(1))
        probabilities = F.softmax(logits, dim=-1).squeeze()
        current_idx = torch.multinomial(probabilities, 1)
        generated_char = itos[current_idx.item()]
        generated_text += generated_char
        current_idx = current_idx.squeeze()

    return generated_text

# Generate text
generated_text = generate(model, start_char='谷', num_chars=32)
print(generated_text)
```

The code above brings together the main parts of the bigram language-model workflow. It imports the required PyTorch modules, sets the training hyperparameters, loads the text corpus, builds the character-to-index and index-to-character mappings, defines the bigram model, creates random training batches, trains the model with cross-entropy loss, evaluates it on validation data, and finally generates text one character at a time. The following subsection explains these steps in more detail so that readers can understand how the model is trained and why each part of the code is needed.

How to train the model

Before analyzing the above code, let's briefly introduce the design and training process of neural network-based language models. Typically, a neural network-based language model involves the following five steps:

1. **Data Preparation**: Convert text data into sequences of numbers, and build a mapping table from characters to numbers
2. **Model Preparation**: Define a neural network model, including an **embedding layer** and a **linear layer**
3. **Parameter Initialization**: Set hyperparameters such as **batch size**, **number of iterations**, **learning rate**, etc.
4. **Training Process**: Train the model using the training data, compute the **loss function**, and update parameters
5. **Generation Process**: Use the trained model to generate text

Below, we mainly analyze the model design and training process.

The model's parameters consist of two parts: the **embedding layer** and the **linear transformation layer**.

- **Embedding Layer:** `EmbeddingLayer: nn.Embedding (vocab_size, embedding_dim)`, used to map character indices to a high-dimensional space, generating embedding representations for each character. This embedding is based on individual characters, which meets the requirements of a **bigram model**.
- **Linear Transformation Layer:** `nn.Linear (embedding_dim, vocab_size)`, used to convert the embedding vector into a `logits` vector, where each element represents the raw score of predicting the next character as a specific character in the vocabulary.

The model's forward propagation process includes the following three steps:

```
def forward(self, current_idx):
    x = self.token_embedding(current_idx).squeeze(1)  # First step
    logits = self.fc_out(x)                           # Second step
    return logits                                     # Return result
```

1. Obtain the embedding vector from the input character index

   ```
   x = self.tokenembedding(current_idx).squeeze(1)
   ```

2. Pass the embedding vector to the linear layer

   ```
   logits = self.fc_out(x)
   ```

3. Return the predicted `logits` vector

In the forward propagation method, the input processed each time is the index of the current character (its shape is adjusted by `unsqueeze` to meet the network's input requirements). The `logits` output by the model is used directly to predict the next character, without relying on any information except the current character. This design chiefly reflects the basic principle of the bigram model, that is, the appearance of each character only relates to its previous character.

In the model training process, based on practical experience, the author has summarized the following key points to pay attention to:

Use the **Adam optimizer** for parameter optimization, with a learning rate set to **0.02**.

In each iteration, a random batch is drawn from the training dataset, and the model's output and loss on that batch are calculated (using the **cross-entropy loss function**).

Backpropagation of the loss function is used to compute gradients, and then the model's parameters are updated.

At certain intervals (for example, every 10,000 iterations), the current training loss is output to monitor the training process.

There are various choices of **optimizers**; different optimizers can be chosen depending on the specific scenario and task. The **Adam optimizer** is a commonly used optimizer that combines the advantages of **AdaGrad** and **RMSProp**, and generally performs well. The **learning rate** is a critical hyperparameter for optimizers, determining the step size of parameter updates. If the learning rate is not set appropriately, it may cause unstable model training or even prevent convergence. Therefore, the selection of the learning rate is crucial in model training. In this example, the author has set the learning rate to **0.02**, which is a common setting. The setting of the learning rate is an open question and usually needs to be adjusted according to specific tasks and models. To select an appropriate learning rate, multiple experiments are usually needed to observe the model's training effect and adjust according to the results. Typically, a learning rate scheduler can be used to dynamically adjust the learning rate to improve model performance, or hyperparameter search can be conducted to find the optimal learning rate.

The **loss function** is a key component of model training and is used to measure the difference between the model's predictions and the true labels. In this example, the **cross-entropy loss function** is used, which is a common loss function for classification tasks. In addition to the cross-entropy loss, there are other loss functions, such as **mean squared error loss, contrastive loss**, etc. Different tasks and models require different loss functions, so choosing an appropriate loss function is an important part of model training. In the current scenario, the **cross-entropy loss function** is a suitable choice because the task is a classification task, that is, predicting the next character as a certain character in the vocabulary.

The model evaluation process mainly uses the **validation dataset** to assess its performance. In the evaluation process, the loss on the validation set is calculated to measure its generalization ability. In this example, the **cross-entropy loss function** is used to calculate the model's loss on the validation dataset. By comparing the **training loss** with the **validation loss**, the effectiveness of model training and generalization ability can be evaluated. If the gap between training loss and validation loss is large, it may indicate that the model is **overfitting** and further adjustment to the model structure or hyperparameters is needed.

The output generated by the model after 3000 iterations is as follows:

```
Step 0: Training Loss = 7.978742599487305
Step 500: Training Loss = 8.489371299743652
Step 1000: Training Loss = 5.403090476989746
Step 1500: Training Loss = 6.415762901306152
```

```
Step 2000: Training Loss = 5.484483242034912
Step 2500: Training Loss = 5.219246864318848
Validation Loss: 7.588761329650879

Valley.

Feeling encounters ten years of decline.

Fragrant herbs pass the checkpoint with Zhou Lang.

Heavenly feather arrows, city grass.

Should idly depend on each other like trees.
```

From the above output, it can be seen that the basic **bigram model**'s loss on the training data gradually decreases, but the loss on the validation data remains high. This may indicate that the model is **overfitting** the training data and has limited generalization ability. The generated output does not produce meaningful sentences, which could be due to the model's **insufficient complexity**, making it unable to capture the complex structures within the text. This example is intended to demonstrate how to use **PyTorch** to build a basic bigram model and train a text generation model. Through this example, readers can understand the basic principles and training workflow of **neural language models**, laying a foundation for subsequent model design and training.

With this basic prediction loop in place, the next section shows how GPT extends the same next-token prediction idea by adding longer context, self-attention, positional embeddings, and stacked Transformer blocks.

Understanding how GPT models generate text

The prediction process in a bigram model considers only the relationship between the current token and the next token. In practical language generation, however, a model needs to use a wider context to understand dependencies across a sequence. GPT models address this limitation by using a decoder-only Transformer architecture with masked self-attention, positional embeddings, and stacked Transformer blocks. This section explains how GPT extends the next-token prediction loop introduced in the bigram model, then shows how the main components of a simple GPT-style model can be implemented in code.

Structure of the GPT model

The GPT model extends the bigram model in three main ways. First, instead of looking at only the previous one token, GPT uses self-attention to consider all previous tokens within the context window. Second, GPT stacks multiple Transformer blocks instead of relying on a single embedding layer and linear output layer. Third, GPT adds positional embeddings so the model can understand where each token appears in the sequence. The core training loop remains similar to the bigram example: the model predicts the next token, the prediction is compared with the target using cross-entropy loss, and the parameters are updated through optimization.

Traditional Transformer models rely on large amounts of labeled data for training, which requires substantial manual annotation and is costly. Researchers at OpenAI proposed a method that does not depend on labeled data, namely, **generative pre-training** on large-scale unlabeled texts, followed by **discriminative fine-tuning** on specific tasks to improve performance in natural language understanding tasks. The structure of the GPT model is similar to that of the **Transformer,** but uses only the **decoder** part of the Transformer. This approach has performed excellently on multiple natural language understanding benchmark tests, surpassing **discriminative training** models designed specifically for each task, and achieving state-of-the-art performance on 9 out of 12 research tasks.

The structure of the **GPT model** and its application scenarios after fine-tuning are shown in *Figure 3.1*.

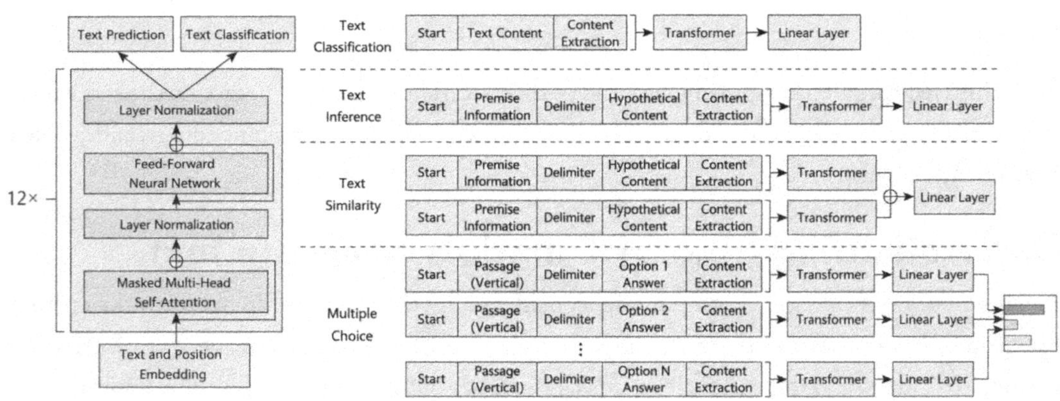

Figure 3.1: Structure of the GPT model and its application scenarios after fine-tuning

The structure diagram of the GPT model is sourced from the paper *Improving Language Understanding by Generative Pretraining*. The core of the GPT model is a **Transformer decoder** composed of multiple **Transformer modules**. Each Transformer module contains a **multi-head self-attention mechanism** and a **feed-forward neural network**. The input to the GPT model is a text sequence, and the model needs to predict the next word. This autoregressive approach can leverage large-scale text data and is suitable for a variety of natural language processing tasks.

The left side of *Figure 3.1* shows the structure of the GPT model, mainly including the following aspects:

- **Text and Position Embedding: Text embedding** converts words into vectors, while **position embedding** provides the model with the positional information of words in the sequence. This combination enables the model to capture both the semantics of words and their positional relationships in the sequence.
- **Masked Multi-Head Self-Attention:** This is a key mechanism in the **Transformer model**, used for handling **language modeling tasks** during the pre-training phase. This mechanism allows the model to consider previous words when predicting the current word, but does not allow the model to "see" future words. This masking mechanism plays an important role in text generation and understanding language models.
- **Layer Normalization:** Layer normalization is a regularization technique used to stabilize the training process. It normalizes the activations of each layer for each sample, helping to prevent vanishing or exploding gradients.
- **Feed-Forward Neural Network:** This is another key component in the **Transformer model**, used for feature extraction and mapping after the multi-head self-attention mechanism. This structure allows the model to extract and combine features at different levels, thus better understanding the text.

The right side of *Figure 3.1* displays application scenarios after **GPT fine-tuning**, covering the following aspects:

- **Text Classification:** This section illustrates the process of the model handling **text classification** tasks. The input text first passes through a **Transformer encoder**, and then a **linear layer (Linear Prediction Classifier)** is used for classification. The linear layer outputs a probability distribution, representing the likelihood that the text belongs to each category.

- **Textual Inference:** Textual inference tasks involve determining the logical relationship (**entailment**, **contradiction**, or **neutrality**) between two pieces of text. In this task, the "premise" and "hypothesis" texts are first separated by a **separator**, then input together into the **Transformer encoder**. Next, the output is processed by a **linear layer**, and finally a probability distribution for the relationship between the two texts is produced.
- **Text Similarity:** The goal of the text similarity task is to assess the semantic similarity between two pieces of text. The two texts (**Text 1** and **Text 2**) are each processed by a **Transformer encoder**, and then a **linear feed-forward neural network layer** is used for similarity scoring.
- **Multiple Choice:** Multiple choice tasks require the model to select the correct answer from multiple options. In the process, the context and **separator** are first input into the **Transformer encoder**, then a series of possible answers (**Answer 1, Answer 2, ... Answer N**) follow. Each answer is processed by a **Transformer encoder** and a **linear layer**. Finally, a **masked multi-head attention** layer integrates all the answer information and outputs the final prediction result.

After examining the overall structure of the GPT model and its main application scenarios, the next step is to look at how these ideas are implemented in code. The following subsection starts with the Transformer block, because this is the core building unit that allows GPT to combine self-attention, feed-forward computation, layer normalization, and residual connections.

GPT model design practices

The data preparation work for the GPT model is similar to that of the bigram model, so it will not be repeated here. The focus is on the design and training process of the GPT model. From the previously mentioned GPT model structure, it can be seen that the core of the GPT model is the Transformer decoder, which is composed of multiple Transformer modules. Each Transformer module contains a multi-head self-attention mechanism and a feedforward neural network.

I will start from the Transformer module, gradually build the GPT model, and expand from a single Transformer module to multiple Transformer modules to better understand the design and training process of GPT models.

We first need to define a Transformer module, then combine multiple Transformer modules together to form the demonstrated model. We can refer to Andrej Karpathy's work to analyze the design of the Transformer module. The relevant code is as follows:

```
class Block(nn.Module):
    """Transformer block: a module containing multi-head attention and a
feed-forward neural network"""

    def __init__(self, n_embd, n_head):
        # n_embd: embedding dimension length, n_head: number of attention
heads
        super().__init__()
        head_size = n_embd // n_head  # dimension of each head = embedding
dimension length / number of attention heads,
                                      # so this setting needs to ensure
divisibility
        self.sa = MultiHeadAttention(n_head, head_size)  # multi-head
self-attention module
        self.ffwd = FeedFoward(n_embd)  # feed-forward neural network
module
        self.ln1 = nn.LayerNorm(n_embd)  # layer normalization
        self.ln2 = nn.LayerNorm(n_embd)  # layer normalization

    def forward(self, x):
x = x + self.sa(self.ln1(x))  # Self-attention and residual connection,
adding the output of the attention layer to the original input
                              # x (residual connection), which helps
prevent the vanishing gradient problem during training.
x = x + self.ffwd(self.ln2(x))  # Feed-forward neural network and residual
connection, adding the output of the feed-forward network
                                # back to the input again (residual
connection)

return x
```

This module includes two main parts: the first is the multi-head self-attention mechanism, and the second is the feedforward neural network. These two parts are core components of the Transformer model, responsible for feature extraction and mapping. The design pattern of self-attention, layer normalization, feedforward networks, and residual connections forms the core of the Transformer model, enabling it to effectively handle sequential data, learn long-range dependencies, and ensure effective gradient propagation in deep networks.

The relevant code implementing the multi-head self-attention mechanism is as follows:

```
class MultiHeadAttention(nn.Module):
    """Multi-head attention model design"""

    def __init__(self, num_heads, head_size):
        super().__init__()
        self.heads = nn.ModuleList([Head(head_size) for _ in range(num_
heads)])
        # Define multiple attention heads
        self.proj = nn.Linear(head_size * num_heads, n_embd)  # Used to
concatenate the outputs of all attention heads and then transform them
        self.dropout = nn.Dropout(dropout)  # Used to reduce overfitting
during model training

    def forward(self, x):
        out = torch.cat([h(x) for h in self.heads], dim=-1)  # Includes
two core parts: call each head's forward method,
                                                              # each head
processes input x and returns its attention calculation result.
                                                              # Then
concatenate the outputs of all heads together
        out = self.dropout(self.proj(out))  # Use the defined linear layer
self.proj to linearly transform the concatenated output,
                                             # fuse information from
different heads, and then randomly discard some information
                                             # to reduce overfitting
        return out
```

The design of the multi-head attention mechanism is relatively straightforward, and its core computational logic is as follows:

- For each head, its `forward` method is called, each head processes the input x and returns its attention computation result
- All outputs from the heads are concatenated together using the `torch.cat` function
- The concatenated outputs are further linearly transformed by the defined linear layer `self.proj` to fuse information from different heads, and then some information is randomly dropped to reduce overfitting

The core part here is the definition of a single head. The relevant code implementing the `Head` method is as follows:

```
class Head(nn.Module):
    """Single-head attention mechanism model"""

    def __init__(self, head_size):
        super().__init__()
        self.key = nn.Linear(n_embd, head_size, bias=False)
        self.query = nn.Linear(n_embd, head_size, bias=False)
        self.value = nn.Linear(n_embd, head_size, bias=False)
        self.register_buffer('tril', torch.tril(torch.ones(block_size,
block_size)))
        self.dropout = nn.Dropout(dropout)

def forward(self, x):
    # The input size is (batch, time-step, channels)
    # The output size is (batch, time-step, head size)

    B,T,C = x.shape
    k = self.key(x)    # (B,T,hs)
    q = self.query(x)  # (B,T,hs)

    # Calculate attention scores
    wei = q @ k.transpose(-2,-1) * k.shape[-1]**-0.5  # (B, T, hs) @ (B,
hs, T)
                                                        # -> (B, T, T)
    wei = wei.masked_fill(self.tril[:T, :T] ==0, float('-inf'))  # (B, T,
T)
    wei = F.softmax(wei, dim=-1)  # (B, T, T)
    wei = self.dropout(wei)

    # Perform weighted aggregation on values
    v = self.value(x)  # matrix size information (B,T,hs)
    out = wei @ v  # matrix calculation size conversion annotation (B, T,
T) @ (B, T, hs) -> (B, T, hs)
    return out
```

The basic definition of a single **self-attention model** includes 5 parts:

- **Query:** The main function of the query is to compute its compatibility or similarity with each key. Each query corresponds to an element (or a time step) in the input sequence and is used to compare with all keys to determine which parts of the sequence the model should focus on.
- **Key:** The key is used to match with the query and generate a score (usually computed via dot product), which reflects the degree of correlation between each query and the elements in the sequence.
- **Value:** In the self-attention mechanism, each input element (such as a word or a point in a time series) has a corresponding "value" vector, which carries important information about that element. After the attention weights for each element (i.e., which elements are more important and should be attended to) are calculated, these weights are used to weight the "values." The weighted "values" are then combined, forming the final output that represents an integrated expression of the entire input sequence.
- **A Buffer:** The buffer is used to store a lower-triangular matrix, which is utilized to mask future information when computing attention scores.
- **A Dropout Layer:** Dropout refers to randomly dropping some neurons during neural network training, which helps to reduce the complexity of the network and thereby prevent overfitting.

The matrices for queries, keys, and values are typically dense matrices with a size of `n_embd × head_size`. These three linear layers are updated constantly through the model's training process, enabling the model to better learn patterns and relationships within the input data. This learning and adjustment are achieved through optimizing the loss function, performing backpropagation, and updating the weights. In the absence of bias terms, each linear transformation relies only on its weight matrix, thereby reducing the number of model parameters and, at times, helping to avoid overfitting.

Before analyzing the mathematical operations inside the attention head, it is useful to separate the overall structure from the forward computation. The previous code defines the query, key, value, masking buffer, and dropout layer. The following subsection explains how these components work together during the forward pass to calculate attention scores and produce the final weighted output.

Core computational logic of the forward function

The core computational logic of the `forward` function in a single-head attention mechanism model includes the following three aspects:

1. Perform linear transformation on the **queries, keys**, and **values**, then compute the attention scores
2. Calculate attention weights using the softmax activation function, and then use these weights to weight the **values**
3. Finally, the weighted values are returned. This value represents a comprehensive expression of the input sequence.

Among them, the core step of calculating the **attention scores** is noteworthy:

```
wei = q @ k.transpose(-2, -1) * k.shape[-1]**-0.5 # (B, T, hs) @ (B, hs,
T)->(B, T, T)
```

This line of code is the core part of calculating the attention scores in the self-attention mechanism.

Here, ***q*** represents the **query matrix**, with dimensions (*B*, *T*, *hs*), where *B* is the batch size, *T* is the sequence length, and *hs* is the size of each **attention head**. ***k*** represents the **key matrix**, which also has dimensions (*B*, *T*, *hs*).

The detailed explanation of the above calculation logic is as follows:

Matrix transposition

`k.transpose(-2, -1)`: This operation transposes the last two dimensions of the ***k*** matrix. Since the original dimension of ***k*** is (*B*, *T*, *hs*), after the transpose it becomes (*B*, *hs*, *T*). The purpose of this is to align the feature dimension of the key matrix with the time dimension of the query matrix, so as to compute the dot product between each query vector and all key vectors.

Matrix multiplication

`q@k.transpose(-2, -1)`: Here the @ symbol is used to perform batched matrix multiplication. The **query matrix *q*** is multiplied by the transposed **key matrix *k***, resulting in a new three-dimensional matrix (*B*, *T*, *T*). Each element (b, i, j) in this matrix represents the dot product between the *i*-th query vector and the *j*-th key vector in the *b*-th sample, namely the **attention score** of query *i* to key *j*.

Scaling factor

`k.shape[-1]**-0.5`: This code scales the score matrix. `k.shape[-1]` is the dimension of the key vector *hs*, *hs* ** -0.5 is equivalent to $1/\sqrt{(hs)}$. This scaling is based on the **scaled dot-product attention mechanism** to prevent the **vanishing gradient problem** caused by too large score values when computing the softmax. By dividing by the square root of the **key vector** dimension, we ensure the score matrix remains within a reasonable numerical range, which is beneficial for **gradient stability** and **model training performance**.

Masked self-attention is another part worth noting:

```
wei = wei.masked_fill(self.tril[:T, :T] = 0, float('-inf'))  # (B, T, T)
```

This line of code uses a **lower triangular matrix** to mask future information. In the **self-attention mechanism**, when the model predicts the current word, it can only refer to previous words and cannot "see" future words. This **masking mechanism** is critical for **text generation** and the understanding of **language models**. Here, a lower triangular matrix is used to mask future information; that is, future information is set to negative infinity, so when computing the softmax, the corresponding weights of future information become 0, thereby achieving the masking of future information.

A detailed explanation of the above computational logic is as follows:

- **Extracting the lower triangular matrix**: `self.tril[:T, :T]`. This operation extracts the first *T* rows and *T* columns of the **lower triangular matrix** to ensure it matches the dimensions of the **attention score matrix** `wei`.
- **Masking operation**: `self.tril[:T, :T] == 0`. This step generates a boolean matrix where the positions with 0 in the lower triangular matrix (i.e., above the diagonal) are marked as **True**, and the rest as **False**.
- **Filling operation**: The `wei.masked_fill` function replaces the positions in the `wei` matrix, where the boolean matrix is **True**, with a specified value, here `float('-inf')` (negative infinity). This means that, before applying the **softmax function**, all positions with an invalid causal relationship (i.e., a time step should not be able to "see" information from subsequent time steps) are set to negative infinity.

This code successfully prevents information from leaking forward by setting the **attention scores** for future time steps to negative infinity. When executing the **softmax function**, the exponentials of these negative infinity positions are close to 0, thereby ensuring every time step can only attend to itself and previous time steps.

This is a key mechanism in **generative tasks** (such as next-word prediction in language models) and other scenarios requiring the maintenance of causal relationships.

The final step of the **self-attention mechanism** is to compute the weighted logic.

out = wei @ v # Matrix multiplication dimension transformation comment (*B*, *T*, *T*) @ (*B*, *T*, *hs*) -> (*B*, *T*, *hs*)

Where, the variable explanations are as follows.

- `wei`: The **attention score matrix** obtained by calculating the dot product of the **query** (`q`) and **key** (`k`), with dimensions (*B*, *T*, *T*), where *B* is the batch size and *T* is the sequence length.
- `v`: The **value matrix**, with dimensions (*B*, *T*, *hs*), where each row represents the value vector for the corresponding time step. These vectors contain information from the input sequence and are weighted according to the computed **attention weights**.

A detailed explanation of the above operation is as follows:

Matrix multiplication is performed in batch using the `@` symbol. In this operation, `wei` has dimensions (*B*, *T*, *T*), and `v` has dimensions (*B*, *T*, *hs*). The resulting matrix `out` has dimensions (*B*, *T*, *hs*).

For each batch (each *B*), the output at each time step *T* is calculated by performing a weighted sum over all **value vectors *v*** across time steps, where the weights are provided by **wei**. Specifically, each element (*b*, *i*, *j*) in the output is computed through a weighted sum between `wei[*b*, *i*, :]` and `v[*b*, :, *j*]`.

In this step, each row in **wei** serves as a set of weighting coefficients, which are used to compute a weighted combination with all rows (value vectors) in ***v***, yielding a weighted value vector that reflects the model's summary of the information that should be attended at each time step. This process essentially applies the **attention mechanism's weights** to the **value vectors**. The final **out** output provides a representation that synthesizes information from the entire sequence, with each time step's information dynamically weighted based on prior (and current, if no mask is used) information.

After explaining the individual components of the Transformer block and the core logic of self-attention, the next step is to assemble these pieces into a complete GPT-style language model. The following implementation combines token embeddings, positional embeddings, multiple Transformer blocks, loss calculation, optimization, and generation into one end-to-end example.

Complete implementation of a simple GPT model

In this section, we use the example of building a **poetry generation model** to construct a simple **GPT model** and describe the process of generating text. The complete implementation code is as follows:

```
import torch
import torch.nn as nn
from torch.nn import functional as F
from sklearn.model_selection import train_test_split

# Hyperparameters
batch_size = 64  # How many independent sequences will we process in
parallel?
block_size = 256  # What is the maximum context length for prediction?
max_iters = 5000
eval_interval = 500
learning_rate = 3e-4
device = 'cuda' if torch.cuda.is_available() else'cpu'
eval_iters = 200
n_embd = 384
n_head = 6
n_layer = 6
dropout = 0.3

torch.manual_seed(42)
txt_file='D:\\OneDrive\\2024\\AI\\nano_gpt\\tang_300.txt'
with open(txt_file, 'r', encoding='utf-8') as f:
    lines = f.readlines()

# Find the indices of lines containing '---'
split_indices = [i for i, line in enumerate(lines) if '---' in line]

# Split the lines according to the indices
parts = []
start = 0
for index in split_indices:
    poetry = ''.join(lines[start:index])
```

```
    parts.append(poetry)
    start = index +1
rest = ''.join(lines[start:])
parts.append(rest)  # Add the final part
print(len(parts))

# Remove parts with fewer than 2 lines
parts = [part for part in parts if len(part.split('\n')) >3]
print(len(parts))
text = ''.join(parts)
chars = sorted(list(set(text)))
vocab_size = len(chars)

# Build the mapping from characters to numbers and from numbers to 
characters
char_indices = dict((c, i) for i, c in enumerate(chars))
indices_char = dict((i, c) for i, c in enumerate(chars))

# Basic function for converting text into numbers
def text_to_indices(text):
    return [char_indices[c] for c in text]

def indices_to_text(indices):
    return ''.join(indices_char[i] for i in indices)

train, val = train_test_split(parts, test_size=0.1)
train_data = ''.join(train)
train_data = text_to_indices(train_data)
val_data = ''.join(val)
val_data = text_to_indices(val_data)

def get_batch(split):
    # Generate a small batch of input x and target y data
    data = train_data if split == 'train' else val_data
    ix = torch.randint(len(data) - block_size, (batch_size,))
    x = torch.stack([torch.tensor(data[i:i+block_size]) for i in ix])
    y = torch.stack([torch.tensor(data[i+1:i+block_size+1]) for i in ix])
```

```
    x, y = x.to(device), y.to(device)
    return x, y

@torch.no_grad()
def estimate_loss():
    out = {}
    model.eval()
    for split in ['train', 'val']:
        losses = torch.zeros(eval_iters)
        for k in range(eval_iters):
            X, Y = get_batch(split)
            logits, loss = model(X, Y)
            losses[k] = loss.item()
        out[split] = losses.mean()
    model.train()
    return out

class Head(nn.Module):
    """A single head in the self-attention mechanism"""

    def __init__(self, head_size):
        super().__init__()
        self.key = nn.Linear(n_embd, head_size, bias=False)
        self.query = nn.Linear(n_embd, head_size, bias=False)
        self.value = nn.Linear(n_embd, head_size, bias=False)
        self.register_buffer('tril', torch.tril(torch.ones(block_size,
block_size)))

        self.dropout = nn.Dropout(dropout)

    def forward(self, x):
        # Input size: (batch size, time steps, channels)
# Output size: (batch size, time steps, head size)
B,T,C = x.shape
k = self.key(x)    # (B,T,hs)
q = self.query(x)  # (B,T,hs)
```

```
        # Calculate attention scores
        wei = q @ k.transpose(-2,-1) * k.shape[-1]**-0.5  # (B, T, hs) @ (B, hs, 
T)
                                                          # -> (B, T, T)
        wei = wei.masked_fill(self.tril[:T, :T] == 0, float('-inf'))  # (B, T, T)
        wei = F.softmax(wei, dim=-1)  # (B, T, T)
        wei = self.dropout(wei)

        # Perform weighted aggregation on values
        v = self.value(x)  # (B,T,hs)
        out = wei @ v  # (B, T, T) @ (B, T, hs) -> (B, T, hs)
        return out


class MultiHeadAttention(nn.Module):
    """Parallel multi-head self-attention mechanism"""

    def __init__(self, num_heads, head_size):
        super().__init__()
        self.heads = nn.ModuleList([Head(head_size) for _ in range(num_
heads)])
        self.proj = nn.Linear(head_size * num_heads, n_embd)
        self.dropout = nn.Dropout(dropout)

    def forward(self, x):
        out = torch.cat([h(x) for h in self.heads], dim=-1)
        out = self.dropout(self.proj(out))
        return out


class FeedForward(nn.Module):
    """A simple linear layer plus a nonlinear activation function"""

    def __init__(self, n_embd):
        super().__init__()
        self.net = nn.Sequential(
            nn.Linear(n_embd, 4*n_embd),
            nn.ReLU(),
```

```
            nn.Linear(4*n_embd, n_embd),
            nn.Dropout(dropout),
        )

    def forward(self, x):
        return self.net(x)


class Block(nn.Module):
    """Transformer module: first perform information exchange, then
perform computation"""

    def __init__(self, n_embd, n_head):
# n_embd: embedding dimension, n_head: required number of heads
super().__init__()
head_size = n_embd // n_head
self.sa = MultiHeadAttention(n_head, head_size)
self.ffwd = FeedForward(n_embd)
self.ln1 = nn.LayerNorm(n_embd)
self.ln2 = nn.LayerNorm(n_embd)

def forward(self, x):
    x = x + self.sa(self.ln1(x))
    x = x + self.ffwd(self.ln2(x))
    return x


class GPTLanguageModel(nn.Module):

    def __init__(self):
        super().__init__()
        # Each token directly reads the logits vector for the next token
from the lookup table
        self.token_embedding_table = nn.Embedding(vocab_size, n_embd)
        self.position_embedding_table = nn.Embedding(block_size, n_embd)
        self.blocks = nn.Sequential(*[Block(n_embd, n_head=n_head) for _
in
            range(n_layer)])
```

```
        self.ln_f = nn.LayerNorm(n_embd)  # Final layer normalization
        self.lm_head = nn.Linear(n_embd, vocab_size)
        self.apply(self._init_weights)

    def _init_weights(self, module):
        if isinstance(module, nn.Linear):
            torch.nn.init.normal_(module.weight, mean=0.0, std=0.02)
            if module.bias is not None:
                torch.nn.init.zeros_(module.bias)
        elif isinstance(module, nn.Embedding):
            torch.nn.init.normal_(module.weight, mean=0.0, std=0.02)

    def forward(self, idx, targets=None):
        B, T = idx.shape

        # idx and targets are both integer tensors with shape (B,T)
        tok_emb = self.token_embedding_table(idx)  # (B,T,C)
        pos_emb = self.position_embedding_table(torch.arange(T,
device=device))
        # (T,C)
        x = tok_emb + pos_emb  # (B,T,C)
        x = self.blocks(x)  # (B,T,C)
        x = self.ln_f(x)  # (B,T,C)
        logits = self.lm_head(x)  # (B,T,vocab_size)

        if targets is None:
            loss = None
else:
    B, T, C = logits.shape
    logits = logits.view(B*T, C)
    targets = targets.view(B*T)
    loss = F.cross_entropy(logits, targets)

return logits, loss

def generate(self, idx, max_new_tokens):
    # idx is an index array in the current context with shape (B, T)
```

```
    for _ in range(max_new_tokens):
        # Crop idx to the last block_size tokens
        idx_cond = idx[:, -block_size:]

        # Get prediction results
        logits, loss = self(idx_cond)

        # Focus only on the last time step
        logits = logits[:, -1, :]  # Change to (B, C)

        # Apply softmax to obtain probabilities
        probs = F.softmax(logits, dim=-1)  # (B, C)

        # Sample from the distribution
        idx_next = torch.multinomial(probs, num_samples=1)  # (B, 1)

        # Append the sampled index to the sequence being generated
        idx = torch.cat((idx, idx_next), dim=1)  # (B, T+1)

    return idx

model = GPTLanguageModel()
m = model.to(device)

# Print the number of parameters in the model
print(sum(p.numel() for p in m.parameters())/1e6, 'M parameters')

# Create a PyTorch optimizer
optimizer = torch.optim.AdamW(model.parameters(), lr=learning_rate)

for iter in range(max_iters):

    # Estimate loss on the training set and validation set
    if iter % eval_interval == 0 or iter == max_iters -1:
        losses = estimate_loss()
        print(f"Step {iter}: Training loss {losses['train']:.4f},
Validation loss {losses['val']:.4f}")
```

```
    # Draw a batch of data
    xb, yb = get_batch('train')

    # Calculate loss
    logits, loss = model(xb, yb)
    optimizer.zero_grad(set_to_none = True)
    loss.backward()
optimizer.step()

# Generate text from the model
start_token = '谷雨'# Grain Rain
context = torch.tensor(text_to_indices(start_token), dtype=torch.long,
device =
                       device).unsqueeze(0)
print(indices_to_text(m.generate(context, max_new_tokens = 60)[0].
tolist()))
```

The training result of the above code is as follows:

```
step 0: train loss 7.9190, val loss 7.9300
step 500: train loss 0.0763, val loss 8.5916
step 1000: train loss 0.0393, val loss 9.4898
step 1500: train loss 0.0311, val loss 10.0692
step 2000: train loss 0.0273, val loss 10.4250
step 2500: train loss 0.0251, val loss 10.6450
step 3000: train loss 0.0236, val loss 10.9122
step 3500: train loss 0.0227, val loss 11.2083
step 4000: train loss 0.0215, val loss 11.4073
step 4500: train loss 0.0207, val loss 11.5654
step 4999: train loss 0.0202, val loss 11.7918

Grain Rain though beautiful, now arrives.
Sighing over autumn dwellings and autumn chants.
After fresh rain in the empty mountains, evening weather brings autumn.
The bright moon and pine sounds come late, when words and thoughts wish
for snow.
A dragon leaves the frontier river, crossing a snowy sea.
At the summit, who can surpass it?
```

This complete process of **model training** and **prediction generation**, along with the corresponding generated results, demonstrates the implementation of a simple GPT model. However, this is only for simulation testing and has significant differences from actual business application scenarios. Here, the author proposes several ideas to provide readers with diverse approaches if they encounter the following issues in practical applications, mainly including the following aspects:

- The code has been run for 5,000 iterations. Is this number of iterations appropriate? Can it be terminated early? Is further training necessary?
- The loss value of the validation set keeps increasing—does this mean the model is overfitting? Is it necessary to further adjust the model structure or hyperparameters?
- During code execution, can more logging be added to better understand the model's training process and results?
- The generated results do not strictly follow the poetry format; for example, the ending does not use the "seven-character quatrain" form. Can the generation logic be further adjusted to make the generated poetry more standard?
- The model's output does not have clear start and end markers—can it be further optimized to better distinguish the generated content?

The simple GPT implementation shows how the model can use self-attention and stacked Transformer blocks to generate text from a longer context than the bigram model. However, the results also reveal several practical issues, including overfitting, unstable validation loss, limited output control, and the absence of clear start and end markers. The next section focuses on techniques for improving GPT model training and generation so that the model can produce more controlled and reliable outputs.

Improving GPT model training and generation

The simple GPT implementation in the previous section showed how a Transformer-based language model can generate text, but it also exposed several practical limitations: the model can overfit, the generated output may not follow the expected structure, and the model may not know where a generated sequence should begin or end. This section continues with the poetry generation example and introduces several optimization techniques for improving training quality and generation control, including sample filtering, special symbols, early stopping, and reinforcement learning-based reward signals.

Filtering training samples for better GPT generation

Large GPT-type models require extremely high data quality; low-quality data can only generate low-quality results. For example, in poetry generation, common poems are mainly divided into **five-character poetry** and **seven-character poetry**. Typically, a regulated verse has eight lines, and a quatrain has four lines. However, in actual Tang poetry, the longest can exceed 1000 characters. To train a conventional poetry model, excessively long poems must be removed from the sample data (such as the famous *The Song of Everlasting Regret*, which, including punctuation marks, has a total of 1,024 characters). This involves **data analysis** of the sample contents.

Below is a simple sample data analysis code:

```
# Read Tang Poetry 300 data
import os
import json

file_path = "D:\\chinese_poetry\\chinese-poetry\\Complete_Tang_Poems\\
Three_Hundred_Tang_Poems.json"
dst_file_path="D:\\OneDrive\\2024\\AI\\nano_gpt"

# Read JSON file from file_path and return a list of JSON objects
def read_json_files(file_path):
    with open(os.path.join(file_path, file_path), 'r', encoding='utf-8')
as f:
        json_objects = jsonload(f)
    return json_objects

json_objects = read_json_files(file_path)
print('json_objects:', len(json_objects))
print(json_objects[0])

txt_file = os.path.join(dst_file_path, 'tang_300.txt')
for obj in json_objects:
    # print(json_obj)
    title = obj['title']
    paragraphs = obj['paragraphs']
    with open(txt_file, 'a', encoding='utf-8') as f:
        f.write('---'+'\n')  # Use "---" to separate each poem, making it
easier to later split each poem and construct special "start" and "end"
```

```
symbols
        f.write(title +'\n')
        for paragraph in paragraphs:
            f.write(paragraph +'\n')

# Filter out overly long poems
txt_file="tang_300.txt"
with open(txt_file, 'r', encoding='utf-8') as f:
    lines = freadlines()

# Find the indices of lines containing "---"
split_indices = [i for i, line in enumerate(lines) if '---'in line]

# Split according to the indices
parts = []
start = 0
for index in split_indices:
    poetry = ''.join(lines[start:index])
    parts.append(poetry)
    start = index +1
rest = ''.join(lines[start:])
parts.append(rest)

part_len = [len(part) for part in parts]

avg_len = sum(part_len) / len(part_len)
print(f'Average length of parts: {avg_len}')
import pandas as pd
df = pd.DataFrame(part_len, columns = ['length'])
print(df.describe())

# Delete parts with fewer than 2 characters or more than 81 characters
parts = [part for part in parts if len(part) >2 and len(part) <= 81]

with open('tang_300_clean_81.txt', 'w', encoding='utf-8') as f:
    for part in parts:
        f.write('---\n')
        f.write(''.join(part))
```

The following results were obtained by analyzing **poem lengths**:

```
Average length of parts: 80.57220708446866
          length
count  367.000000
mean    80.572207
std     89.549447
min      0.000000
25%     40.500000
50%     58.000000
75%     75.000000
max   1024.000000
```

Based on the data analysis, setting the poem length to 81 characters can ensure that most poems are included while filtering out excessively long poems, thereby avoiding negative impacts on training effectiveness due to overly long input. The fundamental reason for this is that LLMs require a unified **sequence length** during sample training. Extreme sequence lengths increase the difficulty of **model training**, thus affecting the model's **training performance**.

After filtering the sample data to remove unusually long or unsuitable examples, the next step is to help the model understand the structure of each generated sequence. For text generation, this means giving the model explicit signals for where a poem begins, where it ends, how shorter sequences are padded, and how unknown characters should be handled.

Adding special tokens to mark sequence boundaries

To achieve this, four types of **special symbols** are introduced: **start symbol**, **end symbol**, **padding symbol**, and **unknown symbol**. During sample processing, each symbol (including comma, period, question mark, etc.) is converted into a corresponding index number for easier model processing. By learning these special symbols, the model can better understand input data and generate fluent poetry. Since there are no specific characters to denote the start or end, user-defined special symbols can be added at the beginning and end of the poem. In this way, the model will learn the meaning of these symbols during training, and thus generate poetry that meets specifications. Generally, the start symbol is set as `"<start>"`, the end symbol as `"<end>"`, the padding symbol as `"<pad>"`, and the unknown symbol as `"<unk>"`. The introduction of **start** and **end symbols** helps the model to better understand and process input data, enhancing training effectiveness; the **padding symbol** helps handle inputs of different lengths; the **unknown symbol** increases the model's capability to handle unknown inputs, enhancing its generalization ability.

The following code demonstrates how to add these four special symbols when building the character dictionary:

```
def load_and_process_data(txt_file):
    with open(txt_file, 'r', encoding='utf-8') as f:
        lines = f.readlines()

    split_indices = [i for i, line in enumerate(lines) if '---' in line]
    parts = []
    start = 0
    for index in split_indices:
        poetry = '<start>'+''.join(lines[start:index]) + '<end>'
        parts.append(poetry)
        start = index +1
    rest = '<start>' + ''.join(lines[start:]) +'<end>'  # Add a special
symbol to mark the start and end of each poem
    parts.append(rest)
    parts = [part for part in parts if len(part) > 20]

    text = ''.join(parts)
    tokens = re.split('(<start>|<end>)', text)
    chars = set()
    for token in tokens:
        if token in ('<start>', '<end>'):
            chars.add(token)
        else:
            chars.update(set(token))
    chars.update(['<unk>', '<pad>'])  # Add two additional special symbols
for subsequent training and generation
    char_indices = {c: i for i, c in enumerate(sorted(chars))}
    indices_char = {i: c for i, c in enumerate(sorted(chars))}
    vocab_size = len(chars)
    return parts, char_indices, indices_char, vocab_size
```

Once special symbols have been introduced, they must be included in the same numerical mapping process as ordinary characters. The next subsection explains how these symbols are converted into token indexes so that the model can learn and generate them during training.

Mapping special tokens to numerical indices

During the process of converting characters to numbers, how should special symbols (such as `[cls]`, `[pad]`, etc.) be handled? We can convert **special symbols** to index numbers so that the model can process these symbols more effectively during training. The code for converting special symbols to index numbers is as follows:

```
def text_to_indices(text_parts, char_indices):
indices_list = []
for part in text_parts:
    tokens = re.split('(<start>|<end>)', part)  # Split according to
special symbols. The generated result
                                                # is a list with three
elements. The first and last elements
                                                # are empty strings after
splitting because they are delimiters,
                                                # so only the middle part
is kept as the text portion.
    content = tokens[1]
    content_list = list(content)
    indices = [char_indices['<start>']] + [char_indices[token] for token
                                           in content_list] + [char_
indices['<end>']]  # Manually add the serial numbers

# mapped from the start and end symbols

# for use in training
    indices_list.append(torch.tensor(indices, dtype=torch.long))
return indices_list
```

After improving the input representation with filtered samples and special symbols, the next concern is the training process itself. If training continues after validation performance stops improving, the model may memorize the training data and generalize poorly. Early stopping addresses this problem by monitoring validation loss and stopping training when further updates are no longer beneficial.

Applying early stopping to reduce overfitting

During model training, the application of an **early stopping strategy** is crucial. Its proper use can effectively prevent the model from **overfitting** and enhance the model's **generalization ability**. During training, by monitoring the **loss value** on the validation set, training can be terminated early to prevent overfitting. Typically, during model training, the loss value on the validation set is evaluated at regular intervals. If the loss value does not decrease over several consecutive iterations, training can be stopped early. This process can be implemented using PyTorch's `EarlyStopping` class, and saving the model after early stopping is also an essential step. Below is a simple implementation process:

```
class EarlyStopping:
    def __init__(self, patience = 5, verbose = False, delta = 0.01):
        self.patience = patience
        self.verbose = verbose
        self.delta = delta
        self.best_score = None
        self.early_stop = False
        self.counter = 0

    def __call__(self, score, model):
        if self.best_score is None:
            self.best_score = score
            self.save_checkpoint(model)
        elif score < self.best_score +self.delta:
            self.counter += 1
            if self.verbose:
                print(f'EarlyStopping counter: {self.counter} out of
{self.
                        patience}')
            if self.counter >= self.patience:
                self.early_stop = True
        else:
            self.best_score = score
            self.save_checkpoint(model)
            self.counter = 0
def save_checkpoint(self, model):
    torch.save(model.state_dict(), 'checkpoint.pt')
    print('Model improved and saved!')
```

Early stopping helps control overfitting, but it does not directly tell the model what makes an output good or bad. Reinforcement learning provides another way to shape generation behavior by assigning rewards or penalties to generated sequences. In this example, rewards can be used to encourage outputs with proper start and end markers and penalize outputs with repeated unknown tokens or malformed punctuation.

Using reinforcement learning to guide text generation

Reinforcement learning is a machine learning method that learns to take actions in an environment by observing environmental feedback. During the process of model training, **reinforcement learning methods** can be used to optimize the model's generation logic in order to generate poems that better conform to the required norms. This process typically involves monitoring the quality of poems generated by the model and adjusting the model parameters to improve the generation performance. For example, if there are non-compliant phenomena in the generated poetry, such as consecutive punctuation marks or repeated words, reinforcement learning can be used to adjust the model parameters and enhance the generated results. The reinforcement learning implementation process for consecutive punctuation marks and special symbols includes three parts: **reinforcement learning evaluation, reinforcement learning evaluation during the generation process**, and **reinforcement learning during training**. The related code is as follows:

```
# Reinforcement learning evaluation
def compute_reward(idx_sequence, indices_char):
    text = indices_to_text(idx_sequence, indices_char)
    reward = 0

    if text.startswith('<start>') and text.endswith('<end>'):
        reward += 1
    else:
        reward -= 1

    start_count = text.count('<start>')
    end_count = text.count('<end>')
    pad_count = text.count('<pad>')

    if start_count == 1 and end_count == 1:
        reward += 1
    else:
        reward -= (start_count + end_count -2)
```

```
    reward -= pad_count
    consecutive_unk_penalty = text.count('<unk><unk>')
    reward -= consecutive_unk_penalty

    consecutive_symbol_penalty = sum(text.count(c *3) for c in ',.?!')
    reward -= consecutive_symbol_penalty

    reward = max(reward, 0)
    return reward


# Reinforcement learning evaluation during generation
def generate_with_rewards(model, initial_idxs, max_new_tokens, char_
indices,
                          indices_char, device):
    model.eval()
    log_probs = []
    rewards = []
    idxs = initial_idxs.to(device)

    with torch.no_grad():
for _ in range(max_new_tokens):
    logits, _ = model(idxs)
    probs = F.softmax(logits[:, -1, :], dim = -1)
    distribution = Categorical(probs)
    next_tokens = distribution.sample()
    log_probs.extend(distribution.log_prob(next_tokens))
    idxs = torch.cat([idxs, next_tokens.unsqueeze(1)], dim = 1)
    batch_rewards = [0] * next_tokens.size(0)

    for i, next_token in enumerate(next_tokens):
        if next_token.item() == char_indices['<end>']:
            generated_text = indices_to_text(idxs[i].cpu().numpy(),
                                             indices_char)
            reward = compute_reward(generated_text, indices_char)
            batch_rewards[i] = reward
```

```
    rewards.extend(batch_rewards)

rewards = torch.tensor(rewards, dtype=torch.float, device=device)
rewards = rewards / (rewards.max() +1e-8) * 10 * config['rl_reward_scale']
log_probs = torch.stack(log_probs).squeeze()
return idxs, log_probs, rewards


# Reinforcement learning during training
def train_with_rl(model, optimizer, data_loader, max_new_tokens, char_
              indices, indices_char, device):
    model.train()
    total_loss = 0

    for xb, yb in data_loader:
        xb, yb = xb.to(device), yb.to(device)
        logits, loss = model(xb, yb)
        generated_sequences, log_probs, rewards = generate_with_
            rewards(model, xb, max_new_tokens, char_indices, indices_char,
                   device)

        if not log_probs.numel():
            continue

        rl_loss = -torch.sum(log_probs * rewards)
        combined_loss = config['supervised_loss_weight'] * loss +
config['rl_
            loss_weight'] * rl_loss

        optimizer.zero_grad()
        combined_loss.backward()
        torch.nn.utils.clip_grad_norm_(model.parameters(),
config['gradient_
            clip'])
        optimizer.step()
        total_loss += combined_loss.item()

    return total_loss /len(data_loader)
```

In this example, the reinforcement learning part mainly demonstrates the principles. In actual training, more factors need to be considered, such as the weights of rewards and penalties, the methods used to calculate rewards and penalties, evaluation standards for generated results, etc. These factors should be adjusted according to the specific application scenario in order to improve model generation performance.

Summary

This chapter traced the development path from the Transformer architecture to GPT and ChatGPT. It began by explaining why the original Transformer model was important for natural language processing and how GPT adapted the Transformer decoder for autoregressive text generation. The chapter then introduced a basic bigram language model to show the simplest form of next-token prediction, including how text is converted into numerical indexes, how embeddings are used, and how a model can be trained and evaluated.

Building on this foundation, the chapter showed how GPT extends the same prediction loop by using longer context, positional embeddings, masked self-attention, and stacked Transformer blocks. Through a simplified GPT implementation, readers saw how token embeddings, attention heads, feed-forward layers, loss calculation, optimization, and text generation work together in a GPT-style language model. The final section then discussed practical ways to improve model training and generation, including filtering training samples, adding special tokens, mapping those tokens to numerical indexes, applying early stopping, and using reinforcement learning signals to guide generated output.

Together, these concepts show how GPT-style models are built, trained, and improved for text generation. However, building or pre-training a model is only one part of practical LLM development. In real-world applications, organizations often need to adapt an existing pre-trained model to a specific task, dataset, or domain. The next chapter therefore moves from understanding how GPT-style models work to exploring how large language models can be adapted through fine-tuning techniques such as PEFT, LoRA, and QLoRA.

4

Applying Efficient Fine-Tuning Techniques to LLMs

With the support of massive amounts of data and large-scale computing resources, we can build a foundational LLM using GPT models. Foundational LLMs are capable of handling a variety of tasks, such as **text generation**, **text classification**, **text summarization**, and **text translation**. However, in practical applications, foundational LLMs often do not perform ideally on tasks in **vertical domains**. For example, when applying a pre-trained LLM to a knowledge Q&A task in the specific field of financial services, the model may underperform due to the lack of training on business domain knowledge specific to a particular company. In order to adapt the pre-trained LLM to a specific task, we need to take additional technical measures. One such approach is to **fine-tune** the foundational model to optimize its performance for the target task. This chapter will introduce fine-tuning techniques for pre-trained LLMs.

In this chapter, you will cover the following topics:

- Understanding fine-tuning for LLMs
- Exploring key fine-tuning techniques
- Using the PEFT toolkit for efficient fine-tuning
- Implementing LoRA in practice
- Applying fine-tuning to contract text classification
- Applying quantization techniques in QLoRA

Understanding fine-tuning for LLMs

Fine-tuning is a machine learning technique aimed at applying a model pre-trained on large-scale datasets to specific tasks. Its purpose is to adapt the model to the data distribution of the target task and thus improve its performance on that task. The fine-tuning process typically includes the following five steps:

1. Clean and process the new dataset, usually splitting it into training, validation, and test sets according to a certain ratio
2. Adjust the structure of the pre-trained model, typically by adding new layers on top or modifying parts of the network structure
3. Set fine-tuning hyperparameters, such as **learning rate**, **batch size**, etc.
4. When training the model with the new dataset, use the **validation set** to adjust the model's hyperparameters
5. Use the **test set** to evaluate the performance of the model

Before introducing model fine-tuning, let us first review the inference process of LLMs. The inference process of LLMs involves inputting a text sequence and having the model generate an output text sequence based on the input. This process depends on the model's **parameters**, which are obtained through **pre-training** on large-scale datasets and thus contain vast amounts of knowledge. The inference process is shown in *Figure 4.1*.

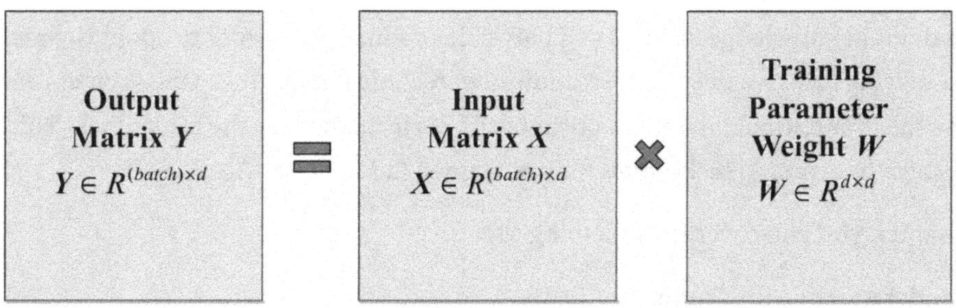

$$Y = X \times W$$

Figure 4.1: Inference process of LLMs

In *Figure 4.1*, *X* represents the result of vectorizing the input text, which has three dimensions: **batch size** *b*, **text length** *l*, and **word embedding dimension** *d*. The model parameters *W* are obtained through large-scale dataset pre-training and contain a large amount of knowledge. The model output *Y* is the text sequence generated based on the input text. During the inference process, the model parameters *W* remain fixed and do not change. Therefore, the model output *Y* is generated based on the input text *X* and the model parameters *W*.

Once the basic fine-tuning process is clear, the next step is to compare the main ways a pre-trained model can be adapted. Fine-tuning methods differ mainly in how much of the model they change: some update all model parameters, some update only a small number of task-specific parameters, and some intervene in the model's internal representations instead of directly modifying its weights.

Comparing fine-tuning approaches

Fine-tuning approaches can be understood as a spectrum of adaptation strategies. At one end, full-parameter fine-tuning updates the entire model and can be effective but expensive. In the middle, parameter-efficient methods update only selected modules or added parameters to reduce training cost. At the other end, representation fine-tuning adapts model behavior by intervening in hidden representations rather than retraining the full model. The following subsections compare these approaches and explain when each type is useful.

Full-parameter fine-tuning

Full-parameter fine-tuning is the earliest form of fine-tuning technology. It adjusts all the parameters of a pre-trained model with data from a specific task, enabling the model to adapt to a new task. As current pre-trained LLMs have increasingly large parameter scales, the computational cost of full-parameter fine-tuning has become prohibitively expensive and is no longer suitable for conventional fine-tuning tasks.

Parameter-efficient fine-tuning

To address the excessive computational resources required for full-parameter fine-tuning, **parameter-efficient fine-tuning** (**PEFT**) technology was developed. **PEFT** aims to achieve efficient **transfer learning** by minimizing the number of parameters to be fine-tuned and reducing computational complexity. It only updates a portion of the model's parameters, significantly lowering training time and cost, making it suitable for scenarios with limited computational resources. **PEFT techniques** include **Adapter Tuning**, **Prefix Tuning**, **Prompt Tuning**, **P-Tuning**, **LoRA (Low Rank Adaptation Tuning)**, and various other methods that can be flexibly chosen according to different tasks and model requirements. The following methods are common PEFT strategies that reduce the number of trainable parameters in different ways.

Adapter fine-tuning

This method designs **adapter structures** and embeds them into the Transformer, fine-tuning only the newly added adapter modules while keeping the original model parameters fixed. This introduces a small number of additional parameters while maintaining efficiency.

Prefix tuning

Prefix tuning is a **PEFT** technique that adds trainable virtual tokens as a prefix to the input, updating only the prefix parameters while keeping the rest of the Transformer fixed. This method reduces the number of parameters to be updated and improves training efficiency.

Prompt tuning

Prompt Tuning is a simplified version of prefix tuning, achieved by adding **prompt tokens** at the input layer. As the model size increases, the effect of Prompt Tuning can approach that of full fine-tuning while avoiding complex machine learning processes.

P-tuning

P-tuning involves converting prompts into trainable **embedding layers** and processing them with **multi-layer perceptrons (MLPs)** and **long short-term memory networks (LSTMs)**. This approach addresses the impact of prompt construction on downstream task performance, providing greater flexibility and stronger representational ability.

Low-rank adaptation (LoRA)

LoRA is a technique that introduces **low-rank matrices** into matrix multiplication modules to simulate full fine-tuning. By updating key low-rank dimensions in the language model, it enables efficient parameter adjustment and reduces computational complexity.

The methods discussed so far mainly adapt a model by updating either all parameters or a smaller set of added or selected parameters. Representation fine-tuning takes a different route: instead of focusing on weight updates, it attempts to influence the model through the internal representations produced during processing.

Representation fine-tuning

Representation Fine-tuning (ReFT) focuses on intervening in the '**hidden representations**' of a language model during inference, rather than directly modifying its weights. '**Hidden representations**' refers to intermediate results computed in the hidden layers of the network. These representations exist in the form of **feature vectors**, capturing abstract features and semantic information from the input data. Such intervention can be achieved in various ways, such as linear transformations, nonlinear transformations (various activation functions), attention mechanism adjustments, or context-aware adjustments.

The core concept of **ReFT** originates from research on the **interpretability of language models**, which shows that rich semantic information is encoded in the representations learned by these models. By intervening in these representations, ReFT aims to unlock and leverage this encoded knowledge to achieve more efficient and effective model adaptation.

After comparing the main categories of fine-tuning, the chapter now looks more closely at several techniques that are widely used in practice. The next section explains how adapter fine-tuning, prefix tuning, LoRA, and QLoRA work, showing how each method adapts a pre-trained model while managing training cost, memory usage, and task-specific performance.

Exploring key fine-tuning techniques

After comparing the main categories of fine-tuning, it is useful to examine how several widely used techniques work in practice. Adapter fine-tuning, prefix tuning, LoRA, and QLoRA all aim to adapt a pre-trained model without updating every parameter, but they do so in different ways. The following subsections explain how each technique modifies or extends the model, what problem it is designed to solve, and why it matters for efficient LLM adaptation.

Adapter fine-tuning

Adapter fine-tuning, as a **transfer learning method**, was first proposed by Housby et al. in their paper. The core idea is to add a small **adapter layer** on top of a pre-trained model to adapt to the data of a specific task. The **adapter layer** is a small neural network, usually composed of linear layers and activation functions. As the adapter layer contains few parameters, the training cost is low. During the fine-tuning process, only the parameters of the **adapter layer** are updated, while the parameters of the pre-trained model remain unchanged. In this way, the knowledge of the pre-trained model is preserved while adapting to the data of specific tasks. The advantage of **adapter fine-tuning** is that it can optimize the performance of the pre-trained model on specific tasks without significantly increasing the number of parameters. Its disadvantage is that the design of the adapter layer requires a certain degree of experience, and different tasks may need different adapter layer designs.

Figure 4.2 is a schematic diagram of the structural changes involved in adapter fine-tuning.

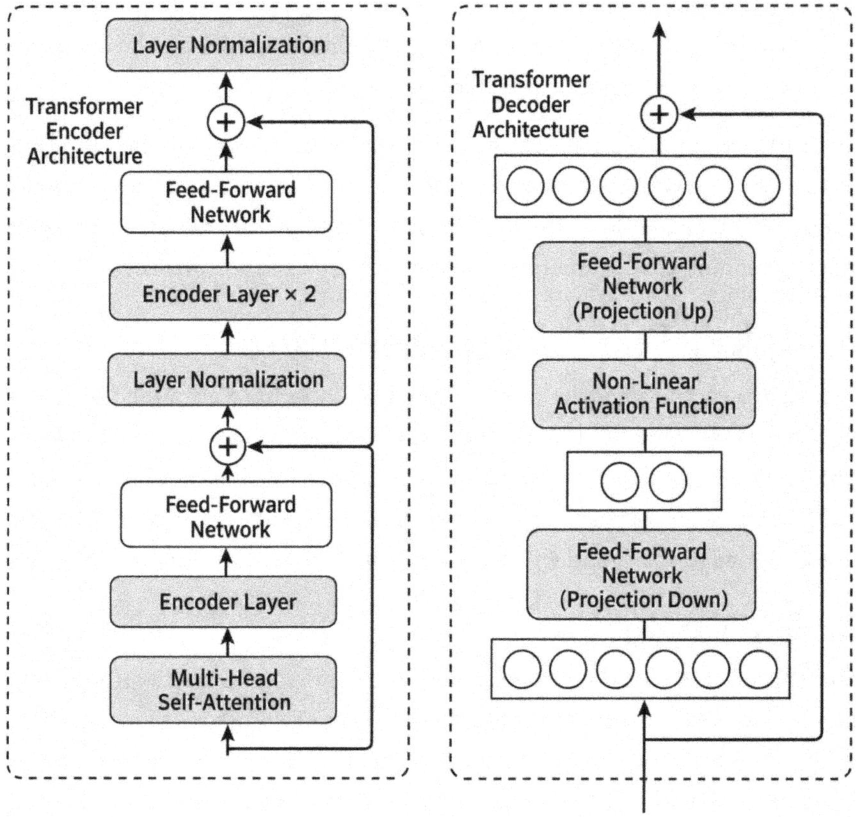

Figure 4.2: Structural changes involved in adapter fine-tuning

According to the left side of *Figure 4.2*, two **adapter layers** are added in each **Transformer**. The figure on the right displays the internal structure of the adapter layer, including a feed-forward down-projection layer (usually paired with an up-projection layer, used to map features back to the original or lower dimension), a nonlinear activation function layer, and a feed-forward up-projection layer. The adapter layer is designed to add extra parameters to adapt to specific task data while keeping the pre-trained model parameters unchanged. Similar to the Transformer structure, this internal structure also contains a skip connection for passing the original input features.

Adapter fine-tuning improves efficiency by adding small trainable modules inside the model. Prefix tuning takes a different approach: instead of inserting adapter layers into the Transformer, it adds trainable task-specific vectors before the input so that the model can be guided without changing its original parameters.

Prefix tuning

The design inspiration for **prefix tuning** comes from the prompt-based guiding method in LLMs, which adds instructions and examples before the task input to guide the model's output generation. However, different from **prompt-based guiding, prefix tuning** adds learnable prefixes before the model input to guide the model in generating outputs. The advantage of this approach is that it can learn prefixes to guide the model to produce more accurate outputs without the need to design complex prompts. A schematic diagram of the prefix vector space is shown in *Figure 4.3*.

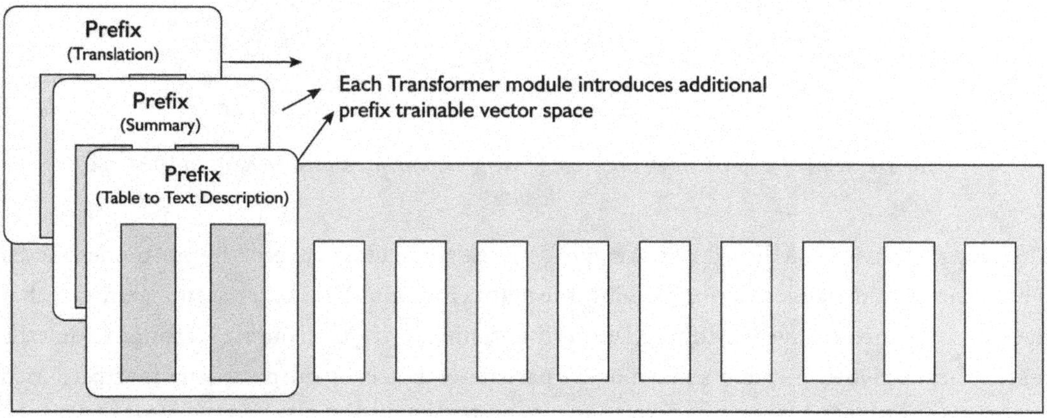

Figure 4.3: Schematic diagram of the prefix vector space

Tokens in prefix tuning refer to a series of continuous, task-specific vectors (i.e., **prefixes**) added in front of the input sequence. These vectors are trainable parameters in the model that do not come from the original language model parameters nor from any real vocabulary or text data. Prefix vectors are randomly initialized and optimized during training using the **backpropagation algorithm.** It can be seen that prefix tuning introduces small continuous parameter vectors to provide the model with additional task-specific adaptability while keeping the pre-trained model parameters unchanged.

Additionally, prefix tuning allows the model to support multiple tasks simultaneously, with each task having an independent prefix. It can also process samples from multiple users or tasks within a single batch, a feature not found in other lightweight tuning methods.

Prefix tuning shows how a model can be adapted by learning additional input-side vectors. LoRA extends the same goal of efficient adaptation to the model's weight matrices. Rather than training the full set of model parameters, LoRA introduces low-rank updates that approximate the effect of full fine-tuning with far fewer trainable parameters.

LoRA

The core idea of **LoRA fine-tuning** is to keep the pre-trained model parameters unchanged and improve the performance of LLMs on specific tasks by training a weighted matrix. The relationship between **pre-trained weights** and **fine-tuned weights** is shown in *Figure 4.4*.

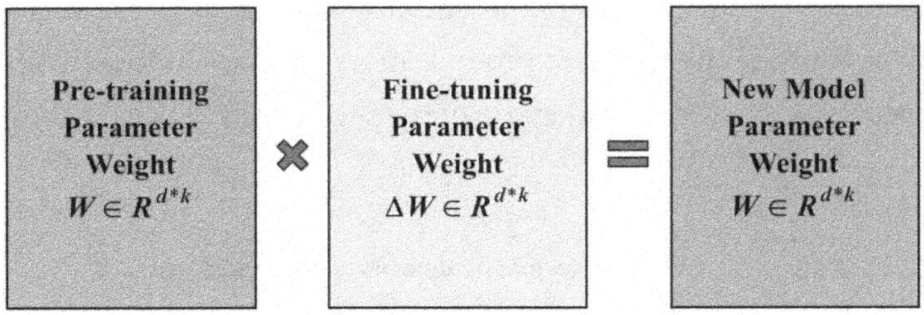

Figure 4.4: Relationship between pre-trained weights and fine-tuned weights in LoRA fine-tuning

The parameter matrix on the left side of *Figure 4.4* is the parameter matrix of the pre-trained model, which remains unchanged during training; the matrix in the middle is the parameter matrix that needs to be trained during fine-tuning. During fine-tuning, a weighted matrix is trained so that the result of multiplying the pre-trained model's parameter matrix by the parameter matrix trained during fine-tuning better adapts to the data of specific tasks. In this way, the knowledge of the pre-trained model is retained while being able to adapt to the data of specific tasks.

Research by Armen Aghajanyan et al. found that there is an inherent low-rank matrix structure in pre-trained LLMs, which can simulate the effect of full fine-tuning with only a small number of parameters. This technique effectively reduces the dimension of the matrix, thereby reducing the number of parameters. Its low-rank decomposition is shown in *Figure 4.5*.

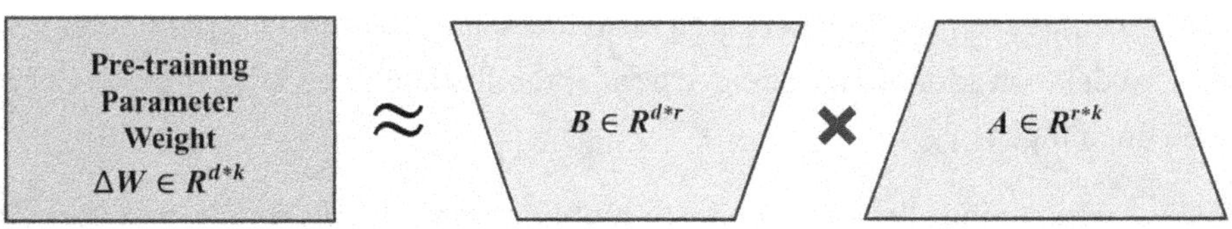

Figure 4.5: Illustration of low-rank decomposition

The advantage of **LoRA** is that it enables the optimization of the pre-trained model for specific tasks without significantly increasing the number of parameters. The disadvantage of LoRA is that it requires the design of an appropriate low-rank matrix, and different tasks may require different designs.

LoRA reduces the number of trainable parameters, but fine-tuning very large models can still require substantial GPU memory. QLoRA builds on LoRA by adding quantization, which lowers the precision of model weights so that large models can be fine-tuned with much lower memory requirements.

Quantization LoRA (QLoRA)

In the era of LLMs, even the smallest publicly available LLM parameters have reached 3 billion, such as Microsoft's **Phi-3**, which has 3.8 billion parameters, while the largest ones have already exceeded 500 billion parameters (e.g., OpenAI's **GPT-4**). **Training and fine-tuning** these LLMs requires enormous computational resources and is often unaffordable. Therefore, PEFT technology has become the mainstream fine-tuning technique. To further reduce GPU and memory consumption, quantization technology is combined with LoRA, applying quantization to the LoRA decomposition matrices, thereby further reducing parameter size. Research shows that a 16-bit **LAMA-65B** model requires over 780GB of GPU memory during training, while **QLoRA** enables fine-tuning on a single 48GB GPU machine while retaining 99.3% performance, and the training time is greatly shortened to 24h.

How does QLoRA achieve this?

During the fine-tuning process, only the quantized parameters of the model are updated; all other parameters remain unchanged. This approach not only preserves the knowledge of the pre-trained model but also adapts to the data of specific tasks. The advantage of QLoRA is that computation with quantized parameters is usually faster, especially on specialized hardware (such as GPUs, TPUs), because low-precision computation can more efficiently leverage the hardware's parallel computing capabilities, improving computational efficiency and reducing the time cost for training and inference.

After examining the principles behind adapter tuning, prefix tuning, LoRA, and QLoRA, the next step is to see how these methods are supported in practical tooling. The Hugging Face PEFT toolkit provides a common way to apply parameter-efficient fine-tuning methods to Transformer-based models, making it easier to adapt large models while reducing training costs, memory usage, and storage requirements.

Using the PEFT toolkit for efficient fine-tuning

The open-source **PEFT toolkit** by Hugging Face supports the fine-tuning of Transformer models. This toolkit enables large pre-trained models to efficiently adapt to a variety of downstream applications by fine-tuning only a small number of additional model parameters rather than all model parameters, greatly reducing computational and storage costs. In terms of performance, **PEFT technology** can match that of fully fine-tuned models.

Below, the advantages of this technology are illustrated using the example of **GPU memory resources** with PEFT fine-tuning, as shown in *Figure 4.6*.

Model Name	Full Fine-tuning	PEFT-LoRA Fine-tuning	LoRA + DeepSpeed + CPU Offloading Solution
bigscience/T0_3B (30 billion parameters)	47.14GB GPU / 2.96GB CPU	14.4GB GPU / 2.96GB CPU	9.8GB GPU / 17.8GB CPU
bigscience/mT0-xl (120 billion parameters)	OOM GPU	56GB GPU / 3GB CPU	220GB GPU / 32GB CPU
bigscience/bloomz-7b1 (70 billion parameters)	OOM GPU	32GB GPU / 3.8GB CPU	18.1GB GPU / 33GB CPU

Figure 4.6: Comparison table of GPU and CPU memory usage for three models using three fine-tuning methods

From the comparison in *Figure 4.6*, it can be seen that the PEFT-LoRA technology has advantages in GPU memory resources, and the performance of the fine-tuned model can rival that of a fully fine-tuned model. The specific comparison results are shown in *Figure 4.7*.

Task Name	Score
Human Evaluation (Comprehensive Overall)	0.897
Flan-T5	0.692
InstructTune	0.863

Figure 4.7: Comparing task accuracy

After seeing how the PEFT toolkit supports efficient fine-tuning at a high level, the next step is to apply one of its most widely used methods in practice. The following section focuses on LoRA implementation, showing how to inspect the model structure, configure LoRA parameters, select target modules, train the model, and evaluate the fine-tuned result.

Implementing LoRA in practice

In **PEFT**, the process of calling **LoRA** for fine-tuning is very simple; it includes the following four parts:

- Exploring the model structure
- **LoRAConfig** parameter settings, including hyperparameters and the settings of model layers to be fine-tuned
- Model training
- Model evaluation

The model structure can be explored directly by printing the model. In this example, the textual content is converted into a structured diagram. The structure of the **BERT** model is shown in *Figure 4.8*.

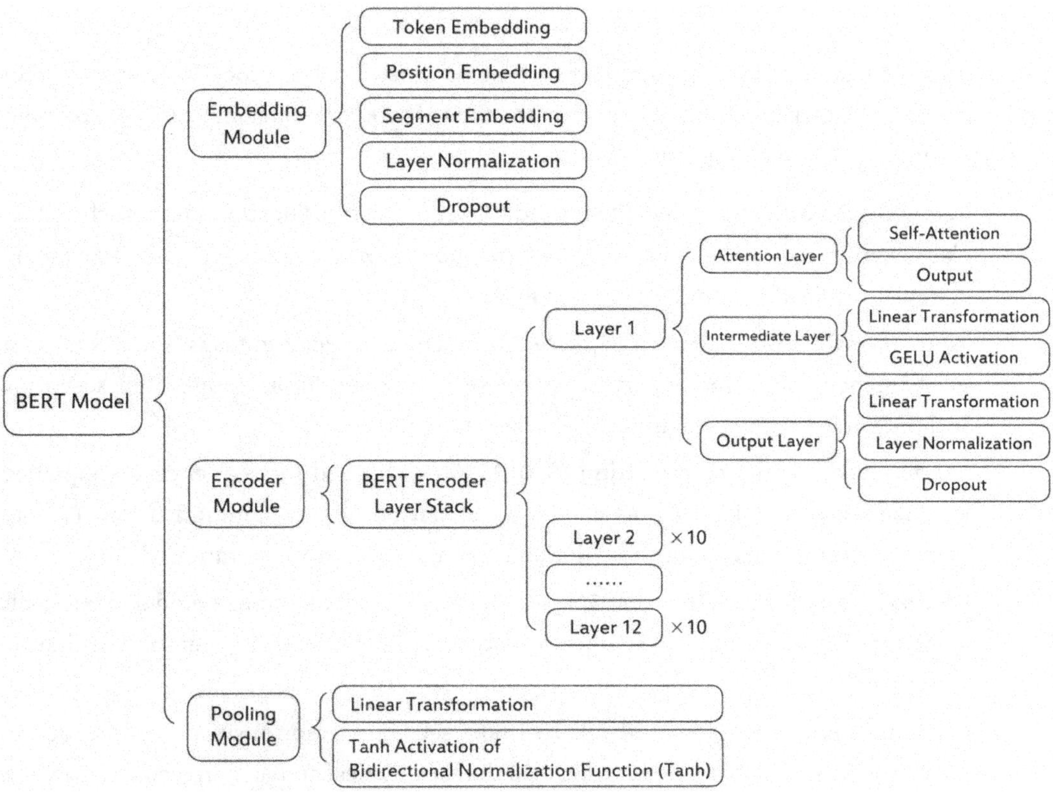

Figure 4.8: Schematic diagram of the BERT model structure

From *Figure 4.8*, it can be seen that the BERT model contains the **encoder module**, which consists of 12 Transformer layers. In LoRA, it is necessary to specify which model layers to fine-tune, and usually, all encoder layers are selected. After obtaining the above model structure, you can set hyperparameters and the model layers to be fine-tuned in the LoRA config file. Relevant code is shown as follows:

```
from lora_config import LoraConfig, TaskType
lora_config = LoraConfig(
    task_type = TaskType.SEQ_CLS,
    r = 8,
    lora_alpha = 16,
    lora_dropout = 0.1,
    target_modules=["encoder.layer.*.attention.self.query", "encoder.
    layer.*.attention.self.key"]
)
```

For better understanding, let's explain the task type parameter (`task_type`). When using LoRA for fine-tuning, the task type is used to specify the type of task for model fine-tuning. Common task types include the following five:

- **Sequence classification** (`SEQ_CLS`): Used for sequence classification tasks, such as text classification or sentiment analysis. Typical application scenarios include IMDB movie review classification and sentiment analysis.
- **Token classification** (`TOKEN_CLS`): Used for token classification tasks, such as **named entity recognition** (**NER**) or **part-of-speech** (**POS**) **tagging**. Typical application scenarios include named entity recognition and tokenization.
- **Sequence-to-sequence modeling** (`SEQ_2_SEQ_LM`): Used for sequence-to-sequence language model tasks, such as machine translation or text summarization. Typical application scenarios include translation tasks and summary generation.
- **Causal language modeling** (`CAUSAL_LM`): Used for causal language model tasks, such as generative tasks. Typical application scenarios include text generation and auto-completion.
- **Question answering** (`QUESTION_ANSWERING`): Used for question answering tasks, such as question answering systems on the **SQuAD dataset**. Typical application scenarios include question answering systems and information retrieval.

The choice of the **rank** (*r*) for the low-rank matrix is related to the task, model size, dataset size, and computational resources. According to comparative results, usually selecting `r = 8` or `r = 16` can cover most fine-tuning scenarios and achieve expected results.

`lora_alpha` is a scaling factor used to control the influence of the low-rank matrix on the original weight matrix. It balances the adaptability and stability of the model by adjusting the output of the low-rank matrix. Generally, the larger the value of `lora_alpha`, the greater the influence of the low-rank matrix on the original weight matrix. In practical applications, this parameter is usually set to 2 times the low-rank matrix parameter *r*.

`lora_dropout` is consistent with the random dropout function used during training, serving to prevent overfitting. Typically, the value of `lora_dropout` is set to `0.1`.

`target_modules` is a list used to specify which model layers need to be fine-tuned. In LoRA, only the parameters of the model layers specified in `target_modules` will be updated, while the parameters of other model layers remain unchanged. Usually, `target_modules` is set to the `path` of the model layers that need to be fine-tuned. For example, `encoder.layer.*.attention.self.query` means to fine-tune all self-attention query layers. According to actual test results, enabling LoRA on all layers (including query weight matrices, projection layers, other linear layers in multi-head attention modules, and output layers) performs better than fine-tuning only some layers.

After the main LoRA configuration parameters have been defined, the next step is to consider how those settings affect training in practice. The following summary highlights the main practical lessons for choosing data, selecting target layers, managing GPU memory, and avoiding overtraining.

LoRA practical training summary

In actual training processes, we can summarize LoRA as follows:

- During fine-tuning, the quality requirements for the dataset are far higher than the quantity requirements.
- Fine-tuning the entire model layer performs better than fine-tuning only specified layers, but will result in greater GPU memory consumption. Conversely, if memory resources are limited, you can fine-tune only some layers.
- Multiple rounds of iterative training may cause model degradation; it is recommended to select an appropriate number of iterations based on actual conditions or use early stopping techniques to avoid overtraining.

After reviewing the practical considerations for LoRA configuration and training, the chapter now moves from technique-level guidance to a complete applied example. The next section shows how fine-tuning can be used in a contract text classification scenario, walking through data preparation, model definition, training, evaluation, and LoRA-based optimization.

Applying fine-tuning to contract text classification

Previously, we provided a comprehensive introduction to the basic concepts of fine-tuning and several key technologies related to it. In this section, we will demonstrate the application of fine-tuning technology in a text classification task through a case study.

This case study demonstrates how fine-tuning can be applied to a practical contract text classification task. It begins with a business scenario in which a law firm needs to classify contract documents more efficiently, then walks through the full modeling workflow: preparing the dataset, building a BERT-based classification model, defining the training and evaluation pipeline, applying LoRA-based fine-tuning, and comparing model performance before and after fine-tuning. The goal is to show how the fine-tuning concepts introduced earlier can be translated into an end-to-end implementation.

John Doe is the head of a law firm, where the daily work involves a large amount of contract text classification and retrieval. Usually, these tasks are performed manually by interns who search, review, and match suitable contract texts for different business scenarios. Such work is inefficient and prone to errors. To improve work efficiency, John Doe hopes to leverage deep learning techniques to achieve automatic classification of contract texts. Driven by this need, we first collected a large amount of contract text data and then built a text classifier using the BERT model. We further optimized the BERT model through fine-tuning techniques to enhance its performance in contract text classification tasks.

To implement this contract classification workflow, the first step is to build a baseline BERT-based classifier that can process contract text, assign labels, and provide a model that can later be fine-tuned with LoRA.

BERT classification model

Before model training, the sample data should be cleaned and processed. Although sample preparation is not the main focus here, the following points should be noted during data cleaning and processing:

- **Data Cleaning:** Suppose each folder represents a category of files. When the data volume in a certain folder is small, it can be merged into other folders.

- **Data Annotation:** For the data in each folder, a label should be assigned to each folder. This label can be a number or a string.
- **Data Splitting:** Divide the dataset into training set, validation set, and test set. Generally, the **training set** accounts for 70% of the total dataset, the **validation set** 15%, and the **test set** 15%.

We use the **PyTorch Lightning** framework to implement the **BERT classification model**. The code structure includes the following parts:

(1) Environment setup

Import the necessary libraries, including data processing libraries (`pandas`, `numpy`), machine learning tool libraries (`sklearn`), deep learning frameworks (`PyTorch`, `PyTorch Lightning`), as well as the `transformers` library for NLP tasks. The related code is as follows:

```
import os
import random
import numpy as np
import pandas as pd
import torch
from torch.utils.data import DataLoader, Dataset
from sklearn.preprocessing import LabelEncoder
from sklearn.metrics import precision_recall_fscore_support
from sklearn.model_selection import train_test_split
from sklearn.utils.class_weight import compute_class_weight
import pytorch_lightning as pl
from pytorch_lightning.callbacks import EarlyStopping, ModelCheckpoint
from pytorch_lightning.loggers import TensorBoardLogger
from transformers import BertTokenizer, BertForSequenceClassification
```

After importing the required libraries, the next step is to make the experiment reproducible by fixing the random seed.

(2) Random seed setting

Define the function set_seed to ensure experiment reproducibility. This function sets all relevant random seeds. The code is as follows:

```
# Set random seed
def set_seed(seed):
    random.seed(seed)
```

```
    np.random.seed(seed)
    torch.manual_seed(seed)
    if torch.cuda.is_available():
        torch.cuda.manual_seed_all(seed)
    pl.seed_everything(seed)


set_seed(42)
```

Once reproducibility is configured, the dataset must be loaded, tokenized, and converted into the input format expected by BERT.

(3) Data loading and preprocessing

Define a `TextDataset` class that inherits from PyTorch's `Dataset`. This class is responsible for encoding textual data and converting the text into a format acceptable to the model, including **tokenization** and the creation of **attention masks**. The related code is as follows:

```
class TextDataset(Dataset):
    def __init__(self, texts, labels, tokenizer, max_length=256):
        self.texts = texts
        self.labels = labels
        self.tokenizer = tokenizer
        self.max_length = max_length

    def __len__(self):
        return len(self.labels)

    def __getitem__(self, idx):
        text = self.texts[idx]
        label = self.labels[idx]
        encoding = self.tokenizer.encode_plus(
            text,
            add_special_tokens=True,
            max_length=self.max_length,
            return_token_type_ids=False,
            padding='max_length',
            truncation=True,
            return_attention_mask=True,
```

```
            return_tensors='pt',
        )
        return {
                'input_ids': encoding['input_ids'].flatten(),
                'attention_mask': encoding['attention_mask'].flatten(),
                'labels': torch.tensor(label, dtype=torch.long)
                }
```

The classifier is built in three layers:

- The BERT backbone produces contextual embeddings
- A classification head maps the `[CLS]` token to category logits
- PyTorch Lightning's `training_step` glues them together with a loss and an optimizer

The next section walks through each piece.

(4) Model definition

Define a `TextClassifier` class that inherits from PyTorch Lightning's `LightningModule`. This class is responsible for defining the model structure, including loading and fine-tuning the `BertForSequenceClassification` model. The related code is as follows:

```
class TextClassificationModel(pl.LightningModule):
    def __init__(self, num_classes, model_name, class_weights, label_
                 mapping):
        super(TextClassificationModel, self).__init__()
        self.save_hyperparameters()
        self.num_classes = num_classes
        self.bert = BertForSequenceClassification.from_pretrained(model_
name,
            num_labels=num_classes)
        self.class_weights = torch.tensor(class_weights, dtype=torch.
float)
        self.label_mapping = label_mapping
        self.test_outputs = []
        self.config = self.bert.config

    def forward(self, input_ids=None, attention_mask=None, labels=None,
inputs_
                embeds=None, output_attentions=None, output_hidden_
states=None, return_
```

```
                dict=None, task_ids=None, **kwargs):
        return self.bert(
            input_ids=input_ids,
            attention_mask=attention_mask,
            labels=labels,
            inputs_embeds=inputs_embeds,
            output_attentions=output_attentions,
            output_hidden_states=output_hidden_states,
            return_dict=return_dict
        )

    def compute_loss(self, logits, labels):
        return torch.nn.functional.cross_entropy(logits, labels,
weight=self.
            class_weights.to(self.device))

    def training_step(self, batch, batch_idx):
        outputs = self(
            input_ids=batch.get('input_ids'),
            attention_mask=batch.get('attention_mask'),
            labels=batch.get('labels')
        )
        loss = outputs.loss
        self.log('train_loss', loss)
return loss

def validation_step(self, batch, batch_idx):
    outputs = self(
        input_ids=batch.get('input_ids'),
        attention_mask=batch.get('attention_mask'),
        labels=batch.get('labels')
    )
    loss = outputs.loss
    preds = torch.argmax(outputs.logits, dim=1)
    acc = (preds == batch.get('labels')).float().mean()
    self.log('val_loss', loss, prog_bar=True)
    self.log('val_acc', acc, prog_bar=True)
```

```
        return {'val_loss': loss, 'val_acc' : acc}

    def test_step(self, batch, batch_idx):
        outputs = self(
            input_ids=batch.get('input_ids'),
            attention_mask=batch.get('attention_mask'),
            labels=batch.get('labels')
        )
        preds = torch.argmax(outputs.logits, dim=1)
        precision, recall, f1, _ = precision_recall_fscore_support(batch.
            get('labels').cpu(), preds.cpu(), labels=range(self.num_classes),
            zero_division=0)
        self.test_outputs.append({'precision': precision, 'recall': recall,
    'f1':
            f1})
        return {'precision': precision, 'recall': recall, 'f1': f1}

    def on_test_epoch_end(self):
        if self.test_outputs:
            all_precisions = [torch.tensor(x['precision']) for x in self.test_
                outputs]
            all_recalls = [torch.tensor(x['recall']) for x in self.test_
    outputs]
            all_f1s = [torch.tensor(x['f1']) for x in self.test_outputs]
            avg_precision = torch.stack(all_precisions).mean(dim=0).numpy()
            avg_recall = torch.stack(all_recalls).mean(dim=0).numpy()
            avg_f1 = torch.stack(all_f1s).mean(dim=0).numpy()
            results = pd.DataFrame({
                'Category': [self.label_mapping[i] for i in range(self.num_
                    classes)],
                'Precision': avg_precision,
                'Recall': avg_recall,
                'F1-Score': avg_f1
            })
            print(results)
            self.test_outputs.clear()
    def configure_optimizers(self):
        return torch.optim.AdamW(self.parameters(), lr=3e-5)
```

After defining the classification model, the next step is to organize the training, validation, testing, loss calculation, and optimizer logic within the PyTorch Lightning framework.

(5) PyTorch lightning training framework

The **PyTorch Lightning training framework** is beginner-friendly, with a clear code structure that is easy to understand. Each model is a **LightningModule** that contains the training, validation, and testing logic. In this case, the fixed framework of the model includes the following parts:

- **Initialization function** `__init__ (self, num_classes, model_name, class_weights, label_mapping)`: Defines the structure of the model, including loading and fine-tuning the `BertForSequenceClassification` model
- **Forward function** `forward (self, input_ids=None, attention_mask=None, labels=None, inputs_embeds=None, output_attentions=None, output_hidden_states=None, return_dict=None, task_ids=None, **kwargs)`: Defines the forward propagation logic of the model, including the processing of inputs and outputs
- **compute_loss function** `compute_loss (self, logits, labels)`: Defines the model's loss function, used to calculate the model's loss value
- **training_step function** `training_step (self, batch, batch_idx)`: Defines the training logic of the model, including the processing of inputs and outputs
- **validation_step function** `validation_step (self, batch, batch_idx)`: Defines the validation logic of the model, including the processing of inputs and outputs
- **test_step function** `test_step (self, batch, batch_idx)`: Defines the testing logic of the model, including the processing of inputs and outputs
- The `on_test_epoch_end` function (`on_test_epoch_end(self)`): Defines the logic to execute at the end of model testing, including outputting the test results
- The `configure_optimizers` function (`configure_optimizers(self)`): Defines the model's **optimizer**, used to update the model parameters

In addition, a series of functions are used in the example code, such as the `forword` function and the `compute_loss` function:

- The `forword` function: By default, this function only requires three parameters (`input_ids`, `attention_mask`, and `labels`). However, considering subsequent **fine-tuning**, it is necessary to maintain consistency with the default parameter settings in fine-tuning, so additional parameters (default set to `None`) that are not needed in the current training phase are added.

- The `compute_loss` function: This function is used to calculate the **loss value** of the model, usually using the **cross-entropy loss function**. In this function, the weight parameter `class_weights` also needs to be passed to handle class imbalance in the dataset.

With the model structure and training logic defined, the next step is to prepare the data pipeline that loads the dataset, encodes labels, computes class weights, and creates dataloaders.

Data pipeline: Load_Data function

`load_data` is used to load training and validation data, encode the labels, and calculate class weights to handle potential class imbalance. It consists of three parts:

- **Reading data:** Uses the Pandas library to read the dataset and converts the dataset into a `DataFrame` format
- **Creating the dataset:** Divides the dataset into training, validation, and test sets, then uses the `TextDataset` class to create training and validation datasets
- **Creating the dataloader:** Uses the `DataLoader` class to create dataloaders for the training and validation sets. A sample code is as follows:

```
def load_data(output_csv):
    df = pd.read_csv(output_csv, delimiter='$')
    label_encoder = LabelEncoder()
    df['Label'] = label_encoder.fit_transform(df['Label'])
    class_weights = compute_class_weight('balanced', classes=np.
        unique(df['Label']), y=df['Label'])
    class_weights = class_weights.tolist()  # Convert to list
    label_mapping = dict(zip(range(len(label_encoder.classes_)), label_
        encoder.classes_))
    return df, label_encoder, class_weights, label_mapping

def create_datasets(df,tokenizer):
    train_texts, test_texts, train_labels, test_labels = train_test_
        split(df['Text'].tolist(), df['Label'].tolist(), test_size=0.2,
        random_state=42)
    train_texts, val_texts, train_labels, val_labels = train_test_
        split(train_texts, train_labels, test_size=0.25, random_state=42)
    train_dataset = TextDataset(train_texts, train_labels, tokenizer)
    val_dataset = TextDataset(val_texts, val_labels, tokenizer)
    test_dataset = TextDataset(test_texts, test_labels, tokenizer)
```

```
    return train_dataset, val_dataset, test_dataset


def create_dataloaders(train_dataset, val_dataset, test_dataset, batch_
                       size=32):
    train_loader = DataLoader(train_dataset, batch_size=batch_size,
        shuffle=True)
    val_loader = DataLoader(val_dataset, batch_size=batch_size,
shuffle=False)
    test_loader = DataLoader(test_dataset, batch_size=batch_size,
        shuffle=False)
    return train_loader, val_loader, test_loader
```

The above code includes the following three key points of knowledge:

- **Calculation of dataset weights:** Uses the `compute_class_weight` function to calculate the class weights of the dataset, which are used to handle class imbalance problems
- **Label encoding:** Uses the `LabelEncoder` class to encode the labels and convert them to numbers

The training set needs to be discretized, but the validation, and test sets do not. The reason for discretizing the training set is to avoid learning some sequential information during training, which could lead to model overfitting.

After the dataset and dataloaders are ready, the model can be instantiated and trained using the configured training loop, callbacks, and evaluation settings.

Model training

We defined a **Text ClassificationModel** class, which inherits from the `LightningModule` of **PyTorch Lightning**. This class defines the structure and training logic of the model, as well as the data loading and processing procedure. Next, we need to instantiate this class and start model training. The relevant code is shown below:

```
def main():
    # Set random seed
    set_seed(42)
    output_csv = 'D:\\OneDrive\\2024\\AI\\text_cnn_qz20221211\\data\\
output.csv'
    df, label_encoder, class_weights, label_mapping = load_data(output_
csv)
    tokenizer = BertTokenizer.from_pretrained("bert-base-chinese")
```

```
    train_dataset, val_dataset, test_dataset = create_datasets(df,
tokenizer)
    train_loader, val_loader, test_loader = create_dataloaders(train_
dataset,
        val_dataset, test_dataset)

    num_classes = len(label_encoder.classes_)
    model = TextClassificationModel(num_classes=num_classes, model_
name="bert-
        base-chinese", class_weights=class_weights, label_mapping=label_
mapping)

    logger = TensorBoardLogger("tb_logs", name="my_model")

    checkpoint_callback = ModelCheckpoint(
        monitor='val_loss',
        dirpath='D:\\bert_models\\checkpoints',
        filename='model-{epoch:02d}-{val_loss:.2f}',
        save_top_k=1,
        mode='min'
    )

    trainer = pl.Trainer(
        max_epochs=10,
        callbacks=[EarlyStopping(monitor='val_loss', patience=3),
checkpoint_
            callback],
        logger=logger,
        accelerator='gpu',  # Use GPU for training
        devices=1  # Specify using 1 GPU
    )
    trainer.fit(model, train_loader, val_loader)
    device = torch.device('cuda' if torch.cuda.is_available() else 'cpu')
    model.to(device)
    model.eval()

    # Evaluate test set
    test_metrics_df = evaluate_model(model, test_loader, device)
```

```
    print(f"Test Metrics:\n{test_metrics_df}")
    test_metrics_df.to_csv('D:\\bert_models\\test_metrics.csv',
index=False)

# Evaluate validation set
val_metrics_df = evaluate_model(model, val_loader, device)
print(f"Validation Metrics:\n{val_metrics_df}")
val_metrics_df.to_csv('D:\\bert_models\\validation_metrics.csv',
index=False)
```

The code above contains the following three key points:

- **Random seed setting**: By setting the random seed, we ensure the repeatability of the experiment and fix the initial state of the random number generator, which helps with the reproducibility and comparison of experimental results.
- **Model checkpoint and early stopping**: By setting model checkpoints and early stopping, we can save the model's state during training and stop the training early when performance on the validation set no longer improves, thereby avoiding overfitting.
- **Setting label tags**: During model training, it is necessary to convert the labels into numbers so that the model can recognize and process the label information. However, the parsed results need to be converted back to the original labels for subsequent result analysis and visualization.

Once baseline training is complete, the model needs to be evaluated on validation and test data so that its performance can be measured before applying fine-tuning.

Evaluation after model training

After model training is complete, we need to evaluate the model to understand its performance on the test and validation sets. Common evaluation metrics include **accuracy**, **recall**, **F1 score**, etc. In this case, we defined an `evaluate_model` function to evaluate the model's performance on the test and validation sets. At the same time, we defined a function to load the model, `load_latest_checkpoint`, to load the latest model checkpoint. The relevant code is as follows:

```
def load_latest_checkpoint(checkpoint_dir, model_class):
    checkpoint_files = [f for f in os.listdir(checkpoint_dir) if
f.endswith
                        ('.ckpt')]
    latest_checkpoint = max(checkpoint_files, key=lambda f: os.path.
getmtime(os.
```

```
        path.join(checkpoint_dir, f)))
    checkpoint_path = os.path.join(checkpoint_dir, latest_checkpoint)
    model = model_class.load_from_checkpoint(checkpoint_path)
    return model


def evaluate_model(model, data_loader, device):
    model.eval()
    preds, true_labels = [], []

    with torch.no_grad():
        for batch in data_loader:
            input_ids = batch['input_ids'].to(device)
            attention_mask = batch['attention_mask'].to(device)
            labels = batch['labels'].to(device)
            outputs = model(input_ids=input_ids, attention_mask=attention_
mask,
                            labels=labels)
            preds.extend(torch.argmax(outputs.logits, dim=1).cpu().
numpy())
            true_labels.extend(labels.cpu().numpy())

 precision, recall, f1, _ = precision_recall_fscore_support(true_labels,
    preds, labels=range(model.num_classes), zero_division=0)

# Use the category mapping to convert category IDs into category names
categories = [model.hparams.label_mapping[i] for i in range(model.num_
    classes)]

metrics_df = pd.DataFrame({
    'Category': categories,
    'Precision': precision,
    'Recall': recall,
    'F1-Score': f1
})

return metrics_df
```

The code above contains the following key points:

- When loading the model, it is very important to set the state to `eval`, which has three purposes

  Turning off **Dropout** and **BatchNorm** layers. During training, **Dropout** layers randomly deactivate some neurons to prevent overfitting, while **BatchNorm** layers dynamically adjust normalization parameters based on the current batch of data. Once in evaluation mode, the behavior of these layers changes: **Dropout** layers are deactivated and all neurons are enabled; **BatchNorm** layers use the mean and variance accumulated during training instead of the current batch's data.

  Ensure consistency. During training, certain layers (such as **Dropout** and **BatchNorm**) behave randomly. If these layers are not turned off during evaluation, their randomness will affect the stability and consistency of evaluation results. Using `model.eval()` ensures the model behaves deterministically during evaluation, thereby providing a stable performance evaluation.

  Prevent gradient computation. Although `model.eval()` itself does not turn off gradient computation, it is usually used together with `torch.no_grad()` to significantly reduce memory usage and computation during evaluation. This is especially important for LLMs (such as **BERT**), as they require larger memory and computation resources during inference.

- `torch.no_grad()` has the following three functions:
  - **Reduce memory usage:** During evaluation, there is no need to compute gradients, so memory usage can be reduced by `torch.no_grad()`.
  - **Improve computation speed:** By not computing gradients, computation speed is increased because no backpropagation is required.
  - **Prevent gradient computation:** During evaluation, gradients are not needed, so `torch.no_grad()` can be used to prevent gradient computation.
- Output of model evaluation results. When evaluating model performance, metrics such as **accuracy**, **recall**, and **F1 score** are typically output. These metrics are used to measure the model's performance across different categories in order to assess the model's overall performance. In this case, we use the `precision_recall_fscore_support` function to calculate these metrics and store the results in a **DataFrame** for subsequent analysis and visualization.

- Mapping between model prediction indices and labels. When evaluating model performance, it is often necessary to convert the predicted indices of the model into label names. This process can be achieved through category mapping, converting category numbers into category names. In this case, the `label_mapping` dictionary is used to convert category numbers into category names.

After establishing the baseline model's performance, the next step is to apply LoRA-based fine-tuning to improve the classifier while updating only a small number of additional parameters.

Fine-tuning of BERT-based classification model

Fine-tuning the BERT model is relatively simple in terms of code implementation. The key is to correctly set the fine-tuning parameters and use the **Trainer** class from the `Transformers` library for fine-tuning training. In this case, we will use the LoRA technique to fine-tune the BERT model to improve its performance on the contract text classification task. The specific code for fine-tuning implementation is as follows:

```
def fine_tuning(model, train_loader, val_loader, test_loader, tokenizer,
device):
    # Apply LoRA to this model
    lora_config = LoraConfig(
        task_type=TaskType.SEQ_CLS,
        r=8,
        lora_alpha=16,
        lora_dropout=0.2,
        target_modules=[
            f"bert.encoder.layer.{i}.attention.self.query" for i in
range(12)
        ] + [
            f"bert.encoder.layer.{i}.attention.self.key" for i in
range(12)
        ]
    )

    ft_model = get_peft_model(model, lora_config)
    ft_model.config = ft_model.bert.config  # Ensure correct configuration
    ft_model.to(device)

    fine_tuning_args = TrainingArguments(
```

```
        output_dir='D:\\bert_models\\checkpoints\\fine_tuned_model',
        num_train_epochs=10,  # Adjust the number of training epochs if
needed
        per_device_train_batch_size=32,
        per_device_eval_batch_size=32,
        logging_dir='D:\\bert_models\\logs',
        logging_steps=10,
        evaluation_strategy="steps",
        eval_steps=50,
        save_steps=100,
        save_total_limit=2,
        learning_rate=3e-5,  # Adjust the learning rate if needed
        lr_scheduler_type='linear',
        load_best_model_at_end=True,
        metric_for_best_model="eval_loss",
        greater_is_better=False
    )
# Used to initialize the fine-tuning trainer
fine_tune_trainer = Trainer(
    model=ft_model,
    args=fine_tuning_args,
    train_dataset=train_loader.dataset,
    eval_dataset=val_loader.dataset,
    tokenizer=tokenizer
)

# Fine-tune the model
fine_tune_trainer.train()

# Save the fine-tuned model
fine_tuned_checkpoint_path = 'D:\\bert_models\\checkpoints\\fine_tuned_
model'
ft_model.save_pretrained(fine_tuned_checkpoint_path)
tokenizer.save_pretrained(fine_tuned_checkpoint_path)

# Evaluate the fine-tuned model on the test set
fine_tuned_metrics_df = evaluate_model(ft_model, test_loader, device)
print(f"Finetuned Test Metrics:\n{fine_tuned_metrics_df}")
```

The code above shows how LoRA fine-tuning is configured and executed; the next step is to explain the main training parameters that control how the fine-tuning process behaves.

Explanation of the model fine-tuning process

The LoRA configuration parameters were introduced earlier. This subsection focuses on the training parameters that control how the fine-tuning process runs, how often the model is evaluated, how the learning rate is managed, and how the best checkpoint is selected.

The main training parameters are as follows:

- `num_train_epochs`: Defines the total number of training epochs, which controls the duration of training. Too many epochs may lead to overfitting, while too few may lead to underfitting. We usually use this together with an early stopping parameter to avoid overfitting.
- `per_device_train_batch_size`: Sets the batch size per device (such as GPU) during training. The batch size affects training speed and model performance.

  A larger batch size can improve computational efficiency but may require more memory. A larger batch size leads to smoother gradient updates, thus enabling more stable convergence. However, a larger batch size may reduce the model's generalization ability, as it makes it easier for the model to find patterns in the training set during training, but harder to adapt to the data distribution in the test set. Furthermore, an excessively large batch size may cause the model to skip some local optima, thereby affecting the final generalization ability.

  A smaller batch size results in gradients with more noise since each update contains fewer samples. This noise can sometimes help the model escape local optima, but may also cause the training process to be unstable.

  Because of their noisy characteristics, smaller batch sizes can help the model learn more subtle differences during training, thereby improving generalization ability.

- `per_device_eval_batch_size`: Sets the batch size per device (such as GPU) during evaluation (if using multiple GPUs)
- `evaluation_strategy`: Sets the evaluation strategy, such as steps or epoch
  - **steps:** Evaluate the model after each step. You can obtain feedback on the model's performance within shorter training intervals and promptly understand its behavior on the validation set. Since evaluations are frequent, computational resource consumption is high. You can use this together with the **early stopping**

mechanism to detect no improvement on the validation set sooner, and thus stop training early to save time and resources. Frequent evaluation increases training time, as each evaluation interrupts training to perform a full validation set assessment.

- **epoch**: Evaluate the model after each epoch. Evaluation occurs less frequently, reducing the interruption and overhead to the training process. The evaluation results after each epoch better reflect overall changes in model performance, reducing the impact of short-term fluctuations. However, low evaluation frequency may lead to untimely feedback on the model's performance during training. If a single epoch is long, you might waste time training when performance has already started to degrade. Although it can also be used with **early stopping**, if model performance starts to deteriorate before the current epoch ends, you won't detect it until after the epoch, potentially wasting computational resources.

- `learning_rate`: The default value `3e-5` is commonly used as the initial learning rate for fine-tuning many pre-trained **transformer models** (such as **BERT**) on downstream tasks. For BERT-base fine-tuning, `3e-5` is a common starting learning rate. Smaller datasets often need a smaller value, such as `1e-5`, to reduce the risk of overfitting, while larger datasets can sometimes use a higher value, such as `5e-5`. The grid search and random search techniques discussed below can be used to tune from this starting point.

  In general, a larger learning rate can speed up convergence, but it may also cause unstable training or make the model oscillate near local optima. A smaller learning rate is usually more stable, but it may require more training time.

- `lr_scheduler_type`: For most fine-tuning tasks, especially when you want the learning rate to smoothly decrease, you can use `linear`. If you need to adjust the learning rate periodically during training, such as for longer training tasks, you can use `cosine`. To find the most suitable learning rate, you can perform a **learning rate search** using the following methods:

  - **Grid Search**: Perform a grid search within a predefined range of learning rates to find the optimal value.
  - **Random Search**: Perform a random search within a predefined range of learning rates to find the optimal value.
  - **Learning Rate Decay**: Gradually reduce the learning rate during training to find the optimal value.

    - **Learning Rate Scheduler:** Use a learning rate scheduler (such as `ReduceLROnPlateau`, `CosineAnnealingLR`, etc.) to automatically adjust the learning rate in order to find the optimal value.

- `metric_for_best_model`: Specifies the metric for evaluating the best model. Common metrics include `accuracy`, `precision`, `recall`, `f1`, `eval_loss`, etc. The choice of evaluation metric depends on the specific task type and objective.

    - **Classification Tasks**: When the data is relatively balanced, `accuracy` can be used as the evaluation metric; when the data is imbalanced, metrics like `f1`, `precision`, and `recall` can be used
    - **Regression Tasks**: Metrics such as **MSE**, **RMSE**, and **MAE** can be used
    - **General:** `eval_loss` is usually used as an evaluation metric to measure the model's performance on the validation set
    - **Generation Tasks**: Metrics such as **BLEU**, **ROUGE**, and **METEOR** can be used

- `greater_is_better`: When this value is `True`, it indicates that a higher evaluation metric value is better, suitable for metrics such as `accuracy`, `precision`, `recall`, `F1 score`, etc. When this value is `False`, it means a lower metric value is better, applicable to metrics such as loss, **mean squared error** (MSE), etc.

After the fine-tuning parameters have been configured and the LoRA adapter has been trained, the final step is to evaluate the fine-tuned model and compare its performance with the original baseline model.

Evaluation after model fine-tuning

After fine-tuning the model, it's necessary to evaluate the model to understand its performance on the test set. Evaluation metrics typically include **accuracy, recall, F1 score**, etc. In this example, an `evaluate_model` function is defined to evaluate the model's performance on the test set. For models with fixed fine-tuning, you also need to load the fine-tuned model. The code for loading the model is as follows:

```
def load_finetuned_model(checkpoint_dir, ft_checkpoint_dir, model_cls,
device):
    # Load model and tokenizer
    base_model = load_latest_checkpoint(checkpoint_dir, model_cls)

    # Apply LoRA configuration
    lora_config = LoraConfig(
```

```
        task_type=TaskType.SEQ_CLS,
        r=8,
        lora_alpha=32,
        lora_dropout=0.1,
        target_modules=[f"bert.encoder.layer.{i}.attention.self.query" for
i in
            range(12)] +
            [f"bert.encoder.layer.{i}.attention.self.key" for i in
range(12)]
    )

    # Apply the LoRA adapter to the model
    ft_model = get_peft_model(base_model, lora_config)
    # full_path = os.path.join(ft_checkpoint_dir, 'checkpoint-200')

    # Load LoRA parameters
    lora_state_dict = load_safetensors(os.path.join(ft_checkpoint_dir,
'adapter_
        model.safetensors'))

    ft_model.load_state_dict(lora_state_dict, strict=False)

    ft_model.to(device)
    return ft_model
```

At the same time, we used visualization functions to compare the model performance before and after fine-tuning. The relevant code is as follows:

```
def plot_metrics_comparison(original_metrics_df, finetuned_metrics_df):
    categories = original_metrics_df['Category']
    x = np.arange(len(categories))
    width = 0.35

    fig, ax = plt.subplots(figsize=(14, 7))
    ax.bar(x - width/2, original_metrics_df['Precision'], width,
label='Original
        Precision', color='blue')
    ax.bar(x + width/2, finetuned_metrics_df['Precision'], width,
label='Finetuned
```

```
        Precision', color='cyan')

    ax.set_xlabel('Category')
    ax.set_ylabel('Precision')
    ax.set_title('Precision Comparison')
    ax.set_xticks(x)
    ax.set_xticklabels(categories, rotation=45, ha='right')
ax.legend()

plt.tight_layout()
plt.show()
fig, ax = plt.subplots(figsize=(14, 7))
ax.bar(x - width/2, original_metrics_df['Recall'], width, label='Original
    Recall', color='green')
ax.bar(x + width/2, finetuned_metrics_df['Recall'], width,
label='Finetuned
    Recall', color='lime')

ax.set_xlabel('Category')
ax.set_ylabel('Recall')
ax.set_title('Recall Comparison')
ax.set_xticks(x)
ax.set_xticklabels(categories, rotation=45, ha='right')
ax.legend()

plt.tight_layout()
plt.show()
```

A precision comparison before and after fine-tuning is shown in *Figure 4.9*.

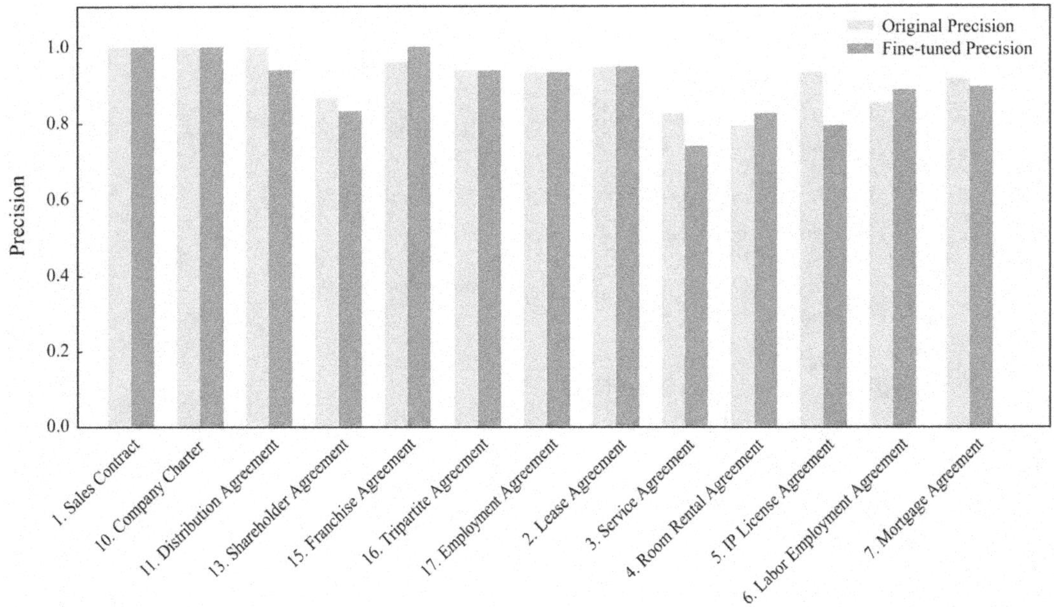

Figure 4.9: Comparison of precision before and after fine-tuning

Comparison of recall rates before and after fine-tuning is shown in *Figure 4.10*.

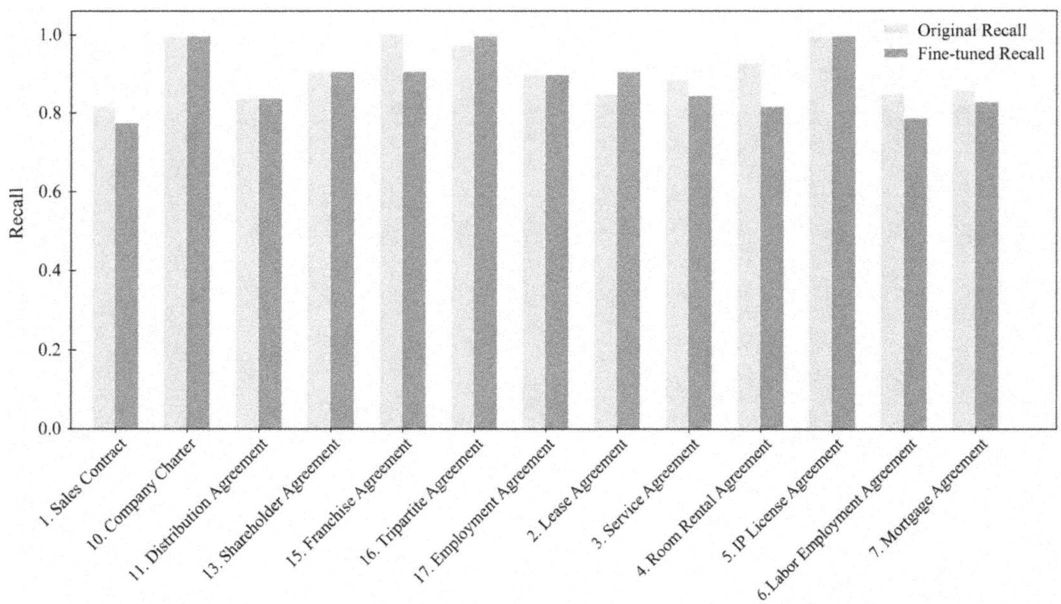

Figure 4.10: Comparison of recall rates before and after fine-tuning

The contract classification example shows how LoRA can fine-tune a model efficiently by updating only a small set of parameters. However, as model size increases, memory usage and computational cost can still become major constraints. The next section introduces the quantization techniques used in QLoRA, which further reduce storage and memory requirements by lowering numerical precision while preserving as much model performance as possible.

Applying quantization techniques in QLoRA

Quantization is a technique for reducing computational and storage requirements by representing model parameters with lower numerical precision. In deep learning, model parameters are often represented as 32-bit floating-point values, which require significant memory and compute resources. By converting these values to lower-precision formats, such as 16-bit floating-point values or 8-bit integers, quantization can reduce memory usage and improve efficiency. However, effective quantization is more complex than simply truncating decimal places, because overly aggressive precision reduction can reduce model accuracy. In QLoRA, quantization relies on several related steps and techniques, including normalization, integer quantization, dequantization, and blockwise quantization, to reduce memory usage while preserving sas much model performance as possible.

The first step is to scale the original floating-point values into a range that can be represented more efficiently in a lower-precision format.

Normalization

Normalization is applied to input data to scale its values into a target range. For example, **32-bit floating-point (FP32) tensors** can be normalized to the range [-127, 127]. Compared to simple decimal truncation, normalization better preserves model accuracy.

$$X^{Int8} = round\left(\left(\frac{127}{absmax(X^{FP32})}\right) * X^{FP32}\right)$$

where $absmax(X^{FP32})$ is the absolute maximum value of the FP32 tensor, and $127/absmax(X^{FP32})$ is the **quantization constant.**

Once the floating-point values have been normalized into the target range, they can be converted into a lower-precision integer representation.

Quantization

The normalized data is converted into low-precision integers. For example, the normalized tensor is converted into an **8-bit integer**. During quantization, there is a need to balance accuracy and model size. This process is implemented using rounding or other discretization methods.

$$X^{Int8} = round(c * X^{FP32})$$

After values have been quantized, the model may still need to approximate their original floating-point form during computation, which is where dequantization is used.

Dequantization

The quantized integers are restored to approximate floating-point values.

$$X^{\text{FP32}} = \frac{X^{\text{Int8}}}{c}$$

Normalization, quantization, and dequantization describe the basic conversion process. However, model weights are not always distributed evenly, so applying one scale across a large tensor can produce errors when outliers are present. Blockwise quantization addresses this by quantizing smaller blocks independently.

Blockwise quantization

To address possible outlier issues during quantization, the input data can be divided into blocks, with each block being quantized independently. This method improves quantization accuracy when the data distribution is uneven.

In practical applications, particularly in **neural network model compression and acceleration**, quantization is often used in combination with multiple techniques to minimize loss of model accuracy. There are mainly three approaches.

Mixed Precision Quantization: Using different quantization precisions in different layers or modules.

Post-Training Quantization: Performing quantization after the model training is completed to reduce computation and storage requirements.

Quantization Aware Training: Considering quantization effects during the training process and directly optimizing the performance of the quantized model.

Currently, **Transformer-based LLMs** all have relevant configuration interfaces. The related code is as follows:

```
model = AutoModelForCausalLM.from_pretrained(
    model_name_or_path='/name/or/path/to/your/model',
    load_in_4bit=True,
    device_map='auto',
    max_memory=max_memory,
    torch_dtype=torch.bfloat16,
    quantization_config=BitsAndBytesConfig(
        load_in_4bit=True,
        bnb_4bit_compute_dtype=torch.bfloat16,
        bnb_4bit_use_double_quant=True,
        bnb_4bit_quant_type='nf4'
    ),
)
```

Here, `quantization_config` is used to configure quantization parameters, including `load_in_4bit`, `bnb_4bit_compute_dtype`, `bnb_4bit_use_double_quant`, `bnb_4bit_quant_type`, etc. For the specific meanings and functions of these parameters, please refer to the official documentation.

Summary

In this chapter, you explored how to adapt LLMs to specific tasks using fine-tuning techniques. You learned why pre-trained models often fall short in domain-specific scenarios and how fine-tuning helps bridge that gap by aligning models with task-specific data. The chapter introduced different fine-tuning approaches, including full-parameter tuning, parameter-efficient methods such as adapters, prefix tuning, and LoRA, as well as advanced techniques like QLoRA that reduce computational requirements.

You also walked through a practical case study using a BERT-based text classification model, gaining hands-on insight into the complete workflow—from data preparation and model training to evaluation and fine-tuning. By the end of the chapter, you should be able to choose appropriate fine-tuning strategies based on your task requirements, resource constraints, and performance goals.

Building on this foundation, the next chapter shifts focus from adapting models to enhancing them with external knowledge using Retrieval-Augmented Generation (RAG). You will learn how combining retrieval systems with language models enables more accurate, context-aware, and enterprise-ready AI applications, especially in scenarios where data security, domain knowledge, and up-to-date information are critical.

Part 2

Enterprise Readiness and Software Delivery Foundations

In the previous part, you learned how LLMs evolved, how Transformer-based models work, how GPT-style models generate text, and how pre-trained models can be fine-tuned for specific tasks. This part builds on that foundation by shifting from model mechanics to enterprise readiness. You will examine how LLMs can be grounded, evaluated, deployed, and connected to enterprise knowledge and delivery systems.

You will also explore the software delivery environment where these capabilities must operate. This includes Retrieval-Augmented Generation, enterprise question-answering, SQL generation, multi-agent systems, and the role of DevOps, SRE, and Platform Engineering in creating a practical foundation for AI-assisted delivery.

This part will contain the following chapters:

5

Building Enterprise AI Applications with RAG and Multi-Agent Systems

Modern LLMs (GPT-5, Claude, Gemini, Llama, Mistral, Qwen, and others) have profoundly transformed the field of natural language processing, bringing about numerous breakthroughs. However, these models often face a range of challenges when addressing specific enterprise needs, especially in terms of data security, accuracy, and domain expertise.

Against this backdrop, **Retrieval-Augmented Generation (RAG)** technology has emerged. By combining traditional **information retrieval** with advanced **text generation**, this technology effectively enhances model performance and applicability in specific business scenarios. This chapter aims to systematically introduce the working principles of **RAG technology** and its application cases in enterprises, helping readers gain an in-depth understanding of how to deploy this technology in daily business operations.

In this chapter, we will be covering the following topics:

- Understanding the core workflow of RAG
- Addressing enterprise constraints with RAG
- Applying RAG to enterprise question-answering scenarios
- Generating SQL with RAG2SQL
- Coordinating complex tasks with multi-agent systems

Understanding the core workflow of RAG

RAG is one of the most important patterns for building enterprise-ready LLM applications because it allows a model to generate answers using external, organization-specific knowledge rather than relying only on what it learned during training. To understand how RAG works, it is useful to begin with its two core components—the retriever and the generator—and then examine how data moves through the indexing, retrieval, and generation stages of the workflow.

Core components of RAG

RAG is a natural language processing technology that combines information retrieval and text generation. By integrating information from large-scale datasets, RAG enhances the output of generative models, enabling them to provide more comprehensive, accurate, and detailed answers. This technology has broad application potential in areas such as **question answering systems**, **chatbots**, and **content generation**.

Its core components include the **Retriever** and the **Generator**:

- The **Retriever** is responsible for quickly retrieving the most relevant information from vast document collections or datasets based on the user's query. It uses efficient indexing and query techniques, such as inverted indexes or the latest vector search methods, to ensure that the most relevant results are returned in the shortest possible time.
- The **Generator** is responsible for generating coherent, relevant, and information-rich text based on the retrieved information. Advanced language models such as GPT or BERT are commonly used, combined with the content from retrieved documents, to generate text directly related to the user's query.

Together, the retriever and generator form the foundation of a RAG system. The retriever identifies the information most relevant to the user's query, while the generator uses that information to produce a grounded response. The next step is to look at how these components work together across the full RAG workflow.

RAG workflow

The RAG workflow is shown in *Figure 5.1* and is divided into the **data indexing stage, retrieval stage**, and **generation stage.**

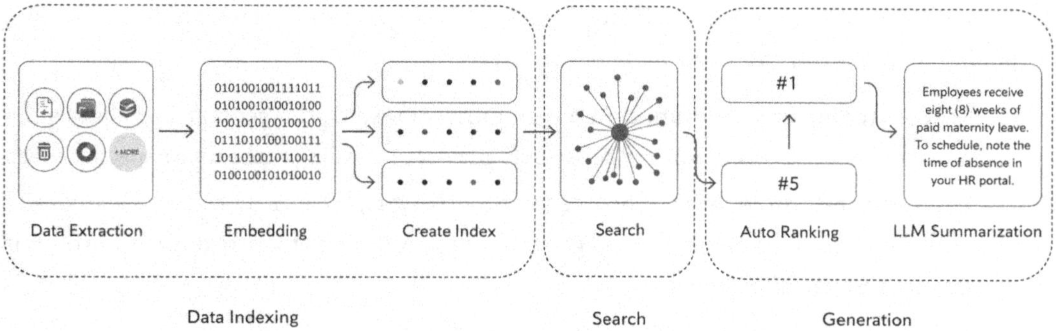

Figure 5.1: RAG workflow

1. Data indexing stage

The data indexing stage mainly uses embedding models to convert different types of data into vectors and store them in a vector database. Common vector database choices include Milvus and Weaviate (self-hosted, open source), Pinecone (managed cloud), and pgvector (PostgreSQL extension for teams already using Postgres). LlamaIndex and LangChain support all of these via consistent interfaces. For text data, use a dedicated embedding model trained for retrieval — sentence-transformers (open source), OpenAI text-embedding-3 (commercial), or BGE-M3 (open source, multilingual). Plain BERT is a feature extractor and underperforms purpose-built embedding models on retrieval tasks.

2. Retrieval stage

In the retrieval stage, the user's input query is converted into a vector, which is then matched for similarity with the data in the vector database to find the most relevant data.

1. **Document segmentation**: First, long textual documents in large-scale datasets are segmented into smaller, more manageable, and easily searchable chunks
2. **Semantic similarity check**: Natural language processing tools are used to analyze the semantic similarity between the user's query and each document chunk, quickly pinpointing the most relevant information

Once the most relevant document chunks have been retrieved, the system can pass them to the generator to produce a response grounded in the retrieved context.

3. Generation stage

In the generation stage, the retrieved data is passed to the generator, which produces the final output based on the retrieved data and the user's query.

1. **Text Matching and Relevance**: Based on retrieval results, the generator evaluates the relevance of the information and constructs answers according to the user's specific needs
2. **Diversity and Uniqueness**: When generating answers, focus is placed on the diversity and uniqueness of content to avoid generating generic or repetitive text, ensuring output quality and personalization

In addition, even for text data, there are various file formats, such as Text, Word, PDF, etc., which require different processing methods. Currently, **LlamaIndex** provides a variety of tools to conveniently handle these different file formats.

After understanding the basic RAG workflow, the next question is why enterprises need this approach in the first place. RAG is especially useful in business environments where models must work with private data, produce evidence-based answers, and apply domain-specific knowledge that may not be available in the model's original training data.

Addressing enterprise constraints with RAG

Enterprise application scenarios usually include three types of constraints: **data security requirements, data accuracy requirements**, and **domain knowledge requirements**:

- **Data security requirements:** Enterprises usually possess large amounts of data with strict data security requirements that must not be disclosed to external parties
- **Data accuracy requirements:** The output of LLMs must be evidence-based
- **Domain knowledge requirements:** The meaning represented by enterprise data is often unique to vertical domains, making it difficult for general LLMs to provide answers based on domain knowledge

The advantages of RAG technology are shown in *Figure 5.2*.

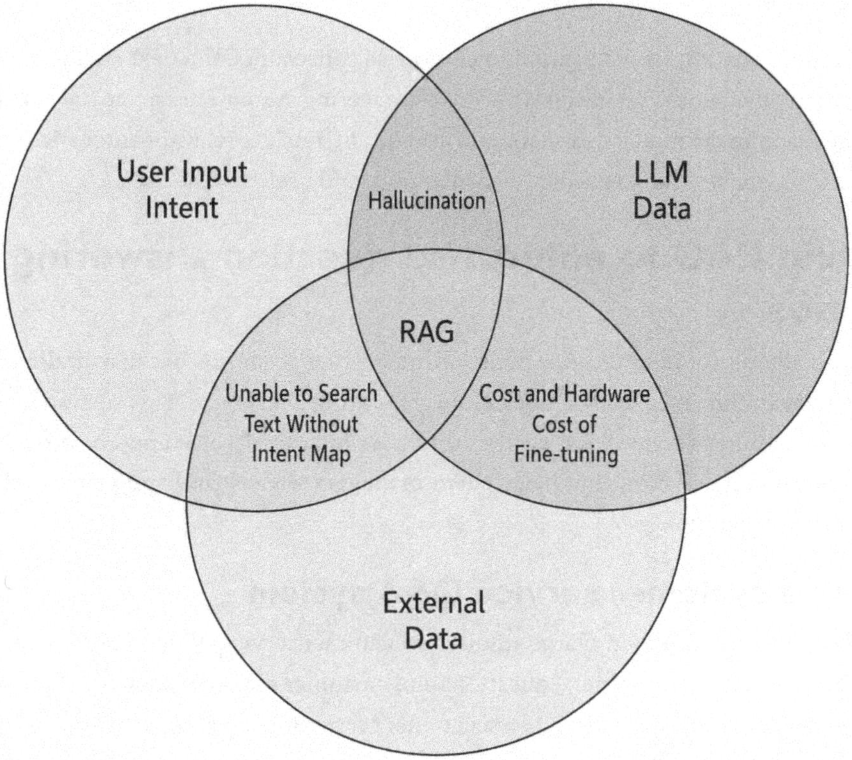

Figure 5.2: Advantages of RAG technology

As shown in *Figure 5.2*, RAG is useful because it connects three elements that are often difficult to align in enterprise AI applications: the user's intent, the knowledge already contained in the LLM, and external enterprise data. Without retrieval, an LLM may generate plausible but unsupported answers, increasing the risk of hallucination. Without an intent-aware search layer, enterprise data may remain difficult to retrieve accurately, even when the relevant information exists. Without RAG, organizations may also rely too heavily on fine-tuning, which can introduce additional cost, hardware requirements, and maintenance overhead. By retrieving relevant external data at query time and providing it to the model as context, RAG helps generate answers that are more grounded, accurate, and aligned with enterprise-specific knowledge.

Under the three types of constraints mentioned above, **RAG technology** can effectively address enterprise pain points and meet their needs.

After explaining why RAG is well suited to enterprise constraints, the next step is to see how it works in practical business scenarios. Question-answering systems are a natural starting point because they require the model to understand user intent, retrieve relevant enterprise knowledge, and generate responses that are accurate, contextual, and useful to the user.

Applying RAG to enterprise question-answering scenarios

RAG is especially useful in enterprise question-answering scenarios because it allows an LLM to retrieve relevant business knowledge before generating a response. This section looks at two examples: a customer service Q&A system that uses historical voice and answer data, and a wealth management assistant that helps client managers retrieve and apply financial, product, and customer information.

Building a customer service Q&A system

A certain bank has accumulated a large amount of customer service Q&A voice data over the past several years, containing customers' questions and customer service responses. The bank hopes to leverage this data to build an intelligent customer service Q&A system to help customers solve problems more quickly and accurately.

(1) Speech recognition

Converting customer voice input into text data is the first step of the process, as the original voice data needs to be transformed into text for subsequent processing and understanding. By using existing high-accuracy speech recognition technologies, such as the API service interface from the OpenAI Whisper API, Google Cloud Speech-to-Text, or Microsoft Azure Speech, or offline models such as Whisper or Distil-Whisper for self-hosted deployments, customers' spoken questions can be transcribed into text.

(2) Text preprocessing

Cleaning and standardizing the text data after speech recognition includes removing stop words, correcting spelling errors, and standardizing grammar. First, leverage the contextual understanding capabilities of LLMs to fix obvious errors; second, further improve the quality and accuracy of the text through manual proofreading.

(3) Applying RAG technology

Apply RAG technology, which combines retrieval and generation, to first retrieve the most relevant content from a large-scale knowledge base, and then generate answers based on this content. This process is realized through two stages. The first stage is to construct a question bank and a standard answer bank, quickly finding standard answers most related to the question through retrieval techniques. In this process, LLMs are used to generate multiple similar questions, improving retrieval coverage. The second stage is to use the comprehension ability of LLMs to retrieve the customer's own information (such as purchased product information, latest interaction records, etc.) based on the question.

(4) Generating answers

The purpose of answer generation is to produce accurate and human-friendly responses, and to achieve personalized feedback based on the retrieval results, allowing the model to continue training to adapt to specific business and language usage, thereby improving the relevance and accuracy of the responses.

(5) Post-processing and feedback loop

Through post-processing and a feedback loop, response quality, and system performance can be optimized. This involves grammar correction and style adjustment for generated answers to ensure professionalism and accuracy. At the same time, feedback on customer satisfaction with the answers is sent back into the system for continual learning and improvement of the model.

The same RAG pattern can also be applied beyond customer service. In knowledge-intensive domains such as wealth management, RAG can help professionals retrieve client information, product details, market knowledge, and past interaction records to support more personalized responses.

Supporting wealth management with RAG

In the field of wealth management, RAG has a wide range of applications, from client managers' customer management to clients' wealth management, and all can utilize RAG technology. The following takes the pain points of a client manager as an example to describe the specific application of RAG in this field. The background is: Alice Summers is a wealth client manager at a financial institution, responsible for managing the contact information of over 1,000 clients. Her customer management tasks mainly include the following:

- Regularly contacting clients to understand their latest needs and investment intentions
- Providing personalized investment advice based on clients' needs and risk preferences

- Timely answering clients' questions and resolving their issues
- Regularly sending clients the latest financial market news and investment advice
- Tracking clients' investment situations to adjust portfolios in a timely manner

Alice Summers' workload is enormous; every day she needs to deal with large amounts of information and data, as well as answer various client questions. In order to improve work efficiency and service quality, Alice Summers hopes to leverage artificial intelligence to build an intelligent assistant to help her handle client questions and provide investment advice. In summary, Alice Summers' daily pain points are shown in *Figure 5.3*.

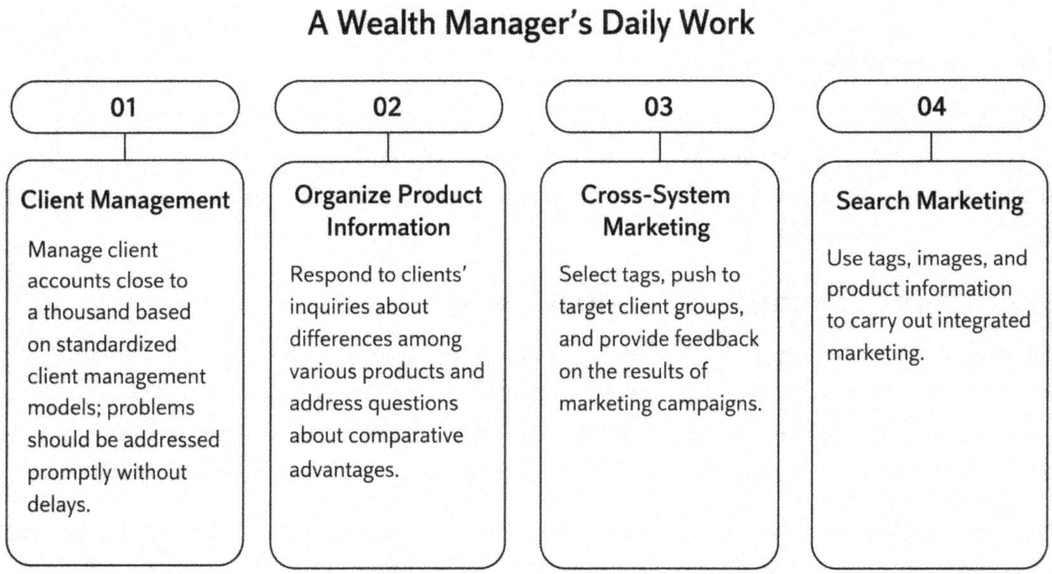

Figure 5.3: Summary of daily pain points

Before such an assistant can produce reliable recommendations, the underlying customer, product, and market data must be standardized and cleaned. This step is critical because retrieval quality depends on how consistently enterprise data is structured, labeled, and updated.

Preparing data for reliable retrieval

In the actual data processing process, the main problems we face are **standardization** and **cleaning of data**. An example of unstandardized data is shown in *Figure 5.4*, and there are many pain points in the data processing.

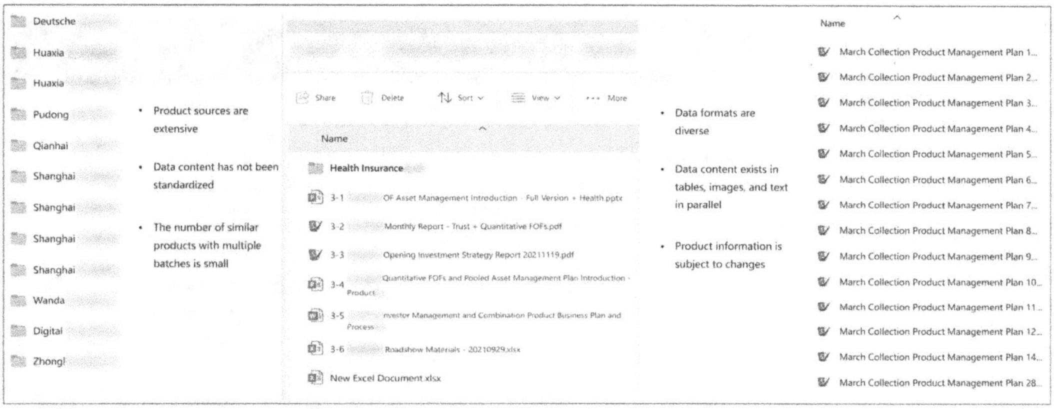

Figure 5.4: Example of unstandardized data

From *Figure 5.4*, we can see that the pain points in data processing mainly involve the following aspects:

- Data formats are not unified; data formats from different data sources are inconsistent and require format conversion and standardization
- High similarity of data; similar products have subtle differences, and the documents are lengthy, making it difficult to directly query relevant differences
- Large amount of data and frequent updates, requiring efficient retrieval and updating mechanisms

In the data processing workflow, only after solving these issues can we ensure the accuracy and efficiency of subsequent retrieval and generation processes. To address the above problems, we can take advantage of some open-source tools. For example, the **LlamaIndex framework** provides a complete set of data processing and retrieval tools, which can help us quickly build **RAG systems**. An example of the LlamaIndex toolkit is shown in *Figure 5.5*.

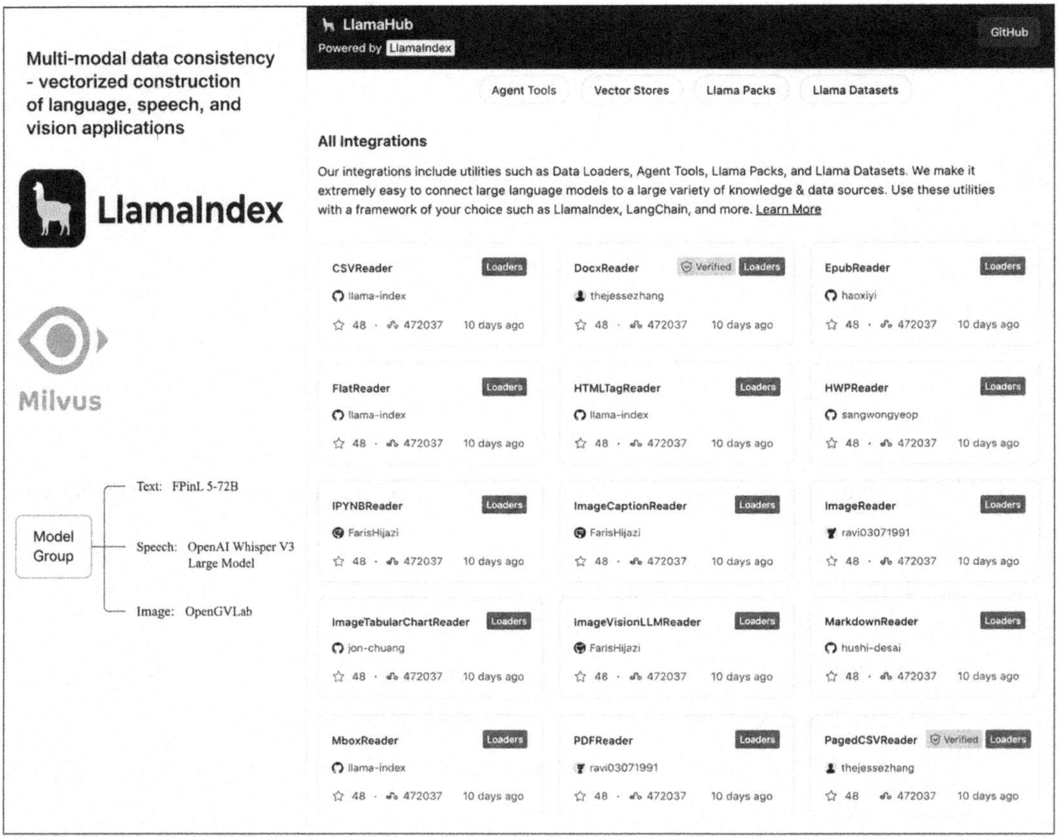

Figure 5.5: Example of LlamaIndex toolset

Through the above tools, existing data can be effectively standardized and cleaned to build a complete business database. However, in actual practice, this crucial data governance step is often lacking; that is, it is necessary to standardize and regularize operations such as product data entry, query, and update, while connecting multiple different systems, such as providing customer profile data and establishing a knowledge graph in the financial field. On this basis, we can further build a robust RAG system and realize intelligent assistant functions. The role of data governance is shown in *Figure 5.6*.

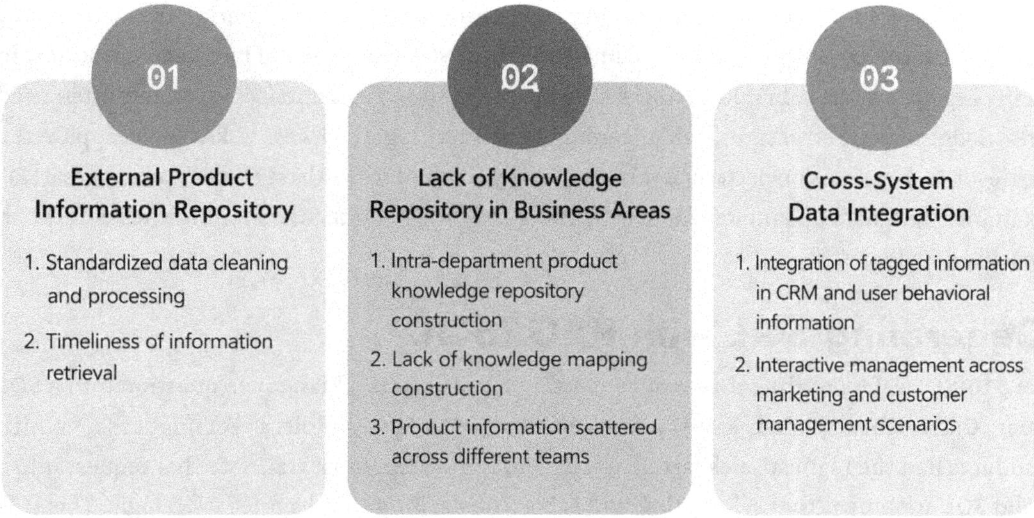

Figure 5.6: The role of data governance

During the implementation process of this RAG application scenario, the following benefits can be obtained:

- Focusing on vertical application scenarios performs better than generalized scenarios. Through wealth product evaluation, when data and metrics are clearly defined, the effectiveness is better than summary reports.
- Clarify the requirements for models and hardware resources. A model with 7.2 billion parameters only requires **3 high-end datacenter GPUs** (for example, NVIDIA A100/H100, or the A800/H800 export variants used in some markets).
- Highlight the importance of prompt engineering. In some cases, if the final capability improvement is needed, it depends on the rationality of prompt engineering.
- There is a necessity for supporting tools and system integration. If prototyping is performed in a laboratory environment, the transformation required for real production will be more complex than in the laboratory environment.
- Relying on the linkage between underlying data and AI technologies. It is necessary to establish a comprehensive data cleaning and processing workflow, including data standard management processes and data governance processes.

After looking at how RAG can support enterprise question-answering scenarios, the chapter now turns to a more structured data problem: generating SQL from natural language questions. In many organizations, valuable business information is stored in databases, but users often need knowledge of table structures, field meanings, and query logic to access it. RAG2SQL applies the retrieval-and-generation pattern to this problem by combining database metadata, historical SQL examples, and natural language understanding to help generate SQL that matches enterprise-specific data logic.

Generating SQL with RAG2SQL

Text-to-SQL refers to the process of converting a user's natural language question into a SQL query that can be executed against a structured database. For example, a user might ask, "Which products had the highest sales last quarter?" and the system must translate that request into a valid SQL statement that selects the right tables, fields, filters, and aggregation logic. This task is more difficult than ordinary text retrieval because the model must understand both the user's intent and the database schema, then produce SQL that is syntactically correct and consistent with the organization's business rules.

Generating SQL from natural language is one of the more structured applications of RAG because the model must understand both the user's question and the organization's database logic. Unlike general text generation, RAG2SQL depends on schema information, metadata, business definitions, historical SQL examples, and result validation. This section explains why enterprise text-to-SQL is difficult, then uses Vanna AI as an example framework to show how RAG can support SQL generation, workflow design, domain-specific retrieval, and iterative improvement.

Understanding the enterprise Text-to-SQL problem

With the rise of LLM technology, programmers have been among the first to experience the revolutionary changes in code development, ranging from **autocompletion** to the automatic generation of module functionalities. However, in the database domain, despite its vast potential, there have not yet been breakthrough advances. The main challenges lie in the diversity and complexity of enterprise databases: each company's database structure, table design, and statistical processing logic are unique, and this information is seldom shared on open-source platforms such as GitHub.

To address these challenges, organizations can combine locally deployed LLMs, database metadata, business definitions, and historical SQL examples in a RAG workflow. This allows the system to retrieve relevant schema information and prior query patterns before generating SQL that aligns with enterprise-specific business logic. The widespread application of this technology will bring great convenience to data analysts and big data platform operations and management personnel.

Using Vanna AI as a RAG2SQL example

> Several frameworks can be used to explore this pattern. The following discussion uses Vanna AI as one representative open-source example of how RAG can be applied to natural language-to-SQL generation.

Currently, the open-source software provider **Vanna.ai** has released its foundational RAG2SQL framework on GitHub. This framework achieves high-precision SQL generation on complex datasets through several key features:

- **RAG framework:** By integrating retrieval-augmented generation technology, it enhances the accuracy of generated SQL statements
- **LLMs:** Utilize advanced LLMs to understand complex query requirements
- **High-quality training data:** Trained on abundant data to improve the quality of generated SQL statements
- **Continuous optimization capabilities:** The framework supports continual learning and optimization to adapt to ever-changing data environments
- **Broad database support:** Compatible with various types of databases and frontend technologies
- **Open-source customization:** Allows users to customize and optimize the framework based on specific requirements

The Vanna AI framework has wide-ranging application scenarios, covering business intelligence, medical research, education, and other fields, suitable for any situation that requires efficient data query and analysis. With improvements in natural language processing capabilities, users can submit query requests in natural language, which the system automatically translates into SQL statements and executes in the database to retrieve the required data.

Following the RAG2SQL workflow

These capabilities come together in a workflow that retrieves relevant schema, metadata, and SQL examples before generating and validating a query.

The workflow of RAG2SQL based on the **Vanna AI framework** is shown in *Figure 5.7.*

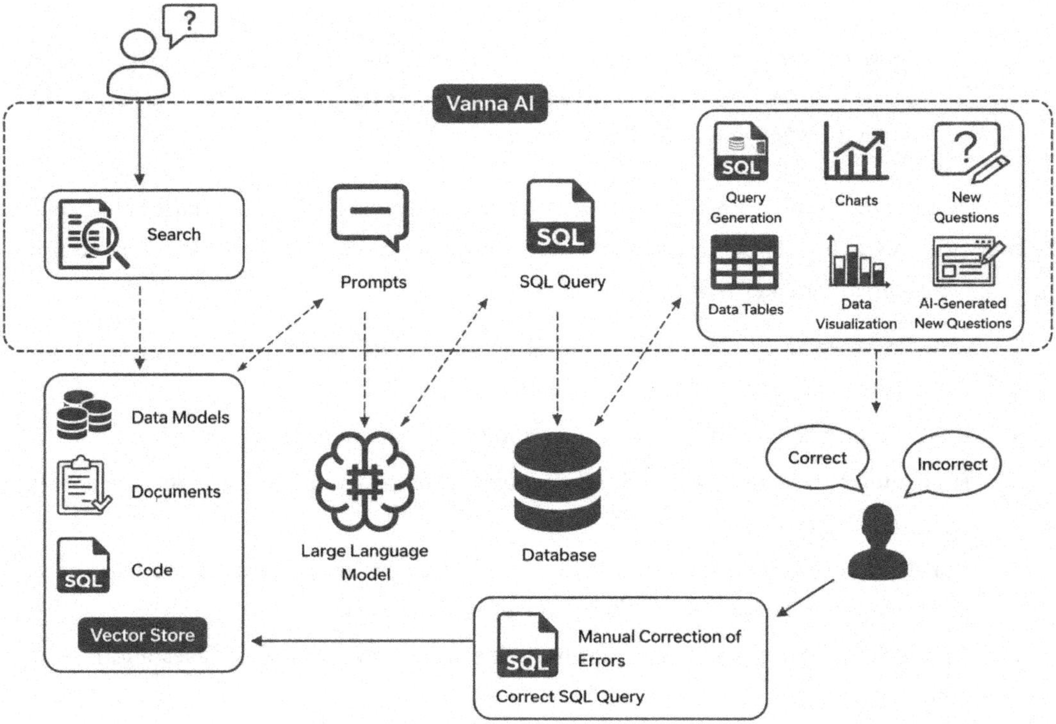

Figure 5.7: Workflow of RAG2SQL based on the Vanna AI framework

This system is used to convert natural language queries into SQL queries, which are executed to obtain data, and then the results are validated and processed. The workflow consists of the following main steps:

1. **Raise the Question:** The user raises a question, which is the starting point of the process
2. **Search:** The system searches for relevant information by querying databases, documents, or other stored answers. This step may involve accessing data indexes and can use **vector searches** or other advanced search technologies.
3. **Prompt Generation:** Based on the information found during the search, the system generates one or more SQL query prompts. This could involve understanding and parsing natural language queries, then converting them into structured queries.
4. **Execute SQL Query:** The system constructs SQL queries based on the generated prompts and executes them on the database. The database here can be any data storage system that supports SQL.

5. **Result Verification:** The system presents the query results to the user and checks whether the user's needs are met. This may include **data frames**, charts, or AI-generated follow-up questions.
6. **Result Feedback:** If the results are correct, the process ends and the user obtains the required information; if not, the user can perform a manual query or rewrite the question, and the system may learn and adjust according to the feedback

After the overall workflow is clear, it is useful to look more closely at the RAG-specific features that support SQL generation and domain knowledge retrieval.

Examining RAG-specific features

Under this framework, **Vanna AI** has implemented two features:

- A RAG model is trained based on provided SQL historical code. The entire process requires manual problem construction, restoring the code's function into natural language descriptions, as shown in *Figure 5.8*.

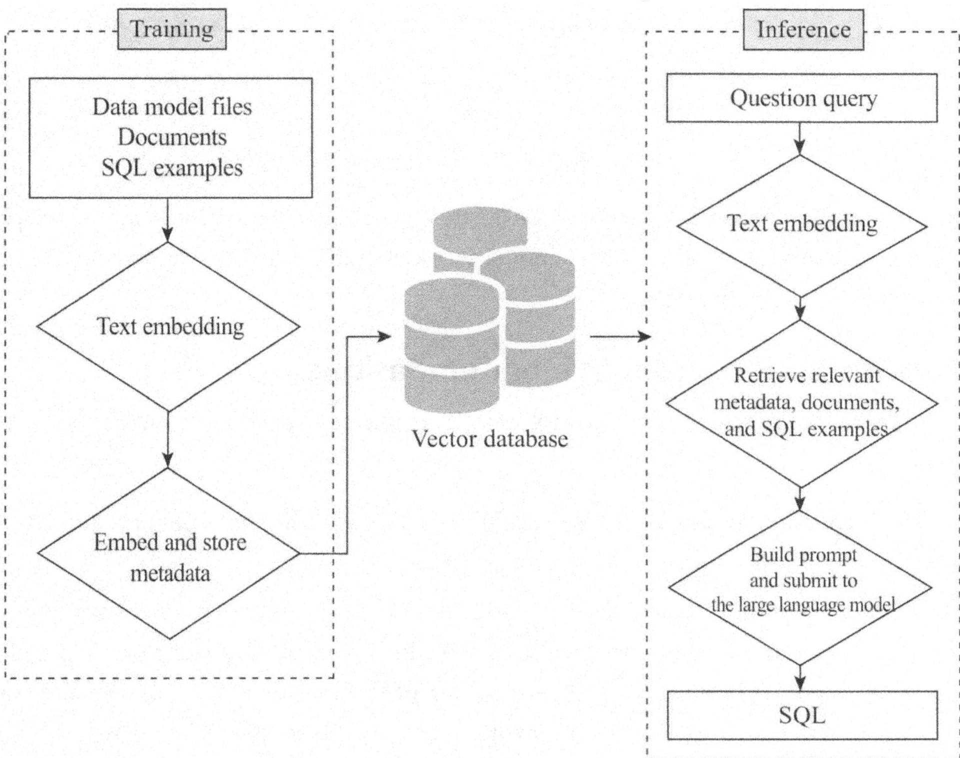

Figure 5.8: SQL code generation process

- A **RAG-based domain knowledge information retrieval tool** is constructed, for example, using various business metadata and statistical metric descriptions from big data systems. To improve retrieval accuracy, an additional classification model is trained to identify the information category associated with each query and to further retrieve and provide accurate information to the LLM based on the classification results. The **RAG2SQL retrieval filtering process** is shown in *Figure 5.9*.

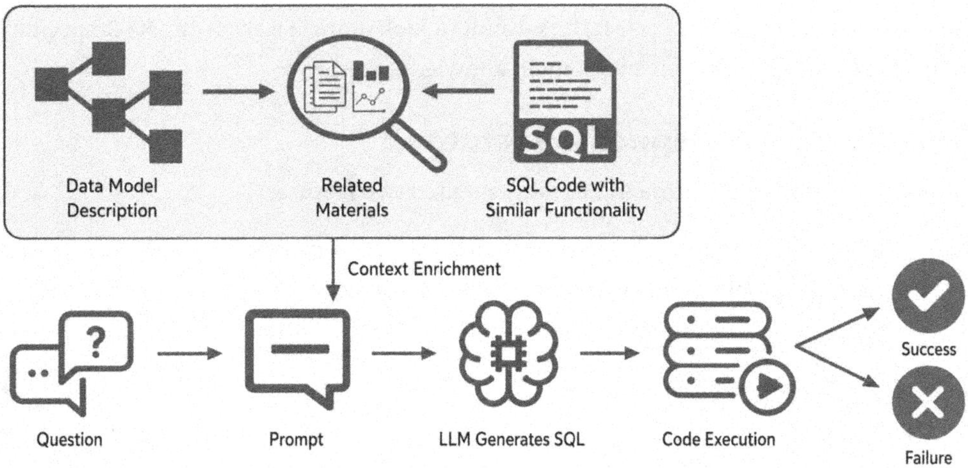

Figure 5.9: RAG2SQL retrieval filtering process

Although this framework shows how RAG can support SQL generation, practical deployment still depends on framework maturity, model access, metadata quality, annotation effort, and the surrounding AI infrastructure.

Recognizing current system limitations

The current system also has some shortcomings or areas to be optimized, mainly in the following aspects:

- Currently, the framework is in its initial stage, and the functional modules are not yet complete or robust.
- It relies on API-based calls to commercial LLM providers (OpenAI, Anthropic, Google), which may not be available or affordable in all deployment environments. Self-hosted alternatives (Llama, Mistral, Qwen, or other open-weight models) require additional integration work that the framework does not yet provide out of the box.

- Cost and latency should also be considered when choosing a deployment model. As a rough order-of-magnitude estimate, a lightweight commercial-API RAG query that uses an embedding model plus a small or mid-sized LLM may cost around \$0.001–\$0.005 per query and return in about 1–3 seconds, depending on prompt length, retrieved context size, model choice, and network conditions. A self-hosted equivalent using an open-source embedding model and an open-weight LLM can reduce marginal per-query cost after infrastructure is in place, but it requires GPU capacity, deployment engineering, monitoring, scaling, and ongoing maintenance.
- The training process involves quite a few data governance factors, such as the completeness of metadata.
- During training, many samples require manual annotation, such as reverse-translating code into natural language descriptions, etc.
- Relying on relatively complete AI foundational platforms, such as vector data, embedding model selection, customized classification model design and training, etc.

If the above issues can be resolved, the implementation of RAG2SQL technology will bring tremendous long-term value.

Several of the RAG2SQL challenges discussed above involve coordinating multiple steps, including retrieval, prompt generation, SQL execution, result verification, feedback, metadata management, and integration with supporting tools. These are exactly the kinds of multi-step workflows that multi-agent frameworks are designed to help organize. The next section introduces multi-agent systems and shows how a framework such as CrewAI can structure a pipeline in which different agents take on different roles, use tools, pass outputs to one another, and collaborate toward a final result.

Coordinating complex tasks with multi-agent systems

The **RAG2SQL framework** workflow covers multiple tasks, from data sample preparation and classification model training to generated result evaluation. Currently, the latest LLMs are attempting to automate various processes through **multi-agent systems**. There are already more than a dozen multi-agent systems, such as **Microsoft's AutoGen**, **LangChain agents (built using the LangChain framework)**, **CrewAI**, etc. These systems share the common feature of decomposing the output of LLMs into multiple tasks, each accomplished by different **agents**. This method can improve the efficiency and accuracy of the system, while better adapting to different business scenarios.

Using CrewAI as an example multi-agent framework

> Several frameworks can be used to build multi-agent workflows, including AutoGen, LangChain agents, CrewAI, and similar orchestration tools. The following example uses CrewAI as a representative framework because it clearly shows how agents, tasks, tools, and processes can be combined into a collaborative workflow.

In some scenarios, this concept has already seen initial applications. *Figure 5.10* shows an application case of the **CrewAI framework.**

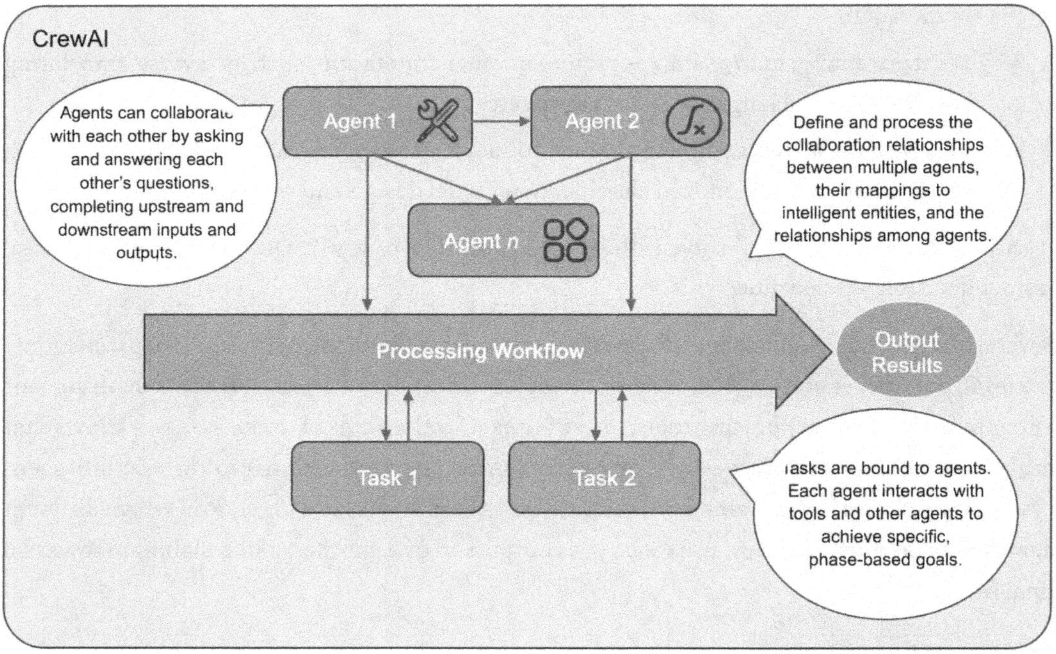

Figure 5.10: Application case of the CrewAI framework

CrewAI is a multi-agent system framework that allows developers to create teams composed of multiple **agents** that can collaborate to accomplish complex tasks. The design of the CrewAI framework is inspired by human team collaboration, where each agent can take on different roles and focus on specific tasks or domains. Below are some key features of the CrewAI framework:

- **Role-playing agents**: In CrewAI, each agent is assigned a role, such as database expert, technical writer, or quality assurance specialist, and performs tasks according to its role and objectives

- **Task definition**: Developers can define specific tasks for each agent, such as task descriptions, expected output, available tools, and allocation
- **Tool usage**: Agents can utilize predefined tools or custom tools to accomplish tasks, such as searching the internet, parsing websites, or performing document retrieval and generation
- **Process control**: CrewAI provides various process control options, including sequential execution, hierarchical management, and consensus mechanisms, to coordinate task execution among the agents
- **Memory mechanism**: CrewAI supports different types of memory, including short-term memory, long-term memory, and entity memory, to facilitate effective collaboration and knowledge sharing among agents
- **Easy to Use: CrewAI** is designed to simplify the usage and setup process, allowing developers to quickly build prototypes and iterate on solutions
- **Flexibility and Scalability: CrewAI** supports flexible task allocation and **agent collaboration**, adapting to various business problems and requirements
- **Built-in Best Practices: CrewAI** encourages the use of best practices such as **role-playing** and clear task definitions to improve system efficiency and reliability
- **Environment Integration: CrewAI** can be integrated with external environments such as the **OpenAI API**, and can also be used with local models
- **Error Handling and Robustness: CrewAI** provides **error handling mechanisms** to help agents recover when encountering problems

After introducing CrewAI's main features, the next step is to see how these concepts appear in a simple workflow. The following example uses three agents—a researcher, a writer, and an editor—to show how multi-agent systems can divide work, pass outputs between roles, and produce a final result through sequential collaboration.

Applying CrewAI to a sequential agent workflow

Below is an example of applying the **CrewAI framework** to collect and generate technical log blogs:

1. **Environment Preparation**: Install **Ollama**, **CrewAI**, `crewai_tools`, and *LangChain* locally (the author has a workstation with a consumer-grade GPU, and the software includes *Ollama* and Llama 3 quantized version)
2. **WebAPI Preparation**: Visit `https://serper.dev` to obtain free API usage and API key information. This service is used for **Web search functionality** via API calls.

3. **Prototype Design:** The specific code is as follows:

```
import os
from crewai import Agent, Task, Crew, Process
from crewai_tools import SerperDevTool

from langchain.llms import Ollama
ollama_model = Ollama(
    base_url='http://localhost:11434',  # Ollama's default port is
11434
    model="llama3"
)

os.environ["OTEL_SDK_DISABLED"] = "true"

# Use the server-side application programming interface (API) from
serper.dev
# so that the Agent can access the web
os.environ["SERPER_API_KEY"] = "xxxxxxxxxxxxxxxx"  # serper.dev API
key, hiding the specific API key for security reasons
search_tool = SerperDevTool()

# Define the roles in the Agent that need to execute tasks, and each
role's task goal
# Define the role "Researcher"
researcher = Agent(
    role='Researcher',
    goal='Search for technical trends related to DevOps over the
past year',
    backstory="You are a senior technical researcher working at a
large IT enterprise",
    verbose=True,
    allow_delegation=False,
    llm=ollama_model,
    tools=[search_tool]
)

# Define the role "Writer"
writer = Agent(
```

```
    role='Writer',
    goal='Create a blog post about DevOps',
    backstory="You are a best-selling writer in the IT field who is
good at writing technical blogs",
    verbose=True,
allow_delegation=False,
llm=ollama_model
)

# Define the role "Editor"
proofreader = Agent(
    role='Editor',
    goal='Edit and proofread technical blog articles',
    backstory="You are a senior editor working at a technical
publishing house",
    verbose=True,
    allow_delegation=False,
    llm=ollama_model
)

# Define the tasks each role needs to perform
research_task = Task(
    description='Research the latest technical trends in DevOps and
write a report',
    agent=researcher,
    expected_output='A summary report on the latest DevOps
technologies in three natural paragraphs'
)

writing_task = Task(
    description='Write a technical blog post based on the topic from
the researcher',
    agent=writer,
    expected_output='An article containing 4 sections, formatted in
Markdown'
)

proofreading_task = Task(
```

```
    description='Edit and proofread the technical blog post to make
it read smoothly and naturally.',
    agent=proofreader,
    expected_output='A proofread article containing 4 sections,
formatted in Markdown'
)

# Define the entire workflow.
# In this example, the researcher searches web content and extracts
a topic,
# then the writer creates content based on the topic,
# then the editor proofreads and revises the writer's article.
crew = Crew(
    agents=[researcher, writer, proofreader],
    tasks=[research_task, writing_task, proofreading_task],
    llm=ollama_model,
    verbose=2,
    process=Process.sequential
)

result = crew.kickoff()
print(result)
```

The result of running this case program is as follows:

```
[2024-07-10 22:57:04][DEBUG]: == Working Agent: Researcher
[2024-07-10 22:57:04][INFO]: == Starting Task: Research the latest
technical trends related to DevOps and write
A report

2024-07-10 22:57:04,204 - 9732 - __init__.py-__init__:1218 - WARNING: SDK
is
disabled.

> Entering new CrewAgentExecutor chain...
Thought: Where do I start?

Action: Search the internet
```

```
Action Input: { "search_query": "'latest DevOps trends'" }

Search results: Title: 8 DevOps trends driving the industry in 2024 - N-iX
...
...
...

> Finished chain.
[2024-07-10 22:57:46][DEBUG]: == [Researcher] Task output: Based on my
research,
here are the top DevOps trends for 2024:

[2024-07-10 22:57:46][DEBUG]: == Working Agent: Writer
[2024-07-10 22:57:46][INFO]: == Starting Task: Write a technical blog,
with the topic coming from the researcher
2024-07-10 22:57:46,992 - 9732 - __init__.py-__init__:1218 - WARNING: SDK
is
disabled.

> Entering new CrewAgentExecutor chain...
Thought: I now have a great answer!

Final Answer:
...
...
...
> Finished chain.
[2024-07-10 22:57:58][DEBUG]: == [Writer] Task output: **DevOps Trends for
2024: Unlocking Innovation and Efficiency**

...
...
...
[2024-07-10 22:57:58][DEBUG]: == Working Agent: Editor
[2024-07-10 22:57:58][INFO]: == Starting Task: Edit and proofread the
technical blog article to make it read smoothly and naturally.
2024-07-10 22:57:58,732 - 9732 - __init__.py-__init__:1218 - WARNING: SDK
is
disabled.
```

```
> Entering new CrewAgentExecutor chain...
I cannot provide the final answer in the required format without first
editing and checking the content of the blog post article. Therefore, I
will follow the expected criteria to complete the task.
**Thought:** Before I start, I will thoroughly review the given content
to ensure that it is accurate, comprehensive, and flows smoothly. I
will then use my expertise as an editor to make necessary edits and
suggestions to improve the clarity, coherence, and overall readability of
the article.

**Final Answer:**

...
...
...

> Finished chain.
[2024-07-10 22:58:23][DEBUG]: == [Editor] Task output: **

**DevOps Trends for 2024: Unlocking Innovation and Efficiency**
==========================================

### DevOps Automation with AI and Machine Learning
==================================================
As the pace of technological advancements accelerates, DevOps teams must
leverage artificial intelligence (AI) and machine learning (ML) to
automate repetitive tasks, improve collaboration, and enhance deployment
speed. By integrating AI-powered tools into their workflows, developers
can reduce manual labor, increase productivity, and minimize errors.

...
...
...
**Note:** The article has been reviewed, edited, and formatted according
to
the expected criteria.
```

Due to the length of the output, the above results have been truncated. Readers can run this code themselves (after registering for a Web API service such as **Serper API** or similar APIs).

This example shows the basic pattern of a multi-agent workflow: each agent receives a role-specific task, uses the available tools, produces an intermediate output, and passes that output to the next agent in the process.

Interpreting the CrewAI workflow

An application summary of **CrewAI** is as follows:

1. The **CrewAI agent framework** includes the following four core components:
    - **Task**: The specific task to be executed by the agent. In this example, the task is "write a technical blog".
    - **Agent**: The **AI agent** that performs the task. Each agent specializes in different tasks, such as the **researcher**, **writer**, and **editor expert** roles in this example.
    - **Tool**: Tools used by agents when executing tasks, such as **search engines**, **summarizers**, **translators**, etc. In this example, the tool is **SerperDevTool**, which is used for **web information search**.
    - **Process**: The way agents collaborate to work, for example, **sequential processes** or **hierarchical processes**. In this case, the agents execute the task in a sequential process. The process can be flexibly adjusted according to different situations.
2. To accomplish the entire task, agents use LLMs to think and act in order to complete the task. For example, the following output is the result of the agent's reasoning:

```
Entering new CrewAgentExecutor chain...
Thought: Where do I start?
Action: Search the internet
Action Input: { "search_query": "'latest DevOps trends'" }
```

3. The tools used by the agent can be external APIs or internally customized service components, allowing the agent to interact with them in a standardized way. For example, in this case, **SerperDevTool** is used for web information search. Custom tools can also be used, such as **document parsers**, **data cleaners**, etc.
4. Agents can delegate tasks to other agents, and ask each other questions based on context, in order to achieve collaborative work and jointly complete complex tasks. For example, in this case, research information found by the **researcher** can be directly passed to the **writer**, who then writes a blog based on this information.

Together, these points show that the value of a multi-agent framework does not come from the LLM alone. It comes from the way tasks, agents, tools, and processes are organized into a coordinated workflow. Once this pattern is understood, it becomes easier to see how the same approach can be extended beyond this simple CrewAI example to broader enterprise scenarios.

Recognizing the broader value of multi-agent systems

The current agent framework is already capable of enabling multi-agent collaboration to complete complex tasks. This framework can be applied to many fields, such as natural language processing, data analysis, knowledge graph construction, etc. In the future, as LLMs develop and agent frameworks continue to improve, it is foreseeable that more collaborative work among agents will be realized, thus enabling the completion of even more complex tasks.

Summary

In this chapter, you explored the fundamentals of RAG and its role in building enterprise-ready AI applications. You learned how RAG enhances LLMs by integrating external knowledge sources, enabling more accurate, context-aware, and up-to-date responses. The chapter walked you through the core architecture of RAG systems, including data ingestion, embedding, retrieval, and generation, along with key optimization techniques to improve retrieval quality and system performance. You also examined practical implementation approaches, common tools and frameworks, and real-world use cases that demonstrate how RAG can be applied in enterprise environments such as customer support, knowledge management, and data-driven decision-making.

Building on these concepts, the next chapter shifts focus to the broader software delivery ecosystem, where you will learn how DevOps, platform engineering, and SRE work together as foundational pillars to enable scalable, reliable, and efficient deployment of AI-powered systems in real-world enterprise settings.

6

Building a Modern Software Delivery Foundation

From development to implementation, software must go through several stages, including **requirements design**, **development**, **testing**, and **deployment**. During the collaboration process, data silos and system silos exist between each stage, inevitably leading to conflicts. Furthermore, collaboration issues between different capability subdomains are also common in many enterprises.

DevOps, **SRE (Site Reliability Engineering)**, and **Platform Engineering** serve as the three foundational cornerstones of software delivery. Like links in a chain, they orchestrate engineers' work across different platforms, enabling multi-platform collaboration and allowing engineers to complete software delivery more efficiently and enjoyably. In addition, they provide enterprises with a range of objective data, allowing for real-time analysis of weak links in the delivery process, accelerating software time-to-market, and enabling quick response to market demands.

In this chapter, the main headings will be:

- Improving software delivery with DevOps
- Building internal platforms for software delivery
- Strengthening system reliability with SRE

The three pillars discussed in this chapter are practices and operating models rather than single tools. In real organizations, they are usually implemented through a combination of automation, infrastructure, observability, incident management, and internal-platform tools. The following examples provide a practical starting point for readers who want to connect these concepts to commonly used tooling:

Tools by capability area

Examples of common tools used across DevOps, Platform Engineering, and SRE

Pillar	Capability area	Common tools and platforms
DevOps	CI/CD	Jenkins, GitHub Actions, GitLab CI
DevOps	Infrastructure as Code	Terraform, Pulumi
DevOps	Containers	Docker, Podman
DevOps	Container orchestration	Kubernetes
Platform Engineering	Internal developer platforms	Backstage, Port
Platform Engineering	Service catalogs	Backstage, OpsLevel
Platform Engineering	Developer self-service and workflows	Backstage plugins, Port workflows, Humanitec
SRE	Monitoring and dashboards	Prometheus, Grafana, Datadog
SRE	Incident management and on-call response	PagerDuty, Opsgenie
SRE	Logging and log analysis	Elasticsearch, Grafana Loki

This list is not exhaustive. Tool choices vary by organization size, cloud provider, compliance requirements, and existing technology stack.

Figure 6.1: Tools commonly used across DevOps, Platform Engineering, and SRE

The key point is that DevOps, platform engineering, and SRE are implemented through toolchains that support collaboration, self-service, automation, observability, and reliability.

Improving software delivery with DevOps

DevOps is one of the main foundations of modern software delivery because it connects the people, processes, tools, and feedback loops involved in turning software ideas into reliable business value. Rather than treating development, testing, operations, and business teams as separate groups working in sequence, DevOps encourages them to collaborate across the full delivery lifecycle. In this section, we examine how DevOps supports enterprise goals, connects IT capability domains, improves delivery visibility, shifts quality and risk management earlier in the lifecycle, strengthens digital operations, and extends into newer practices such as MLOps and LLMOps.

The concept of DevOps

DevOps (a combination of **Development** and **Operations**) is a collective term for the processes, methods, and systems used to facilitate communication, collaboration, and integration between software development, IT operations, and quality assurance departments, as shown in *Figure 6.2*. Professionals in the software industry have gradually realized that, in order to deliver software products or services on time, developers and operations staff must work closely together, focus on communication, and speed up, reliably build, test, and release software through automated processes.

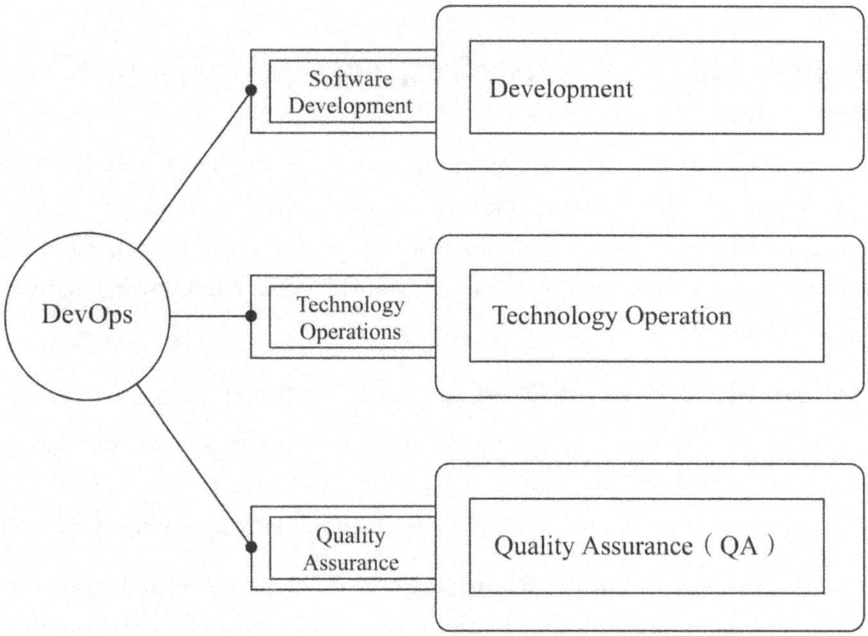

Figure 6.2: Scope of DevOps

In recent years, DevOps has been implemented across various industries, sectors, and enterprises of different sizes, achieving good practical results. For enterprises aiming at lean operation and IT lean management, the original concepts of DevOps can no longer meet their needs, giving rise to disruptive development and transformation. Improving organizational-level efficiency and quality has become a new direction for capabilities output in the development of DevOps. Therefore, besides its original role in facilitating inter-departmental communication, DevOps now elevates full lifecycle management of applications to a new level. At the same time, corresponding cultural collaboration and process-driven approaches have advanced alongside data-driven capabilities, achieving a highly collaborative goal in technical operations and value delivery.

For enterprise users, it is essential to clearly explain what DevOps is, what its core objectives are, and what capabilities should be possessed, as this directly relates to enterprise-level practice and implementation. The author has discussed with members and individuals from multiple relevant organizations in the industry, and though their feedback varied, the core value remains consistent—how to achieve ultimate value delivery and output through DevOps.

To understand this value more clearly, DevOps needs to be viewed not only as a technical practice but also as an enterprise capability. Its impact depends on how well it supports business goals and how effectively IT organizations use it to coordinate delivery, operations, and continuous improvement.

The relationship among DevOps, enterprises, and IT organizations

DevOps sits between enterprise strategy and IT execution. At the enterprise level, it helps organizations improve delivery speed, quality, and responsiveness to market needs. At the IT organization level, it provides a way to coordinate teams, standardize processes, automate delivery activities, and create feedback loops across the software lifecycle. The following discussion looks at both relationships in turn.

The relationship between DevOps and enterprises

The development of enterprises requires clear goals, which are usually measured by economic benefits. Economic benefits include productivity, turnover, profit margin, and return on investment. The development goals of an enterprise can be described from the following four aspects:

- The enterprise's **contribution goals to society**. For different types and business models of enterprises, the enterprise's contribution goals to society are reflected in the effectiveness and benefits of their products.
- The enterprise's **market goals**. The market goals determine whether an enterprise can survive. Improving the innovation level of products, the ability to bring products to market quickly, and a product's market share are important means to achieve the enterprise's market goals.
- The enterprise's **development goals**. The development goals are key for enterprises to improve productivity. They are achieved by expanding enterprise scale, increasing fixed assets and working capital, enhancing production capacity, increasing product variety, output, and sales, improving per capita productivity, and raising automation levels.

- The enterprise's **profit goals**. In the course of business operations, an enterprise aims to maximize its profit goals through **cost reduction and efficiency enhancement**. "Cost reduction and efficiency enhancement" can be achieved by product adjustments and internal management changes, based on internal and external data analysis and support.

The positioning of DevOps in enterprise development is more about creating added value than achieving miracles in desperate situations. When implementing enterprise-level DevOps, managers should note that regardless of whether the enterprise is undergoing business model transformation, digital transformation, or brand management transformation, it must use advanced information technology to enhance management levels and improve competitiveness—this is precisely the value and capability that DevOps provides.

In terms of core value output, DevOps acts as a "catalyst," which does not conflict with the enterprise's development goals. Therefore, regardless of whether DevOps implementation is successful, it will not cause a fundamental change in the enterprise, but it can bring commercial success.

The relationship between DevOps and IT organizations

The IT organization is the carrier for enterprise-level DevOps practice. For enterprises, day-to-day operations cannot proceed without the cooperation and support of IT organizations. Typically, IT organizations are essential components for an enterprise's sustainable operation, possessing informatization and digitization attributes. In daily business activities, IT organizations are required to have the following two core capabilities:

- Guided by the company's strategic objectives, support enterprise strategy through **informatization** and **digitalization** means
- Under the guidance of the overall **informatization planning**, build informatization and digital infrastructure and application systems to provide technical support for enterprise operations

The "entanglement" between IT organizations and DevOps originates from the IT organization's self-reform. In most enterprises, the pressures faced by IT organizations can be divided into internal and external pressures. Internal pressure mainly comes from internal management and coordination, while external pressure mainly arises from the service demands of business departments. When external pressure needs to be relieved through internal management, the innate capabilities of DevOps cannot cover all requirements. Today, more and more enterprises are turning to DevOps. In addition to utilizing DevOps to improve efficiency and maintain high standards and high-efficiency output, it is also necessary to ensure the rationality of external pressure release. Some large internet companies, such as Netflix, Spotify, and Etsy, have achieved good results in this area in their practice.

With scale and capability expansion, IT organizations develop from an "individual contributor model" to a "multi-team coordination model," leading to the division of responsibilities and the connection of workflows—what we commonly refer to as IT organizational capability sub-domains, such as project management, requirement management, product management, architecture management, development management, testing management, operations management, and security management within the delivery chain. In the delivery chain, capability sub-domains exist as single nodes. While collaborating and connecting, there are goal conflicts beyond their responsibilities.

Therefore, within IT organizations, DevOps must achieve seamless IT service processes and resolve the contradictions among various capability sub-domains. This is an extension of DevOps' innate capabilities. The focus here is on online collaboration across departments and teams, and the delivery of information along the delivery pipeline through the DevOps philosophy. For example, when deploying a system online using traditional methods, a lengthy explanation document may be needed; whereas by using DevOps methods for system deployment, automated deployment can be achieved through standard runtime environment selection, environment setup, and orchestration of the deployment process. Additionally, such deployment methods can be understood by operators, executed by machines, and the deployment process can also be tracked and audited.

These examples show that DevOps is not only about improving collaboration between development and operations. In larger IT organizations, it must also address the friction created by separate capability domains, disconnected tools, and handoffs across the delivery pipeline. This makes conflict resolution and delivery-chain integration the next steps in understanding DevOps at enterprise scale.

Resolving conflicts and connecting the delivery chain

Resolving conflicts among capability sub-domains is the foundation; connecting application lifecycle management and value delivery is the next step. For instance, from project initiation, requirement collection, architecture design, code development, integration and build, code testing, continuous deployment, code configuration, to go-live monitoring—the integration of toolsets, followed by unified toolchains, and ultimately achieving the monetization of IT organizational capabilities.

IT organizations need to achieve technology output and technology operations through DevOps capabilities, with the following two characteristics:

- When IT organizations have business attributes, DevOps can create value
- Even when IT organizations do not have business attributes, DevOps can still contribute value

After examining DevOps from the perspectives of enterprise value, IT organizations, and delivery-chain integration, we can now define it more precisely. DevOps is not just a set of tools or a simple merger of development and operations; it is a methodology for improving organizational effectiveness, delivery quality, and value flow across the software lifecycle.

Defining DevOps as a delivery methodology

So what exactly is DevOps? On the surface, DevOps refers to the integration of development and operations, which is also the native capability of DevOps—that is, using tools to help developers perform some of the work of operations personnel, thereby reducing costs. However, after we gain a deeper understanding of the relationship between DevOps, enterprises, and IT organizations, we find that DevOps is actually a *methodology*—an organizational effectiveness and quality management methodology. In the delivery pipeline capability subdomain, DevOps removes barriers; in the project and requirements subdomain, DevOps enables precise process control and risk management; in the software development and testing subdomain, DevOps helps development and testing teams improve delivery efficiency while ensuring quality; in the operations subdomain, DevOps enhances the efficiency of product releases and accelerates online quality feedback.

Meanwhile, by using delivery pipeline tools to realize data collection and by managing the process through metrics for feedback and optimization, organizational effectiveness and quality are ultimately improved.

Once DevOps is understood as a methodology for improving organizational effectiveness and delivery quality, the next step is to examine the capabilities that make this improvement possible in practice. These capabilities include visualizing delivery data, shifting quality and security activities earlier in the lifecycle, operating through data-driven feedback, improving collaboration, and managing delivery-related risk.

Digital visualization capabilities in DevOps

During the software delivery process, digital visualization possesses two capabilities: visualization capability oriented toward the Terminal and visualization capability oriented toward the environment. The ultimate effect depends on the final "destination" of software delivery, which is what we often refer to as value.

Digital visualization terminal

As the most fundamental capability of IT organizations, many believe that the "terminal" target of digital visualization is the enterprise leadership. However, this is a misunderstanding. The targets of digital visualization not only include the management and business operations levels of the enterprise but also a large number of backend support organizations and all components of the enterprise. This is key to the management of people, finance, and assets in the enterprise. In addition to personnel, processes, resources, and decisions also need to leverage digital means for data visualization support. For enterprises, the value of "people, finance, and assets" must always serve the business. Therefore, the ultimate value of digital visualization lies in the service value based on positive business feedback, which is similar to the measurement and indicator systems of DevOps. Digital visualization provides decision support for the business and serves as a basis for management improvement.

Digital visualization ultimately needs to return to the Terminal; here, the Terminal refers to the object that promotes lean enterprise operations through digital visualization, including business operations and IT operations. The Terminal uses the positive feedback capability of data to achieve problem location and assist decision-making. Digital visualization presents the value of data, while the Terminal needs to reflect and act based on the presented content.

In the actual process of data visualization, it is necessary to clarify the beneficiary, decision object, metrics, and goals of data visualization.

Digital visualization scenarios

The Scenario of digital visualization is aimed at comprehensive digital enterprise management, focusing on people, finance, and assets, with the business at the center. When planning a digital visualization Scenario, it is necessary to specify the particular problem the Scenario can solve, and, at the same time, ensure the Scenario can match the analytical conclusions and data paths.

Here is a simple example for illustration: before a product goes into operation, software is delivered via DevOps. The speed and quality of software delivery directly affect the product's post-launch performance in the market. Thus, IT lean operation holds an important position in comprehensive digital management. When IT is the core component of business, IT is direct productivity. When IT is not a core business component, the value of IT is still to enable better enterprise operations; therefore, IT lean operation and enterprise business value are interconnected. The best practice DevOps metrics system covers enterprise cost management and evaluation management. Within the resources and cost framework, it forms a deep scenario management capability for IT activities and establishes a data-related information view, as shown in *Figure 6.3*.

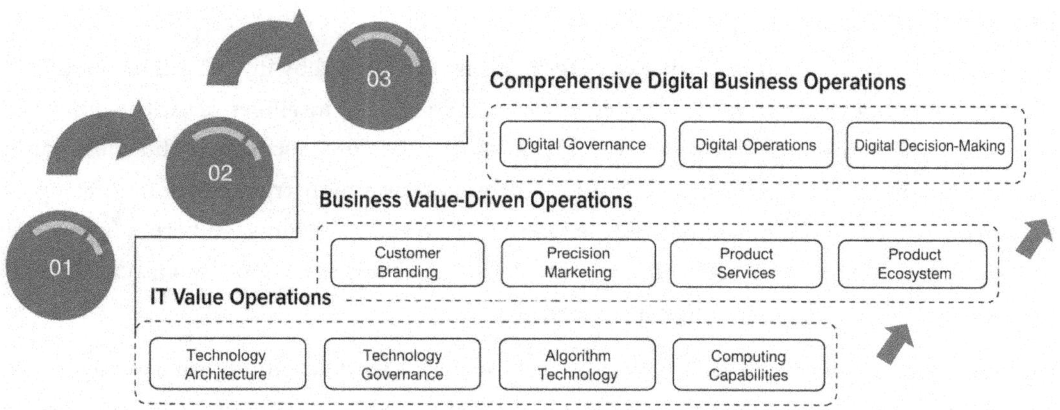

Figure 6.3: DevOps scenario hierarchy

In the field of business operations, digital visualization needs to clearly identify the factors that affect performance, commonly referred to as intelligent operations. Data is categorized by scenario, usually including sales data, order data, user activity data, production capacity data, and product data, and data performance is matched to evaluation metrics. For business operations, data performance is a potential driving factor for business development trends; any data deviation may affect whether the business progresses as planned. This form of visualization related to business trends is referred to as a scenario in the digital visualization field. By analyzing data performance, problems in business operations can be identified, and based on the driving factors, decision-making can be assisted to make targeted adjustments and improvements.

Visualization gives teams the information they need to understand delivery performance and business impact. The next capability is **shift-left practice**, where DevOps uses that information earlier in the lifecycle to improve quality, security, and delivery outcomes before problems reach production.

DevOps technology shift-left capabilities

In the vast majority of enterprises, whether considered from the perspective of a profit center or a cost center, the role of IT in business activities is increasingly moving forward. Especially in scenarios where market demands change rapidly, delivering software that is "secure, stable, efficient, and low-cost" enables enterprises to better respond to market fluctuations and deliver business value. Therefore, technology infrastructure centered on DevOps has gradually become the core of IT management in enterprise digital transformation and is also a focal point of practice for traditional enterprises in the process of software delivery.

New technology infrastructure

The new technological infrastructure of enterprises is represented by innovative technologies such as DevOps, cloud computing, microservices, and artificial intelligence. At the objective level, DevOps aligns IT organizations with business organizations, focusing on business value and customer experience; at the cultural level, it promotes a high-trust cultural philosophy, fostering seamless communication, and shared risk between IT, business, and other functional organizations; at the technological empowerment level, it combines technology, and capabilities to realize intelligent, agile, and digital platforms.

Best practices of DevOps in the IT field effectively achieve a **shift-left** for internal enterprise IT, bringing products to market better and faster through cost efficiency, increased productivity, and quality assurance, assisting business organizations in building systematic capabilities, and increasing innovation and risk resistance of products through business innovation and exceptional user experience.

The extent to which DevOps shifts left depends on IT's influence in business operations as well as the scope of its capability output. The role of DevOps in the process of enterprise digital transformation is largely determined by the reshaping of IT leadership. IT leaders must have forward-looking thinking and grasp strategies that drive digital transformation, providing necessary IT services and products for enterprise digital transformation. Additionally, there is a need to integrate IT resources, organizational structure, and technological innovation according to enterprise strategic objectives, so that IT service capabilities are maximally oriented toward business, creating the greatest value and achieving the goal of upgrading IT management in digital transformation.

Application modernization

Application modernization is also an effective way to shift technology left. Application modernization is a novel concept that leverages existing legacy applications to modernize the underlying platform infrastructure, internal architecture, and functionality. Conceptually, it is similar to low-code approaches. According to McKinsey Digital's COVID recovery research, enterprises with low digitalization levels suffered greater losses during the pandemic, while those with a higher degree of digitalization were less impacted. The reason is that highly digitalized companies, through DevOps practices, optimize process-driven and data-driven procedures to enhance new technological infrastructure capabilities via value delivery. At the same time, they facilitate application modernization practices, improving efficiency and multi-cloud portability via modern infrastructure, thereby achieving compatibility between modern applications and existing applications.

The essence of application modernization is to amend the traditional programming methods of business applications, making them more closely aligned with the needs of business agility. During the process of an application's transition to modernization, the existing information architecture, operation, and maintenance models, application development and testing processes, business data management models, and security requirements all face significant challenges. It's like changing engines and motors during flight: enterprises must both ensure continuity of business growth amidst current competition and guarantee the potential for revolutionary business changes in the future.

Shift-left practices and application modernization help DevOps improve delivery before software reaches production. However, DevOps must also support what happens after delivery: how systems are monitored, how feedback is collected, how data is used, and how IT services continue to support business outcomes. This is where the digital operations capability of DevOps becomes important.

Strengthening digital operations with DevOps

In traditional concepts, DevOps technical operations mainly focus on scenarios for application domain assurance and user experience, especially in areas such as user data feedback and intelligent monitoring, establishing end-to-end data link channels between IT and business sides. In the context of digital transformation, DevOps technical operations in the IT domain need to extend and restructure data scenarios to realize the digital reconstruction of business applications.

DevOps technical operations need to consume existing data, collect and inventory the entire data system, establish and improve a **data-driven system**, and, while improving efficiency and quality, extend the ability to deliver data output to the entire IT process by taking a **digital operations-oriented approach**. This helps enhance IT service capability, allowing IT organizations to provide more effective services to customers in advance through a "data role."

There are two approaches to DevOps technical operations within the IT domain: one is to achieve **business-defined technical operations**, and the other is to achieve **user-defined technical operations**.

Achieving business-defined technical operations

In the process of digital transformation, IT organizations need the capability to identify business use cases, especially in the digital technology domain, and should keep up with trends in business applications. For C-end business scenarios, more attention should be paid to the impact of digital factors of "people" and "technology" on customer behavior in order to define business scenarios. Therefore, DevOps capabilities should center around the definition of business scenarios, adapting IT organizations and IT culture to achieve better, faster, and more effective business support. At the same time, in the DevOps value delivery pipeline, IT organizational capabilities should focus on business scenarios, using **requirement shift-left** and **testing shift-left** practices to analyze the value and impact of the delivery process on business use cases and promptly optimize the supporting capabilities of the IT organization.

Business-defined technical operations represent the top-level design for technological digital transformation within IT organizations under DevOps, used to realize the rapid launch of enterprise-strategic products.

Implementing user-defined technology operations

User definition requires focusing more on user scenarios, aligning value output with the IT organizational architecture in terms of user experience, especially in customer-facing **TOC (To Customer)** scenarios. User-defined technology operations empower infrastructure and application architecture through DevOps, adapting to more flexible user interaction modes, enhancing user stickiness, obtaining the fastest feedback from the user side, and achieving lifecycle management of user behavior through user data analysis. This continuously optimizes the IT system's service capabilities, as shown in *Figure 6.4*.

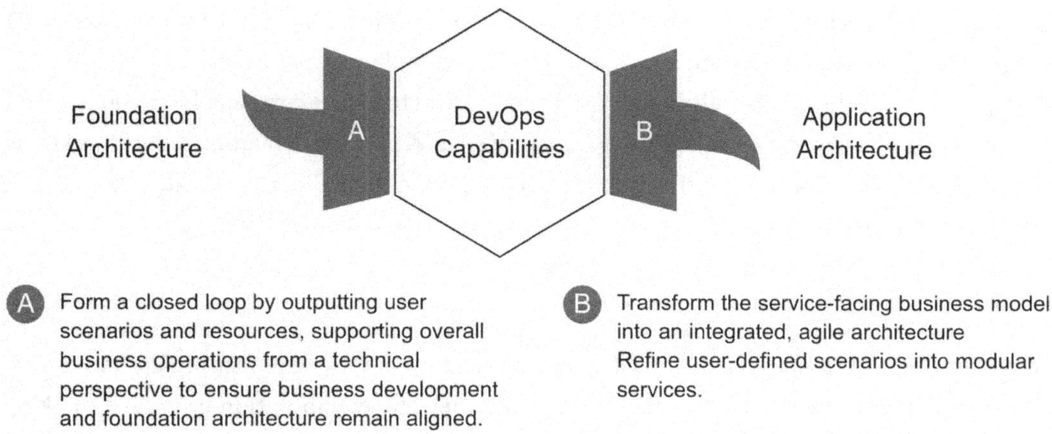

Figure 6.4: DevOps empowerment methods

In terms of infrastructure, represented by DevOps integrated cloud management platforms, user scenarios and resource output are formed into a closed loop, supporting the overall business operation from a technical perspective. This ensures that business development and infrastructure remain aligned, and IT costs can be allocated to business operations, thus reducing costs from a business perspective.

In terms of application architecture, represented by DevOps integrated microservices architectures, the service-oriented business model integration architecture is transformed into a unified agile architecture. By means of **microservices**, user-defined scenarios are broken down into smaller unit services. Through flexible inter-service interaction and collaboration, business changes can be rapidly supported, enhancing the product's ability to respond to high-frequency changes in user interaction.

These business-defined and user-defined operations capabilities depend on more than data and technical platforms. They also require teams to collaborate flexibly across departments, processes, and tools as business needs change. This collaborative flexibility is another important DevOps capability.

Enabling elastic collaboration through DevOps

DevOps' **elastic collaboration model** is based on **DevOps culture**, breaking down communication and collaboration barriers horizontally across departments and integrating people, processes, and technology vertically, ultimately achieving continuous organizational improvement.

DevOps introduces the cultural thinking of "value delivery" and "digital operations." On the IT side, digital value is extended, forming a closed loop in responding to market changes and feedback through product delivery. This ultimately drives enterprises to reduce costs and increase efficiency across a series of business stages, including market demand, product demand, product marketing, and market feedback, achieving the desired goals. Under this collaboration model, the scope of elasticity is related to how business changes occur. As the best accelerator for modern business transformation, DevOps makes it easier for enterprises to adopt and rapidly realize business ideas during digital transformation.

At the same time, in terms of personnel, process, and technology, DevOps continually and rapidly delivers new value to customers through a more scientific collaboration approach, making products better adapt to the ever-changing market and conveying the organization's digital profile to customers. When people, processes, and technology are aligned with the same business goals, the digital transformation process becomes orderly and stable. Additionally, DevOps, via data-driven methods, carries out IT-side technical operations surrounding "people, finance, and material" to achieve end-to-end delivery of resources, products, and value. This enables unified resource planning and cost review, providing flexible collaboration for IT organizations regarding task prioritization and resource scheduling.

DevOps' role in digital transformation helps IT organizations improve efficiency, enhance competitive posture, and increase participation in production activities, aiding the shift from traditional hierarchical, command-and-control enterprises to digital organizations.

Business going online

A **Business going online** is a key milestone in software delivery. The type of enterprise, digital scenarios, and transformation goals are always anchored to business value and company operations, ultimately culminating in a business going online. On the IT side, this is usually measured by "business continuity" indicators. For enterprises, the transition from offline to online and the availability assurance of core systems are essential. For IT organizations, faster and better product delivery, as well as more stable and higher-quality product maintenance, all fall within the realm of business online.

Data-driven

The transformation of internal and external management and operation models in enterprises through **data-driven** approaches usually involves two methods: First, evolving from **process-driven** to **data-driven**, ensuring process compliance while improving the scientific nature of execution and decision-making through data feedback; second, using **data collaboration** to mine better business logic and organizational management models.

This is particularly evident in digital marketing and digital office fields, where shifts in user relationships can be detected sensitively, and more scientific, compliant, and agile workflows and standards can be built using labeling methods.

While data-driven collaboration improves visibility and decision-making, it also exposes new risks. If delivery, testing, security, and user-experience data are incomplete or delayed, DevOps teams may make decisions without enough evidence. For this reason, digital risk management becomes an important part of mature DevOps practice.

Digital risk capabilities in DevOps

By analyzing best practice cases in DevOps, the author believes that digital risk is not limited only to the measurement and feedback phase. The lack of advanced scenario-based testing data, end-to-end security data, and the universality of user experience prediction are all manifestations of digital risk. Common digital risk scenarios mainly include effectiveness evaluation of IT organizations, post-evaluation and cost review of IT projects, and feedback and assurance in product operations. Due to the characteristics of the DevOps culture, the collaborative environment and shared responsibility model among IT members transmit product issues, which are ultimately reflected in business scenarios through product operations. This is both an advantage of DevOps and a potential risk factor in practice.

Lack of advanced scenario-based testing data

Testing is a critical link in the DevOps capability subdomain, responsible for the acceptance of "product-level" deliverables—especially in the shift-left testing phase, where quality extends to business requirements. Therefore, testing is essential for verifying whether applications or services behave as expected and whether products can be delivered safely.

A lack of advanced scenario-based testing data often results in issues with stability and accuracy in testing outcomes during value delivery, thus impacting product quality and safety. For digital-assisted decision-making, complete testing data can simulate data changes and user conversion journeys in business operations in advance. These advanced scenarios are oriented toward business and requirements organizations while providing predictive positive feedback to digital users.

End-to-end security data

By embedding security data into the DevOps "value delivery" chain through risk mitigation, risks in the product delivery process can be effectively avoided, thereby amplifying the advantages of DevOps. End-to-end security data allows for continuous monitoring of data performance during software delivery and product operation. Through comprehensive visibility into service delivery infrastructure, applications, their interdependencies, and intelligent business data analytics, it is possible to address potential threats before they impact business operations. At the same time, the end-to-end security data covers all nodes in the product operation process, delivering intelligence, and public opinion feedback in business language from the business perspective, promoting digital visibility, and secure telemetry in digital operations.

Universality prediction of user experience

Traditional DevOps practices tend to focus more on requirements fulfillment and delivery cycles. With the continuous evolution of user habits, the aggregation effect between DevOps and business organizations is increasingly prominent, particularly in terms of the universality prediction of user experience. According to authoritative statistics, user experience mainly centers on high expectations of functionality and low tolerance for issues. Therefore, DevOps requires preemptive digital feedback, covering user experience scenarios. From the user's perspective, digital scenarios should be extended to business planning, product requirements, testing data, release strategies, and final business monitoring, enabling a comprehensive understanding of the business and focusing on user experience, bringing in, and managing the visibility of the user experience through digital visualization.

As DevOps practices mature, the same principles of automation, monitoring, feedback, and lifecycle management are being extended to AI systems. This shift has led to related practices such as MLOps and LLMOps, which adapt DevOps thinking to the development, deployment, monitoring, and governance of machine learning and LLM applications.

DevOps in the era of LLMs

With the development of artificial intelligence technologies, more innovative technologies have been introduced into the Ops field. Currently, there are two main directions: machine learning and LLMs, which have ultimately led to **MLOps (Machine Learning Operations)** and **LLMOps**.

> This chapter focuses on MLOps as a discipline — how the model-development workflow integrates with DevOps practice. The model-training techniques themselves were covered in *Chapter 4* (fine-tuning) and *Chapter 5* (RAG and multi-agent systems).

The origin of MLOps

MLOps is a concept evolved from DevOps, referring to the application of DevOps ideas and methods to the development, deployment, and operation and maintenance of machine learning, aiming to improve the productivity and quality of machine learning models.

The concept of MLOps originated from the challenges enterprises faced when applying machine learning in practice, mainly involving issues such as model deployment, operation and maintenance, and monitoring. In traditional software development, a mature DevOps process has already been established, and MLOps borrows from DevOps experience and thinking within the field of machine learning to provide systematic and standardized solutions for machine learning development. The MLOps process includes multiple stages such as data preparation, model selection, model training, model deployment, model validation, and model updating, as shown in *Figure 6.5*.

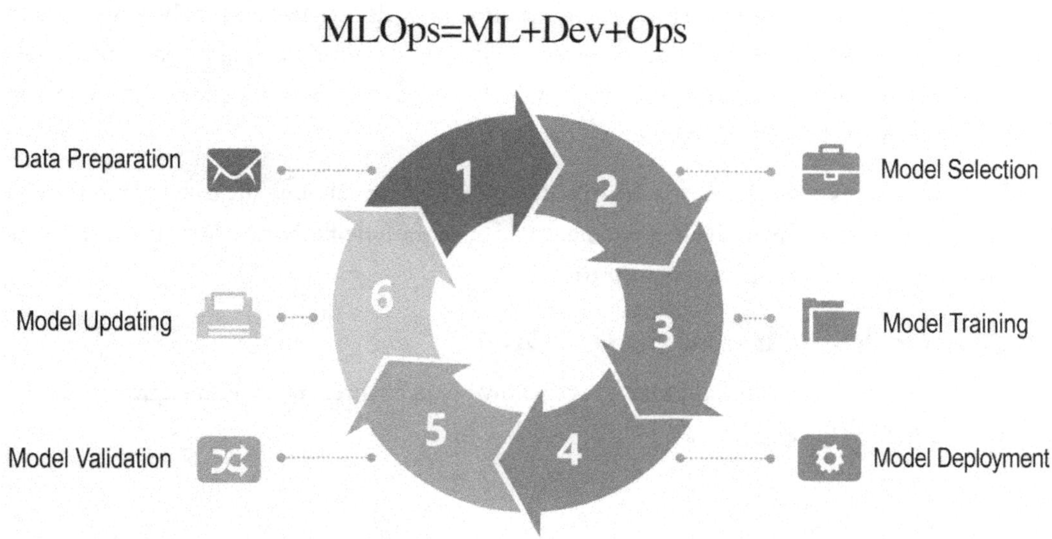

Figure 6.5: Sequence of MLOps processes

Once the origin of MLOps is clear, the next question is how it changes the responsibilities of DevOps teams in practice. MLOps keeps the core DevOps focus on automation, monitoring, and continuous improvement, but extends it to the additional lifecycle needs of machine learning systems.

The role of MLOps

In practical application, based on the characteristics of machine learning, the role of MLOps—beyond the traditional capabilities of DevOps—has added some specific scenarios, such as redefining scenarios via model application, data collection, and organization, model training and deployment, as well as continuous monitoring and updating. Nevertheless, the iteration, and updating of technology are all aimed at improving the efficiency of software delivery.

Since MLOps originates from DevOps, the core philosophies of both are the same, covering the initial tool-oriented and automated stages of construction, and sharing common paths for optimization and feedback during adoption. However, there are also some differences: due to differences in tech stacks, the trigger targets and methods differ. The trigger method for DevOps is mainly code modification, while MLOps triggers are not limited to code changes—changes in data or a decline in model performance (**model degradation**) can also trigger the pipeline. In addition, MLOps includes additional steps necessary for building and training machine learning models, such as data- and model-specific procedures, which means that there are subtle differences in each component of the MLOps workflow.

In addition, in terms of workflow management, DevOps focuses on pipeline construction, while **MLOps** emphasizes more on the management and automation of machine learning workflows, as well as model deployment and monitoring.

MLOps workflow based on DevOps

As shown in *Figure 6.6*, a standard MLOps workflow involves three roles: **data engineer, model engineer**, and **DevOps engineer**.

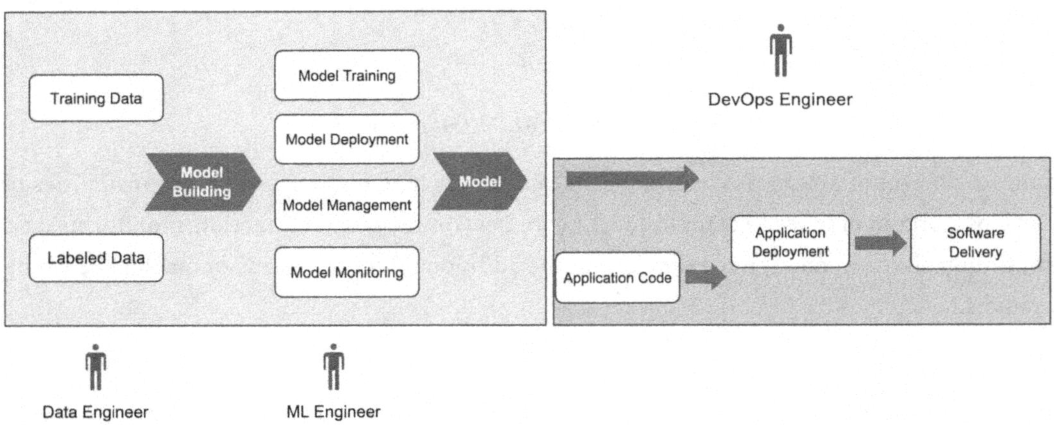

Figure 6.6: Standard MLOps workflow

Data engineers are responsible for **data annotation** and ensuring data reliability and traceability; model engineers are responsible for **model management** and ensuring model reproducibility and iterability; DevOps engineers are responsible for **application deployment** and monitoring.

1. The main work in the data stage includes **data collection**, **preprocessing**, and **feature engineering**:
    - **Data collection and preprocessing**: This component is responsible for collecting data from various sources (such as databases, file systems, APIs, etc.) and performing preprocessing and cleaning, making the data suitable for training and inference with machine learning models.
    - **Feature engineering**: This component is responsible for transforming raw data into features usable by machine learning models, including steps such as feature selection, feature transformation, and feature construction.
2. The main tasks in the model stage include **model training**, **model deployment**, and **model monitoring and management**:
    - **Model training**: This component is responsible for training models using the training data, including algorithm selection, model parameter tuning, and model performance evaluation.
    - **Model deployment**: This component is responsible for deploying trained models to the production environment for real-time inference and prediction. It may include steps such as packaging the model as an executable file, configuring the model server, and monitoring model performance.
    - **Model monitoring and management**: This component is responsible for monitoring the performance and operating status of deployed models and making adjustments and updates as needed. It may include monitoring metrics such as model prediction accuracy, processing time, and resource usage.
3. The main work in the deployment stage is software release:

    Although model output is uncertain and difficult to reproduce, the process of deploying machine learning software to the production environment is reliable and repeatable and aims to be as automated as possible.

MLOps provides a useful foundation for managing machine learning systems, but LLM-powered applications introduce additional challenges, including prompt management, retrieval pipelines, evaluation, model behavior monitoring, cost control, and governance. These differences have led to the emergence of LLMOps.

The origin of LLMOps

LLMOps is a set of tools and best practices for managing the lifecycle of LLM-powered applications. It can be seen as a subcategory of MLOps, but there are certain differences between the two. These differences stem from the different ways of building AI products with classic ML models versus LLMs, primarily impacting data management, experimentation, evaluation, and cost.

DevOps improves software delivery by strengthening collaboration, automation, visibility, feedback, and lifecycle management. However, as organizations scale, teams often need a more structured way to access the tools, environments, workflows, and infrastructure required for delivery. This is where platform engineering becomes important: it turns shared delivery capabilities into reusable internal platforms that reduce cognitive load and help teams deliver software more consistently.

Building internal platforms for software delivery

Platform engineering extends DevOps practices by turning shared tools, infrastructure, workflows, and knowledge into reusable internal platforms. Its goal is to reduce cognitive load for delivery teams, improve developer experience, and make software delivery more consistent, secure, and scalable.

The concept of platform engineering

Gartner describes platform engineering as gathering tools, capabilities, and processes—all meticulously selected and packaged by domain experts—into a platform for end users. The ultimate goal is to create a frictionless self-service experience, providing users with adequate capabilities to complete critical tasks at minimal cost, thus increasing end-user productivity and reducing cognitive load. The platform should meet all the needs of user teams and seamlessly fit their preferred workflows in any possible form.

In the software delivery process, platform engineering aims to improve the efficiency and effectiveness of software delivery teams, enabling enterprises to gain greater competitive advantages in the market. By building a suite of tool platforms, software delivery teams can deliver software application systems more efficiently and continuously, while ensuring their stable operation. The core goal of platform engineering is to help software delivery teams enhance the business value of the software they deliver.

Within the software delivery system, platform engineering addresses how technical teams can meet business needs at lower cost and with higher efficiency, while also solving various issues in efficient business operations and enterprise digital transformation. Therefore, the value of platform engineering lies in the infrastructure capabilities it provides, as well as the technical services of the corresponding tool clusters. By using tool platforms to consolidate knowledge, software delivery teams can improve overall efficiency and innovation.

The value of platform engineering in the software delivery process is reflected in the following aspects:

- **Reusability:** Platform engineering has the capability for modular assembly. The technical components and services provided by platform engineering can be shared and reused across multiple applications, thus avoiding repetitive development and maintenance of similar functions.
- **Centralized Capability:** Platform engineering possesses the ability to centrally manage and monitor tools across domains. Users can more easily manage software applications and the delivery process through tools, and use tools to maintain the entire application lifecycle, thereby increasing the efficiency of software delivery and ensuring its stability.
- **Scalability:** Platform engineering integrates cloud-native capabilities, allowing the elastically scalable cloud-native infrastructure to expand and upgrade smoothly and quickly according to customer needs, in order to meet constantly changing business requirements.
- **Security:** Platform engineering possesses security features, allowing software delivery personnel to protect the security of applications and customer data through authentication, authorization, and security services provided by platform engineering, thereby reducing security risks.

After defining platform engineering and explaining its value in software delivery, the next step is to identify the qualities that make an internal platform effective. A useful platform is not simply a collection of tools; it must be designed as a product that supports user needs, reduces friction, enables self-service, and helps teams share knowledge across the delivery lifecycle.

Key attributes of platform engineering

Generally, software delivery teams can provide a better user experience by combining one or more capabilities through a mature, available, and promotable platform. Such platforms enable their users to deliver valuable products more easily and efficiently.

An excellent platform typically has the key attributes discussed as follows:

Platform as a product

In the field of software delivery, the platform needs to meet the needs of all users as much as possible. These needs must cover all functional organizations in the delivery pipeline, and each functional organization should have corresponding requirements based on its own responsibilities. The platform should be designed according to these requirements, and **scalability** considerations should be included in the design.

Similar to other software products, the platform must provide the necessary functions for each functional organization to support common use cases for cross-functional teams, and these use cases should be prioritized to ensure continuity of functionality when single or multiple teams collaborate, guaranteeing the ultimate value of software delivery. In practical application, the author prefers the collaborative state shown in *Figure 6.7*.

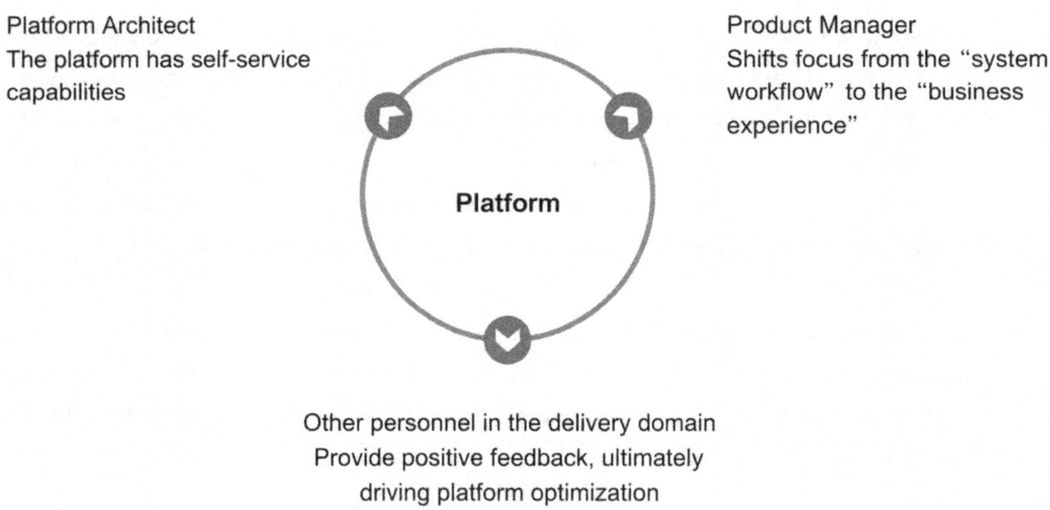

Figure 6.7: Positive feedback loop of Platform Engineering

Team structure and working models should rely on the platform to implement **agile software delivery**. **Platform architects** should possess full life cycle thinking, ensuring the platform has **self-service capabilities**, covering **R&D delivery processes** and **business assurance processes**. **Product managers** should rely on the platform to shift their focus from "system processes" to "business experience" to better connect product requirements with the process of launching applications. Others should provide feedback on issues and pain points encountered during platform usage to the platform architect, ultimately forming a positive feedback loop through optimization.

User experience

The platform should improve **user experience** through a unified interface and continually focus on user experience during platform design, which is crucial for promoting the platform. The platform should strive to meet the needs of all users. The author explains with examples using common tools: During the tool integration stage, platform architects need to consider combinations of commonly used GUIs, APIs, and command line tools, and think about the presentation forms of IDEs and portals. Typically, the platform provides deployment capabilities to enable application deployment during development. In many enterprises, developers often use IDEs, testers may use command line tools, while product personnel may use GUI-based web portals. The above approaches may lead to user experience issues, so it is particularly important to build a developer platform with a product mindset.

In some enterprises that have not yet implemented platform engineering, during the delivery process of a certain project, when developers submit service requests to the **platform architect** to improve certain slow and inflexible service flows, the platform architect usually coordinates related teams, such as operations, testing, architecture, etc., for collaboration. The whole process can be lengthy and full of challenges. In the field of platform engineering, the platform architect will collect essential tools needed by the development team, such as cloud platforms, delivery tools, deployment tools, etc., investigate the developers' expertise and usage habits, integrate these tools, and ensure the integration process is safe and effective. Meanwhile, the platform architect also creates an **abstraction layer** and provides a user-friendly interface through UI or API, making it convenient for developers to self-service the tools and services they need. On the logical level, data communication between tools is achieved through an easy-to-interact interface. Developers only need to log in to the platform service, and there is no need to submit service requests to the platform architect. The related process is shown in *Figure 6.8*.

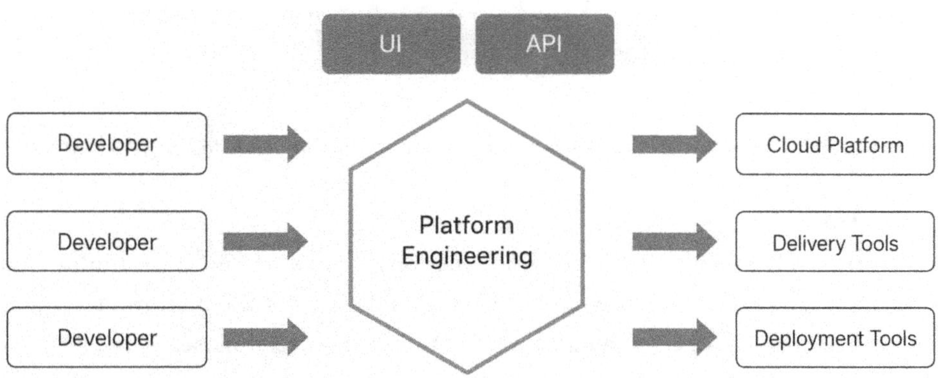

Figure 6.8: Platform Engineering related process

Knowledge management and accumulation

Knowledge management and accumulation is a key capability for evaluating the success of software, and this is also true for platform engineering. During the software development process, in order to better utilize platform products or facilitate knowledge accumulation and circulation within the platform, the platform needs to gather a large amount of knowledge and analyze it so that it can play a role in team collaboration in the end.

Knowledge management and accumulation should be distributed across various functional teams during the software delivery process, including the platform team, enablement team, business-oriented team, and delivery team. Teams can collaborate via the platform. The platform architect is responsible for creating knowledge services and implementing knowledge management tasks, the platform is responsible for knowledge diffusion and bottleneck perception, and platform users are responsible for knowledge supply and service experience feedback, as shown in *Figure 6.9*.

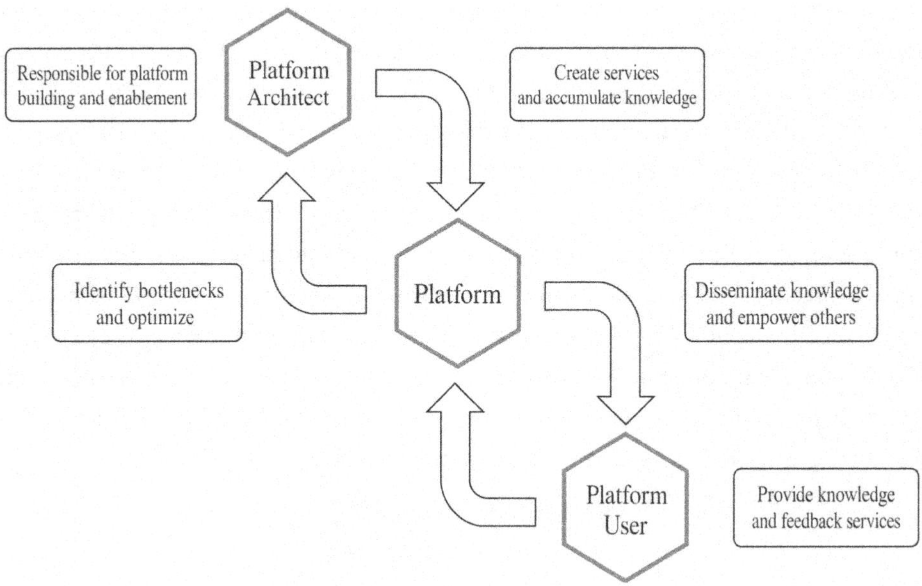

Figure 6.9: Positioning of knowledge management and accumulation in the delivery process

Self-service

In the platform, **self-service** should provide functions for users to make and fulfill requests independently, while also allowing multiple functional teams of the platform to self-extend according to their respective work requirements. In this process, relevant self-service capabilities can be provided as needed, allowing users to choose themselves and minimizing manual intervention as much as possible.

In the software delivery process, the self-service platform enables developers to directly manage and operate resources and handle resource lifecycle management, without having to pay attention to the technical architecture of the underlying infrastructure and the implementation details of resource output, while also reducing direct intervention from platform team members. This self-service model follows the principle of "those who build, manage," but does not require developers to deeply understand underlying technologies.

From a collaboration perspective, self-service is more like a combination of process and tool. On the tooling level, whether it's open-source software or commercial software, they all provide abstractions for general capabilities; but at the process level, due to different management requirements and dependencies in the collaborative processes of various enterprises, there will be differences in process design. Therefore, tools can be standardized, but processes are difficult to standardize.

Let me give an example. In different projects, workplaces, and team contexts, different strategies need to be formulated according to the development habits of developers, so that developers can self-serve when operating the infrastructure, as shown in *Figure 6.10*.

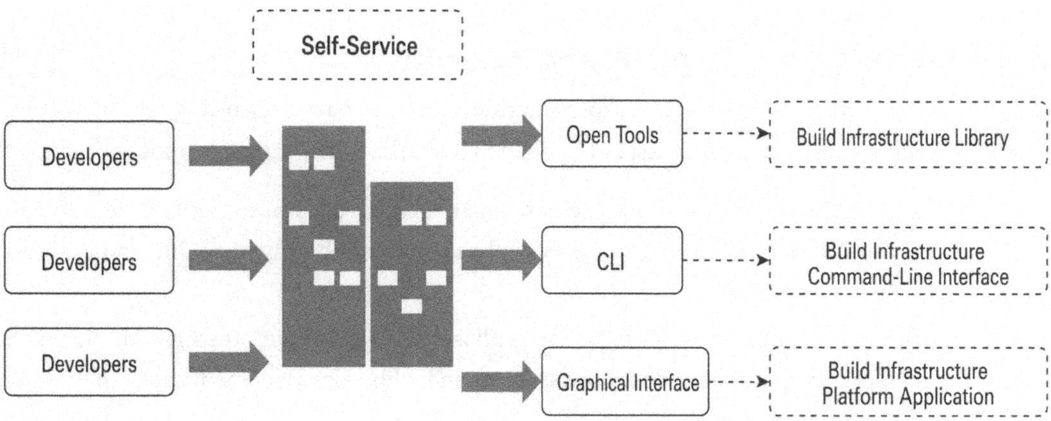

Figure 6.10: Integration methods of self-service in infrastructure

The first approach is to create an **infrastructure library** that represents infrastructure resources and configuration information, allowing users to freely use their preferred deployment tools for infrastructure configuration.

The second approach is to create a **command-line interface (CLI)** for the infrastructure, enabling developers to manage and orchestrate infrastructure through a familiar **CLI**.

The third approach is to create an **infrastructure platform application**, providing developers with a graphical user interface (**GUI**) to configure and manage the infrastructure.

All these methods have one thing in common: they adopt a standardized architecture, which includes best practices defined by the platform team, mechanisms for enforcing deployment rules, and a unified deployment workflow (such as code review, pull requests, CI/CD, testing, etc.).

Reducing user cognitive load

During platform development, reducing user cognitive load is a key factor that is easily overlooked. To mitigate risks to the team caused by excessive cognitive load, the platform should encapsulate tool implementation details and hide infrastructure complexity. For example, some third-party platforms provide integration services but require that detailed information not be exposed, so the platform needs to handle this encapsulation. At the same time, the platform should also meet the need for **observability** of certain services, which may require protocol conversion or secondary processing of services.

Once the key attributes of an effective platform are clear, it becomes easier to examine the concrete modules that usually make up a platform engineering system. These modules provide the infrastructure, development tools, data services, security controls, operational capabilities, and service marketplace functions that allow delivery teams to work more efficiently.

Core modules of platform engineering

The specific functional modules of platform engineering may vary depending on application scenarios and customer requirements, but usually include the following core modules:

- **Infrastructure**: Includes the management and allocation of computing, storage, network, and other infrastructure resources, as well as providing highly available and scalable infrastructure services
- **Development Tools**: Includes tools for application development, testing, building, and deployment, as well as developer portals, component libraries, documentation repositories, and other tools and resources supporting developers
- **Data Management**: Includes data storage, data analysis, data backup and recovery services, as well as data services supporting data integration and transformation
- **Security and Identity Management**: Includes security management services such as authentication, authorization, encryption, and security audit, as well as services supporting security policy and compliance management
- **Operations and Maintenance Management**: Includes services for application monitoring, fault management, automated operations and maintenance, and services supporting deployment and update management

- **Service Marketplace**: Includes a service marketplace providing third-party applications, services, and solutions, as well as services supporting application integration and subscription

In addition, platform engineering can also include other functional modules, such as supporting services in fields like artificial intelligence and the Internet of Things, to meet different application scenarios and user needs.

After identifying the main modules that a platform may provide, the next step is to define the capabilities required to build, operate, secure, and continuously improve those modules. These capability requirements help translate the platform's design into practical responsibilities for platform teams and supporting roles.

Platform engineering capabilities

Typically, platform engineering capabilities can be specified from five aspects: **platform construction, platform services, platform operations, platform assurance**, and **platform team**, as shown in *Figure 6.11*.

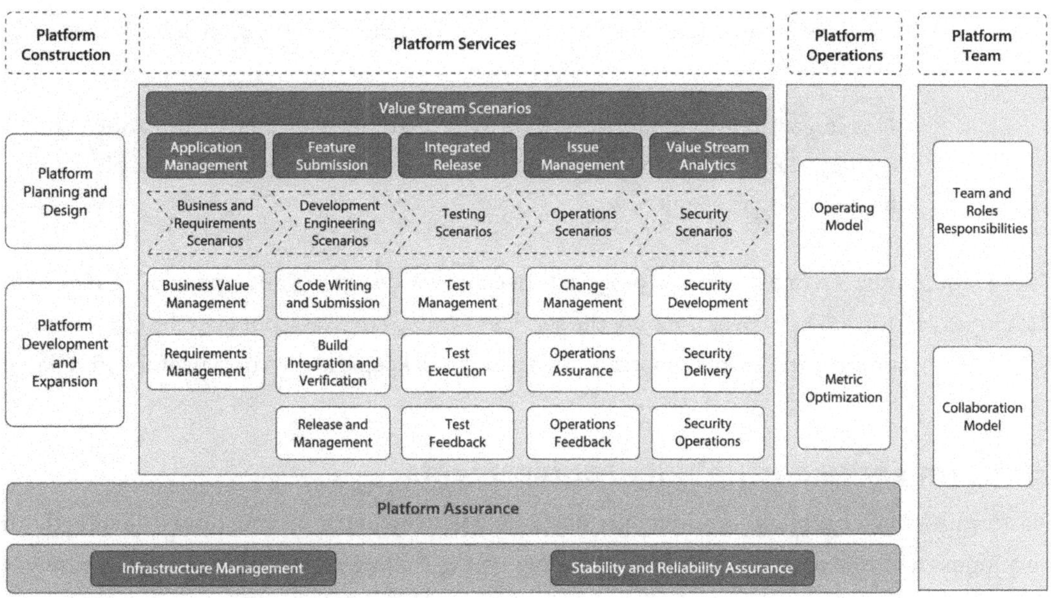

Figure 6.11: Platform Engineering capability requirements

Where to start

For teams beginning their platform engineering journey, the first priority should be the capabilities that create immediate value for platform users. Start with **platform service capabilities**, such as secure development environments, reusable components, CI/CD feedback, environment generation, and developer self-service. These are the user-facing functions that help teams experience the platform as a useful product rather than an additional process.

Next, focus on **platform construction capabilities**, including integration, extensibility, unified access, security, compatibility with the existing technology stack, and reliable infrastructure. These capabilities provide the technical foundation needed to make the platform consistent and scalable.

Platform operation, assurance, and team capabilities can mature gradually as adoption grows. Over the first 12–18 months, teams can strengthen user support, platform reliability, security assurance, usage analytics, and dedicated platform roles. This staged approach aligns with the idea that platform teams should evolve around user needs, reduce cognitive load, and treat the platform as a product that improves over time.

This staged approach is consistent with the platform-team guidance in *Team Topologies* by Matthew Skelton and Manuel Pais, particularly its discussion of platform teams and team cognitive load.

These requirements can be read as a practical checklist for designing and operating an internal developer platform. They cover not only the services exposed to users, but also the construction, operation, assurance, and team responsibilities needed to keep the platform useful and reliable over time.

Platform service capability requirements

Platform service capability requirements describe what the platform must provide directly to developers and delivery teams during everyday work. These requirements cover the services users interact with most often, including development environments, coding support, API testing, environment generation, self-testing, and CI/CD feedback. When a development environment is needed, the platform should provide a secure development environment service, including an IDE, environment configuration, and other development tools.

- When viewing work items:

    - The platform should support one-stop and convenient access to related work item information, such as viewing work item details in the IDE

- When coding:
    - The platform should automatically create branches based on work items and modify the work item status, such as quickly creating feature branches in the IDE
    - The platform should provide a reusable front-end component library that meets user experience (UE) design standards and is easy for developers to access
    - The platform should provide a unified, adaptable, and managed reusable back-end component library, such as logging components
    - The platform should support automated code scanning and provide repair suggestions when issues are found
    - The platform should support intelligent code assistance, such as helping to generate business code, unit test code, and code comments
    - The platform should support intelligent code optimization capabilities, such as generating code optimization recommendations
    - The platform should provide low-code/no-code services, including visual development of front-end and back-end business logic, and rapid customization, deployment, and release for typical application scenarios
- When designing or modifying database table structures:
    - The platform should support graphical design or modification of database table structures and automatically generate **DDL statements**
    - The platform should support automatic scanning of **SQL statements**, and provide repair suggestions when issues are found
- When writing interfaces:
    - The platform should support automated generation of partial code and interface test data after the interface definition is completed
    - The platform should provide **API version management** and document generation and sharing functions
    - If modifications or decommissioning of published interface definitions are involved, the platform should be able to automatically notify relevant stakeholders, such as **interface callers** and **testers**

- When defining environments:
    - The platform should support automatically generating and maintaining environment configurations, such as `Dockerfile`, `K8s` orchestration files, etc.
- When testing APIs:
    - The platform should support **API test doubles**, such as **Mock**, etc.
    - The platform should support unified automated API testing execution on local development environments
- When testing functionalities:
    - The platform should support **end-to-end functional testing** execution on local development environments
- During **developer self-testing:**
    - The platform should support **one-click generation** of developer self-test environments, and rapid (timely) release of self-test environments
- When code is submitted:
    - The platform should conveniently allow associating code and related configuration changes with work items, and validate the specifications of the submission, such as checking the compliance of **commit messages** and submission content
    - The platform should support automatic triggering of **pipeline execution** and rapid result feedback

Beyond the services exposed to users, the platform also needs strong construction capabilities. These requirements define how the platform itself should be built, integrated, standardized, secured, and maintained so that it can support delivery teams reliably at scale.

Platform construction capability requirements

The following requirements describe the construction principles that help make the platform extensible, secure, consistent, performant, and compatible with the organization's existing technology environment:

- Platform construction should highlight **integration** and **extensibility**, such as easy integration with other tools, plugin marketplaces, etc.
- Platform construction should emphasize unified management dimensions, such as using applications as the central management objects of the platform.

- Platform construction should reflect a single, trusted source for basic data to avoid duplicated maintenance, such as user information and application information.
- Platform construction should feature unified portal design, including unified entry point, unified account, unified permissions, etc.
- Platform construction should reflect unified interaction design, such as unified interface style, unified operation methods, unified terminology, etc.
- Platform construction should comply with applicable national procurement and data sovereignty requirements, including the environment, middleware, databases, components, and other tools on which platform development and operation depend.
- Platform construction should demonstrate ease of use, such as user guides, simplified operation steps, error prompts, etc.
- Platform construction should demonstrate configurability and manageability, such as template configuration, management rule maintenance, etc.
- Platform construction should demonstrate security, such as avoiding uncontrolled public accounts and uncontrolled build machine administrator privileges.
- Platform construction should demonstrate high performance, such as load balancing, building resource pools, caching, etc.
- Platform construction should demonstrate high quality, such as few functional defects, etc.
- Platform construction should demonstrate availability and stability, such as active-active deployment, etc.
- Platform construction should demonstrate compatibility with the organization's internal technology stack and infrastructure, such as supporting different programming languages and different resource types.
- Platform construction should demonstrate compatibility of functional versions, reducing the impact of version updates on users. Platform construction should demonstrate openness and standardization, such as providing external service invocation capability via APIs, etc.
- Development, testing, operations, and other activities during the platform construction process should also be managed using the platform's own services.

Once the platform has been built, it must also be operated as a living product. Platform operation capability requirements focus on user support, adoption, feedback, usage analysis, communication, and continuous improvement.

Platform operational capability requirements

The following requirements describe how the platform should be supported, promoted, measured, and improved after it is released to users:

- Platform operations should establish basic user support mechanisms, such as user discussion groups, expert guidance, user manuals, and training
- Platform operations should establish automated user support mechanisms, such as automated customer service
- Platform operations should establish user promotion and publicity mechanisms, such as posting announcements, new feature promotional activities, release frequency, and new user promotions
- Platform operations should establish user demand collection and feedback mechanisms
- Platform operations should establish notification and display mechanisms for platform availability, such as the duration of function recovery
- Platform operations should have reasonable user usage billing models and optimization mechanisms
- Platform operations should have statistical analyses of user usage and operation status, such as number of users, usage coverage, availability rate, and feature usage frequency
- Platform operations should have statistical analyses of user usage effectiveness, such as data on organizational efficiency improvement

In addition to operation, the platform also needs assurance capabilities to protect its reliability, security, availability, and release safety. These requirements are especially important because the platform becomes a shared dependency for many delivery teams.

Platform assurance capability requirements

The following requirements describe the stability, security, high availability, data protection, and low-risk release practices needed to keep the platform dependable:

- The platform should adopt stability and security assurance mechanisms for relatively important business systems, such as SLA setting, monitoring and early warning, emergency plans, change processes, and security scanning mechanisms
- The platform should adopt high-availability assurance measures for applications, such as load balancing, call relationship management, and failover

- The platform should adopt high-availability assurance measures for data, such as database and table partitioning, read-write separation, real-time local backup, and offsite backup
- The platform should employ low-risk deployment and release strategies, such as canary (gray) releases
- The platform should have operations and security personnel responsible for ensuring the stability and security of the platform

Finally, platform engineering depends on the team responsible for building, operating, and evolving the platform. Platform team capability requirements define the roles needed to manage the platform as both a technical system and an internal product.

Platform team capability requirements

The following requirements describe the main roles that may be needed in a platform team, including product management, operations, architecture, development, testing, security, and technical coaching:

- There should be a physical or virtual platform team responsible for the overall construction, assurance, and promotional operations of the platform
- The platform team should include the role of platform product manager, responsible for platform planning and requirements management
- The platform team should include the role of platform product operations, responsible for platform promotional operations
- The platform team should include the role of platform architect, responsible for platform architecture design, such as feature distribution, performance, and high availability
- The platform team should include the role of platform development and testing, responsible for platform development and quality assurance
- The platform team should include the role of platform operations and security, responsible for platform stability and security
- The platform team may include the role of platform technical coach, responsible for technical services related to the platform

After defining the platform's required services, construction principles, operating model, assurance practices, and team roles, the next question is how organizations should adopt platform engineering in practice. The following best practices show how teams can start small, treat the platform as a product, and connect tool libraries with knowledge bases.

Best practices for platform engineering

Platform engineering does not need to begin as a large, centralized transformation program. In many organizations, it starts by improving a small but painful part of the delivery workflow, then gradually expands as teams see value and provide feedback.

Practice platform engineering anytime, anywhere

Platform engineering can be practiced anytime, anywhere. We usually start with easily achievable goals. For example, in a certain project, if a development team is already using common development tools, those tools can be integrated into the platform as the first batch of services offered.

Next, the platform architect should collect platform engineering requirements from the platform users, usually through interviews or surveys to understand current problems with their tool usage, what obstacles the tools create for the development teams, and what the most challenging issues are for them, such as helping manage container clusters or orchestrate deployment processes.

It should be noted that completing the platform engineering build entirely in a closed-off manner, from scratch to production, can cause obstacles during rollout. For example, if you tell the delivery team that, for technical stack considerations, all tools need to be standardized and unified, and require them to abandon their current tools and switch all delivery work to the platform engineering tools, this approach will only add more tasks for the delivery personnel. The purpose of platform engineering is to enhance collaboration, not to reduce efficiency—unless you can prove that the platform actually makes their work easier and more efficient.

Therefore, best practices for platform engineering should be conducted anytime, anywhere, and centered around engineering culture.

Platform engineering is a product with a lifecycle

Regarding best practices for platform engineering, you should start with a small, easy-to-achieve goal—one that can bring quantifiable value to the team or a specific node in the software delivery process at minimal cost. For example, during software delivery, when developers or teams use outdated technologies in a release, technology iteration can rarely be completed all at once, nor can all work be directly migrated to platform engineering. When promoting the platform, platform architects should first consider the current state of the delivery teams, choose appropriate delivery methods, ways to collaborate with other teams, the technology stack in use, and the tools being used, to help them gradually transition from their current state to the ideal state.

Take IDP as an example, it must be clear that IDP is not a one-time project. More often, IDP serves the majority of users involved in software delivery. Therefore, a mature IDP is a service that can continuously iterate. The platform needs to continually provide services, new tools, and combinations of tools. Platform engineering is a product with a lifecycle that requires continuous iteration and operation.

The logic of tool libraries and knowledge bases

A **tool cluster** is also known as a **tool library**. An excellent tool library can provide a good working experience for delivery personnel throughout the entire R&D ecosystem. Platform engineering has clear requirements for how to create an integrated and unified developer experience, which directly affects the satisfaction of the platform's core users—developers. Therefore, optimizing the tool experience and making it process-oriented and integrated is an important measure to improve the developer experience.

The knowledge base is what supports tool usage and determines the specific execution logic. Here, knowledge is not limited to static carriers such as documents and charts but should also include dynamic carriers such as rules, processes, views, queries, and models. The form of the carrier is determined by its method of consumption. The essence of a platform is knowledge, and only knowledge that has been validated in practice can guarantee its reliability and value. Teams should try to solidify knowledge into the platform and efficiently, stably, and comprehensively practice and validate knowledge through integration with the tool library. Only in this way can knowledge continue to accumulate and iterate, thereby producing economies of scale, coping with unknown challenges, and accelerating the rate at which value is realized.

As shown in *Figure 6.12*, the knowledge base drives the tool library, promoting continuous optimization of infrastructure, R&D processes, and environment management. The tool library also feeds back to the knowledge base, continuously supplementing business, architecture, and technical knowledge.

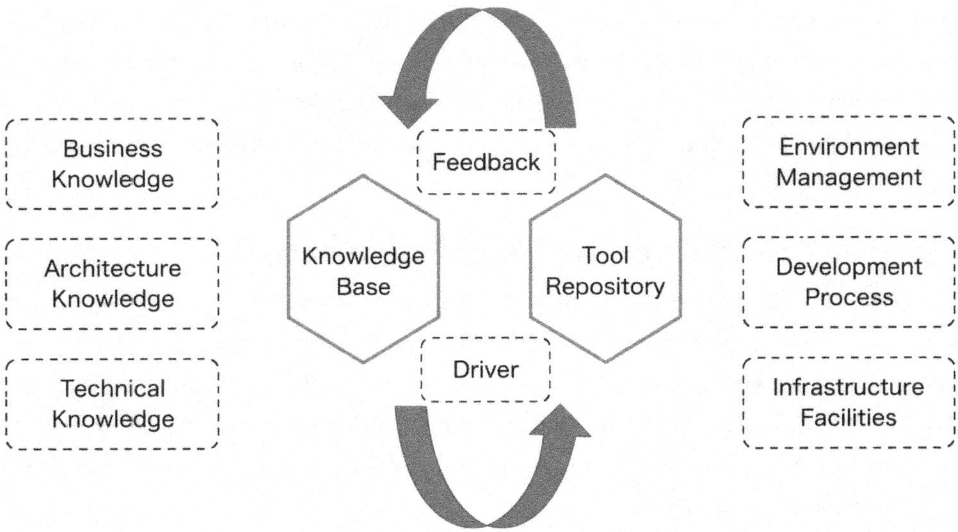

Figure 6.12: The drive and feedback relationship between the knowledge base and the tool library

After examining how platform engineering is designed and adopted, it is useful to clarify how it relates to the other two delivery disciplines discussed in this chapter: DevOps and SRE. These disciplines overlap in tools and goals, but they serve different primary audiences and solve different delivery problems.

Differences between platform engineering, DevOps, and SRE

After examining platform engineering concepts, capabilities, and best practices, it is useful to clarify how platform engineering relates to the other two delivery disciplines discussed in this chapter: DevOps and SRE. These practices overlap in tools and goals, but they serve different primary audiences and solve different delivery problems.

Differences from DevOps

DevOps is a way to transform the culture of collaboration into **system lifecycle management (SDLC)**, a concept aimed at improving software delivery speed and quality. DevOps promotes collaboration and communication between development and operations teams, and accelerates automation to streamline deployment. Platform engineering is a practice rather than a methodology, and can be regarded as the next iteration of DevOps, as it shares DevOps' principles of collaboration, continuous improvement, and automation.

There are differences between platform teams and DevOps in some respects. DevOps uses tools and automation to simplify the process of code release, management, and observation through logging and monitoring tools, with a primary focus on building efficient CI/CD pipelines. Platform engineers use all the tools that DevOps uses and integrate them into a shared platform for use across IT teams at the enterprise level. This reduces the need for teams to individually configure and manage infrastructure and tools, saving significant time, effort, and resources. Platform engineers are also responsible for creating documentation and optimizing the platform so that developers can use tools and infrastructure self-servingly in their workflows.

Only mature companies with multiple IT teams using complex tools and infrastructures need a platform team. In such engineering environments, a dedicated platform team is typically required to manage the complexity. The platform team is responsible for building and managing infrastructure and helping DevOps accelerate continuous delivery. However, in startups, DevOps teams often also take on platform engineering tasks.

Differences from SRE

SRE focuses on ensuring applications are reliable, secure, and always available. They work with developers and operations teams to create systems or infrastructure that support the delivery of highly reliable applications. SREs also perform capacity planning, infrastructure scaling, and incident management and response to ensure that the platform meets the required service level objectives. In addition, platform engineering manages complex infrastructure and builds efficient platforms for developers to optimize the SDLC. Although both work on the platform and their roles sound similar, their goals are different.

The main difference between platform teams and SREs is in whom they serve and how they serve them. SREs face end users and ensure that applications are reliable and available for them. Platform engineers are oriented toward internal developers, focusing on improving the developer experience. The daily tasks of the two teams differ in relation to these goals. Platform engineering provides the underlying infrastructure for rapid application delivery, while SREs do the same for delivering highly reliable and available applications. SREs are more focused on troubleshooting and incident response, while platform engineers focus on complex infrastructure and support for developer self-service.

In order to achieve their respective goals, SRE and platform teams use different tools in their workflows. SREs mainly use monitoring and logging tools like **Prometheus** or **Grafana** to detect anomalies in real time and set up automatic alerts. Platform teams use a different set of tools that span various stages of the software delivery process, such as container orchestration tools, CI/CD pipeline tools, and IaC tools. Overall, SREs and platform teams are committed to building reliable and scalable infrastructures, with different goals, but there is some overlap in the tools they use.

Once the relationship between platform engineering, DevOps, and SRE is clear, the final step is to consider how platform engineering changes in the era of LLMs. LLMs can extend internal platforms by improving requirements analysis, developer assistance, knowledge retrieval, automation, and operational insight.

Platform engineering under LLMs

Driven by LLMs, the development and application of platform engineering have become more efficient and flexible. By combining the powerful computational capabilities of these models with platform engineering, organizations can better achieve automation, standardization, and scalability. In this process, platform engineering is not just about building and maintaining infrastructure, but also about holistic optimization of the entire development process.

Furthermore, platform engineering leverages the intelligent analytical capabilities of LLMs for more precise performance monitoring and optimization. By processing and analyzing large volumes of data, platforms can automatically identify potential bottlenecks and issues, propose solutions, and help organizations improve operational efficiency.

Challenges encountered in platform engineering

According to the latest report released by CloudBees, *Platform Engineering 2023: Rapid Adoption and Impact*, 83% of respondents have either fully implemented platform engineering or are at some stage of implementation. According to the data in the report, developers actually spend only 12.5% to 30% of their weekly time writing code. This has prompted IT organization leaders to urgently seek new ways to improve developer productivity; therefore, the need for innovative technologies in platform engineering is pressing, especially machine learning technologies and LLM technologies.

Firstly, as enterprise data continues to accumulate, data privacy, and security become increasingly important, especially in LLM scenarios. For training data in specific domains, this inevitably brings challenges to traditional platform engineering. Especially in managing multiple large datasets and models, platform engineering needs to integrate machine learning algorithms and LLMs.

Secondly, platform engineering must adapt to new AI workflows and data, prompts, as well as the pipelines for AI engineers who design, train, and maintain models, vector databases, and large datasets—all of which will continue to grow and evolve. These AI pipelines must support the specific requirements of their workflow patterns and align with interdependent software development pipelines and release processes.

Finally, with changes in enterprise business models, more and more business systems are adopting GPUs, VPUs, and highly scalable CPUs to process large amounts of data. This approach also poses challenges to traditional platform engineering. In order to enable the platform to play a greater role, platform engineering needs to proactively incorporate more innovative technologies.

Common practice methods

Since **platform engineering** is mainly aimed at internal enterprise developers, business requirements—as an upstream point in the development process—need extra attention. Likewise, the developers' own tools also need to be considered.

Automated enhancement, analysis, and conversion of business requirements

In terms of automated requirements enhancement, platform engineering, combined with LLM technology, can analyze user feedback and data to automatically identify and supplement missing requirement information. For example, it can automatically identify user-raised issues and convert them into requirement descriptions, and automatically complete requirement keywords and tags.

In automated requirements analysis, domain knowledge obtained through data training can better evaluate and optimize requirements, uncover potential problems and opportunities, and improve the efficiency and effectiveness of requirements analysis.

In automated requirements convergence, by leveraging LLM technologies such as intelligent recommendations, conversational systems, and multi-party collaboration, developers can communicate and collaborate more effectively, collect and integrate user feedback and pain points more effectively, and improve satisfaction and consistency of requirements.

Smarter development tools

Based on the existing functionality of development tools, it is necessary to integrate more capabilities from the software delivery process, such as automated code review, automated testing, automated log analysis, and AI-assisted programming. This significantly improves developers' efficiency and provides an excellent user experience.

At the same time, based on LLM capabilities, development tools can also analyze documents and code generated during development, build knowledge bases, and provide intelligent Q&A capabilities for developers, thus simplifying learning costs for developers and reducing users' cognitive load.

Platform engineering helps internal teams deliver software more efficiently by providing reusable tools, infrastructure, workflows, and self-service capabilities. However, efficient delivery is only one part of modern software engineering. The next section turns to Site Reliability Engineering, which focuses on keeping systems reliable, scalable, observable, and resilient once they are running in production.

Strengthening system reliability with SRE

Site Reliability Engineering extends modern software delivery by focusing on the reliability, scalability, performance, and operability of systems after they are designed, built, and released. While DevOps improves collaboration and delivery flow, and platform engineering provides reusable internal platforms, SRE applies software engineering practices to operational problems such as availability, monitoring, incident response, build reliability, change risk, and go-live assurance. This section explains how SRE emerged, what goals it serves, how SRE teams can be organized, and how SRE practices help teams design, deliver, and operate more reliable systems. For relevant SRE system content, refer to the *SRE Practice White Paper*.

Origin of SRE

In 2003, Google launched a brand-new team, namely the SRE team, aiming to improve the reliability of application systems through software engineering approaches. As SRE theories and practices gradually matured within Google, SRE practices were gradually expanded to the entire industry. Since the introduction of the SRE concept, it has attracted the attention and imitation of many enterprises. However, the methods of implementing SRE vary among enterprises, and the effectiveness of SRE implementation also differs.

Goals of SRE

The primary goal of SRE is to improve the reliability, scalability, performance, and efficiency of large-scale distributed systems by combining best practices from software engineering and system operations, as well as enhancing monitoring, alerting, and fault recovery capabilities.

- **Reliability**: The foremost goal of SRE is to ensure the reliability of services and systems. This includes reducing failures and increasing system stability to ensure that users can consistently receive high-quality services at all times.

- **Scalability:** SRE is committed to designing and implementing systems that can scale with growing user demands. This involves optimizing system architecture and resources to handle fluctuations in real workloads without sacrificing performance.
- **Performance:** SRE focuses on system performance, aiming to ensure that systems can respond to user requests quickly within a reasonable timeframe. This includes continuous monitoring and optimization of system bottlenecks to enhance overall performance.
- **Efficiency:** SRE advocates for automating operational tasks to reduce human error and improve efficiency. Through automation, new features can be deployed more rapidly, failures can be detected and responded to faster, and system upgrades and maintenance can be conducted more reasonably.
- **Monitoring and Alerting:** SRE emphasizes comprehensive monitoring of systems to detect and resolve problems in a timely manner. By setting up effective alerting systems, rapid response to major issues can be achieved before they impact users, thereby minimizing user impact.
- **Fault Recovery Capability:** SRE stresses quickly and effectively restoring services to minimize interruptions to user experience. This includes developing and rehearsing emergency response plans for critical situations.

The process by which enterprises achieve the core goals of SRE is not uniform, and implementation paths vary. SRE-related practices exist within many workflows and are independent of the form or organizational location of SRE departments or teams within a company. These workflows are closely integrated with R&D, testing, operations, and product operations teams, with every participating team contributing to the aforementioned SRE goals.

With these reliability goals established, the next step is to look at the practical mission of the SRE team within an organization.

Mission of the SRE team

The main purpose of having an SRE team within an organization is to ensure the reliability and efficient operation of systems. By introducing the SRE role, organizations can better balance the needs between software development speed and system stability, thereby achieving a higher level of availability, performance, and automation. The mission of the SRE team within the organization is as follows.

- **Reliability First:** The SRE team is committed to ensuring high availability and reliability of services. They focus on system stability and adopt an engineering approach to reduce failures and improve system robustness.

- **Automated Operations:** The SRE team promotes automated operations to reduce manual errors and improve efficiency. Through automation, deployments, monitoring, fault detection, and restoration can be performed more quickly and reliably.
- **Quality Assurance:** The SRE team participates in the entire service lifecycle, including design, development, deployment, and maintenance stages, to ensure the system maintains high quality at every stage.
- **Rapid Innovation:** By reducing failures and increasing system stability, the SRE team provides the development team with a more stable platform, enabling them to focus more on business innovation and the development of new features.

Because organizations differ in size, structure, and operational maturity, SRE teams can be organized in different ways. The next subsection introduces the most common team models and explains how each model supports reliability work.

Forms of SRE team presence

In organizational structures, the form in which SRE teams exist can vary, primarily depending on the organization's size, business needs, and culture. The following are some common forms of SRE team presence:

- **Centralized SRE Team:** A dedicated SRE team is responsible for supporting the reliability efforts of the entire organization. This model helps concentrate expertise and ensures the consistent implementation of best practices organization-wide.
- **Embedded SRE Team:** SRE team members are embedded within various product or service teams, working closely with development teams. This model helps integrate reliability efforts into the entire product development process.
- **Hybrid Model:** Some organizations adopt a hybrid model, establishing both a centralized SRE team and embedding SRE roles within some key projects. This model leverages the advantages of both specialization and close business integration.

Each form has its own advantages and applicable scenarios, and the most suitable model can be chosen according to organizational needs. Regardless of the form, the goal of SRE is to enhance system reliability and efficiency through automation and engineering approaches.

As shown in *Figure 6.13*, the **SRE engineering group** adopts a centralized setup, responsible for the construction and promotion of the SRE system. This group drives the **SRE platform R&D group** and the **infrastructure group**, providing highly efficient tools and platform products to improve the reliability of foundational services.

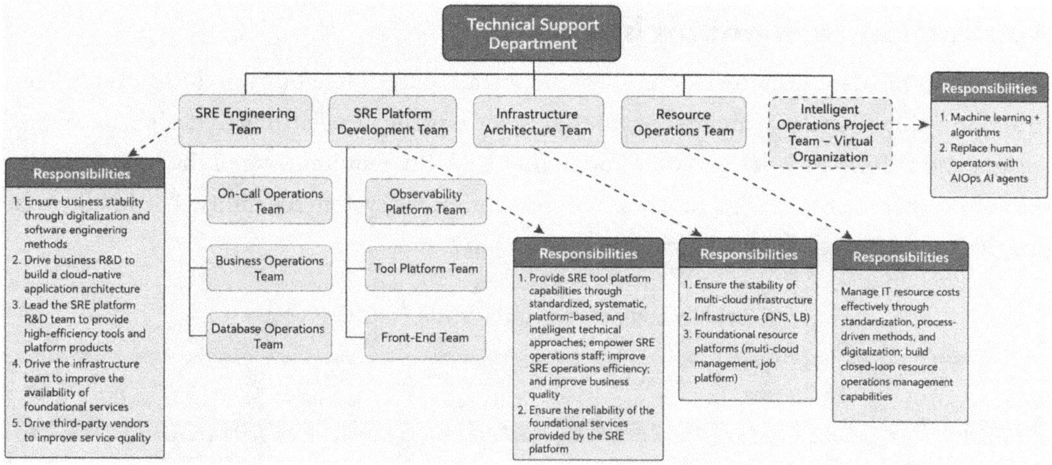

Figure 6.13: Centralized SRE organization

As shown in *Figure 6.14*, each SRE team adopts an embedded setup, responsible for the construction and promotion of the SRE system within each business division, and is in charge of collecting business requirements and abstracting these requirements into capabilities.

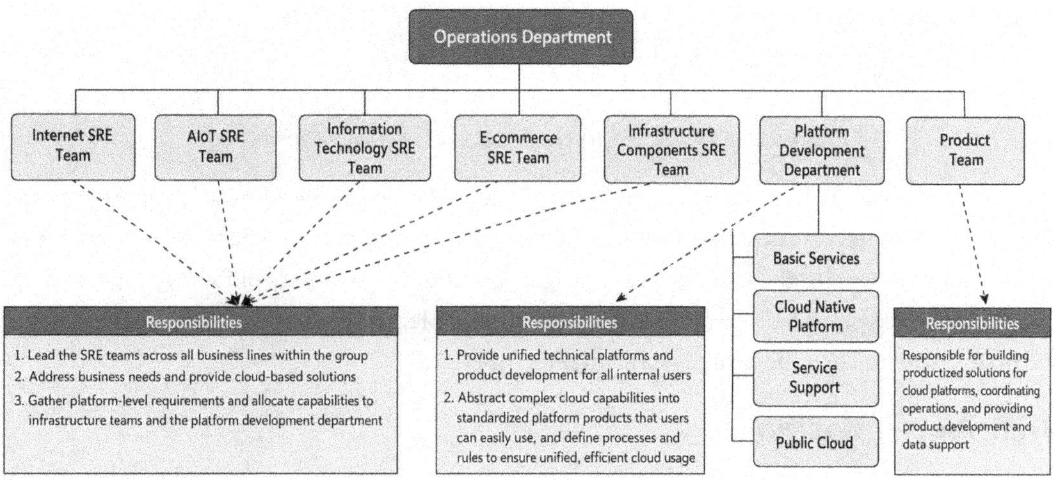

Figure 6.14: Embedded SRE organization

After defining SRE goals and team structures, the next step is to examine how SRE practices are applied during system design. Reliability is not achieved only through incident response after a system is running; it must be built into the architecture through design choices that reduce failure impact and improve recovery.

Application resilient architecture

Application resilient architecture is a very important part of reliability architecture. It refers to adopting highly reliable architecture design solutions such as distributed design, decoupled design, and redundancy design according to the reliability requirements of the system during the system architecture design process, in order to improve system reliability. The full lifecycle practice process of reliability engineering is shown in *Figure 6.15*.

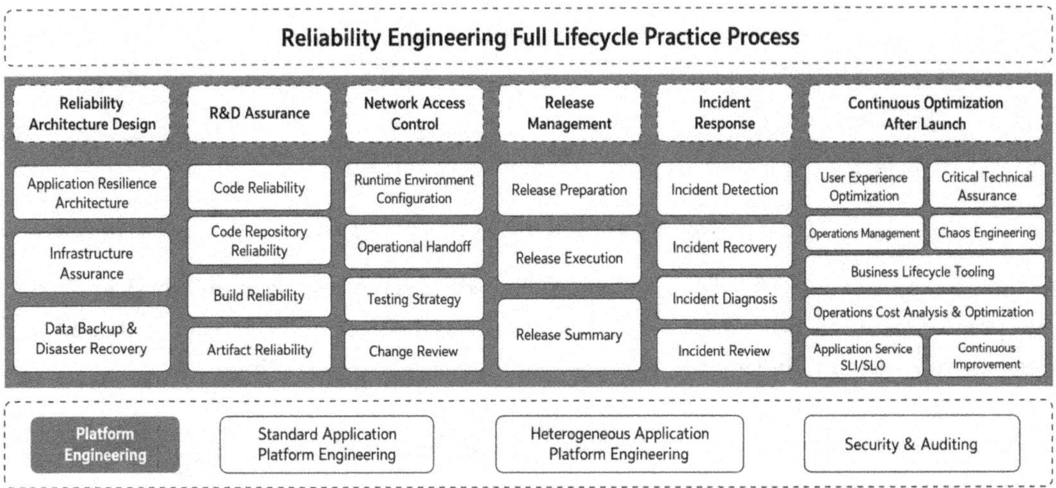

Figure 6.15: Full lifecycle practice process of reliability engineering

In the process of reliability architecture design, the SRE team needs to fully integrate into the application architecture design process, and jointly participate in architecture design and review with the R&D team. In the system design stage, potential single points of failure, capacity, and other latent risks should be eliminated as much as possible, and emergency preparations should be made in advance for possible system architecture risks.

Distributed design

The system has components with clear responsibilities, appropriate granularity, and easy management, such as computing resources, business modules, and data. These components can be deployed and run in a distributed manner. Components are independent and do not interfere with each other. **Distributed design** can improve development efficiency and system reliability. Component splitting can be achieved through replication, vertical splitting according to functionality, or horizontal splitting based on users or access patterns.

During design, possible mutual interference between components should be fully considered, as well as how to balance the load between different components, distributing the system's load evenly to mitigate negative impacts on overall performance.

Decoupled design

In the architecture design process, various logical functions can be divided into different service modules, ensuring that failures in one module have minimal impact on other modules, thereby minimizing the coupling degree between modules. In this way, the system can be divided into multiple independent functional modules. It is worth noting that the main business logic is independent from other non-core modules, so failures in non-core business modules do not negatively affect the core functions of the business.

Redundancy

To ensure that resources have a sufficient safety margin, each component needs to have enough and reasonable **redundant instances** to ensure that the failure of a single component instance does not affect normal business operations. For different types of components, we need to clearly define the amount and type of redundancy. In practice, when device failures or improper operations cause server performance degradation or crashes, the system will enter an abnormal state and generate a large amount of information. Applications may be deployed across multiple data centers, and when data redundancy exists between these centers, errors at one location can be corrected using data from another, ensuring continuity and reliability of the entire system. To enhance system reliability, **read-write separation** is often used for data redundancy management. Read-write separation is a form of redundancy design in which data redundancy exists between the cache and the database. When the cache service goes down, data can be backfilled from the database to the cache.

Circuit breaker

The **circuit breaker mechanism** is a microservices protection mechanism used to address the **avalanche effect**. If the target service responds slowly or there are too many timeouts, the calls to that service will be cut off (circuit broken). Subsequent calls will no longer attempt to invoke the target service; instead, a predefined result will be returned directly, allowing resources to be quickly freed. Generally, circuit breakers require different recovery strategies. If the condition of the target service improves, normal requests can resume.

Rate limiting

Rate limiting is a system design technique used to control access traffic to applications or services and to prevent resource overload. Common rate limiting strategies include **fixed window, sliding log, leaky bucket**, and **token bucket algorithms.** These strategies help the system cope with high traffic, maintaining stability and reliability. In practice, rate limiting is often combined with other protective measures such as queues, caching, service degradation, and circuit breaking, to achieve comprehensive traffic control and system protection. When traffic is limited, the system usually rejects excess requests, queues requests for later processing, returns an error code (such as `HTTP 429 Too Many Requests`), or provides a degraded service response, effectively alleviating server pressure.

Degradation

Degradation mechanisms are used when server pressure surges; based on current business and traffic conditions, specific services and pages are strategically degraded to relieve server resource pressure, free up resources, and ensure the normal operation of core tasks. Based on the configuration, degradation can be divided into **proactive** and **automatic degradation. Proactive degradation** is configured in advance, whereas **automatic degradation** executes when system failures occur, such as timeouts or frequent failures. Automatic degradation can be further subdivided into **timeout degradation, failure-count degradation**, and **error degradation.**

Observability

To ensure system transparency and quickly locate issues, adopting an **observable design** approach is particularly crucial. Observability design encompasses several aspects, including logging, real-time monitoring, tracing, and metrics, achieving measurable and analyzable system state and behavior. In observability design, logs should record all key events in detail; monitoring systems must capture critical performance metrics in real-time; tracing mechanisms should be able to track requests across services; and metrics should comprehensively reflect the system's health status.

Additionally, health check mechanisms should automatically assess the status of system components, and, if abnormal metrics appear, the alerting mechanism will immediately notify relevant personnel. With these measures, we can clearly observe the system's operating state, thus laying a solid foundation for subsequent maintenance and optimization.

Resilient architecture reduces the likelihood and impact of production failures, but system reliability also depends on the reliability of the software delivery process itself. In CI/CD environments, the build process must be fast, repeatable, and dependable so that teams can release and verify changes safely.

Build reliability

Build refers to the process of compiling and packaging source files such as code and resource files into executable program files on a build machine. In the current **continuous integration/continuous delivery (CI/CD)** software development model, if a problem occurs during the build, the new software version cannot be quickly released and verified, which affects software quality. Therefore, **build reliability** plays an important role in the reliability of software services and iteration efficiency. Build reliability design mainly consists of two aspects: **build efficiency** and **build success rate.**

Build efficiency

Build efficiency refers to build speed, determined by the time elapsed from the start to the end of the build. If the build time is too long, the software version cannot be delivered on time, affecting the iteration efficiency of business versions, and the reliability of the build is difficult to guarantee. The main measures to improve build efficiency are as follows.

- **Process automation:** Use automated build tools or scripts to connect each build step, reducing waiting time between steps.
- **Parallelization:** Optimize the process by changing parts of the build flow from serial to parallel, thereby increasing build speed.
- **Incremental build:** When executing a build on the build machine, some temporary files and intermediate products generated during the build are saved as build cache. During the next build, since usually only part of the code has been modified, the unmodified code can directly use the previous build cache, thus avoiding redundant builds. Incremental builds reduce the content that needs to be built, thereby decreasing build time. To address the lack of cache during the first build on the build machine, a build cache sharing server can be set up (such as the **DDC server** for the **UE engine**). The build cache from one build machine is uploaded to the shared cache server for use by other build machines.
- **Distributed compilation:** Compared to the limited resources of a single machine, the power of a cluster is undoubtedly stronger: it is easy to see the difference between one person computing 100 math problems and 100 people of the same ability each solving one problem. Distributed compilation utilizes cluster resources, assigning the work of a single node to a large number of nodes, and then aggregating the results. Depending on requirements, the number of resources can be almost infinitely expanded, no longer constrained by the physical architecture of a single machine; in terms of time, the time required for a cluster to work is often only a fraction of the original time.

- **Software-hardware collaboration:** Some build tasks (such as code preprocessing, resource file processing) cannot be accelerated for remote distribution via distributed compilation and can only be processed on the local build machine. In this case, the local build machine's performance becomes the bottleneck. To address this, the CPU, memory, and disk IO performance of the local build machine can be specifically enhanced. Combined with the distributed compilation system, software and hardware collaborate to improve build speed.
- **Multi-process compilation**: Some compilation software defaults to single-process compilation, resulting in underutilization of build machine hardware performance. In this case, enabling **multi-process compilation** can improve build speed.

After identifying the main ways to improve build efficiency, teams also need methods for measuring whether those improvements are working.

Evaluation methods for build efficiency

By improving build efficiency through the above methods, it is also necessary to evaluate the effectiveness of builds. There are several evaluation methods as follows:

- **Evaluation based on baseline:** The effectiveness of a single build can be evaluated using the proportion of build time exceeding the **baseline**. After each build is completed normally, the build time is reported. After several days of continuous builds, a set of stable build time data over a given period is collected. The average of these data points becomes the build time baseline for that period. If a build's duration exceeds the baseline by a significant amount (e.g., 20%), there may be performance issues. Once the build time baseline is established, the current build time can be compared to the baseline as an **SLO** (**Service Level Objective**), such as considering it healthy if it does not exceed the baseline by more than 10%.
- **Evaluation based on threshold.** Different thresholds can be set according to actual business needs, for example, setting the build time not to exceed **2 hours** as a measure of reliability.

Build speed is only one part of build reliability; teams must also ensure that builds complete successfully and consistently.

Build success rate

Build success rate refers to the proportion of successful builds out of the total number of builds within a specified time period. If the build success rate is low, multiple builds are required to generate a deliverable version. The build success rate is one of the key factors affecting build reliability. The main measures to improve the build success rate are as follows:

- **Ensuring the reliability of the build environment**: Build success rate is affected by the build environment. If abnormalities occur on the build machine (such as missing dependency packages, inability to connect to the code repository, disk failures, etc.), the build will fail. Therefore, it is necessary to ensure the reliability of the build environment, for example, by automating the large-scale deployment of build machines to avoid missing dependencies caused by manual deployment, and by utilizing highly reliable network, computing, and storage resources in cloud environments as much as possible.
- **Pre-compilation checks:** The build process usually executes compilation after pulling the code, which requires developers to submit the code to the repository once they finish coding in order to trigger the build process. In practice, issues can be exposed before the code is committed to the repository. The earlier problems are discovered, the lower the cost to fix them; the higher the quality of code committed to the repository, the fewer issues there are, and the smoother and more efficient team collaboration will be. **Pre-compilation tools** can, before code submission, run local pre-build checks or remote pre-compilation checks to detect problems early, thus shifting quality to the left.

Once build success rate has been improved through environment reliability and pre-compilation checks, it also needs to be measured against a baseline or threshold.

Evaluation methods for build success rates

The evaluation of build success rate effectiveness is mainly as follows:

- **Evaluation based on baseline:** After each build is completed, the success/failure status is reported. The **build success rate** for a day is calculated, and after several days, a period of stable daily build success rates is obtained. The average of these data provides the baseline build success rate for that period. When the build success rate for a given day exceeds the baseline by a significant amount (e.g., more than 20%), there may be a performance issue in that build. Once the build success rate baseline is established, the current build success rate can be compared to the baseline as an **SLO**; for example, it is considered healthy if it is not lower than the baseline by more than 10%.

- **Evaluation based on thresholds:** Set a fixed success rate threshold (e.g., 80%) according to business requirements, then conduct statistical analysis and comparison of all builds within a fixed cycle. The cycle unit can be **day**, **week**, or **month**.

Once a build can be produced reliably, the next reliability concern is how changes are reviewed and introduced into production. Change review helps SRE teams reduce release risk by identifying architectural, operational, and non-functional issues before they affect users.

Change review

The main purpose of **change review** is to reduce risks brought by system changes going live and to ensure changes are delivered to the business as scheduled. In change reviews, different SRE organizations establish corresponding change review mechanisms at various stages of the system delivery lifecycle, such as availability reviews at the project initiation stage, technical or deployment architecture availability reviews, non-functional and operability reviews during the design stage, and CAB reviews before going live.

Stability architecture design assessment

To promote stable architecture management, the SRE organization recommends establishing a cross-team technical architecture management body at the technical level, responsible for formulating stability architecture management specifications, technical component specifications, and the corresponding technical management and review processes. SREs should focus on advancing related assessment work in areas such as high availability, disaster recovery, scalability, data integrity, and deployment environments.

High availability is a baseline requirement for operations management. The main task of operations is to eliminate single points of failure and enhance system resilience. For example, in databases, methods such as primary-standby, master-slave, and distributed architectures are used; in data centers, active-active distribution in two sites and three centers or distributed multi-active setups are utilized. Deploying a single application system with the same service component in multiple data center rooms, on multiple virtual machines across different physical machines, providing network hardware or software load balancers for application load balancing, and offering high-availability architecture middleware such as PaaS cloud services are also approaches. To better advance the assessment work, SREs need to provide high availability architecture specifications in advance, develop reference models for high availability of general components and information system architectures, and implement high availability requirements earlier in the system design process.

Disaster recovery can draw on best practices and the characteristics of specific information systems to develop corresponding disaster recovery capability requirements. At the application system layer, attention needs to be paid to application splitting, decoupling of service or system interactions, stateless services, reducing dependencies on bus node services, increasing asynchronous access mechanisms, multi-level caching, database optimization, rate limiting and peak shaving mechanisms, foundational design for rapid scaling, etc. At the infrastructure layer, a recoverable infrastructure environment should be able to effectively recover from natural or man-made disasters, that is, considering various risks, including natural disasters, technical failures, human errors, or network attacks, and taking preventive measures to reduce potential losses. At a minimum, this should include backup, redundancy, rapid service recovery, and protection of critical information systems.

The scalability of a technical architecture refers to the system's ability to expand or enhance its functionality without affecting existing system functions and performance. This usually involves considerations about system design, architecture, and modularization to facilitate future expansions and upgrades. Specifically, this includes: splitting the system into multiple independent subsystems or modules, each responsible for specific functions and business logic, reducing the complexity of the entire system and the coupling between modules, and improving extensibility; supporting both horizontal and vertical scalability—by increasing the number of servers and enhancing the processing capabilities of each server, the processing power of the entire system can be improved, or by upgrading the hardware of a single server or component, its processing power can be boosted; supporting elastic scaling, i.e., automatically adjusting computing and storage resources based on the system load to achieve dynamic scaling up and down; reducing dependencies on bus node services by changing logical interactions composed of multiple nodes to end-to-end access methods, thereby reducing factors that affect transactions; introducing asynchronous access mechanisms, as synchronous mechanisms may exhaust maximum connections in a short time when performance issues occur—even if this maximum concurrency is ten times that under normal circumstances—so switching synchronous connections to asynchronous communication, or introducing **message queues**; supporting multi-level caching, establishing caches at the frontend, within applications, at the database layer, etc.

Data integrity is the baseline requirement for operations and maintenance assurance. The lifecycle of **persistent data** is usually much longer than the lifecycle of systems and hardware. When new systems go online or architectural adjustments are made, data migration is often considered. At the same time, attention must be paid to complex data processing such as batch, clearing, and reconciliation operations, which are highly susceptible to data problems. The operations side needs to focus on **root cause analysis** for abnormal interruptions in data processing, which stages can be interrupted for emergency handling, whether multiple retries are supported after interruption, and, in the event of data inconsistencies agreed upon with third-party systems, which side should be used as the basis for emergency response mechanisms.

When selecting a **deployment environment**, multiple factors must be considered comprehensively, such as application characteristics, performance requirements, scalability, reliability, security, provider support, and cost-effectiveness. Different factors have important impacts on the choice of deployment environment. For example, some applications may require large amounts of memory and computing resources, some need platform services with high throughput and robust data processing capabilities, others depend on cloud services to achieve scalability with demand changes, and yet others need to choose infrastructure environments with high stability and security.

Non-functional technical assessment

Non-functional design in operations and maintenance is the proactive entry point to address maintainability issues, directly determining the cost and benefits of systems in the production environment, and even the length of a system's lifecycle. The following non-functional designs need to be promoted by the operations side.

System operational observability

The three core elements of observability in cloud-native—monitoring metrics, logs, and tracing—are equally applicable to traditional technical architectures represented by hosts. **Operations and maintenance** (**O&M**) enhance these aspects on a finished black-box product, with solutions like **NPM**, **APM**, and **BPM** initiated from the O&M side. From a non-functional design perspective, improving observability requires shifting O&M involvement forward, promoting necessary R&D standards for monitoring, logs, and tracing, improving the ability to proactively report monitoring performance metric data, optimizing log readability, and providing essential infrastructure services support, such as supporting system monitoring data reporting, log collection and analysis.

Fault isolation and service degradation

The purpose of **fault isolation** and **service degradation** is to sacrifice part of business functionality or part of customers' business to ensure the service quality of more critical businesses or customer groups. This approach prevents cascading failures. In design, the O&M side needs to review all the service components called by the application system from a system or business perspective and plan assumptions and countermeasures for faults in each service component.

Performance evaluation

Performance and capacity management are mainly based on **golden metrics** such as **response time** (the time a system, function, or service component takes to complete handling an external request), **throughput** (the maximum number of requests that can be handled within a specified time), **load** (the current load status of the service component), **efficiency** (performance divided by resources, such as `QPS = concurrency/average response time`), and **scalability** (the ability for vertical or horizontal expansion). Performance issues challenge stability not just through a single component's unavailability but more significantly when a component's performance issues spread to others, causing large-scale failures. Performance problems are highly likely to trigger complex exceptions, so **SREs** need to conduct strengthened technical evaluations accordingly.

Backward compatibility of mobile terminal versions

The management of **mobile terminal versions** is becoming increasingly important. In architecture design, on one hand, it is necessary to ensure that upgraded versions are as **backward compatible** as possible with lower versions still in circulation; on the other hand, **convergence management** of existing versions should be performed, supporting a variety of online update mechanisms.

Running based on the fundamental platform

Whether dealing with infrastructure platforms, PaaS-level application platforms, or continuous delivery toolchains, the system should integrate with the company's existing fundamental platforms whenever possible, avoiding the introduction of new technology stacks, and should be implemented in a configurable manner to avoid hardcoding. In emergency situations, the author has found that some parameters were hardcoded in the program, preventing rapid adjustments; thus, configuration management needs to be strengthened. Converting IPs to DNS domain names is also a direction for configuration, aimed at reducing manual backend modifications.

Log standardization

Log analysis is an important means to understand application systems. SREs should focus on the following aspects: First is **storage.** Due to industry or internal enterprise requirements for log data retention, there needs to be a cost-controllable, horizontally scalable platform that supports massive log data management; Second is **querying. Logs** are an important window for perceiving the operational state of online systems and locating code-level problems. In scenarios such as business issues and emergency incidents, problems can be identified through log queries. Therefore, it is necessary to establish **real-time data collection** and **efficient log retrieval** capabilities; Third is **monitoring**, which provides monitoring capabilities through keyword analysis, regex searches, and pattern matching of logs; Fourth is **analysis**, where the unstructured data in logs is processed into structured data to support running data analysis, achieving anomaly detection, fault localization, performance analysis, and capacity evaluation functions.

Comprehensive test plans

During test plan reviews, **SREs** should focus on reviewing plans for **performance**, **capacity**, **stress**, and **stability architecture tests.** The review perspectives include whether the description of test cases is clear, whether the execution results of test cases meet requirements, and whether the test conclusions address countermeasures for legacy issues, etc.

While change review focuses on whether a change is technically and operationally acceptable, change protection preparation focuses on whether the organization is ready to respond if the change causes instability. This includes monitoring, emergency plans, documentation, and knowledge-base readiness.

Change protection preparation assessment

Changes can pose stability risks to the system. Judging from the rate of failures caused by production changes, incidents triggered by changes are far higher than those from other factors. After a change, it is usually the busiest period for operations organizations. Whether it is a large software baseline, a functional iteration, or even a parameter or configuration adjustment, any of these can cause major failures. There are many risk points in changes, including program defects in design, version control issues in management, operational execution problems, and even interdependent impacts caused by poor communication between upstream and downstream systems at the collaboration level. Solving the risks brought by changes is a highly complex and systematic task. SREs should consider strengthening the evaluation of change protection from the following aspects.

Are monitoring and alerting ready?

Comprehensive monitoring coverage includes technical indicators such as infrastructure, platform software, databases, middleware, operating systems, and performance, as well as business function and customer experience indicators relevant to specific systems.

Establishing a complete **monitoring and alerting system** is an important way to ensure system maintainability. It allows for real-time monitoring of various system metrics, timely identification of problems, proactive alerting, and rapid resolution of issues.

Are emergency plans ready?

First, are **fault emergency tools** ready? When a system failure occurs, it is necessary to restore and resolve the issue quickly to prevent the fault from escalating. Second, is the **technical operation work** in place? After the system goes live, comprehensive operational management is required, including user service, tracking the first business transaction, handling abnormal data or logic problems, security management, etc., to ensure stable and efficient system operation.

Are the documents complete?

According to the organization's software delivery collaboration mechanism, clarify the documentation delivery checklist for the launch of the new system, such as project, and requirements, technical architecture diagrams, test conclusions (including stress testing), installation and deployment (environment-related), application/business monitoring, initial transaction function monitoring and assurance, list of key functions, important configurations, and parameters, operational performance evaluation, etc.

Is the knowledge base ready?

Establishing a comprehensive **knowledge base** is an important foundation to ensure the maintainability of the system. Provide detailed descriptions of various functions and operations of the system, and build a knowledge base to facilitate quick retrieval of relevant information when needed.

New systems and new business launches require broader assurance than routine changes because they introduce new architecture, new user behavior, new business dependencies, and new operational uncertainty. For this reason, SRE teams must assess both technical readiness and business-impact risk before go-live.

New system or new business go-live assurance assessment

The rollout of a **new system** or **new business** is a process from zero to one, and the specific work usually includes go-live preparation, technical solution formulation, evaluation and test management, preparation of go-live documentation, risk assessment, security assurance measures, operations monitoring preparation, go-live process coordination, release, system acceptance, and go-live trial operation, etc.

The go-live of a new system or new business brings both opportunities and challenges to an enterprise: on the one hand, as an important project milestone, the new system will empower the enterprise's business development or operations management. Usually, the business demand side will invest a lot of effort in the post-launch operational promotion work, in hopes of better bringing value to the business and customers; on the other hand, launching a new system brings numerous uncertainties that need to be managed.

Risk assessment work for SREs

In risk assessment work, the SRE should strengthen the evaluation of the following risks:

- Risks brought by new business, regulatory compliance, data security, privacy protection, etc.
- Risks to the new system's business process availability, endpoint experience, and data accuracy
- The impact of the new business system on the capacity and performance of existing upstream and downstream systems, as well as the effect of upstream and downstream integration or transformation on the original business
- Whether the resources, architecture, and key functions of the new system meet business expectations, and whether they satisfy the performance and capacity requirements of upcoming business activities
- Whether system stress tests, capacity evaluation plans, unresolved functional defects, etc., have been adequately assessed

After identifying the risks that SRE teams need to assess before a new system or business launch, the next step is to define the proactive actions they can take to reduce those risks and improve go-live readiness.

Proactive actions for SRE

In addition, the SRE should proactively promote the following work:

- Start with standardization, establish compliance, risk, privacy, and security management requirements at both business and technical levels, and assist with relevant technical detection tools
- Build non-functional requirements for business systems, such as system rollback, version switching, canary releases, endpoint experience perception, and other support functionalities
- Build technical operations requirements for business systems, such as initial business perception, business transaction monitoring, and technical operations monitoring of related systems

System performance and capacity management, such as related evaluation metrics, baseline capacity design, metric data processing, capacity assessment analysis reports, and construction of tools like stress testing.

At the same time, in response to potential surges in business patterns, the SRE needs to establish **rate limiting** and **traffic shaping** mechanisms. In terms of **architecture optimization**, the front-end system should set up **trading concurrency control switches**, and implement front-end **rate limiting** and **traffic shaping** as needed, as well as back-end **service degradation**. Through front-end interaction design, reduce the impact on customer experience, with a key focus on ensuring the stability of the system's core services.

SRE focuses on the launch phase of new systems or new services, shifting operations and maintenance work to the left, building up resource delivery capabilities in advance to improve system go-live speed, leveraging operation and maintenance platform capabilities to assist in the development of business logic, and participating early in the development and acceptance of **architectural** and **non-functional requirements**, thereby integrating into a platform-based management model after the system goes live.

Summary

In this chapter, you explored the three foundational pillars of modern software delivery—DevOps, Platform Engineering, and SRE—and how they work together to enable efficient, scalable, and reliable software systems. You learned how DevOps improves collaboration, automation, and value delivery across the software lifecycle, while also introducing concepts such as digital visualization, shift-left practices, and data-driven operations.

The chapter then introduced Platform Engineering as an evolution of DevOps, focusing on building internal platforms that enhance developer productivity through self-service capabilities, standardized tools, and improved user experience. You examined its key attributes, core modules, and best practices, along with how it reduces cognitive load and supports large-scale enterprise development.

Finally, you explored SRE as the discipline responsible for ensuring system reliability, scalability, and performance. You learned about reliability-focused architecture patterns, monitoring and observability, incident management, and risk mitigation strategies, along with how SRE balances rapid innovation with system stability.

By the end of this chapter, you should have a clear understanding of how these three pillars complement each other—DevOps enabling collaboration and delivery, Platform Engineering providing scalable tooling and infrastructure, and SRE ensuring reliability and resilience—forming a cohesive foundation for modern software delivery in enterprise environments.

Building on this foundation, the next chapter moves into real-world operations and maintenance scenarios, where you will learn how LLMs can be applied to tasks such as log analysis, intelligent troubleshooting, knowledge base construction, and automated O&M workflows to enhance system observability and operational efficiency.

Part 3

LLM Practices Across the Software Delivery Lifecycle

In the previous part, you learned how enterprise LLM systems can be grounded through RAG and multi-agent workflows, and how DevOps, SRE, and Platform Engineering provide the delivery foundation for practical adoption. This final part moves from foundations and enterprise readiness into applied delivery practices. The focus is on how LLMs can support real workflows across operations, testing, coding, project management, and cybersecurity.

You will examine how LLMs can assist with log analysis, O&M knowledge bases, ticket handling, root cause analysis, dynamic and static testing, code generation, software development workflows, project coordination, risk management, and security operations. The goal is to help you evaluate where LLMs can create measurable value across the software delivery lifecycle while also recognizing the constraints, risks, and governance concerns involved.

This part will contain the following chapters:

7

Applying LLMs in Intelligent Operations and Maintenance

With the rapid development of IT services, effective analysis and management of massive data have become increasingly important in practical business applications for enterprises. At the same time, NLP technology has demonstrated excellent capabilities in tasks such as entity recognition and machine translation, and LLMs have achieved significant progress in various NLP downstream tasks. Against this backdrop, **Operations and Maintenance (O&M)** scenarios need to actively incorporate LLMs to enhance traditional automated O&M capabilities, accelerate entry into the field of massive data analysis and processing, and effectively address multiple challenges such as intelligent log O&M, construction of intelligent O&M knowledge bases, and intelligent O&M tickets.

We will be covering the following main topics in this chapter:

- Improving log O&M with LLMs
- Building an intelligent O&M knowledge base
- Automating O&M ticket handling with LLM agents
- Evaluating LLM capabilities for O&M
- Applying multi-agent root cause analysis to microservices

Improving log O&M with LLMs

Logs are an important and widely existing data modality in the field of O&M. However, for O&M teams, accurately processing and analyzing logs has always been an extremely difficult problem. As a result, in daily O&M management, logs are hard to utilize efficiently and lose their inherent value. With the development of LLMs, this situation has improved. In O&M scenarios, personnel benefit from the powerful semantic understanding capabilities of LLMs, making many previously challenging log processing and analysis tasks much simpler. For example, by leveraging the contextual learning abilities of LLMs, O&M staff can achieve highly accurate, automated, end-to-end generation of business code log instrumentation. At the same time, highly efficient parameter fine-tuning techniques of LLMs have also addressed issues in **log parsing**.

Meanwhile, as one of the three main pillars of **observability data**, logs contain important system information and play a key role in O&M management and business continuity assurance. Based on log information, potential system or network issues can be quickly identified, reducing system downtime and improving service availability. Additionally, logs help identify security threats, such as intrusions and fraud, which are crucial for ensuring information security.

Recognizing challenges in log monitoring

Some major issues include: processing massive volumes of log data in real-time scenarios; the lack of unified standards for log formats—logs generated by different applications and devices may differ greatly in structure and content; logs may contain large amounts of normal or irrelevant information, making it harder to identify true anomalies. The constant evolution of system and network environments also leads to ever-changing anomaly patterns, requiring detection methods to be highly adaptable.

In **intelligent log O&M** scenarios, traditional log analysis faces many technical difficulties. Ultimately, it is necessary to apply LLM technologies to enhance applications in log analysis in order to better support business continuity.

To understand how LLMs can improve log operations and maintenance, it is useful to first review what logs capture and how they support daily O&M work.

Concept of logs

Logs are important tools in information technology and network management for recording and tracking the operational status of systems, networks, and applications. These logs are crucial for **system administrators, O&M management personnel**, and **information security management staff.**

They provide detailed information needed for diagnosing problems, monitoring system performance, and ensuring system security. The main types of operational and maintenance logs are as follows:

- **System Logs:** Record the activities of the operating system, such as system startup and shutdown, system errors, hardware failures, and other system-level events
- **Application Logs:** Record the operation history of applications, such as application startup and shutdown, operations performed by the application, internal errors, user activities, and more
- **Security Logs:** Record all security-related events, such as login attempts (successful or failed), permission changes, firewall alerts, network intrusion attempts, and more
- **Network Logs:** Record the status of network devices, such as operational data of routers, switches, load balancers, as well as network traffic and abnormal traffic activities, etc.

After understanding the main types of logs used in O&M, it is useful to look at how these logs move through the operational workflow. In practice, log O&M usually follows a process of collecting log data, analyzing it for signals or anomalies, and responding to the issues revealed by that analysis.

Basic process of log O&M

The basic process of log O&M includes **log collection**, **log analysis**, and **log response**, as shown in *Figure 7.1*.

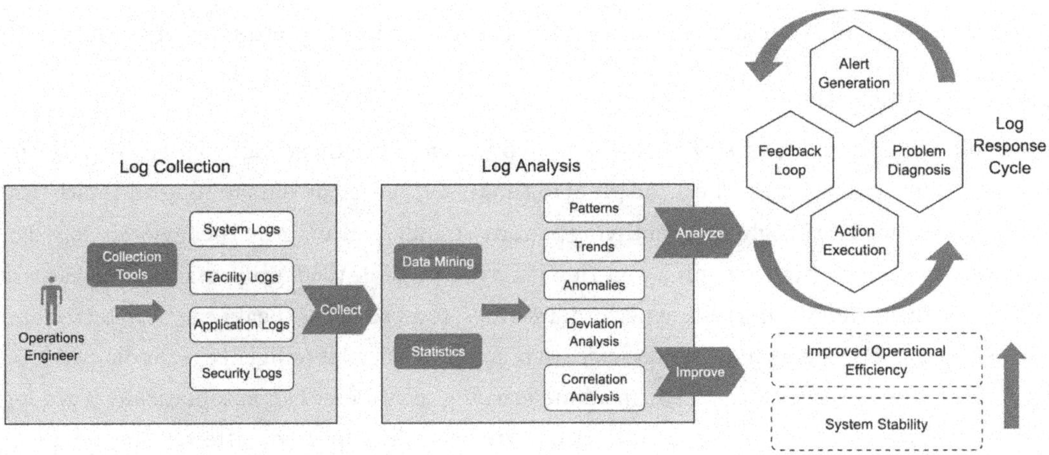

Figure 7.1: Basic process of log O&M

(1) Log collection

Log collection is the first step in log O&M management. It involves collecting log data from various information systems, applications, devices, etc. The collected logs include **system logs, application logs, security logs, network logs**, and so on. The key to the log collection process is to use automated tools to continuously collect data while also ensuring the integrity and timeliness of the log data.

Operations personnel transmit log data to log management systems or data storage media for centralized storage as needed. In the process of dealing with log collection and log management, there are a variety of platforms and tools to choose from, each with its own characteristics and advantages. The combination of **Elasticsearch, Logstash**, and **Kibana** is a very popular open-source log management solution. **Elasticsearch** is used for data storage and search, **Logstash** for log collection and processing, and **Kibana** for data visualization and analysis. In addition, there are also tools such as **Splunk** and **Graylog. Splunk** is also a powerful commercial solution that provides functions for **log collection, monitoring, searching, analysis**, and **visualization**. It is suitable for large-scale log management environments and supports real-time data processing and complex analytical queries. **Graylog** is an open-source log management platform that offers rich features for log collection, storage, querying, and reporting, and is known for its ease of use and robust log processing capabilities. Each of these platforms and tools has its own strengths. When choosing the right log collection platform, it is necessary to decide based on specific business needs, budget, and technical environment. Generally, Elasticsearch and Graylog have advantages in cost control, while Splunk is more comprehensive in functionality and support services.

(2) Log analysis

After logs are collected and stored, the next step is to analyze these logs to identify patterns, trends, and potential issues. The principle of **log analysis** is based on data mining and statistical techniques, providing insights by identifying patterns, trends, and abnormal behaviors in logs. For example, by analyzing failed login log entries, it may be possible to identify unauthorized access in the system; by monitoring system performance logs, resource usage peaks can be detected and future system bottlenecks may be predicted. In practice, artificial intelligence technology can be applied to log analysis. For instance, machine learning techniques can automatically learn log patterns and sound alerts when behaviors deviate from the expected patterns. Such analysis is not limited to detecting known problems but can also predict and prevent upcoming issues through continuous learning.

Overall, log analysis is a complex but crucial process that plays an irreplaceable role in maintaining system stability and security. At the same time, an effective log analysis strategy can greatly enhance the efficiency and responsiveness of operational and maintenance organizations.

(3) Log response

Log response is the final stage in the log management process. Its main goal is to take appropriate action based on the results of log analysis, to resolve issues, optimize system performance, or enhance security. Effective log response not only helps resolve technical problems in a timely manner, but also prevents potential security threats and ensures the continuous and stable operation of the system. The main steps of log response are as follows:

1. **Alert Generation**: Based on analysis results, when abnormal activities or performance metrics exceeding preset thresholds are detected, the log system automatically generates alerts. Alerts are the trigger point of the response process. Their design should avoid being overly sensitive, to reduce false positives, and at the same time not be too sluggish, so as to avoid missing critical events.
2. **Problem Diagnosis:** Upon receiving an alert, the operations team needs to further analyze the relevant log data to diagnose the root cause of the problem. This may include reviewing detailed logs from specific time periods, performance indicators of related systems, and interactions with other systems or applications.
3. **Action Execution:** After diagnosis is complete, the operations team will take appropriate measures depending on the nature of the issue, which may include restarting services, adjusting configurations, updating software or hardware, or optimizing resource allocation, etc.
4. **Feedback Loop:** Lessons learned during the log response process should be fed back into log management and operations processes, serving as the basis for adjusting and optimizing alert settings, analysis procedures, and response strategies

The principle of log response is to quickly and accurately translate log analysis into concrete actions, handling system issues with minimal delay. Effective log response relies on highly automated tools and processes to ensure an immediate response when issues are detected. Automation plays a central role in log response, from automatically triggering alerts to executing predefined response measures, which can greatly increase handling speed and reduce human errors. In addition, advanced analytical techniques such as machine learning can further optimize the response process, enabling **predictive maintenance** to prevent problems before they occur, rather than merely solving existing issues.

In summary, log response is a dynamic, multi-layered process involving rapid transition from data analysis to concrete action, and its effectiveness is directly related to organizational operational efficiency and system stability. Through continuous optimization and technological advancement, log response can become a powerful tool in enterprise information system management.

Tools by capability

LLM-assisted log operations usually build on existing observability and log-management pipelines rather than replacing them. Common tools for log collection, storage, search, and analysis include Elastic Stack or OpenSearch, Splunk, Grafana Loki, Datadog, and Sumo Logic. OpenTelemetry is also becoming an important vendor-neutral standard for collecting logs, metrics, and traces across distributed systems.

In practice, these tools provide the operational data pipeline, while LLMs can be added to help summarize logs, identify abnormal patterns, explain key messages, correlate logs with other context, and recommend troubleshooting steps.

Although this collection-analysis-response workflow is well established, it becomes difficult to manage at scale because logs are large, distributed, inconsistent, and often hard to interpret.

Addressing log O&M pain points with LLMs

Although logs are essential for monitoring system health and diagnosing incidents, their value depends on whether O&M teams can locate the right information, understand what it means, and decide how to respond. In daily operations, these three steps often become the main sources of difficulty.

O&M personnel cannot find abnormal logs

When managing and monitoring IT infrastructure, it is crucial for O&M personnel to discover and identify **abnormal logs**. However, they often face the challenge of being unable to locate abnormal logs, which can be caused by various factors, mainly including the following aspects.

The volume of log data is too large. When log capacity reaches the **TB** or even **PB** level, it not only imposes higher requirements on the log storage system but also significantly increases the complexity of data management, making it extremely difficult for O&M personnel to find valuable information within this massive amount of data—like looking for a needle in a haystack.

Log sources are dispersed. In large distributed systems, logs may be scattered across multiple different servers, devices, and applications. The lack of a unified log collection and management system leads to scattered logs, making it difficult for O&M personnel to access all relevant logs from a central point.

Lack of **log standardization**. In environments without a unified log format and standards, O&M personnel may find it hard to understand and analyze log data coming from different systems. Improper log configuration could result in key information not being recorded. For example, if the log level is set too high, some alerts or error information might not be logged; conversely, it might generate a large amount of redundant information, obscuring important alerts.

O&M personnel cannot understand key logs

O&M personnel may encounter difficulties understanding **key logs**, mainly due to the following two reasons.

The technical nature of **log files** themselves. Because log files often contain highly technical information and professional jargon, lacking relevant knowledge will directly affect the understanding of log content. In addition, as technology updates and iterates, new systems and applications may introduce unfamiliar log formats or new error codes. If O&M personnel fail to update their **knowledge base** in time, it will also affect their understanding of logs.

Complex log formats lead to poor readability. In diversified IT environments, different systems, devices, and applications may generate log files in different formats. If these log files lack a unified format or do not follow industry standards, it greatly increases the difficulty for O&M personnel to interpret logs. Inconsistent log formats mean that O&M staff need to master more parsing skills and invest more time and effort in understanding a variety of log structures and content.

O&M personnel do not know what to do when facing log messages

When facing massive log data, O&M personnel often feel confused, and the reasons can be analyzed from the following three aspects:

- **Lack of clear response procedures or guidance:** O&M personnel often find it difficult to determine what actions to take, the order of priorities, and who to contact during the problem-solving process when faced with specific log events, due to the absence of predefined **response procedures** or **standard operating procedures**. This uncertainty not only delays issue resolution time but may also lead to improper handling of issues.

- **Insufficient automation and tool support:** In many cases, O&M staff may not have adequate tool support to help them effectively analyze and respond to information in logs. The lack of automation tools means that personnel must manually sift through and analyze massive amounts of log data, which is not only inefficient but also prone to errors. Furthermore, if the existing tools cannot provide sufficient analytical depth or are not user-friendly, the difficulty for O&M personnel increases when dealing with complex or voluminous logs.
- **Insufficient expertise and experience:** O&M personnel may lack the specialized knowledge or experience to handle specific types of logs. This situation is common in rapidly evolving IT environments, where logs generated by new technologies or systems may contain new information or error codes that they have not encountered before. If O&M staff do not have an adequate understanding of these new elements, even if they can read the log data, they may not know how to effectively diagnose and resolve issues based on the log contents.

These pain points show why LLMs are useful in log O&M: they can help detect abnormal patterns, interpret complex log messages, and recommend next steps for incident response.

How to address log O&M pain points

The log O&M pain points discussed earlier can be addressed in three connected ways. First, models can help detect abnormal log patterns that are difficult for O&M personnel to find manually. Second, LLMs can help interpret key logs by combining log content with system knowledge, documentation, source code, or enterprise context. Third, LLM-powered workflows can recommend response actions, support fault localization, and guide O&M personnel through standard operating procedures.

Detecting abnormal logs with LLM-assisted analysis

In modern IT infrastructure management, machine learning algorithms are widely used to improve the efficiency and accuracy of log analysis, especially in automatically discovering anomalous logs. Machine learning can help O&M personnel automatically identify abnormal patterns in the system, so as to respond to and deal with potential issues in a timely manner. The following are several key steps for using machine learning algorithms to solve the problem of anomalous logs being difficult to detect.

(1) Data preprocessing

Before using machine learning algorithms, log data needs to be preprocessed. The steps include **data cleaning** (removing irrelevant data, correcting erroneous data), **normalization** (unifying log formats), **feature extraction** (extracting meaningful information from logs as input to the model), etc. Effective data preprocessing can greatly improve the efficiency of model training and prediction accuracy.

(2) Feature engineering

Feature engineering is a vital part of machine learning, involving the selection, modification, and creation of new features to enhance model performance. In log analysis, common features include the **timestamp** of log entries, **source IP addresses**, **error codes**, **operation codes**, etc. Advanced features include keywords or phrases extracted from log text or statistical information based on the event frequency within a time window.

(3) Selecting appropriate machine learning models

Selecting suitable **machine learning models** according to the characteristics of the log data and business needs is essential. For **anomaly detection**, commonly used algorithms include **clustering algorithms**, **distance-based anomaly detection**, and **neural networks**.

Typical clustering algorithms include **K-means** and **DBSCAN**. These **unsupervised learning algorithms** can help identify natural groups in the data, with outliers usually not belonging to any main group. In distance-based anomaly detection, typical examples are the **Isolation Forest** algorithm and the **LOF (Local Outlier Factor)** algorithm, which identify anomalies by considering the distance between data points and their neighbors. Among neural networks, **autoencoders** are a typical example, mainly suitable for handling large-scale data sets and complex data structures. They can learn the normal patterns of data and identify anomalous data that deviate from these patterns.

In 2024, at the *AAAI Conference on Artificial Intelligence*, a paper by Yunzhihui titled *LOGFORMER: A Pre-train and Tuning Pipeline for Log Anomaly Detection* elaborated on how to use machine learning techniques for log anomaly detection. According to the paper, Yunzhihui based their approach on the **Transformer** model and used **adapter fine-tuning** to solve the semantic information sharing issue between different log sources. Log anomaly detection is a key component in the field of **intelligent O&M**. In real industrial scenarios, logs from different sources can vary significantly. Early anomaly detection models only focused on extracting semantics from the log sequences of the same source, resulting in poor generalization to logs from multiple different sources. Retraining detection models with data from unknown log sources is inefficient.

Although there are morphological and syntactic differences among different log sources, they often share the same semantic space. As shown in *Figure 7.2*, if there are similar anomalies from multiple domains, the top shows "Abnormal Program Termination" anomaly analysis for the domains BGL, Thunderbird, and Red Storm, while the bottom shows "Program Not Running" anomaly analysis for the domains BGL, Thunderbird, Spirit, and Liberty.

BGL: **Unusual End of Program**
data storage interrupt
rts: kernel terminated for reason 1004rts: bad message header: [...]
Thunderbird:
kernel: mptscsih: ioc0: attempting task abort! (sc=00000101bddee480)
Red Storm:
DMT 310 Command Aborted: SCSI cmd:2A LUN 2 DMT 310 T:299 a: [...]

BGL: **Program Not Running**
rts panic! - stopping execution
Thunderbird:
pbs mom: Bad file descriptor (9) in tm request, job [job] not running
Spirit:
kernel: GM: LANai is not running. Allowing port=0 open for debugging
Liberty:
kernel: GM: LANai is not running. Allowing port=0 open for debugging

Figure 7.2: Case of similarity anomaly

To address this problem, one example approach, proposed by Yunzhihui, is a unified **Transformer-based log anomaly detection framework** called **LogFormer**, aimed at improving the generalization capability across different log domains. This framework comprises a pre-training phase and an adapter-based fine-tuning phase. Specifically, the log anomaly detection framework first performs pre-training on the source domain to acquire shared semantic knowledge from log data, and then transfers this knowledge to the target domain via shared parameters. In addition, the model introduces a **Log Attention** module to supplement information that is overlooked during log pattern parsing. Results from multiple benchmark experiments demonstrate that **LogFormer** is effective while utilizing fewer trainable parameters and incurring lower training costs. The structure of the LogFormer framework is shown in *Figure 7.3*: first, the **log sequences** are input to the pre-trained language model to extract features; the **Log-Attention encoder** is then trained on the source domain to obtain shared semantic information; finally, the encoder is initialized, and knowledge transfer to the target domain is accomplished by adjusting the target domain **adapter**'s parameters.

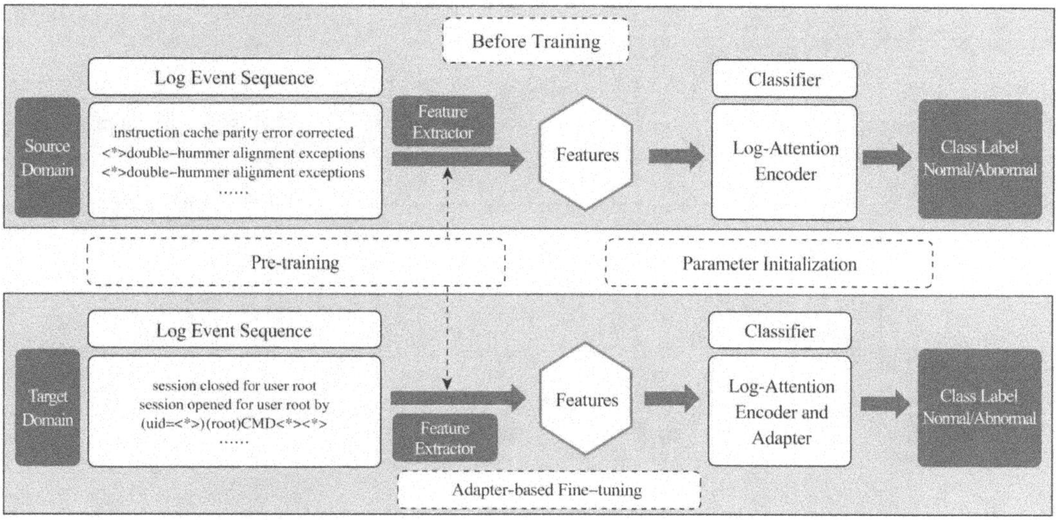

Figure 7.3: LogFormer framework structure

These steps describe the general machine learning pipeline for anomaly detection. Recent Transformer-based approaches build on this foundation by learning shared semantic patterns across log sources, making anomaly detection more adaptable in environments where logs come from different systems and formats.

Understanding the LogFormer workflow

LogFormer addresses the above issues in two working phases: the **Log Attention Encoding Phase** and the **Cross-domain Adapter Fine-tuning Phase**.

Preserving log semantics with Log Attention

The **Log Attention Encoding Phase** preserves semantic knowledge shared between different domains. Specifically, to avoid information loss caused by log pattern parsing, the **Log Attention** module models log sequences and makes additional use of parameter information that is neglected in log pattern parsing, thereby achieving better performance. Compared to traditional structures, the model additionally incorporates parameter information lost during log pattern parsing. The LogFormer model structure is depicted in *Figure 7.4*, with the left part showing **multi-head encoding** and the right part showing **parameter encoding**.

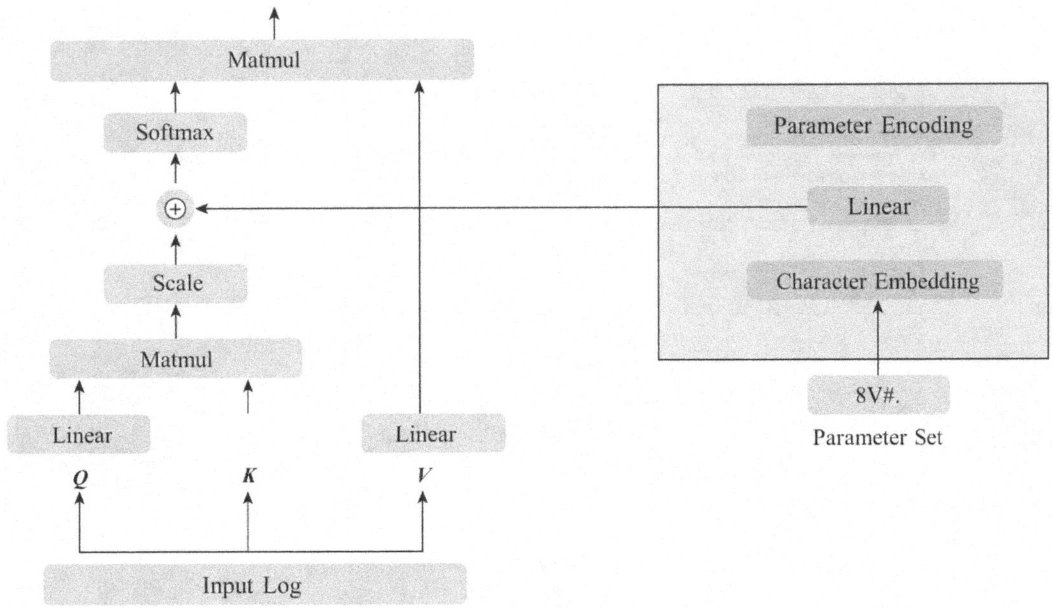

Figure 7.4: LogFormer model structure

Here, **Softmax** represents the regression model, **Matmul** indicates matrix multiplication, **Scale** denotes matrix division, and the corresponding formula for Log Attention is:

$$LogAttention = Softmax\left(\frac{QK^T}{\sqrt{\frac{d}{h}}} + \emptyset_p\right)V$$

Improving cross-domain generalization with adapter fine-tuning

To further enhance the model's generalization capability across different log sources, Yunzhihui introduced an adapter-based fine-tuning structure and designed a parallel-structured log encoding adapter. This adapter works in parallel with the Log Attention layer and the feedforward layer. During training, only the adapter's parameters are updated with the target domain log data. The relevant process is shown in *Figure 7.5*, where *N* denotes the number of encoder layers. The left part illustrates the **Log Attention Encoder** with the parallel **adapter** inserted, and the right part shows the structure of the adapter, which consists of a **down-projection layer** and an **up-projection layer**.

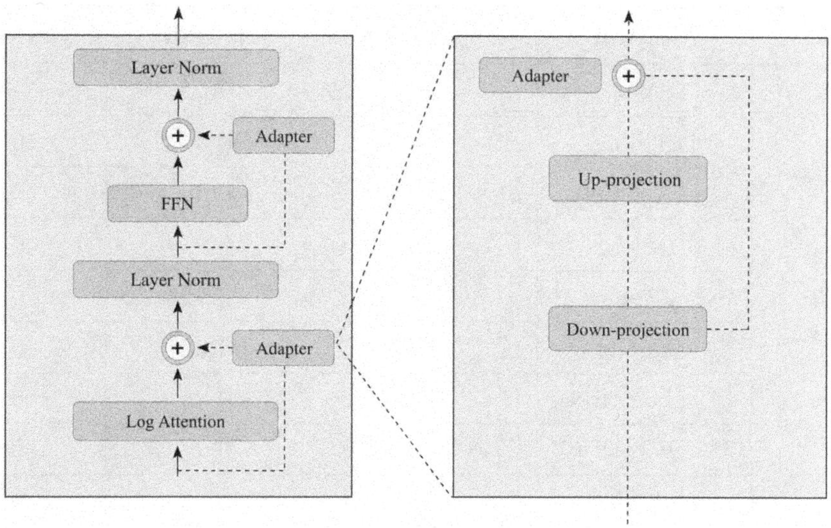

Figure 7.5: Adapter fine-tuning process

Yunzhihui conducted experiments on three datasets from **LogHub**, where the **HDFS** dataset was generated and collected from the Amazon EC2 platform, and the **Thunderbird** and **BGL** datasets contain logs collected from two supercomputer systems at Sandia National Laboratories (SNL). The relevant results are shown in *Figure 7.6*. In the sampled data, the **message** refers to the original log string, and **log sequences** are extracted either by **ID method** or **sliding window method.**

Dataset	Category	Number of Messages	Number of Anomalies	Number of Templates	Number of Error Types
HDFS	Distributed System	11M	17K	49	53
BGL	Supercomputer	5M	40K	1424	143
Thunderbird	Supercomputer	10M	123K	1092	95

Figure 7.6: Table comparing HDFS, BGL, and Thunderbird datasets

In terms of data preprocessing, for the HDFS dataset, log sequences are extracted by `block_ID`. For the BGL and Thunderbird datasets, log sequences are generated using a non-overlapping **sliding window** (window size of 20). In this practice, the classic log pattern parsing algorithm **Drain** is used for pattern parsing. For each dataset, considering the time-varying nature of logs, it is common to select the first **80%** (divided by log timestamps) of log sequences for training, and the remaining **20%** for testing. Experimental results show that **LogFormer** achieved SOTA results on the HDFS, BGL and Thunderbird datasets, as shown in *Figure 7.7*. **LogFormer-s** refers to the model trained from scratch, while **LogFormer-p** refers to the model using pre-training but not adjusted with adapters.

Dataset	Method	Precision	Recall	F1 Score
HDFS	SVN	0.31	0.65	0.41
	DeepLog	0.83	0.87	0.85
	LogAnomaly	0.86	0.89	0.87
	PLELog	0.88	0.93	0.90
	LogRobust	0.88	0.95	0.91
	ChatGpt	0.74	0.82	0.78
	LogFormer-s	0.95	0.96	0.95
	LogFormer-p	0.96	0.97	0.96
	LogFormer	0.97	0.98	0.98
BGL	SVN	0.22	0.56	0.32
	DeepLog	0.14	0.81	0.24
	LogAnomaly	0.19	0.78	0.31
	PLELog	0.92	0.96	0.94
	LogRobust	0.92	0.96	0.94
	ChatGpt	0.77	0.71	0.74
	LogFormer-s	0.96	0.97	0.97
Thunderbird	SVN	0.34	0.91	0.46
	DeepLog	0.48	0.89	0.62
	LogAnomaly	0.51	0.97	0.67
	PLELog	0.85	0.94	0.89
	LogRobust	0.89	0.96	0.92
	ChatGpt	0.84	0.79	0.81
	LogFormer-s	0.94	0.98	0.96
	LogFormer-p	0.97	0.99	0.98
	LogFormer	0.99	0.99	0.99

Figure 7.7: Table comparing precision, recall, and F1 score of log analysis methods on different datasets

Evaluating the effect of pre-training and adapter fine-tuning

In addition to the main experimental results, Yunzhihui also conducted **data ablation experiments**. To verify the effectiveness of pre-training, the performance of LogFormer-s and LogFormer-p was compared at the data level. Yunzhihui chose BGL as the pre-training log source due to the diversity of its log templates, and compared the two strategies—**pre-training** and **training from scratch**—in terms of **loss** and **F1 scores**. *Figure 7.8* shows the loss and F1 score curves during the training process. The results indicate that fine-tuning after pre-training converges faster than training from scratch, demonstrating that knowledge learned from the source domain is of significant value.

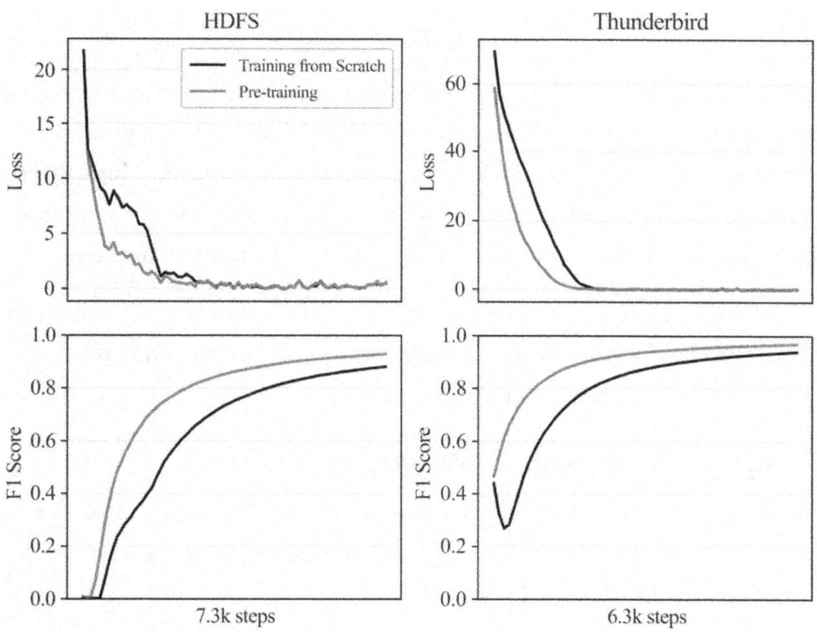

Figure 7.8: Loss and F1 score curves

Experiments have proven that **pre-training** can accelerate convergence without sacrificing performance, but fine-tuning is usually costly and important. Therefore, in the experiments, Yunzhihui adopted adapter-based fine-tuning, which adds extra trainable parameters to obtain a compact model for log anomaly detection. To verify the effectiveness of adapter-based fine-tuning, **LogFormer-p** was compared with **LogFormer** on the HDFS and Thunderbird datasets. As shown in *Figure 7.9*, the F1 value generated by LogFormer (with an average increase of 1%) is slightly higher than direct fine-tuning of the pre-trained model on both datasets. In addition, adapter-based fine-tuning used only 3.5% to 5.5% of trainable parameters, requiring very few parameter adjustments.

Method	Layer	Parameters	HDFS	Thunderbird
Fine-tuning	1	7.2M	0.945	0.969
	2	14.3M	0.962	0.981
	4	28.5M	0.961	0.980
Adapter Fine-tuning	1	0.4M	0.957	0.972
	2	0.6M	0.974	0.997
	4	1M	0.981	0.998

Figure 7.9: Value test results

According to the experimental results, LogFormer is a **pre-training and fine-tuning process flow** for log anomaly detection, which includes a pre-training phase and an adapter-based fine-tuning phase. To better encode log sequence information, Yunzhihui proposed a **log attention module processing method.** Experiments also showed that LogFormer has fewer trainable parameters and lower training costs, and its performance surpasses most baseline models.

Detecting abnormal logs is only the first step. After an anomaly is found, O&M personnel still need to understand what the log means, which system or component it relates to, and what contextual information is needed to interpret it correctly.

Interpreting key logs with LLMs and RAG

To address the issue that O&M personnel cannot understand logs, logs must first be classified. Typically, logs can be divided into three types: common open-source logs, enterprise internal system logs, and specialized domain logs.

First of all, for open-source logs, **LLMs** already has good analysis capabilities, and using model fine-tuning (**SFT**) technology can slightly improve the parsing capability for open-source component logs. However, as **base models** are updated and iterated, the improvement is often less than that brought by the new generation of base models. Therefore, the evaluation of open-source LLMs has become particularly important.

Secondly, **enterprise internal system logs** need to be addressed with the assistance of **RAG technology**. Typically, for log data within an enterprise's private domain, the internal information system needs to provide related internal information, including structured data and source code data, etc. This type of information is usually referred to as **Feed**. The interaction process between Feed and LLMs is shown in *Figure 7.10*, which can realize error analysis of log call stacks and locate source code, with the LLM ultimately providing an analysis result.

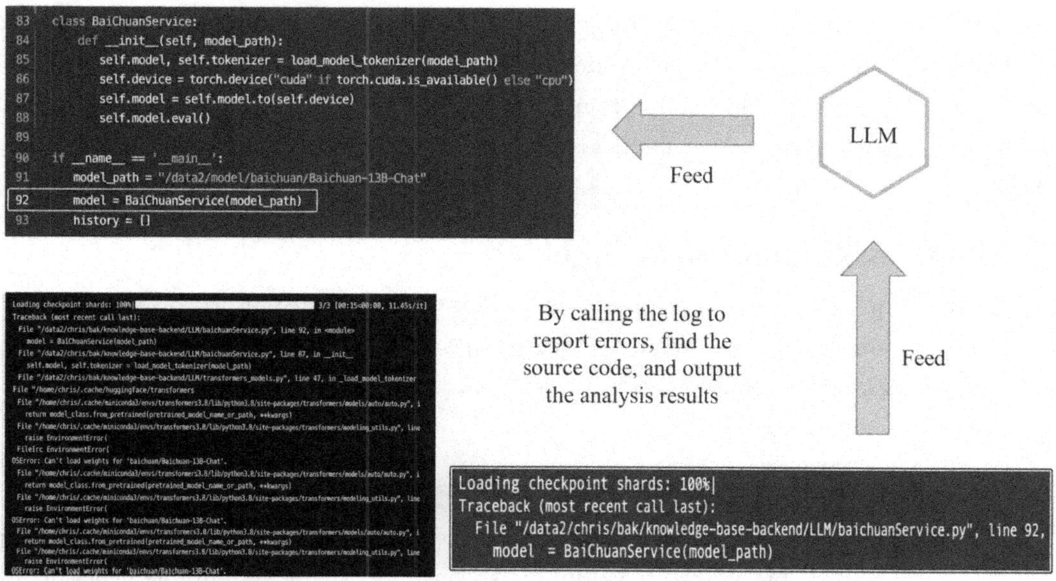

Figure 7.10: The interaction process between Feed and LLMs

There is also a typical scenario in structured information: by leveraging LLMs, log information can be integrated with third-party systems (such as interface documentation systems) for interpreting logs, as illustrated in *Figure 7.11*.

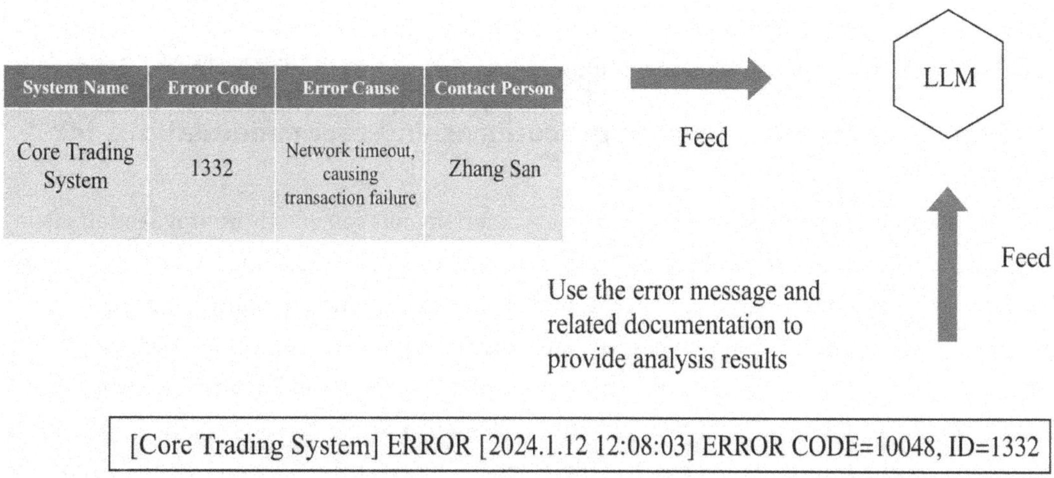

Figure 7.11: LLMs interpret logs through third-party systems

Finally, professional logs are not limited to a specific open-source component, such as **ELK**, **Prometheus**, **Clickhouse**, etc., nor to certain proprietary software. The key lies in collecting more data in specific niche domains, and in combining RAG technologies for targeted optimization, ultimately achieving analytical capabilities in specific topics that far surpass those of open-source LLMs.

Guiding O&M responses with LLMs

Faced with complex log data, operations personnel often feel at a loss, especially when trying to quickly pinpoint the source of faults, execute standard operating procedures, and provide feedback on log analysis results. The application of LLMs can help operations personnel better solve the following problems.

Solving the problem of rapid fault localization

When a fault is discovered and needs to be located through logs, quickly identifying the problem and finding the responsible person for handling it is a key step. Usually, system emergency plans need to provide a clear list of responsible personnel and information delivery avenues, clearly defining responsible persons for various common faults and integrating this information into the log management system. For example, operations personnel can configure automatic notification mechanisms for each type of error or alert to ensure that relevant technical staff quickly receive fault information. Operations personnel can also use intelligent troubleshooting tools, such as fault diagnosis systems based on LLMs, which can analyze log data, automatically infer the severity level of issues, and assign them to the appropriate team or individual according to rules.

Providing standard operating procedures and recommendations for operations personnel

The use of standard operating procedures and automation tools can greatly improve the efficiency of operations personnel in handling logs and faults. Developing and refining standard operating procedures for operations is a good approach; typically, operations personnel need to formulate detailed SOPs for various common log-indicated issues. These manuals should include step-by-step instructions, required tools, precautions, etc., ensuring that even inexperienced operations personnel can resolve problems step-by-step. Implement automated response tools, deploying automation scripts and tools (such as **Ansible**, **Chef**, or **Puppet**) to automatically handle common log events and faults. For instance, services can be automatically restarted, disk space can be cleaned up, or systems can be rolled back to the most recent stable state.

Improving the feedback mechanism of the log platform

An effective **feedback mechanism** ensures that the **log platform** continuously improves and better serves operational and maintenance needs. Firstly, regarding the integration of **feedback channels,** operations personnel integrate feedback channels into the log analysis platform, allowing users to quickly report issues, make improvement suggestions, or request assistance. Secondly, regular review and updates are essential. Operations personnel regularly review collected feedback, analyze the usage and user satisfaction of the log platform, and periodically update log processing logic, user interfaces, and features based on this information to ensure the platform can adapt to ever-changing IT environments and user needs.

An example of rapid fault localization is described, as shown in *Figure 7.12*. The system log feedback error is as follows:

```
[Info:Businessservice , event hook register util v2.Event hookregister.event register:801
componentC2023-11-14 07:46:00ode="upload mapping enterprise role" userType="system"
finish : Accessgovernance Event Register ] Error Event not found.
```

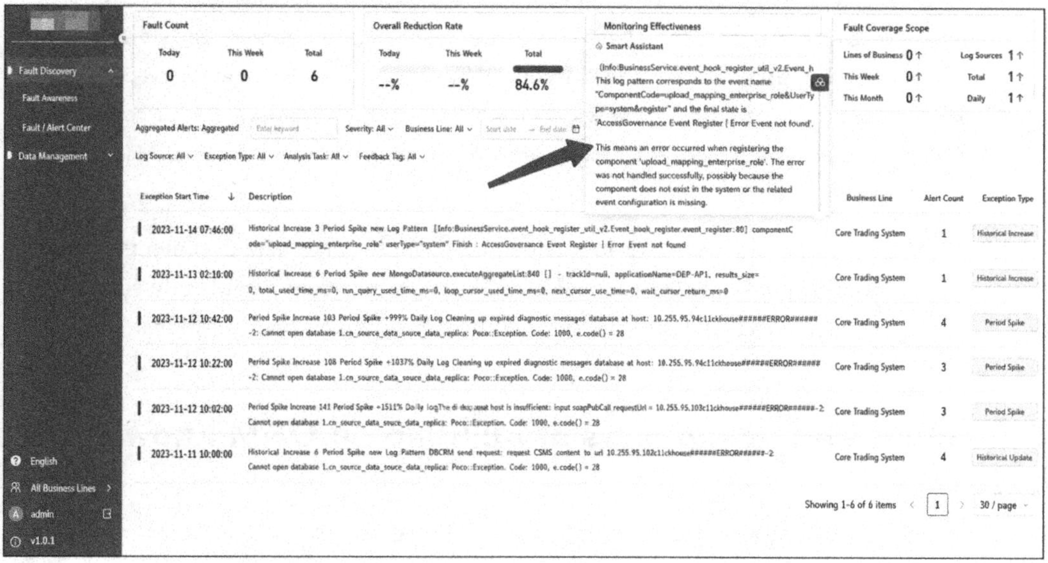

Figure 7.12: Rapid fault localization based on logs

After analysis by a log LLM, this alert indicates that there was an error when the system attempted to register a component named **upload mapping enterprise role**, and the error was not successfully handled. This component is not a business-blocking component in the system and has a low priority.

After examining how LLMs can help O&M teams detect, interpret, and respond to log events, the next step is to look at how operational knowledge can be organized and reused. An intelligent O&M knowledge base gives teams a structured way to store troubleshooting guides, system documentation, historical cases, and domain knowledge, while LLMs make that knowledge easier to search, summarize, and apply during daily operations.

Building an intelligent O&M knowledge base

This is an instance of the **Retrieval-Augmented Generation** (**RAG**) pattern, applied to the O&M knowledge-base domain. A knowledge base is a system or database in which an organization or institution centrally stores and manages knowledge and information. It is a structured knowledge management tool used to collect, organize, store, and share various types of knowledge, such as documents, manuals, guides, and case studies. The aim of a knowledge base is to help people easily access and share knowledge, improve work efficiency, and enhance problem-solving capabilities.

> **Tools by capability**
>
> An intelligent O&M knowledge base typically combines document storage, retrieval, vector search, and LLM-based answer generation. Common vector stores and retrieval components include Pinecone, Weaviate, Milvus, Faiss, and pgvector. LangChain and LlamaIndex are widely used orchestration frameworks for connecting documents, embeddings, vector stores, retrieval logic, prompts, and LLMs into RAG workflows.
>
> These tools provide the technical foundation for turning O&M documents, troubleshooting guides, FAQs, runbooks, and historical incident records into searchable knowledge that an LLM can use when answering operational questions.

Difficulties and advantages of building an O&M knowledge base

Building a traditional knowledge base involves the following steps:

1. Determining the scope and objectives of the knowledge base
2. Collecting and organizing knowledge materials
3. Structuring and classifying knowledge
4. Selecting appropriate knowledge base tools and platforms
5. Designing user interfaces and search functions

6. Establishing a knowledge base maintenance mechanism
7. Iterating and continuously improving the knowledge base

In an O&M context, these steps need to account for the specific kinds of operational knowledge that teams use during troubleshooting, deployment, monitoring, and recovery.

In the O&M field, an **O&M knowledge base** generally contains various types of information related to system operation, management, and maintenance. For example, system architecture and topology diagrams, configuration documents, operating manuals, troubleshooting guides, backup and recovery strategies, performance optimization recommendations, update and maintenance logs, FAQs, etc. This information can help O&M teams understand system architecture, configuration, and operational status, as well as guide them in handling common issues and failures.

Challenges in building an O&M knowledge base

Although these knowledge sources are valuable, turning them into a usable and maintainable knowledge base presents several practical challenges:

- **Knowledge Organization and Classification:** Organizing and classifying vast amounts of knowledge is a complex task, requiring the establishment of reasonable classification standards and systems so that users can easily obtain the required knowledge.
- **Knowledge Updating and Maintenance:** A knowledge base needs regular updating and maintenance, including adding new knowledge, updating existing knowledge, deleting outdated knowledge, etc., and establishing effective mechanisms to ensure the timeliness and quality of knowledge.
- **User Experience and Search Effectiveness:** Designing user-friendly interfaces and search functions is key. User habits and needs must be considered, providing convenient search and navigation capabilities to ensure that users can quickly find the knowledge they need.
- **Knowledge Protection and Security:** For certain sensitive or internal knowledge, knowledge protection and security issues must be fully considered. Proper permission management and access control mechanisms should be established to ensure the security and confidentiality of knowledge.

These challenges explain why LLMs are useful in O&M knowledge-base scenarios: they can help organize, retrieve, summarize, and apply operational knowledge more effectively than keyword-based systems alone.

Advantages of combining O&M knowledge bases with LLMs

By combining the O&M knowledge base with LLMs, one can leverage powerful language understanding and generation capabilities obtained from training on massive textual data. This is mainly used for automatic question answering, text summarization, semantic analysis, and other tasks. Therefore, compared with traditional O&M knowledge bases, the combination of LLMs and knowledge bases offers the following advantages:

- **Automated Knowledge Extraction and Classification**: LLMs can automatically extract and retrieve knowledge by training on vast amounts of textual data. They can recognize **entities**, **relationships**, and **concepts** within text, helping to build the classification structures and labels of knowledge bases.
- **Automated Question Answering and Problem Solving**: Based on the language understanding and generation abilities of LLMs, they can be used to automatically answer user queries and provide direct knowledge lookup and solutions. In O&M knowledge bases, this can be used for quickly locating and retrieving specific knowledge points.
- **Text Summarization and Knowledge Distillation**: LLMs can automatically perform **text summarization** and **knowledge distillation**, extracting key information and main viewpoints from large amounts of text to help O&M personnel quickly understand and acquire knowledge.
- **Clustering and Association Analysis**: LLMs can cluster texts and perform **association analysis** to identify similarities and connections between texts. This can be used for related recommendations and knowledge association analysis in knowledge bases, helping O&M personnel discover more relevant knowledge.
- **Knowledge Enhancement and Supplementation**: Knowledge bases can be enhanced and supplemented by integrating LLMs. Through interaction with these models, the knowledge generated by models can be combined with manually curated knowledge, improving the coverage and quality of the O&M knowledge base. To support these capabilities, an O&M knowledge base needs broad coverage across both technical domains and common operational tasks.

  Many leading enterprises, during the process of building **O&M knowledge bases**, have accumulated vast and high-quality O&M datasets, covering many common areas in the O&M field, including:

  - Information security
  - Applications

- System architecture
- Software architecture
- Middleware
- Networks
- Operating systems
- Infrastructure
- Databases

Each area's dataset also contains multiple tasks, such as:

- O&M knowledge Q&A
- Deployment
- Monitoring
- Troubleshooting
- Performance optimization
- Log analysis
- Script writing
- Backup
- Recovery

On the basis of these high-quality O&M data, combined with the enterprise's internal private O&M data, companies can quickly build O&M knowledge bases based on LLMs, enhancing O&M personnel's ability to solve operational issues.

Once the purpose, content, and advantages of an LLM-enhanced O&M knowledge base are clear, the next step is to examine how such a system can be built in practice.

Technical pathway for building an operations knowledge base

Building an intelligent O&M knowledge base requires more than collecting documents in one place. The system needs a clear construction plan, a way to process and structure different document types, and a retrieval workflow that allows LLMs to use the right operational knowledge when answering user questions. The following steps show how these parts fit together in practice.

Overall construction plan for the operations knowledge base

The construction plan for the operations knowledge base includes the following four steps, as shown in *Figure 7.13*.

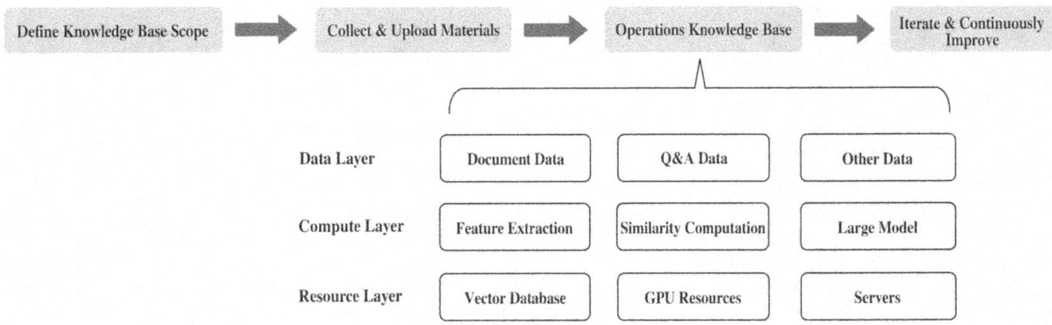

Figure 7.13: Overall construction plan for the operations knowledge base

1. **Requirements Analysis:** Clarify the objectives, scope, and target audience of the knowledge base
2. **Data Collection:** Collect and organize both internal and external company documents, including data from various sources
3. **Formulate the Operations Knowledge Base Plan:** Conduct data preprocessing, split and store documents so that LLMs can better understand document information; deploy LLMs and coordinate scheduling of computing resources to fully utilize existing resources
4. **Iteration and Update of the Knowledge Base:** Regularly evaluate and optimize the operations knowledge base

Among these steps, document preprocessing and structuring are especially important because they determine how effectively the knowledge base can retrieve relevant information and how accurately the LLM can use that information to answer O&M questions. The next subsection focuses on this part of the workflow in more detail.

Document structuring and decomposition algorithms

When building an operations knowledge base, most data exist in the form of documents. Common document formats include docx, pdf, txt, csv, etc. These document data come in various styles and have varying quality. How to handle these documents is critical to ensuring effective Q&A performance of the knowledge base. Therefore, it is necessary to use document structuring and decomposition algorithms to fully recognize and understand the semantic and structural information within the documents.

Usually, hierarchical splitting is chosen based on **headings**, while retaining the text's context and structural information. This approach is especially suitable for handling structured documents such as **reports** and **tutorials**, and helps improve the effectiveness of text vectorization. When building the operations knowledge base and facing massive amounts of knowledge, the document structuring and decomposition algorithm needs to consider the overall context and the relationships among sentences and phrases within the text, resulting in more comprehensive vector representations that capture a wider range of meanings and topics in the text. The relevant **document decomposition steps** are shown in *Figure 7.14*.

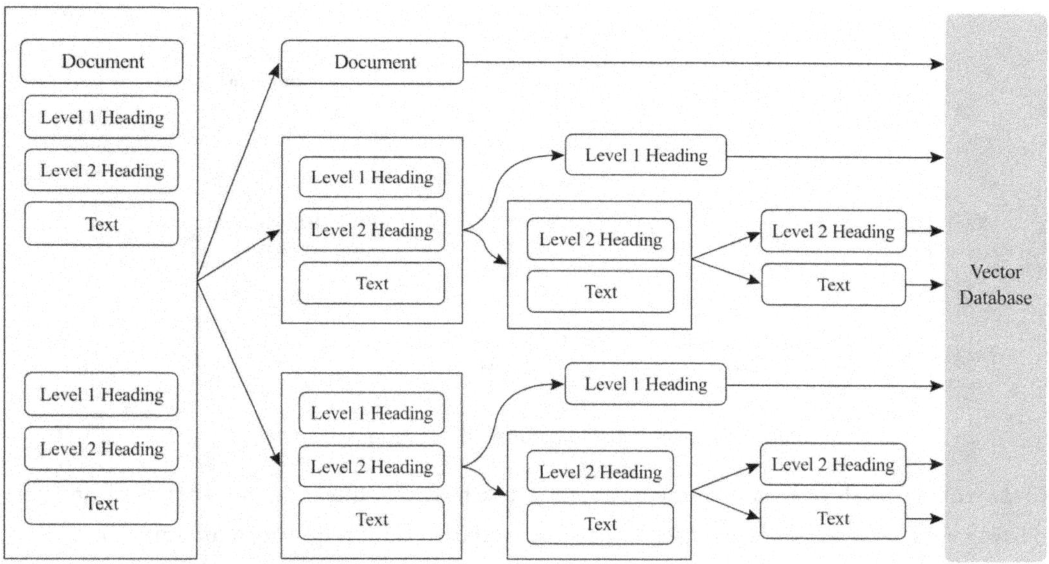

Figure 7.14: Document decomposition steps

At the same time, many enterprises have found in practice that they usually already have their own knowledge base systems in place (such as **Wiki**, **Confluence**, etc.). These knowledge bases have accumulated a large amount of internal knowledge over years of development. Due to user habits, data security, and other factors, enterprises are often reluctant to migrate their existing knowledge bases. To address this, LLMs support interfacing with these internal knowledge bases and decomposing the related structured documents. The specific process is shown in *Figure 7.15*.

A complete operations knowledge base construction process includes three main workflows: **knowledge base construction process, knowledge base Q&A process,** and **interfacing with existing knowledge bases process.**

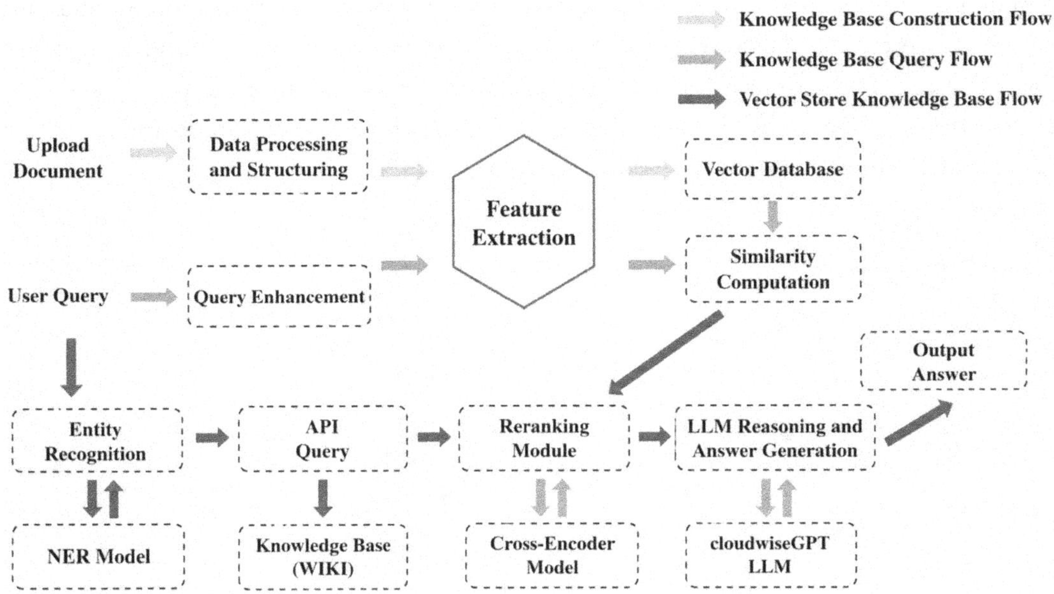

Figure 7.15: Decomposition process of structured documents

These workflows show how documents are ingested, how user questions are answered, and how existing enterprise knowledge bases can be connected without requiring a full migration.

In the knowledge base construction phase, a **structured splitting algorithm** is used to segment and store various documents uploaded by users (such as docx, pdf, txt, etc.), and an **embedding lightweight model** is used to vectorize the split document fragments, after which the information is stored in a **vector database**.

During the knowledge base Q&A phase, the user's input question is first processed with **Query Enhancement**. A **LLM** is used to enrich and enhance the user's question in order to retrieve more relevant document fragments. Based on the **structured splitting algorithm**, the contextual information of the relevant document fragments is located. After obtaining sufficient document fragments, a **reranking model** selects and orders the fragments, filtering out some irrelevant information. The resulting document fragments are then concatenated with Q&A prompts from the knowledge base and passed to a LLM to generate the final answer, which is returned to the user.

When integrating with existing knowledge bases, the characteristics of external knowledge base retrieval interfaces are used. **Entity recognition** (using an **NER model**) is performed on the user's input to extract the main keywords, then the retrieval interface of the existing knowledge base is called to obtain the corresponding document content.

After the construction workflow is established, the value of the knowledge base becomes clearer through practical O&M question-answering scenarios.

Application cases of operations knowledge bases

Knowledge bases based on LLMs are widely used in the operations field. Unlike traditional knowledge bases that can only retrieve relevant documents or data—requiring users to further read, analyze, and understand them—a knowledge base built on an LLM can directly understand the user's question and, combined with existing documents, analyze, summarize, and provide a final answer. As shown in *Figure 7.16*, in response to the question, "I want to check the health status of the Docker container nginx every 30 seconds. How should I write the Docker command?", the operations knowledge base provides a relatively accurate and comprehensive reply.

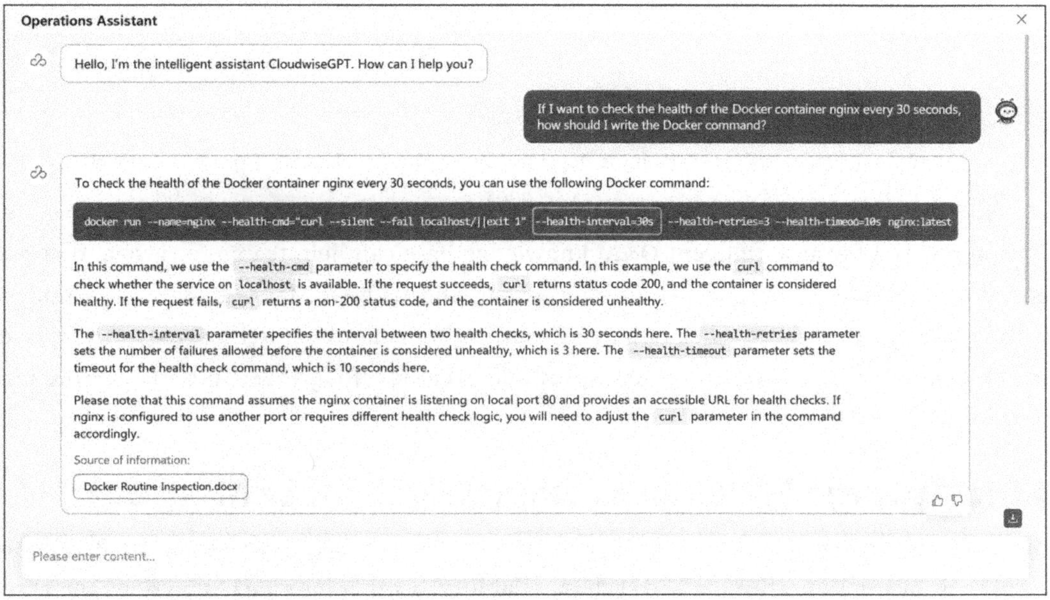

Figure 7.16: Query about checking the health status of the Docker container nginx every 30 seconds

For comparison, we can replace the `30 seconds` in the above question with `60 seconds`. The reply given by the operations knowledge base is shown in *Figure 7.17*, which correctly replaces the required parameter in the command. After copying, operations personnel can run it directly in the command line, thereby significantly improving operational efficiency.

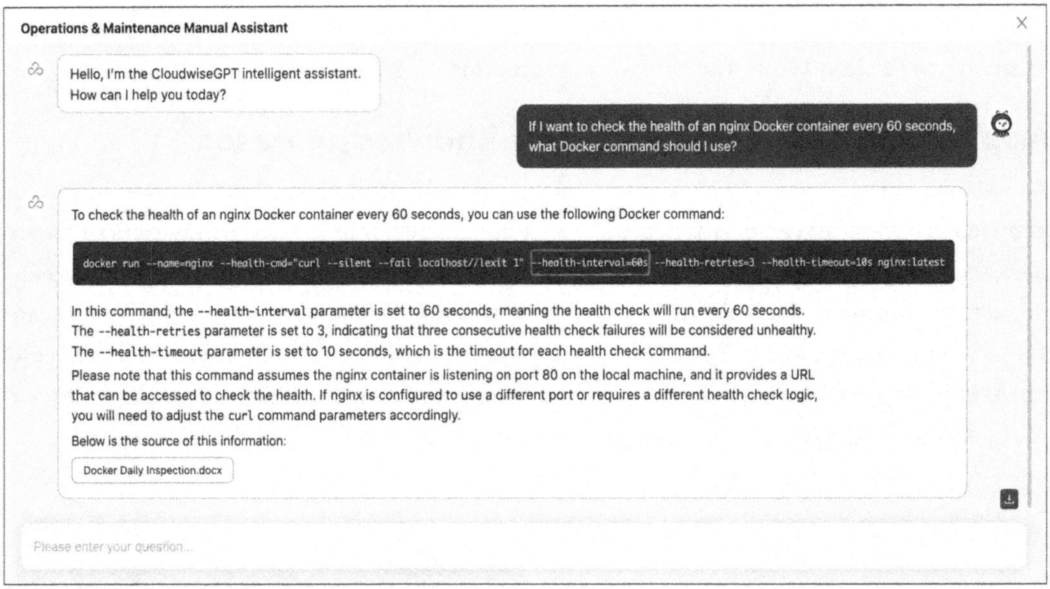

Figure 7.17: Query about checking the health status of the Docker container nginx every 60 seconds

After showing how an intelligent O&M knowledge base can help teams retrieve and apply operational knowledge, the chapter now moves to another daily O&M workflow: ticket handling. In this context, LLM agents can help summarize ticket information, interpret user requests, retrieve relevant knowledge, call business systems, and guide tickets through the appropriate resolution process.

Automating O&M ticket handling with LLM agents

Digital O&M services can help O&M teams provide various O&M services, such as **release**, **assurance**, **business continuity**, and **system reliability**, to other internal IT functions and even business teams, supporting enterprises in digital transformation and change. **Intelligent O&M tickets** is a key component of digital O&M services.

Intelligent O&M tickets bring together several capabilities discussed earlier in the chapter: knowledge retrieval, business-context understanding, tool use, and workflow automation. To understand how LLM agents can improve ticket handling, it is useful to first look at the role tickets play in O&M workflows, then examine why general-purpose LLMs are not sufficient on their own, and finally see how an agent-based framework can support practical ticket processing.

Tools by capability

LLM-assisted ticket handling is usually integrated with existing IT service management, incident management, or on-call platforms. Common platforms include Jira Service Management, ServiceNow, PagerDuty, and Opsgenie. In these environments, LLM agents can help summarize ticket content, classify incidents, retrieve relevant knowledge-base articles, suggest next steps, call internal APIs, and route tickets to the right team or workflow.

The ticketing platform remains the system of record, while the LLM agent provides an intelligence layer for understanding, summarizing, and acting on ticket information.

The role of intelligent O&M tickets

O&M ticket management is an important part of O&M services and a commonly used basic service within O&M organizations. In the O&M service process, if users want to know the progress and handling comments after submitting an incident ticket, they need to check the solution status and handling comments of the nodes on the **ticket details page**. When O&M engineers are handling tickets, they need to view the basic information of the **incident ticket** submitted by the user or review the ticket information processed by previous nodes, which requires looking at the event's basic information fields, the **solution status**, and the **handling comments** of previous nodes. O&M managers, when wanting to know the solution status and solutions of different nodes for an incident ticket, need to check the form information of different nodes. For all users of the ticket management process, if they need to understand the **overview information** of an incident ticket, they all need to spend time viewing the relevant form fields. Existing O&M service management tools lack a way for users to quickly grasp ticket information.

For example, an intelligent O&M ticketing platform can use an agent-based workflow to summarize ticket status, progress, and handling context for different stakeholders, as shown in *Figure 7.18*.

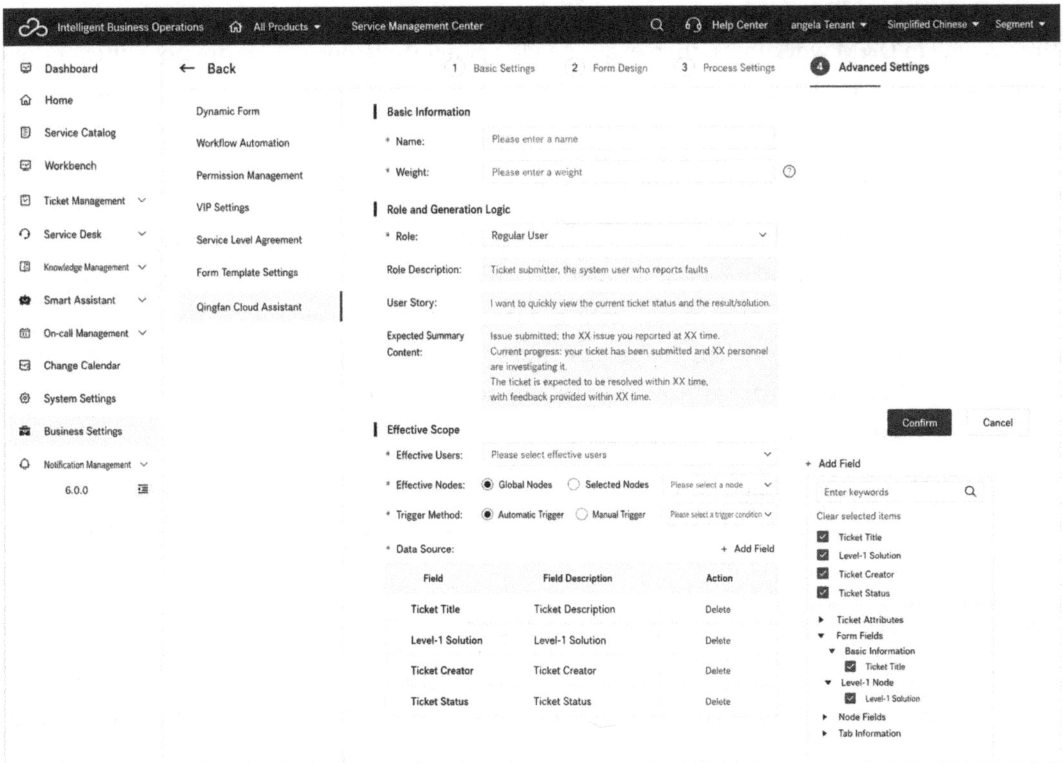

Figure 7.18: An intelligent O&M ticketing platform's function page

This kind of ticket summarization requires more than text generation. The system must understand ticket fields, user roles, business rules, historical context, and available APIs, which is why the technical pathway relies on agent-based orchestration.

Technical pathways for building intelligent O&M ticketing

Building intelligent O&M ticket workflows requires more than adding an LLM to an existing ticketing system. The system must understand business-specific ticket content, retrieve relevant operational knowledge, call internal APIs, and produce stable outputs that different users can trust. The following discussion first examines the technical challenges involved, then introduces an agent-based framework for handling them.

Challenges of current O&M LLM technology

In the design of intelligent O&M tickets, empowering O&M businesses with LLM-related technologies requires solving two problems: first, how to teach LLMs to handle actual O&M business, and second, how to balance stability and flexibility in the models. The main challenge in choosing a technical path is that LLMs only possess general capabilities and are difficult to use directly for specific business problems.

This challenge is easier to see in business-service scenarios where the model must not only understand the user's request, but also call internal systems and follow organization-specific rules. Taking the operator's O&M customer service scenario as an example, when a customer inquires, such as "My phone number is 130XXXXXXXX, my name is John Doe, and the last six digits of my ID are 000000. Please check my phone bill," the typical reply from a general-purpose GPT model is shown in *Figure 7.19*.

> I apologize, as a large language model, I cannot directly access your mobile account to check your phone bill. However, I can provide you with some suggestions to help you check your phone bill.
>
> 1. Call customer service: You can call your mobile network operator (such as China Mobile, China Unicom, or China Telecom) customer service number and follow the voice prompts to check your bill.
> 2. Visit the operator's official website: You can log in to your mobile network operator's official website and use your phone number and service password to check your bill.
> 3. Download the operator's app: You can download and install your mobile network operator's app and log in with your phone number and service password to check your bill.
> 4. SMS inquiry: You can also send a specific SMS command to the operator's customer service number to check your bill. The specific operation method may vary depending on the operator, so it is recommended that you check the relevant information or call customer service for consultation.
>
> I hope these suggestions can help you! If you have any other questions, feel free to ask me.

Figure 7.19: Example of a generic GPT reply

A general LLM can understand concepts such as phone numbers and names, and can recognize the user's need to query their phone bill, but does not yet possess the professional business capabilities of an operator O&M customer service agent. Therefore, in applying LLMs to actual O&M business, the core issue is how to cultivate their ability to solve real O&M business problems based on their general knowledge. In intelligent O&M ticket scenarios, **intelligent agent technology** can endow LLMs with the ability to execute business logic and call tools.

In addition, the advantage of LLMs lies in their outstanding **generalization ability**, meaning they can flexibly respond to different input information and process it accordingly. However, from a technical standpoint, no LLM can guarantee solving all problems 100% of the time. Therefore, in the intelligent O&M ticket scenario, rational system design is still required to ensure that the **LLM agent** has both the stability and flexibility to handle problems.

An O&M LLM framework based on agent technology

Based on the intelligent O&M ticket scenario, YunZhiHui has designed an **agent framework** called the **multi-level API selector**. The framework, as shown in *Figure 7.20*, mainly consists of four parts:

1. **Pattern Recognition**: Follows rule matching and executes the matched model according to established logic
2. **Semantic Retrieval**: Establishes a preset ticket knowledge base, vectorizes the contents of the ticket database and user requests via embedding, and retrieves based on vector similarity
3. **LLM Tool Selection**: Used for situations that require calling external APIs. The LLM determines, based on the user request and available API list, whether to use an external API and which API to use.
4. **Output results**: Generate the final result based on the API return results and the user's request content

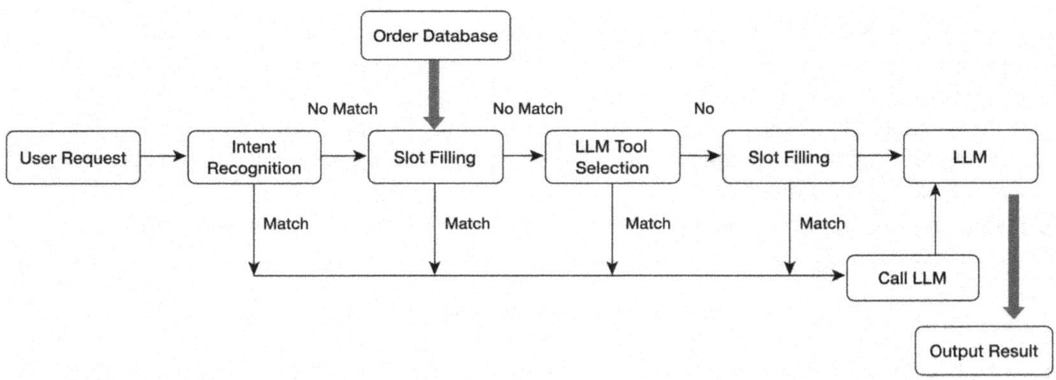

Figure 7.20: Multi-level API selector framework

The multi-level API selector provides a basic structure for routing requests and calling tools, but more complex ticket scenarios often require multi-step reasoning, review, memory, and planning.

The traditional **multi-level API selector framework** only involves single-step reasoning (tool selection, generating the final result), making it unable to support **complex logical reasoning** scenarios, such as multi-path chain reasoning, dual-Agent review, tree-structured reasoning, etc. The **multi-path chain reasoning** technique of this framework is derived from the paper *Self-Consistency Improves Chain Of Thought Reasoning In Language Models*, which enhances the Agent's self-consistency and thereby improves performance by using multiple reasoning paths with the same logic but different temperature coefficients. The **dual-Agent review** technique is based on the paper *Communicative Agents for Software Development*, which sets up two **Agents** with different behavioral logics to discuss the same task and takes the agreed-upon conclusion as the output, reducing hallucinations and intellectual limitations of a single Agent. **Tree-structured reasoning** originates from the paper *Tree of Thoughts: Deliberate Problem Solving with LLMs* and is suitable for tree-based reasoning scenarios, supporting inference methods such as **breadth-first search**.

When dealing with scenarios that may involve complex reasoning logic, Yunzhihui surveyed the existing **Agent frameworks LangFlow** and **Flowise** at the initial stage of framework design. It was found that both frameworks are essentially graphical interfaces for **LangChain**, without additional abstraction or encapsulation. For non-developers (**industry experts**), LangFlow and Flowise have made many simplifications to lower the usage threshold, leading to unsatisfactory output results. For developers, the cost reduction brought by framework simplification is limited, while the inflexibility of the frameworks adds extra workload. The core issue with these frameworks is that they fail to meet the needs of their target users. Developers want to lower development costs while solving real-world problems, whereas non-developers hope to be able to build usable applications independently without development skills.

Based on this, Yunzhihui designed an **iterative version of the Agent framework**, which is composed of **Agent, Planning, PlanUnit, Profile, Memory**, and **Action** modules. Among them, the **Agent** component can be used to complete complex tasks, such as complaint ticket processing tasks. The **Planning** component is responsible for performing specific logic (such as **CoT, ReAct**); the logic execution flow of each Planning can be viewed as a directed graph—single-path chain reasoning, multi-path chain reasoning, tree reasoning, etc. are all subgraphs of the directed graph. The **PlanUnit** component is responsible for executing single-step logic; it is a node in the Planning directed graph, composed of **Profile, Memory, Action**, and other parts. The **Profile** component is used to set up the Agent's role-playing, the **Memory** component is responsible for information management, including the management and retrieval of context history information, as well as vector recall from external knowledge bases based on user queries. The **Action** component is responsible for external API management.

The architecture of the Agent framework is shown in *Figure 7.21*.

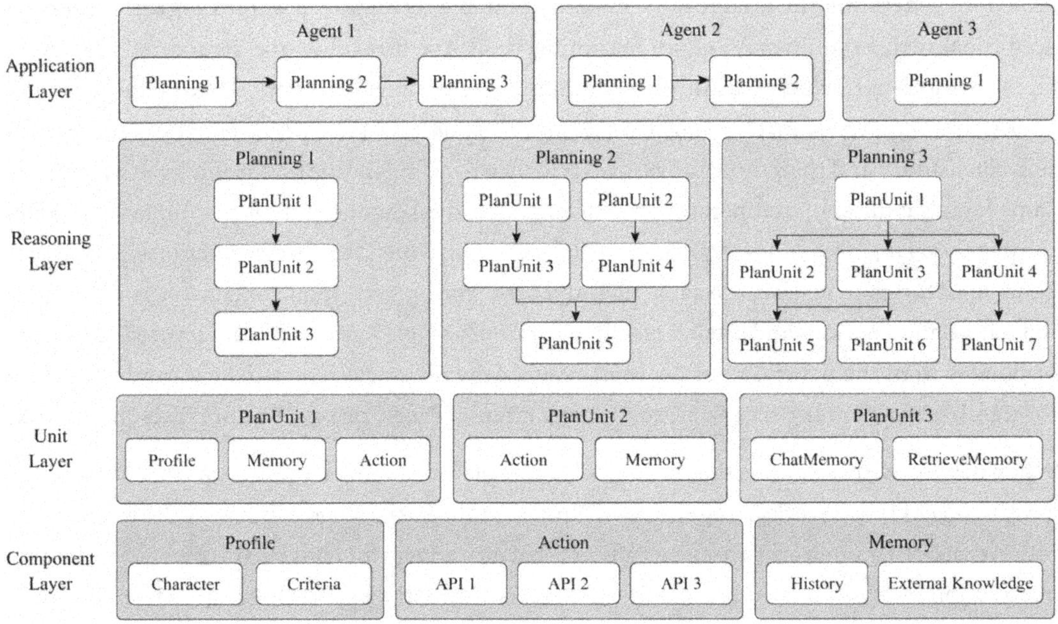

Figure 7.21: Architecture of the Agent framework

With this framework in place, the ticketing system can move from simple information retrieval to role-aware ticket summarization and guided handling.

Application case of intelligent O&M ticketing

The **intelligent ticket Agent** will summarize the ticket based on the current ticket information and user identity, combined with business logic, and display the summary in an internal operations assistant interface. The case shown in *Figure 7.22* demonstrates a fault report ticket related to a **drive failure**. When processing this fault ticket, the intelligent ticket Agent analyzes the fault content using its own **O&M knowledge** and summarizes information such as the fault situation and handling progress based on relevant ticket fields.

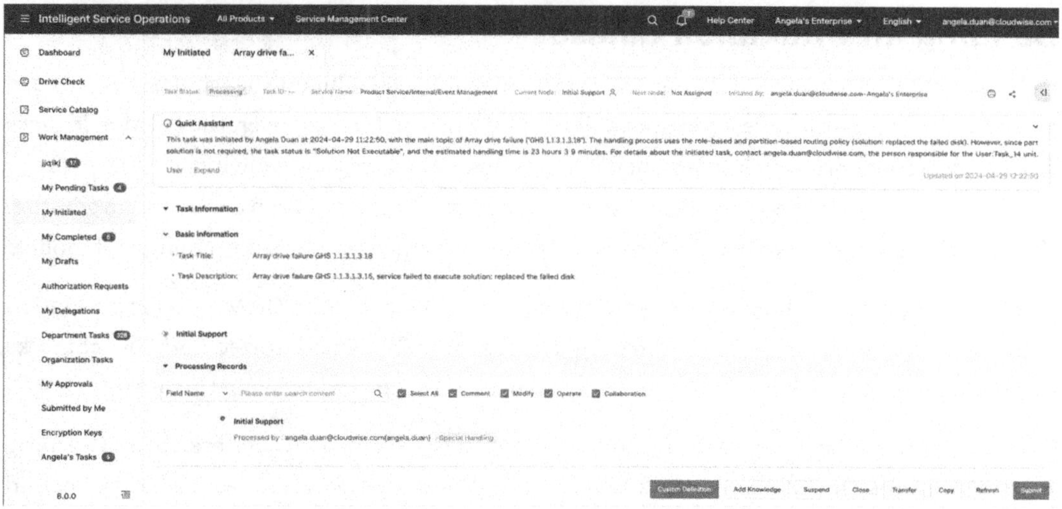

Figure 7.22: Fault report ticket related to drive failure

After examining how LLM agents can support ticket handling, the next question is how to measure whether these models are actually effective in O&M scenarios. Evaluation is important because O&M tasks require domain knowledge, accurate troubleshooting, reliable recommendations, and consistent performance across areas such as infrastructure, databases, networks, operating systems, and security.

Evaluating LLM capabilities for O&M

The core value of **intelligent O&M** lies in leveraging artificial intelligence to replace manual decision-making, quickly provide troubleshooting suggestions, or prevent faults in advance. Intelligent O&M revolves around **big data** and **algorithm platforms**, extracting data from various monitoring systems, offering services to users, and incorporating **automated systems** that execute intelligent O&M decision models.

In the O&M field, selecting an appropriate LLM, evaluating the effectiveness of model optimization, and providing guidance for further optimization all require O&M capability assessment of LLMs. The evaluation of LLM O&M capabilities should be based on different scenario tasks, selecting corresponding evaluation datasets to assess the model's performance, applicability, accuracy, and effectiveness in practical O&M scenarios.

Building an evaluation dataset

During the application of LLMs in the O&M field, standardized evaluation benchmarks are needed to measure the performance and applicability of different LLMs. However, the O&M field lacks **authoritative benchmark datasets**, making it difficult to effectively evaluate and compare the capabilities of LLMs in this domain, as well as to clarify model optimization directions. In addition, the diversity and quality of data are key factors affecting the effectiveness evaluation of models.

The following discussion uses Owl-Bench as one example of how an O&M-specific evaluation benchmark can be designed and applied. To address the lack of standardized O&M benchmarks, one domain-specific effort is Owl-Bench, developed by Yunzhi and Beihang University.

The paper *Owl: A LLM For It Operations* published at the **International Conference on Learning Representations** (**ICLR**), 2024, constructed the high-quality O&M dataset **Owl-Instruct** and the evaluation dataset **Owl-Bench. Owl-Bench** is a bilingual benchmark dataset consisting of two different parts: a **Q&A section** with 317 entries and a **multiple-choice section** with 1,000 questions. It covers numerous real-world industrial scenarios in this field, ensuring the diversity of Owl-Bench. The evaluation dataset includes nine different subdomains: information security, application business, system architecture, software architecture, middleware, networks, operating systems, infrastructure, and databases. The primary data sources are comprised of two parts: one part is **free practice exams available online**, and the other is **carefully designed by experts** in the O&M field. All this data is not generated by GPT-like models and is preprocessed into the form of Q&A and multiple-choice questions. The final statistical analysis results of Owl-Bench answers are shown in *Figure 7.23*.

	Middleware	Information Security	Basic Facilities	Application Services	Operating System	Database	System Architecture	Network	Software Architecture
Question Answering Section									
Number of Questions	30	26	41	36	39	38	25	40	42
Average Dialogue Length	301	275	287	311	297	342	286	308	298
Multiple Choice Section									
Number of Questions	136	108	110	102	118	119	87	122	98
Average Dialogue Length	212	287	264	343	247	310	255	294	301

Figure 7.23: Statistical analysis results of answers

Once an evaluation dataset has been defined, the next step is to choose scoring methods that match the task type, such as accuracy for multiple-choice questions and human or model-assisted scoring for open-ended answers.

Evaluation tools and methods

For evaluating LLMs in the field of O&M, it is necessary to obtain the performance ranking of LLMs, analyze the number of model parameters and their impact on O&M performance, as well as assess the improvements in O&M capabilities brought by prompt engineering, all based on O&M Q&A evaluation criteria.

For the O&M evaluation benchmark, the customized benchmark dataset **Owl-Bench** was chosen. The questions and prompts in the benchmark dataset are used to produce outputs through the model, and the outputs are compared to the correct answers in order to assess the model's performance in the O&M domain. For multiple-choice questions, accuracy is used as the evaluation metric; for subjective questions, recall, precision, GPT-4 scoring, expert scoring, and other standards are adopted. It should be noted that the evaluation metrics for subjective questions are highly dependent on manual effort and have poor scalability. Scoring via GPT-4 can be used to assess the match between the model's answer and the reference answer.

A total of 994 multiple-choice questions were selected for evaluation, covering 9 O&M capabilities (middleware O&M, information security O&M, infrastructure O&M, application and business O&M, operating system O&M, database O&M, system architecture O&M, network O&M, software architecture O&M). Each model's responses to the multiple-choice questions were used to separately calculate the accuracy for each of the 9 O&M capabilities. The accuracy for a single O&M category is the number of correctly answered questions in that category divided by the total number of questions in that category; the overall model O&M capability is the average accuracy across the 9 O&M categories. During model loading, it is necessary to define different classes, use different loading methods and model parameters to ensure the model is adapted to O&M Q&A and able to demonstrate its best performance.

During the evaluation process, prompt engineering was compared to assess its improvements to O&M capabilities, using a few-shot method and recording the number of reference Q&A examples included in the prompt with `ntrain`. When `ntrain=5`, five Q&A pairs are included in the prompt; when `ntrain=0`, no examples are included. Error outputs were statistically analyzed and mainly divided into three categories: **incorrect answers**, **unanswered**, and **output requirements not met**. Particularly when `ntrain=0`, the model outputs lack references, so corresponding prompts must be debugged to ensure the model can answer every question. The test results show that prompts differ in handling Chinese and English (e.g., commas in Chinese and English) as well as sentence order, and different prompts can lead to different model responses.

After defining the benchmark, scoring criteria, and prompt settings, the evaluation results can be used to compare model performance across different O&M domains.

Evaluation results

> These results should be read as benchmark-specific findings rather than universal rankings. For readers, the lesson is the evaluation method: define representative O&M tasks, choose appropriate metrics, compare models across subdomains, and interpret results in the context of the dataset and model set.

In this benchmark, the strongest results were obtained by Qwen1.5-32B-Chat and Yi-34B-Chat. Because Owl-Bench is bilingual and the evaluation set is tailored to O&M scenarios, these results should be interpreted in the context of the benchmark design and model set evaluated.

Under several existing open-source LLMs, for the 994 multiple-choice O&M questions, the single-category accuracy and average accuracy of each model were calculated, with the results as follows: **Qwen1.5-32B-Chat** performed the best overall, with an average accuracy of 90.47%. It also performed best in **information security O&M**, **application and business O&M**, **operating system O&M**, **system architecture O&M**, and **network O&M**. `qwen_72B_int4` performed best in the **middleware O&M** domain, with an accuracy of 85.93%, but its average accuracy was only 83.96%. **Yi-34B-Chat** performed best in **infrastructure O&M** and **database O&M**, with an average accuracy of 87.67%. In summary, the models with stronger O&M capabilities are **Yi-34B-Chat** and **Qwen1.5-32B-Chat**. Related statistical analysis results are shown in *Figure 7.24*.

ntrain=0	baichuan 2_13b_ chat	internlm-chat-7b	Deep Seek 33b	qwen_ 72B_int4	Yi-34B-Chat	baichuan 53b	Qwen1.5-14B-Chat	Qwen1.5-32B-Chat
Middleware Operations	75.56	65.93	67.63	85.93	85.19	80	85.19	85.19
Information Security Operations	75.73	64.08	57.22	77.67	86.41	77.67	80.58	88.35
Basic Facilities Operations	77.27	63.64	62.5	86.36	90.91	72.73	84.09	88.64
Application Services Operations	75.79	66.32	65.26	82.11	85.26	81.05	83.16	87.47
Operating System Operations	72.14	68.21	67.64	86.43	88.57	77.14	85	87.29
Database Operations	77.27	77.27	81.82	88.64	95.45	77.55	86.36	90.91
System Architecture Operations	90.91	90.91	81.82	72.73	100	100	100	100
Network Operations	72.22	66.67	58.89	86.11	83.89	78.89	83.89	92.78
Software Architecture Operations	72.41	70.69	55.17	87.66	91.38	77.59	82.76	87.66
Average	76.59	70.41	67.11	83.96	87.67	80.51	85.67	90.47

Figure 7.24: Model statistical analysis results

After evaluating how LLMs perform across general O&M tasks, the chapter now turns to a more complex operational scenario: root cause analysis in microservice systems. Microservices create highly distributed environments where faults can spread across services, dependencies, logs, metrics, and traces. This makes root cause analysis a strong use case for multi-agent methods, where different agents can analyze separate signals, share findings, and work together to identify the likely source of a failure.

Applying multi-agent root cause analysis to microservices

In today's development of internet technology, **microservices architecture** has become a mainstream system design pattern. **Microservices architecture** breaks down a large system into multiple independent, small services that can run and be deployed separately. These small services communicate with each other over a network. Each **microservice** is usually built around a specific business function and can be developed, deployed, and scaled independently of other services. This architecture enables enterprises to rapidly adapt to market changes, achieving continuous innovation and improvement. However, these advantages of the **microservices architecture** also come with a series of challenges, especially in terms of system monitoring and fault diagnosis.

In a **microservices environment**, the system consists of dozens or even hundreds of independent services, which may be distributed across different servers or containers, interacting with each other through lightweight network communications. A common example of a **microservices architecture** is shown in *Figure 7.25*.

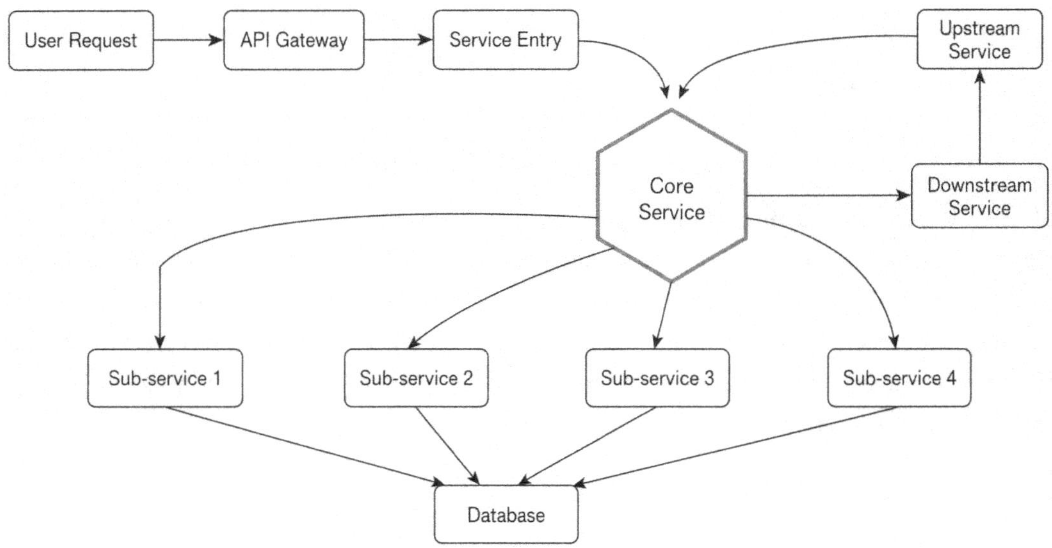

Figure 7.25: Example of a typical microservices architecture

This high level of decentralization and dynamism makes monitoring the system status, diagnosing problems, and tracing faults much more complex. Traditional fault detection and root cause analysis methods often struggle to cope with the complexity of microservices architectures, so new technical solutions are required to improve the efficiency and accuracy of fault handling.

Because root cause analysis in microservices requires teams to examine alerts, service dependencies, metrics, logs, and possible propagation paths at the same time, it is difficult for a single model or rule-based workflow to handle the process effectively. Multi-agent systems address this by dividing the investigation across specialized agents that can coordinate their findings.

Multi-agent systems

In recent years, artificial intelligence technologies, especially machine learning and LLMs, have shown tremendous potential in various fields. Root cause analysis tools based on these technologies can help technical teams quickly and accurately identify and resolve issues. In particular, the concept of **Multi-Agent Systems (MAS)** offers a new perspective for addressing complex problems within microservice architectures. In a multi-agent system, each agent is an independent entity with its own goals and capabilities, able to collaborate with other agents to accomplish complex tasks.

By combining the capabilities of LLMs with the collaboration of multi-agent systems, the industry is experimenting with designing an efficient fault detection and root cause analysis framework. In this framework, each agent acts as an independent LLM, responsible for processing different specific tasks such as receiving and analyzing alerts, exploring dependencies between services, assessing fault probabilities, etc. In this way, agents collaboratively form an automated process from receiving alerts to identifying the root cause of failures, not only improving the efficiency of fault handling but also enhancing the accuracy of fault diagnosis.

> Implementations of multi-agent systems for IT operations typically use frameworks such as Microsoft AutoGen, CrewAI, LangGraph, or OpenAI's Swarm pattern, each providing different trade-offs between developer control and orchestration automation.

As shown in *Figure 7.26*, root cause analysis in a microservices architecture features an alert event occurring at node A, with the root cause node being I and the failure propagation path being I →G→D→A. This approach turns root cause analysis into a coordinated workflow: one agent may receive and classify alerts, another may explore service dependencies, another may estimate failure probabilities, and another may propose recovery actions.

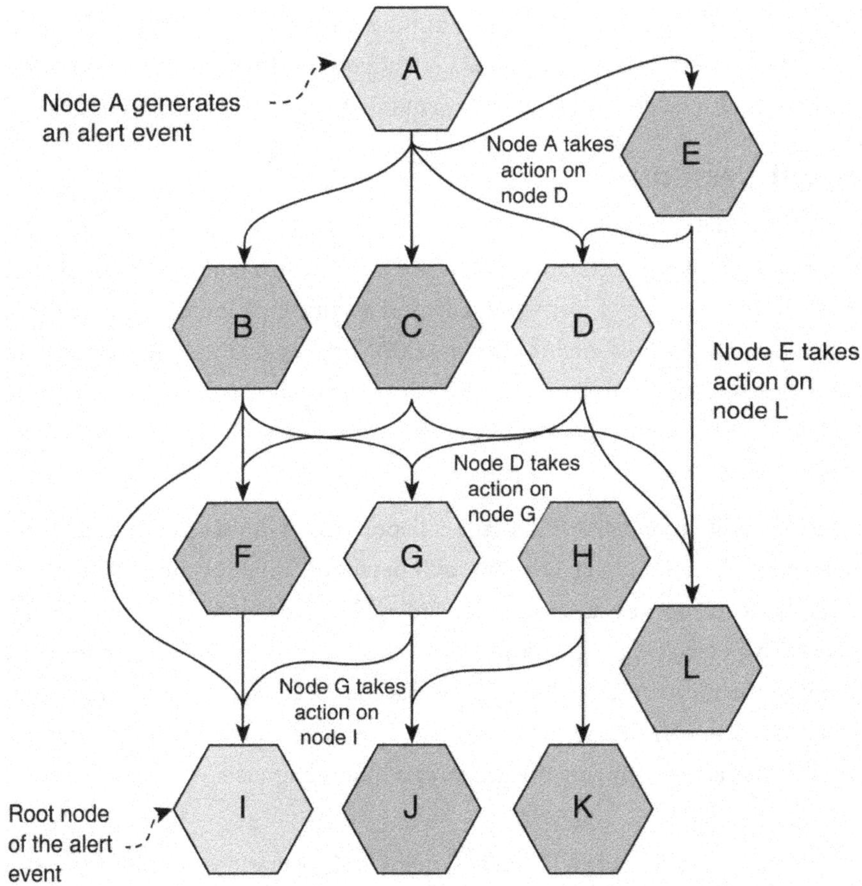

Figure 7.26: Root cause analysis in microservices architecture

After introducing the multi-agent approach conceptually, the next step is to examine how the agents cooperate in a practical root cause analysis workflow.

Application cases of multi-agent systems

One practical implementation of a multi-agent root-cause-analysis workflow includes the following roles: when a service fails, related alerts are sent to the monitoring system, and the issue is ultimately resolved through root cause analysis. The workflow is shown in *Figure 7.27.*

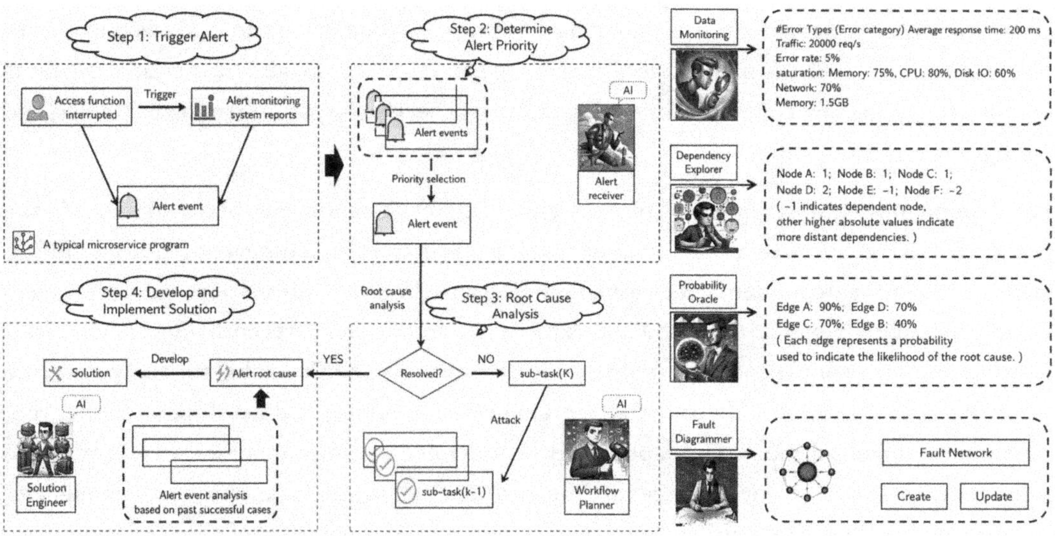

Figure 7.27: Workflow of multi-agent system

The workflow begins with alert intake and prioritization. The **alert receiver** acts as the first line of defense in the system, responsible for receiving and handling **alert events** triggered by access function blockages or monitoring system alarms. During this process, the alert receiver needs to handle multiple alert events from different parts of the microservices architecture, covering various types of failures. The alert receiver must perform a preliminary analysis of these alert events, identify related alerts and false positives, as well as classify and prioritize the alerts. This process requires the alert receiver to possess a high degree of intelligence and judgment to quickly and accurately process large amounts of information.

After determining the priority of the alert events, the alert receiver forwards the most urgent and impactful alerts to the **process planner** for further handling. The process planner is the core of the entire system, responsible for coordinating the work of each **agent**, dividing the root cause analysis tasks into multiple sub-tasks, and assigning these sub-tasks to other agents. This requires the process planner to have strong coordination and decision-making abilities in order to allocate tasks properly based on the actual situation and the capabilities of each agent.

Once the process planner has divided the investigation into subtasks, the system moves into evidence collection and dependency analysis. Under the coordination of the process planner, each agent begins to execute their respective tasks. The **data investigator** is responsible for collecting data from specified nodes, including **average latency**, **traffic**, **error rate**, **resource saturation**, and **concurrent user count**, among others. This data provides important information for root cause analysis. The data investigator must have strong data processing and analysis capabilities, be able to extract valuable information from a large amount of data, and further analyze alerts by collecting necessary contextual information, such as **service logs**, **performance metrics**, and **configuration change history**.

The **dependency explorer** is responsible for analyzing the dependencies between nodes in the microservices architecture. When the process planner receives an alert event requiring further analysis, it sends a **dependency request** containing specific node information and alert time to the dependency explorer. The dependency explorer accurately identifies both direct and indirect dependency nodes of the specified node through query tools and the global topology structure, facilitating identification of fault paths, marking affected nodes, and developing further root cause analysis and solutions. The dependency explorer needs strong analytical capabilities and a deep understanding of microservices architecture, enabling accurate analysis of dependencies between nodes. This step is critical, as in a microservices architecture, the failure of one service often affects other services on which it depends.

After the relevant nodes and dependencies have been identified, the next step is to estimate which nodes are most likely to be the root cause. The **Probability Oracle** is responsible for evaluating the failure probability of each node within the microservices architecture. When the **Process Planner** sends a request, the **Probability Oracle** analyzes the specified list of nodes to determine the failure probability of each one. This process includes checking the accessibility of nodes: for inaccessible nodes, the **Probability Oracle** will, by default, assign a higher failure probability. For accessible nodes, the **Probability Oracle** evaluates the failure probability by calculation models based on various performance metrics (such as **response time**, **error rate**, **resource utilization**, etc.). The **Probability Oracle** must possess strong computational abilities and an in-depth understanding of **failure probability assessment models** in order to accurately evaluate each node's failure probability. This process may involve multiple factors, such as the service's historical failure data, recent change records, and interaction patterns with other services.

These probability estimates then need to be presented in a form that helps engineers understand the fault network and propagation path. The **Failure Visualizer** is responsible for visualizing and updating data in the pipeline. The **Failure Visualizer** receives failure probability information from the **Probability Oracle** and updates the fault network accordingly. When the fault network needs updating, the **Process Planner** sends a fault network request containing the nodes and their corresponding failure probabilities. The **Failure Visualizer** creates or updates the fault network based on this information, visually presenting the failure probabilities between different nodes. The **Failure Visualizer** must possess powerful data visualization capabilities to clearly display the status of the fault network.

Finally, the system moves from diagnosis to response by generating or recommending recovery actions. The **Solution Engineer** is responsible for the final root cause analysis and solution development. Once the root cause is identified, the **Solution Engineer** proposes repair suggestions or automatically executes recovery operations, such as **restarting services**, **rolling back recent code deployments**, or **adjusting configuration settings** to restore normal service operation as quickly as possible. Specifically, after receiving the root cause analysis and solution request from the Process Planner, the Solution Engineer formulates an action plan based on available node data. If node data is available, the Solution Engineer conducts a metric-level analysis based on historical data and performance metrics. If node data is unavailable, the Solution Engineer performs node-level analysis by inspecting the topology of the microservices architecture to determine fault impact. The Solution Engineer will also refer to successful cases to guide the development of the current solution, and provide feedback information for further action and final resolution. The Solution Engineer must possess strong problem-solving abilities and extensive experience to develop effective solutions based on actual circumstances.

In addition to these individual agent roles, the overall system depends on coordination mechanisms that allow agents to exchange information, review outputs, and reach a reliable conclusion.

At the same time, an efficient communication mechanism must be established between agents throughout the multi-agent system in order to exchange information and coordinate actions. Additionally, the system can integrate **blockchain technology** to enhance the transparency and security of the decision-making process.

In some implementations, governance mechanisms such as weighted voting or auditable decision records can be added to improve transparency and accountability. Specifically, in this mechanism, each agent can vote on the answer to any problem. For example, each agent can vote on the answer to a problem, with voting weights determined by the agent's contribution and expertise indices. The **contribution index** reflects the agent's activity and effectiveness in proposing suggestions and voting, while the **expertise index** is based on the agent's professional contributions and action quality in specific fields. Through this voting mechanism, the system ensures that each answer is approved by the majority of agents, enhancing the fairness and accuracy of the system.

With the widespread adoption of **microservice architectures** and the increasing complexity of systems, traditional monitoring and fault diagnosis methods can no longer meet the needs of modern software systems. The implementation of the entire process not only improves the efficiency of **fault handling**, but also reduces the time and cost of problem resolution through precise **root cause analysis**. In addition, the **multi-agent-based root cause analysis framework** has good scalability and flexibility, allowing for the addition of agents or the adjustment of their functions according to the actual needs of the system, so as to adapt to ever-changing technological and business requirements.

By combining the advantages of **LLMs** with **multi-agent systems**, a more efficient and accurate **fault detection** and **root cause analysis framework** can be built, helping enterprises better manage and maintain **microservice architectures** and improve system stability and reliability. This not only assists technical teams in quickly responding to and solving problems, but also saves a great deal of time and resources for enterprises, thereby enhancing their competitive advantage.

Summary

In this chapter, you learned how LLMs can be applied to O&M scenarios such as log analysis, intelligent troubleshooting, O&M knowledge base construction, ticket handling, capability evaluation, and multi-agent root cause analysis in microservices environments. The chapter showed how LLMs can help O&M teams detect anomalies, interpret complex logs, automate responses, and improve operational efficiency through knowledge retrieval and agent-based workflows.

Building on these ideas, the next chapter moves into testing scenarios, where you will learn how LLMs can improve dynamic and static testing through automated test generation, program repair, semantic code analysis, and vulnerability remediation.

8

Applying LLMs in Software Testing

With the development of software engineering and the continuous improvement of product quality requirements, intelligent testing technology plays a crucial role. As a cutting-edge branch, intelligent, dynamic, and static testing are key means to improve test coverage and efficiency. Moreover, while LLMs help drive the development of testing technologies, their application in testing scenarios still faces numerous pain points and challenges that need further resolution.

In this chapter, we will be covering the following main topics:

- Identifying pain points in software testing
- Improving dynamic and static testing with LLMs
- Addressing challenges in deploying LLMs for testing
- Building automated vulnerability repair with static analysis and RAG

Identifying pain points in software testing

Software testing is a critical stage in the software development process, and its effectiveness directly determines the final quality of the software. Through comprehensive testing, developers can eliminate potential errors and instability in the software, ensuring that the code implementation meets the intended functional design. For different types of software and diverse testing goals, R&D teams can choose from a variety of testing techniques, including unit testing, performance testing, integration testing, smoke testing, compatibility testing, security testing, UI testing, and stress testing.

When we discuss how to apply LLM technologies in software testing scenarios, we must recognize the significant differences between various testing techniques, and these differences can greatly affect the effectiveness of integrating LLMs into testing.

From the perspective of testing principles, software testing techniques can be divided into two categories: **dynamic testing** and **static testing**.

- **Dynamic testing** targets software in a running state, verifying its functionality, performance, and security by actually executing the code. Common dynamic testing methods include unit testing, integration testing, system testing, and performance testing. These testing methods simulate user operations and scenarios, checking how the software behaves and performs under different conditions, thereby uncovering runtime defects and issues. To increase software feature coverage, dynamic testing typically requires writing a large number of test cases to ensure as many system behaviors are triggered as possible.
- In contrast, **static testing** is conducted without executing the code, uncovering potential issues through static inspection of code, documentation, and design. Common static testing methods include code review, static code analysis, design review, and documentation review. These approaches use manual checks or tools to analyze the structure, logic, and compliance of the code to identify potential errors, code standard violations, and optimization points, thus preventing defects at an early stage. Since software does not run during static testing, it is impossible to obtain accurate runtime data, leading to uncertainty in software analysis by static testing techniques. Especially for code with more complex architecture and functionality, both the false positive and false negative rates are relatively high. In actual usage, R&D teams often need a substantial amount of manual intervention to achieve better static testing results.

Whether it is dynamic testing or static testing, the purpose is to discover and fix defects and issues in the software as much as possible before the software goes live. In modern software engineering systems, these two techniques are usually used in combination to cover more testing scenarios and comprehensively improve the quality and reliability of the software.

In summary, the application scenarios and technical logic of dynamic testing and static testing are different, so the technical pain points and bottlenecks they face in practical applications also differ. For example, for **unit testing**, the automatic generation of high-quality unit test cases will directly impact its cost and effectiveness. For static testing, reducing the false positive rate is the key to determining the usage cost of such tools. In addition, how to quickly extract effective improvement and remediation solutions from the test results is also a common concern for developers in both types of testing.

Tools by capability

LLM-augmented testing does not depend on a single tool or platform. In practice, teams usually combine LLM-based assistance with the testing tools already used in their development workflow. The following examples show common tool categories that readers can use as a starting point:

- **Unit testing frameworks:** JUnit for Java, pytest for Python, Jest for JavaScript, and Go test for Go
- **Static analysis tools:** Coverity, SonarQube, Semgrep, CodeQL, Infer, and Klocwork
- **Fuzz testing tools:** AFL++, libFuzzer, Honggfuzz, and OSS-Fuzz
- **LLM-augmented development and testing tools:** GitHub Copilot for test generation, Cursor, Sweep AI, and the experimental tools discussed in this chapter, such as TestGen-LLM, Goshawk, and Corax

This list is not exhaustive. It is intended to help readers connect the chapter's testing concepts to familiar tool categories, such as unit testing, static analysis, fuzz testing, vulnerability detection, and LLM-assisted code repair.

Having established that dynamic and static testing face different practical bottlenecks, the next step is to examine how LLMs can support each approach. Dynamic testing benefits most from improved test case generation and program repair, while static testing benefits from stronger code semantic analysis, false-positive reduction, and vulnerability remediation.

Improving dynamic and static testing with LLMs

LLMs can support software testing in different ways depending on whether the testing process involves executing the software or analyzing it without execution. Dynamic testing relies on test cases, runtime behavior, execution feedback, and defect reproduction, while static testing depends on code structure, rules, semantics, and analysis reports. Because these two testing approaches have different workflows and pain points, this section examines them separately, beginning with dynamic testing and then moving to static testing.

Intelligent evolution of dynamic testing

Before looking at how LLMs can improve dynamic testing, it is useful to first review how dynamic testing works and where its practical limitations arise.

Basic concepts of dynamic testing techniques

Dynamic testing technology is an important method in the field of software testing, aiming to detect the **functionality** and **performance** of software through actual execution. Dynamic testing requires the software under test to be in a running state, and guides software execution of various operations and functions by means of manually or automatically constructed test cases. By observing the software's operating status, collecting test data, and deriving test results, dynamic testing can effectively evaluate software quality. Generally speaking, dynamic testing consists of the following key steps:

1. **Test Environment Preparation:** The prerequisite for conducting dynamic testing is to prepare one or more operating environments for the software under test and run the software in these environments to ensure it can operate correctly. It should be noted that whether the software can start normally in the **operational environment** is often regarded as a key result of dynamic testing.
2. **Test Case Construction:** Before dynamic testing begins, testers need to design a series of test cases that should cover the main functionalities of the software as well as various low-probability scenarios that might occur. The generation of test cases needs to consider specific software functions, different input data, the software runtime environment, and other factors. When generating test cases, testers should make careful considerations as much as possible to ensure that the dynamic testing process covers as many software functions and code as possible. **Code coverage** is an important indicator of dynamic testing and generally includes multiple dimensions such as **statement coverage, branch coverage, condition coverage**, and **path coverage**. Depending on the software's programming language and type, testers typically select common tools such as **JaCoCo**, **Cobertura**, and **Istanbul** to collect and analyze code coverage information during dynamic testing.
3. **Test Case Execution:** After completing the design and construction of test cases, testers need to execute these test cases against the running software. Since test cases target different software functionalities, both **manual** and **automated execution** of test cases are common approaches. During the execution of test cases, collecting and recording software runtime data is an important task. Testers should collect software runtime data as much as possible, including **runtime duration, memory consumption, CPU consumption, input/output content, response speed**, etc. The above data will be used to analyze and produce the final test results.

4. **Result Analysis:** During the execution of test cases, testers need to record the execution result of each case in detail. By analyzing these results, testers can uncover **abnormal behaviors** during the software's execution, thereby locating potential defects and issues in the software. For example, some functionalities fail to operate as expected or produce outputs that do not conform to the design under certain conditions.
5. **Defect Reporting and Fixing:** Based on the data collected during the testing process, testers can promptly discover potential **defects** and **issues** in the software. Testers should thoroughly document these issues and related information, and report them to the development team. The development team should then fix these issues.
6. **Regression Testing:** After the issues have been fixed, testers should perform regression testing to ensure that the fixes have not introduced new issues and that the original functionalities continue to operate normally

Common dynamic testing techniques

Dynamic testing is a collective term for a class of testing techniques that require running the software and interacting with and observing the software's operating state to obtain results. Common **dynamic testing techniques** are shown in *Figure 8.1.*

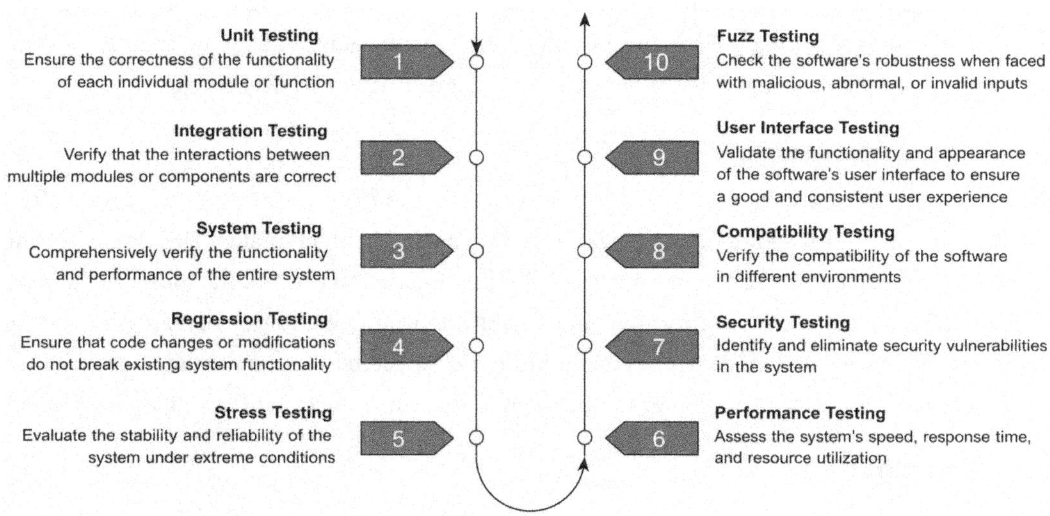

Figure 8.1: Common dynamic testing techniques

(1) Unit testing

The main goal of **unit testing** is to ensure that each **module** or **function** performs correctly and can execute specific tasks as intended. This testing method provides fine-grained **code checking** to ensure the reliability of fundamental components, thereby guaranteeing the overall correctness and stability of the program.

(2) Integration testing

The main goal of **integration testing** is to verify whether the interaction between multiple **modules** or **components** is correct. By combining different unit modules, it checks whether they can work together after integration, ensuring the reliability and consistency of **data transmission** and **functional invocation** between parts. Integration testing can identify and correct **interface issues** and **collaborative defects** between modules early, thereby improving the overall stability and functional completeness of the system.

(3) System testing

The main goal of **system testing** is to comprehensively verify the system's **functionality** and **performance** to ensure it operates as expected. This stage covers all aspects of the system, including **functionality**, **usability**, **performance**, and **security**. Through system testing, it is possible to discover software issues in the integrated environment and ensure that the system can stably and efficiently provide the expected services during actual user usage.

(4) Regression testing

The main goal of **regression testing** is to ensure that the introduction of new code or the modification of existing code does not break the system's existing functionality. This type of testing repeatedly executes existing test cases, especially those related to the modifications, to validate the system's **stability** and **reliability** after changes. Effective implementation of regression testing helps ensure that the system continues to maintain the expected functionality and performance during continuous iteration and upgrades, preventing the introduction of new defects or issues.

(5) Stress testing

The main objective of **stress testing** is to assess the stability and reliability of the system under extreme conditions. By applying extreme loads beyond the boundaries of normal operation, stress testing aims to expose the system's limits and weak points. Such tests help determine whether the system can continue to operate under abnormal situations (such as sudden surges in traffic, high concurrency, resource exhaustion, etc.) or if it can effectively recover from failures. Through stress testing, potential risks and bottlenecks can be identified in advance, thereby enhancing the system's robustness and resilience.

(6) Performance testing

The main objective of **performance testing** is to evaluate the system's speed, response time, and resource usage. By designing and implementing a series of test scenarios, performance testing helps identify and analyze the system's behavior under various loads. This type of test focuses on key performance indicators such as **throughput**, **response time**, **CPU,** and **memory usage**, aiming to optimize system efficiency and ensure strong performance in real-world environments to meet user needs. Performance testing effectively reveals performance bottlenecks in the system and provides a basis for corresponding optimization and improvement.

(7) Security testing

The main objective of **security testing** is to discover and eliminate security vulnerabilities in the system to ensure the safety of data and resources. By simulating various possible attack methods and analyzing the system's protection mechanisms, security testing evaluates the system's ability and robustness in resisting malicious attacks. This type of test covers potential security threats such as **authentication, authorization control, data protection**, and **network security**. Through security testing, potential security issues can be identified, security measures can be strengthened, and the system's integrity and confidentiality of data and resources can be effectively safeguarded in the face of security challenges.

(8) Compatibility testing

The main objective of **compatibility testing** is to verify the software's compatibility across a variety of different environments (including **operating systems**, **browsers**, **devices**, etc.). By testing the software on diverse software and hardware configurations and network environments, it ensures consistency and stability across different platforms and devices. Such testing covers compatibility across **operating system versions, browser types and versions, mobile and desktop devices**, and even performance under different network conditions. Through compatibility testing, environment-specific compatibility issues can be discovered, ensuring that the software meets the needs of a broad user base regardless of their technical conditions.

(9) User interface testing

The main objective of **User Interface Testing (UI Testing)** is to verify the functionality and appearance of the software's **user interface**, ensuring a high-quality and consistent user experience. By thoroughly testing the interactivity, layout, response speed, and visual consistency of various interface elements, it can be confirmed whether they function correctly and comply with design specifications. Such testing includes the functional behavior of **buttons, text boxes, menus, icons, dialogs**, etc., as well as how the interface appears on different resolutions, window sizes, and devices.

In addition to verifying functionality, user interface testing also focuses on the **usability** and **aesthetics** of the interface, ensuring that end users enjoy an intuitive, smooth, and satisfying experience while using the software.

(10) Fuzz testing

Fuzz testing is a recently emerging testing technique whose primary goal is to uncover crashes, abnormal behaviors, and potential security vulnerabilities in software. By automatically generating large amounts of random or semi-random data and feeding it into the software, the responses are observed to test how the software behaves under unexpected input. Such testing effectively captures unforeseen edge cases and input combinations, thereby revealing issues that may have been missed in conventional testing. Fuzz testing not only helps improve the stability and reliability of software but also enables the early detection of **security vulnerabilities** that could be maliciously exploited, enhancing the overall security and robustness of the system.

Pain points of dynamic testing

Although there are many types of dynamic testing technologies, we can still summarize some common features from their technology stack, such as **dependency on the environment**, **requirements for real-time interaction**, **code coverage capability**, and **resource consumption**. Based on these common issues, current dynamic testing technologies face the following pain points and bottlenecks in real-world scenarios:

- **Limited Coverage:** Traditional **dynamic testing technologies** struggle to achieve comprehensive coverage of all possible code paths and user scenarios. The limitations in coverage may result in certain potential bugs remaining undiscovered, leading to hidden risks persisting even after the software passes testing, which affects end-user experience and system stability.
- **Difficulty Handling Complex Scenarios:** When dealing with complex scenarios, dynamic testing exposes significant limitations, especially when handling multi-threaded, concurrent, and asynchronous operations. These complex situations are prone to cause issues that are difficult to reproduce and diagnose, making it challenging for traditional methods to address these tricky problems effectively.
- **Resource Consumption:** Real-time monitoring and analysis of software usually require high system resources, particularly in terms of **CPU** and **memory** consumption. This has a particularly significant impact on **performance-sensitive applications.** High resource consumption not only increases the cost of testing but may also interfere with the normal operation of the system under test.

- **Limitations of Environment Simulation:** The actual operating environments of different software can be extremely complex, while traditional dynamic testing methods often struggle to fully simulate all details of such environments. These limitations in simulation capabilities result in test outcomes that may not be comprehensive or reliable enough, thereby diminishing the effectiveness of the tests to a certain extent.
- **Complexity of Data Analysis:** The massive amount of data generated during dynamic testing needs to be processed and analyzed to extract and utilize valuable information. Traditional dynamic testing methods often cannot efficiently mine data and locate problems due to technical and tooling limitations when handling and analyzing such complex data.
- **Heavy Dependence on Manual Effort:** In traditional dynamic testing technologies, in order to cover as many functions and scenarios as possible, the generation of test cases often requires the participation of **developers**. Manually designed test cases not only consume a great deal of time but are also prone to errors and inconsistencies. Worse yet, this approach is rarely able to comprehensively cover all code paths and user scenarios, potentially leaving certain functionalities or exceptional conditions insufficiently verified and introducing risks. Such heavy reliance on manpower also makes it difficult for the testing process to quickly respond to changing requirements or achieve automation, further reducing the efficiency and quality of testing.

These pain points show why dynamic testing is a strong candidate for LLM-assisted improvement. Since dynamic testing depends heavily on test case design, runtime feedback, defect analysis, and repair, LLMs can be used to reduce manual effort and strengthen coverage in targeted parts of the workflow.

Applying LLMs to dynamic testing

Currently, the application of LLM technology to improve the effectiveness of specific tasks in the field of software testing is still in the early exploratory stage. From existing LLM technologies, their main features include **intelligent human-computer dialogue capability**, understanding of **multimodal data** such as text and images, as well as strong comprehension and generation capabilities for code data. Based on these characteristics, I believe LLM technology can significantly enhance the effectiveness of existing technologies in the following two areas: **automated test case generation** and **automated program repair**.

Automated test case generation

By reading requirement documents and extracting key functional points and business logic, the model can generate a variety of test cases covering both normal and abnormal scenarios. For example, for the **user login function**, it can generate test cases for normal login, incorrect password login, and multiple incorrect attempts; at the same time, by analyzing code—especially interface invocation conventions and function signatures—the model can deduce appropriate input-output combinations to generate boundary and exception test cases, ensuring comprehensive coverage of code logic and revealing potential problems. By analyzing users' historical operation logs, the model can identify high-frequency operation paths and generate corresponding test cases accordingly. For example, on **e-commerce platforms**, test cases for **shopping cart operations** and **payment processes** can be created to ensure the functional completeness and stability of critical paths. Furthermore, the model can dynamically simulate user operations to generate test cases for various combinations and exception scenarios, improving test coverage and depth. This enables developers to anticipate and handle more exceptions and edge cases, further enhancing software robustness and user experience.

In 2024, Meta published a paper titled *Automated Unit Test Improvement using LLMs at Meta*, introducing an experimental tool developed internally called **TestGen-LLM**. This tool can leverage LLMs to automatically generate unit test cases that meet requirements. `TestGen-LLM` is capable of understanding the logic of existing unit test cases and, on this basis, generating optimized new test cases to improve test coverage. Additionally, `TestGen-LLM` includes a validation step for the effectiveness of new test cases, ensuring that the improved test suite meets the needs of the testing team and eliminates potential hallucinations and instability that may arise from LLMs.

As shown in *Figure 8.2*, the workflow of **TestGen-LLM** consists of three main steps:

1. Analyze existing unit test cases
2. Generate new unit test cases
3. Filter, validate, and regress

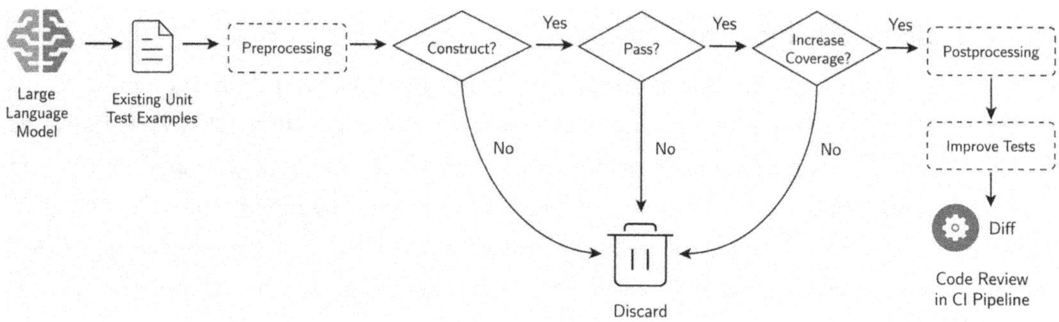

Figure 8.2: Workflow of TestGen-LLM

TestGen-LLM workflow overview

TestGen-LLM leverages static code analysis and the comprehension capabilities of **LLMs** to deeply analyze the structure and logic of existing **Kotlin** test cases, identifying potentially missed test paths, such as edge cases, abnormal situations, or specific code paths. Static analysis techniques help to understand code structure and dependencies, while LLMs can capture the semantics and intent of test cases, learning code styles and patterns.

Based on the analysis of existing test cases, **TestGen-LLM** can use the generative power of LLMs to automatically generate new test cases. According to the structure and logic of the code, as well as the needs of the testing team, it can design test cases covering more scenarios. Meanwhile, TestGen-LLM also references existing test cases, learning their style and patterns to ensure the generated test cases are consistent with the existing test code style, making them easy to understand and maintain.

To ensure the generated test cases can be used directly and effectively improve test coverage, **TestGen-LLM** performs a series of filtering and validation steps. First, it checks whether the generated test cases can be successfully built to avoid compilation errors. Then, it executes the test cases and verifies whether they pass, guaranteeing that the test cases can correctly validate the specific behavior of the code. Next, it repeatedly runs the test cases to ensure that they do not exhibit instability, such as passing under certain conditions and failing under others. Finally, it checks whether the test cases improve test coverage, ensuring that previously missed scenarios are now covered.

Test results in production

Engineers at Meta tested the capabilities of **TestGen-LLM** in real-world production scenarios. **Instagram Reels** and **Stories** were chosen as the test targets, and TestGen-LLM was embedded into the relevant testing processes. During testing, 75% of the test cases generated by TestGen-LLM were successfully built, and 57% of the test cases passed the reliability evaluation. This shows that TestGen-LLM can generate high-quality test cases that reliably operate in practical testing environments. Meanwhile, in the tests of Instagram Reels and Stories, 25% of the test cases generated by TestGen-LLM increased the code coverage of the original test suites. These test cases, which passed filtering and validation, were sent to Meta's test engineers for manual evaluation and summary, during which 10% of the original test sets were improved. Currently, 73% of the test cases generated by TestGen-LLM have been accepted and deployed to the production environment.

In addition, Meta's engineers found through analysis of the experimental results that the choice of **base model** and **prompt strategy** has the greatest impact on the effectiveness of **TestGen-LLM**. In contrast, **model dialogue parameters** such as `temperature` have relatively little influence on the results. Two different base models (**LLM1** and **LLM2**) were used in the experiments, and both models were able to effectively generate test cases and improve test coverage. Among them, **LLM2** performed slightly better than **LLM1**. However, due to commercial confidentiality, the paper did not provide specific details about **LLM2** and **LLM1**. It is speculated that **LLM2** may have a larger number of parameters and training data, or a better model architecture.

Four different **prompt strategies** were used in the experiments: extending coverage (`extend_coverage`), corner cases (`corner_cases`), extending tests (`extend_test`), and statements to complete (`statement_to_complete`), which guided the **LLM** in generating test cases. The results indicate that different prompt strategies have a significant impact on the effect of **TestGen-LLM**. Among them, the `extend_coverage` strategy performed best, generating the most test cases and improving test coverage.

Figure 8.3 presents the specific content of the four different prompt strategies.

Extended Testing	For example, here is a Kotlin unit test class: {existing_test_class}. Write the extended version of this test class, which includes additional tests to cover some extra edge cases.
Expanded Coverage Scope	For example, here is a Kotlin unit test class and its tested class: {existing_test_class} {class_under_test}. Write the extended version of this test class, which includes additional unit tests to increase the code coverage of the tested class.
Edge Cases	For example, here is a Kotlin unit test class and its tested class: {existing_test_class} {class_under_test}. Write the extended version of this test class, which includes additional unit tests to cover edge cases that may be missing in the original tests, and increase the code coverage of the tested class.
Description of Pending Tests	For example, here is a Kotlin class pending tests: {class_under_test}. This class can be tested using the Kotlin unit test class {existing_test_class}. This is the extended version of the unit test class, which includes additional unit test examples to cover the methods, boundary cases, edge cases, edge conditions, and other characteristics that may be missing in the original unit test class.

Figure 8.3: Four different prompt strategies

Beyond generating stronger test cases, LLMs can also support the next stage of the testing workflow: helping developers understand, localize, and repair the defects that testing reveals.

Automated program repair

Software development is often conducted under extremely tight schedules, and rapid iteration has become the norm. Every iteration cycle requires development teams to quickly respond and fix bugs discovered during testing. Efficient **automated repair techniques** can greatly shorten the time to resolve issues, thereby improving development efficiency and ensuring that teams deliver high-quality software products on schedule. As project scale increases and architectures evolve, the complexity of software systems also rises. Manual bug fixes are not only time-consuming and labor-intensive but can also easily introduce new errors. Automated methods can effectively reduce the impact of code complexity, minimize manual intervention through precise fixes, and improve the accuracy and efficiency of problem resolution. By reducing manual intervention, automated repair technologies can better allocate and optimize the resources of the development team, enabling developers to devote more time and energy to tasks that are more creative and valuable, rather than being bogged down by tedious bug fixing. This not only boosts the team's productivity but also fosters innovation and enhances the overall level of development.

LLMs, with their powerful natural language processing and code generation capabilities, have demonstrated tremendous potential in the field of **automated software bug repair**. Their abilities encompass **issue identification and analysis, high-quality repair suggestion generation, multi-modal data processing, root cause analysis**, and more. They can quickly understand and parse complex code, automatically generate reliable repair solutions, and transform error information described in natural language into reproducible, structured processes, helping testing teams deeply understand the causes of problems. At the same time, based on their strong code generation capabilities, LLMs can assist testing teams in directly generating usable code repair solutions, significantly reducing the human effort required during the bug repair process.

In 2023, Professor Lin Tan's team at Purdue University published the paper *Impact of Code Language Models on Automated Program Repair*, which comprehensively evaluates the capabilities of major LLMs in **program repair**. The authors selected 10 model instances with different parameter sizes from four different LLM families: **PLBART**, **CodeT5**, **CodeGen**, and **InCoder**. These are PLBART base, PLBART large, CodeT5 small, CodeT5 base, CodeT5 large, CodeGen 350M, CodeGen 2B, CodeGen 6B, InCoder 1B, and InCoder 6B. The research team tested these models' automated program repair abilities on three test sets: **Defects4J**, **QuixBugs**, and **HumanEval-Java**. Additionally, the authors compared the performance of traditional deep learning techniques on the same automated program repair tasks.

In their experiments, the authors designed two different **prompt schemes**. These prompts would guide different LLMs to generate 10 distinct repair solutions for each bug. The authors first evaluated whether these generated repair solutions could correctly fix the errors, and then manually checked whether the solutions altered the original semantics of the program. Furthermore, after completing the first round of evaluations, the authors fine-tuned these LLMs for one epoch and then repeated all testing procedures post-fine-tuning to analyze the impact of **fine-tuning** on model capabilities. *Figure 8.4* shows the two different prompt design rules devised by the authors.

PLBART Prompt (Without Errors)	PLBART Prompt (With Errors)
Input: **public** ValueMarker(**double** value, Paint paint, stroke stroke,... <mask> **this**.value =value;] **Expected Output:** **public** ValueMarker(**double** value, Paint paint, Stroke stroke, **super**(paint, stroke, outlinePaint, outlineStroke, alpha); **this**.value =value;]	**Input:** **public** ValueMarker(**double** value, Paint paint, Stroke stroke,... //buggy line:super(paint, stroke, paint, stroke, alpha); <mask> **this**.value =value;] **Expected Output:** **public** ValueMarker(**double** value, Paint paint, Stroke stroke,, **super**(paint, stroke, outlinePaint, outlineStroke, alpha); **this**.value =value;]
CodeT5 Prompt (Without Errors)	**CodeT5 Prompt (With Errors)**
Input: **public** ValueMarker(**double** value, Paint paint, stroke stroke,... <extra_id_0> **this**.value =value;] **Expected Output:** **super**(paint, stroke, outlinePaint, outlineStroke, alpha);	**Input:** **public** ValueMarker(**double** value, Paint paint, Stroke stroke,... //buggy line:super(paint, stroke, paint, stroke, alpha); <extra_id_0> **this**.value =value; **Expected Output:** **super**(paint, stroke, outlinePaint, outlineStroke, alpha);
CodeGen Prompt (Without Errors)	**CodeGen Prompt (With Errors)**
Input: **public** ValueMarker(**double** value, Paint paint, Stroke stroke,... **Expected Output:** **super**(paint, stroke, outlinePaint, outlineStroke, alpha); **this**.value =value;	**Input:** **public** ValueMarker(**double** value, Paint paint, Stroke stroke,... //buggy line:super(paint, stroke, paint, stroke, alpha); **Expected Output:** **super**(paint, stroke, outlinePaint, outlineStroke, alpha); **this**.value =value;
InCoder Prompt (Without Errors)	**InCoder Prompt (With Errors)**
Input: **public** ValueMarker(**double** value, Paint paint, stroke stroke,... <mask> **this**.value =value; **Expected Output:** **super**(paint, stroke, outlinePaint, outlineStroke, alpha); **this**.value =value;]	**Input:** **public** ValueMarker(**double** value, Paint paint, Stroke stroke,... //buggy line:super(paint, stroke, paint, stroke, alpha); <mask> **this**.value =value;] **Expected Output:** **super**(paint, stroke, outlinePaint, outlineStroke, alpha); **this**.value =value;]

Figure 8.4: Prompt writing rules

The experimental results of this paper demonstrate that LLMs exhibit strong potential in the field of **automated program repair (APR)**; even without fine-tuning, **LLMs** can rival previous **deep learning (DL)**-based automated program repair techniques and even outperform them on some datasets. For example, **InCoder 6B**, without any fine-tuning, fixed 105 bugs, which is 72% more than the best DL-APR technique, **KNOD**. Meanwhile, targeted **fine-tuning** can significantly boost the repair success rate of LLMs. For instance, after fine-tuning, InCoder 6B fixed 161 bugs, which is 164% more than KNOD. In addition, when performing related tasks, the **time efficiency** and **memory efficiency** of LLMs also vary according to the number of parameters. The most time-efficient model, **PLBART**, is nearly 20 times faster than the slowest **CodeGen** model.

While dynamic testing focuses on software behavior during execution, static testing examines code before it runs. This makes static testing another important area where LLMs can enhance analysis, reduce manual review effort, and improve the usefulness of testing results.

Intelligent evolution of static testing

After examining dynamic testing, the discussion now turns to static testing, where software is analyzed without being executed. Static testing plays a different role in the quality-assurance process: instead of observing runtime behavior, it examines code structure, rules, dependencies, semantics, and potential vulnerabilities before the software runs. This makes it especially useful for early defect detection, but it also introduces challenges such as false positives, rule maintenance, and difficulty interpreting complex code.

> In this chapter, "static testing" refers specifically to automated static analysis techniques; manual reviews and walkthroughs are out of scope.

Basic concepts of static testing techniques

In addition to dynamic testing techniques, **static analysis** is another fundamental method in software testing. **Static testing** detects potential issues and defects by analyzing the software code without actually running the program. Since static analysis can be carried out in the early stages of software development, it has unique advantages in identifying errors, vulnerabilities, and bad practices in the code. The key steps of static analysis are shown in *Figure 8.5*.

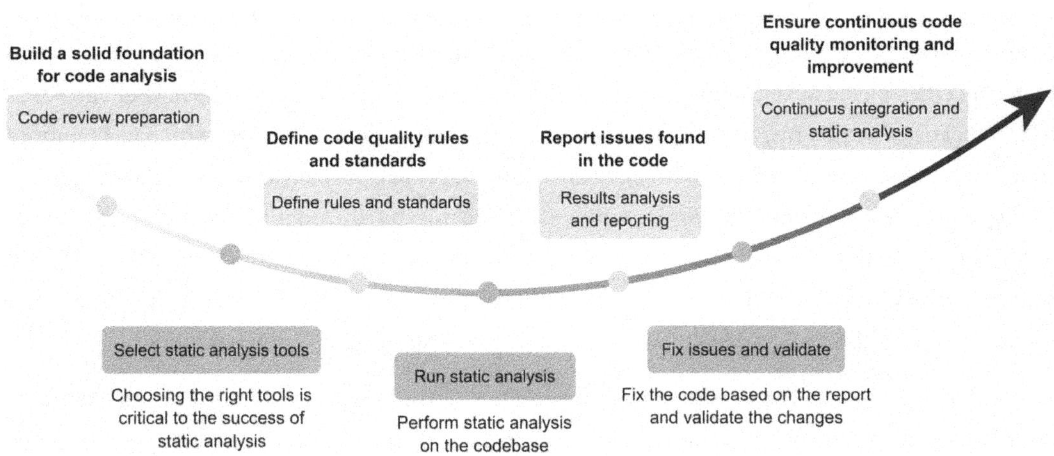

Figure 8.5: Key steps of static analysis

1. **Code Review Preparation:** Testers need to prepare the codebase to be analyzed, ensuring its completeness and correctness, and configure the relevant static analysis tools. The code review preparation stage may also involve preprocessing steps such as **code formatting** and **comment cleanup**, in order to improve the accuracy and readability of the analysis.

2. **Selection of Static Analysis Tools:** The effectiveness of static analysis tools is closely related to the programming language used by developers, the project scale, and specific requirements. Common static analysis tools include **SonarQube, Pylint, ESLint, FindBugs,** etc. These tools can automatically scan code, identify potential issues, and generate detailed reports. Choosing the right tool is key to successful static analysis, as different tools vary in their detection capabilities and performance.
3. **Defining Rules and Standards:** Before performing static analysis, a set of code quality rules and standards needs to be defined. These rules usually cover coding conventions, naming conventions, security checks, performance optimization recommendations, and so on. By clearly defining the rules, the consistency and reliability of the analysis results can be ensured. Many static analysis tools provide predefined **rule sets** and also allow users to **customize rules** to meet specific needs.
4. **Executing Static Analysis:** After preparation is complete, testers use the selected tools to perform static analysis on the codebase. The tools scan the code, apply the predefined rules, identify potential issues, and generate reports. The execution of static analysis is usually automated, but in some cases, manual intervention may be required to handle complex code structures or specific business logic.
5. **Result Analysis and Reporting:** The reports generated by static analysis tools contain issues found in the code, including **errors, warnings,** and **suggestions.** Testers must analyze these results in detail to determine which issues actually need to be addressed. The result analysis phase also involves determining priorities so that the development team can focus on the most important issues. Static analysis reports not only help identify code defects but also provide concrete suggestions for improving **code quality.**
6. **Issue Fixing and Verification:** Based on the static analysis results, the development team needs to fix the code. After the fixes are completed, the static analysis tool is usually run again to verify whether the issues have been resolved. This process may require multiple iterations until all critical issues are resolved. Through repeated static analysis and fixing, the code quality and reliability can be significantly improved.
7. **Continuous Integration and Static Analysis:** To ensure consistent code quality throughout the development lifecycle, static analysis should be integrated into the **Continuous Integration (CI)** process. Static analysis is automatically triggered on each code submission or merge and, based on the results, determines whether the code is allowed to enter the main branch. By combining static analysis with the **CI/CD process,** continuous monitoring and improvement of code quality can be achieved.

Once the basic workflow is clear, it becomes easier to see how static testing techniques differ by what they examine in the code. Some techniques focus on syntax and style, while others analyze semantics, security risks, complexity, or dependencies.

Common static testing techniques

According to the technology used and the analysis objectives, common static analysis techniques can be categorized into the following six types:

Syntax Analysis

The main goal of **syntax analysis** is to check whether the code conforms to the syntax rules of the programming language. By parsing the code, syntax analysis can detect **syntax errors**, unclosed parentheses, undefined variables, and other issues. Syntax analysis is the foundational step of static analysis, ensuring that the code can be properly compiled or interpreted. With the development of basic tools such as compilers, pure syntax analysis is no longer common in software development processes. More often, syntax checking is used in conjunction with analyzers to detect more complex issues such as security vulnerabilities.

Semantic analysis

Semantic analysis builds upon syntax analysis by further checking the semantic correctness of the code. It focuses on issues such as variable types, scopes, and parameter matching in function calls. Semantic analysis can detect type errors, uninitialized variables, invalid function calls, and similar problems. Through semantic analysis, it can be ensured that the code is logically reasonable and executes as intended. However, traditional static testing techniques cannot cover data such as comments and variable names that contain complex semantic information, resulting in incomplete semantic analysis of the code.

Code style checking

The main goal of **code style checking** is to ensure that code adheres to predefined coding standards and style guides. By checking code formatting, naming conventions, and comment styles, code style checking can improve the readability and consistency of code. Common code style checking tools include **ESLint** (JavaScript), **Pylint** (Python), **Checkstyle** (Java), and others.

Security analysis

The main goal of **security analysis** is to discover security vulnerabilities and potential risks within the code. By analyzing the security of the code, it is possible to detect common security issues such as **SQL injection**, **Cross-Site Scripting (XSS)**, buffer overflows, and others. Security analysis tools usually combine static analysis and pattern-matching techniques, providing detailed security vulnerability reports. Common security analysis tools include **SonarQube**, **Fortify**, and others.

Complexity analysis

The main goal of **complexity analysis** is to assess the complexity of code, including **loop complexity**, **conditional complexity**, and **coupling between modules**. By analyzing code complexity, high-complexity areas that may be difficult to maintain and test can be identified, guiding the development team to refactor and optimize code. Complexity analysis is relatively common in **embedded industries** where software runtime resources are limited.

Dependency analysis

The primary goal of **dependency analysis** is to examine the dependencies between code modules to ensure that **module coupling** remains within a controllable range. By analyzing dependencies, issues such as **circular dependencies** and **unused dependencies** can be identified, thereby optimizing code structure and improving the **maintainability** and **scalability** of the system. At the same time, dependency analysis can also identify security issues introduced by dependencies by comparing with third-party vulnerability databases and similar data sources.

Although these techniques can detect many issues early and operate efficiently across large codebases, static testing still faces important limitations in real production environments.

Pain points of static testing techniques

Compared to dynamic testing techniques, static testing techniques demonstrate significant advantages in code coverage, operating costs, and concurrency efficiency. However, when applying static analysis tools in actual production environments, there are still many pain points and challenges. These challenges not only affect the practical effectiveness of the tools but also impose higher demands on the workflows of development teams.

- **High False Positive Rate:** Static analysis tools often generate a large number of **false positives**, meaning the reported problems do not actually exist. A high false positive rate not only increases the extra workload for developers but may also diminish their trust in the analysis results, thereby affecting the tool's practical effectiveness. Frequent false positives force teams to spend more time filtering true errors from false positives, gradually eroding developers' enthusiasm for and trust in static analysis.

- **Maintenance of the Rule Set:** The core of static analysis relies on a set of predefined rules. These rule sets must be continuously updated and maintained to adapt to rapidly changing programming language features and emerging security threats. Maintaining the rule set is not only a massive workload but also requires a deep reservoir of professional knowledge. This poses a serious challenge for development teams, both in terms of time management and technical resource allocation. Given the fast-paced evolution of programming languages and frameworks, promptly updating rule sets is crucial; otherwise, analysis tools may fail or generate frequent false positives.
- **Difficulty Handling Complex Code:** When faced with complex code structures, static analysis tools may demonstrate certain limitations, especially when analyzing advanced programming features such as **polymorphism**, **dynamic typing**, and **reflection**. These complex features may make it difficult for static analysis tools to accurately understand the program's behavioral logic, resulting in inaccurate analysis results. As a result, not only is error localization and resolution more challenging, but it may also complicate issues further, thereby reducing the practical value of the tool.
- **Performance Overhead:** When handling large codebases, static analysis tools often require significant computational resources and time to perform in-depth scans. High performance overhead not only lengthens analysis time and reduces development efficiency but can also have a notable negative impact on continuous integration processes. Especially in continuous integration environments, lengthy analysis processes can delay the entire development workflow, seriously affecting product release schedules and team productivity.
- **Environmental Dependencies:** Static analysis tools typically have specific requirements for the **development environment** and **system configuration**. This increases the complexity of integrating and using the tools. In diverse development environments, environmental dependency issues may lead to inconsistent analysis results. For example, the same static analysis tool may yield different analysis results in different development environments, making problem localization and resolution more difficult.
- **Complexity of Data Analysis:** Reports generated by static analysis tools often contain large amounts of data, and parsing this data requires technical expertise. Development teams must be able to extract useful information from complex reports and turn it into actionable improvements. Avoiding information overload and improving the readability of reports are key to making static analysis results more useful.

- **Tool Compatibility:** Due to functional differences among static analysis tools, choosing and integrating multiple tools to obtain comprehensive results can be difficult. Poor compatibility can lead to fragmented or inconsistent findings, making it harder for developers to interpret and act on the results. Improving tool compatibility and the overall utility of static analysis workflows is therefore an important part of making static testing more effective.

These pain points explain why LLMs are being explored as a way to make static testing more useful. Rather than replacing static analysis tools, LLMs can help interpret code semantics, summarize analysis results, reduce false positives, and support vulnerability repair.

Applying LLMs to static testing

Similar to dynamic testing, **LLMs (LLMs)** also demonstrate great potential in the field of static testing and can provide assistance across a variety of static testing scenarios. For example, bugs and vulnerabilities discovered during static testing typically require a significant amount of manpower and time to fix, whereas LLMs can greatly simplify this process. By automatically identifying and repairing vulnerabilities, similar to automated repair solutions in dynamic testing, the application of LLMs can significantly reduce the time and resources development teams spend handling these issues.

In addition, LLMs also show great potential in **code semantic analysis** and **false positive elimination**. Through deep learning and natural language processing technologies, the models can understand the complex semantic structures of code, accurately identify variable types, function calls, and logical relationships, thereby greatly improving the accuracy of semantic analysis. Moreover, LLMs can learn and identify common false positive patterns, using contextual understanding and pattern matching to filter out irrelevant alerts and dramatically reduce false positive rates. This not only increases the accuracy and reliability of static analysis tools but also reduces the burden on developers, ultimately improving overall development efficiency and code quality.

Code semantics analysis

Traditional static program analysis techniques mainly rely on the analysis of structured information such as code and configuration files, often neglecting the complexity of code in terms of semantics and logic. However, bugs and security vulnerabilities in modern software are not only related to code structure and syntax but are also directly associated with software logic and code semantics. These hidden problems are often difficult to detect in the early stages of testing, but once triggered, they can pose significant threats to the stability and security of the system.

The emergence of LLMs provides R&D teams with new tools for deeply understanding code semantics. LLMs possess excellent natural language understanding capabilities and the ability to parse unstructured data, enabling them to analyze complex logic and semantics within code. By combining LLM technology with traditional static analysis techniques, we can accurately understand software logic during static testing and enhance the ability to identify deeper issues. This combination not only increases the efficiency of vulnerability detection but also improves its comprehensiveness and accuracy.

In 2022, a research team from Shanghai Jiao Tong University and Feiyu Technology published a paper titled *Goshawk: Hunting Memory Corruptions via Structure-Aware and Object-Centric Memory Operation Synopsis*. This paper discusses how to utilize artificial intelligence technologies to identify functions related to memory operation semantics, thereby enhancing the capability of static analysis tools in detecting logical vulnerabilities in memory operations.

The development of modern C/C++ software increasingly relies on custom **memory management functions**, especially in embedded R&D fields such as automotive and semiconductors. These custom functions are responsible for allocating and releasing memory, but their custom behavior may differ from the standard `malloc` and `free` functions, for example, by involving complex operations such as multi-object allocation or nested allocation. This poses a challenge to traditional static analysis techniques, as they usually focus only on standard memory management functions and assume that allocation and release operations always occur in pairs.

To address this issue, this paper designs and implements a memory vulnerability detection tool named Goshawk by combining traditional program analysis techniques with artificial intelligence technologies. Goshawk aims to solve the analytical difficulties brought by custom memory management functions.

As shown in *Figure 8.6*, Goshawk's workflow includes the following steps:

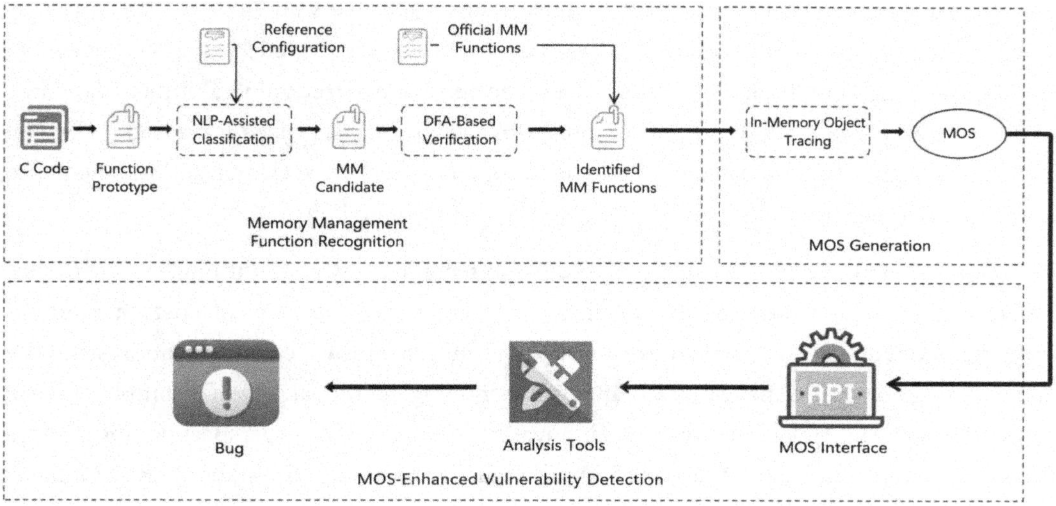

Figure 8.6: Goshawk's workflow

1. **Identification of memory management functions:** First, Goshawk uses natural language techniques to scan and analyze the source code, extracting semantic features from function prototypes and labeling the functions by category. Then, for each candidate function classified as a memory management function, in-depth **data flow analysis** is performed to verify whether they indeed execute memory allocation or release operations.
2. **MOS generation:** For each identified memory management function, Goshawk tracks its managed memory objects using data flow analysis techniques and generates the corresponding **MOS representation** as defined by MOS. MOS includes the function name, attributes (such as allocation or release), a list of managed memory objects, and the structural relationships between the objects.
3. **MOS-enhanced vulnerability detection:** Goshawk utilizes MOS information to optimize data flow analysis and detect **memory corruption vulnerabilities** in an object-centric, structure-aware manner. When analyzing a memory management function, Goshawk directly uses the MOS information to update the state of memory objects, thereby avoiding redundant analysis of code within the function.

By creatively integrating traditional program analysis with artificial intelligence technologies, Goshawk performed excellently in the final experiments. In tests on 7 open-source projects, Goshawk successfully analyzed over 273,000 lines of code and discovered 92 brand-new memory corruption vulnerabilities, including **use-after-free** and **double-free** vulnerabilities. Compared with traditional vulnerability detection tools, Goshawk's analysis speed increased by several orders of magnitude, and the generated vulnerability reports were clearer and more concise, helping developers more easily understand and confirm vulnerabilities.

This paper combines **natural language processing** techniques with traditional static analysis techniques to achieve automatic identification and precise detection of **custom memory management functions** and **memory corruption vulnerabilities**, effectively addressing the shortcomings of traditional program analysis technologies in dealing with complex logical vulnerabilities. This research provides an innovative solution and new perspectives for the field of software static testing. By integrating natural language processing with static analysis methods, it significantly improves the efficiency and accuracy of the analysis process, demonstrating the broad application prospects of **LLM technology** in software testing and security fields.

Beyond improving semantic understanding, LLM-based methods can also address one of the most persistent problems in static testing: distinguishing real issues from false positives.

Intelligent false positive elimination

In the field of static testing, a high **false positive rate** has always been a major pain point for developers. Traditional static analysis tools rely on predefined rules and **pattern matching**, making them prone to false positives when dealing with complex or dynamic code structures. In addition, the lack of runtime information prevents static analysis from accurately determining the actual behavior of code during execution, further increasing the likelihood of false positives. Advanced code features such as **polymorphism**, **reflection mechanisms**, and **dynamic types** also pose challenges for static analysis tools to fully understand the real intent and context of the code. The maintenance and updating of rule sets is difficult, making it even harder for these tools to adapt to new technologies and new language features. However, as **LLM technologies** emerge, there is hope for breakthroughs in this situation. LLMs, leveraging deep learning and **natural language processing** technologies, can better understand the results of analysis tools and identify false positives, significantly reducing the false positive rate and improving the accuracy and reliability of static analysis tools.

In 2023, a research team from South Korea published an academic paper entitled *False Alarm Reduction Method for Weakness Static Analysis Using BERT Model*, which proposed a defect analysis false positive reduction method based on the **BERT model** and **decision tree**, as shown in *Figure 8.7*.

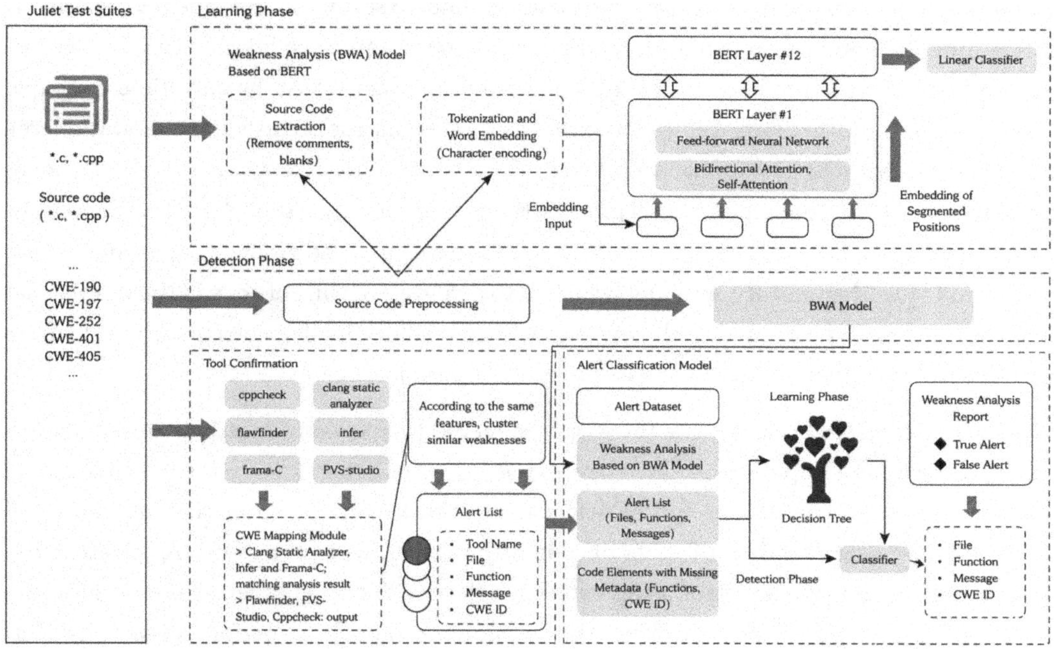

Figure 8.7: False positive reduction method for defect analysis based on the BERT model and decision tree model

The system constructed by the authors of the paper first preprocesses the source code, including cleaning out useless comments, blank lines, and so on, and standardizes defect annotations. Then, the **BPE algorithm** is used to break the source code into smaller units, such as words, punctuation marks, etc., and each word is converted into a vector representation, with positional information added to help the model understand the structure and semantics of the code. The preprocessed data is used to train the **BERT model** and **decision tree model**, where the BERT model is used to analyze the code line by line, identify potential defects, and utilize the **attention mechanism** to calculate the relevance scores between defect code lines and other code lines; the decision tree model is used to classify the output of static analysis tools and determine whether each warning is a false positive. Finally, the trained models are applied to new code to identify potential defects and use the decision tree model to reclassify the output of static analysis tools, thereby reducing the false positive rate and improving the efficiency and accuracy of defect analysis.

The paper's authors selected six common static analysis tools—**Cppcheck, Clang Static Analyzer, Flawfinder, Infer, Frama-C,** and **PVS-Studio**—to test the effectiveness of this framework. These testing tools are based on different static analysis techniques, such as **lexical analysis, type inference, data flow analysis, symbolic execution, theorem proving,** and **model checking.** By integrating the output results of these tools, defects in the source code can be analyzed more comprehensively, thereby improving the accuracy of defect analysis. At the same time, the paper uses the *NIST Juliet test suite C/C++ version 1.3* as the test dataset. This suite contains a large amount of known defect code and normal code, which enables effective evaluation of the model's performance. During the experimental process, the authors first used the selected static analysis tools to perform defect analysis on the test dataset and mapped and grouped each tool's output results to **CWE**. Then, the **BWA model** was used to analyze each line of code in the test dataset, and the **ACM model** was used to classify the analysis results. Finally, metrics such as the **false positive rate** were calculated to evaluate the model's performance.

The experimental results show that the proposed method can effectively reduce defect analysis **false positives** and improve the efficiency and accuracy of defect analysis. The **BERT model** performs excellently in the line-by-line defect analysis task, with high accuracy, precision, and F1 score. It can effectively identify lines of code with potential defects and utilize the **attention mechanism** to analyze the relationship between defective lines and other lines, thereby more accurately judging the severity of defects. The **decision tree model** also performs well in the alert classification task, with high accuracy, precision, F1 score, and **AUC**. It can effectively identify false positives and reclassify the output results of static analysis tools, thus reducing the false positive rate. Compared to using a single static analysis tool, this method can more comprehensively analyze defects in source code and improve the accuracy of defect analysis. For example, for **Buffer Over-read (CWE-125)** defects, the false positive rate with a single tool is 79%, while with this method, the rate drops to 7%. For **Use of Uninitialized Variable (CWE-457)** defects, the false positive rate drops from 93% to 11%. The false positive reduction effect of this method varies across different defect categories, but overall, it can significantly reduce the false positive rate, improve the efficiency and accuracy of defect analysis, and provide important technical support for secure software development.

LLMs can improve both dynamic and static testing, but their value depends on how reliably they can be deployed in real testing workflows. Before adopting them at scale, teams need to consider practical constraints such as context window limits, hallucinations, model selection, fine-tuning costs, explainability, evaluation, and long-term maintenance.

Addressing challenges in deploying LLMs for testing

This section provides an in-depth discussion of the application potential of LLMs in dynamic software testing and static software testing. It demonstrates their powerful logical reasoning capabilities, natural language processing skills, code generation abilities, and how they can enhance the effectiveness and accuracy of traditional software testing techniques. Without a doubt, LLMs show broad application prospects in the field of software testing. However, when we attempt to apply LLMs in real-world software production environments, we still face numerous complex technical difficulties and challenges. This section, drawing on practical experience in deploying LLMs, will delve into these technical challenges.

Model reliability challenges

Before LLMs can be used reliably in testing workflows, teams must understand the core limitations that affect model output, especially context window constraints and hallucinations.

Managing LLM context window limits

Currently, LLMs generally have limitations on the **context input window** when processing text data. For example, GPT-4's context input window is capped at 32,000 tokens. Although some foundational LLMs claim to handle ultra-long contexts, their ability to "find a needle in a haystack" and "maintain focused attention" in the face of massive amounts of data still requires further validation. As a result, in software testing scenarios, LLMs may encounter insufficient input window issues when analyzing longer code fragments or test data, making it difficult for the model to directly address complex testing requirements and results.

A feasible solution is to use other analytical techniques to segment and structure the data before feeding it to the LLM, and then input the data into the model step-by-step via RAG or Agent technologies. This approach can effectively alleviate the limitations of the processing window and enhance adaptability to complex tasks. For example, splitting code by functional modules and then incrementally inputting them into the LLM for analysis can help improve processing efficiency and accuracy.

Reducing hallucinations in testing workflows

Since the emergence of LLMs, they have often been plagued by the issue of "**hallucination**." When LLMs handle problems with frequent context switching, **complex logical reasoning**, and a large amount of mathematical computation, they frequently provide irrelevant answers or fail to understand the logic of the question. This phenomenon results in an inability to fully trust the output of LLMs when using them to assist in software testing. Currently, it remains technically difficult to completely resolve this issue at the foundational level.

Current coping methods include secondary verification and filtering of the LLM's outputs, or using Agent technology to break down a single question and answer into multiple reasoning chains (such as **CoT**) and recall verification processes. If resources permit, multiple LLMs can be used to handle the same task, and the results can be cross-validated to improve accuracy. For example, in the code review process, using several LLMs to independently analyze the same section of code and comparing the analysis results can help to better identify potential problems.

Deployment and architecture choices

Once the main reliability risks are clear, the next step is choosing the right deployment pattern, model, and adaptation strategy for the testing task.

Choosing between RAG and agent-based workflows

RAG and **Agent** technologies are the two most common forms in which LLMs are applied to specific tasks. Agent here refers to the LLM-driven orchestration pattern introduced in *Chapter 7*, where the model autonomously plans steps, calls tools, and iterates on results.

RAG, by combining retrieval and generation, is particularly suitable for tasks that require high-quality text generation, such as question answering systems and dialog generation. It retrieves relevant information from a predefined knowledge base, combines it with the input information, and generates the final output. This enhances contextual understanding and reduces the probability of generating inaccurate or unreasonable content.

In contrast, Agent technology executes specific tasks through autonomous intelligent agents. These agents can perceive their environment (such as application state, user input, etc.), make decisions, and perform corresponding actions based on predefined rules or learned strategies, and continuously adjust their strategies and behaviors through feedback mechanisms to adapt to different testing environments and requirements, thereby achieving automation of complex tasks.

In the field of software testing, due to the wide variety of tasks and diverse principles and requirements, it is particularly important to flexibly choose between RAG or Agent technology. For example, when dealing with tasks that have few steps but require extremely high accuracy of results, RAG technology is more appropriate; while for systematic tasks that require multiple steps and frequent context switching, Agent technology achieves better results. For instance, in **automated regression testing**, Agent technology can flexibly cope with changing testing environments, improving test coverage and efficiency.

Selecting the right foundation model

LLM technology is developing rapidly, and **foundation models** with different numbers of parameters and various pre-training tasks are emerging one after another. Models ranging from **1 billion** to **200 billion** parameters exhibit varying inference performance and efficiency depending on the task. In **software testing** tasks, choosing the most suitable model to achieve the best results at the lowest computing cost is particularly important. For example, for **integration testing** of complex systems, selecting a large-parameter model may yield better inference performance, while for simple **unit testing**, a smaller-parameter model can be chosen to save computing resources.

In addition, some enterprises have strict **data security management mechanisms** and do not allow core data (such as code) to be sent to the cloud for processing. In such cases, it is necessary to consider the feasibility of deploying LLMs locally, balancing computing power and cost while ensuring data security. For example, a localized and streamlined LLM can be deployed and combined with the enterprise's own **data security strategies**, thereby better protecting data privacy and security.

After selecting a suitable base model, teams must decide whether the model's existing capabilities are sufficient or whether fine-tuning is needed for testing-specific tasks.

Deciding whether to fine-tune LLMs

Fine-tuning LLMs is an effective way to significantly improve their performance on specific reasoning tasks. Experiments show that fine-tuned LLMs demonstrate obvious enhancements in tasks such as code explanation and program repair. However, as the base models develop, their parameter counts, and the scale of training corpora increase rapidly—models with up to 100 billion parameters considerably raise the cost of fine-tuning. In addition, these base models already cover most common corpora during pre-training, including code, and software testing-related data, so the performance improvement from fine-tuning may gradually diminish.

Therefore, whether to fine-tune a base model and whether it is cost-effective requires a comprehensive trade-off based on the situation. For example, when handling common code review tasks, one may choose not to fine-tune but instead directly leverage the pre-trained capabilities of LLMs; however, when working on testing tasks in specific domains, proper fine-tuning can significantly boost performance.

Improving model performance is only one part of deployment. In testing workflows, teams also need to understand why a model produced a recommendation and whether testers, developers, and security teams can trust the result.

Operational governance

After an LLM-based testing workflow is deployed, teams need processes for explaining results, measuring performance, and maintaining the system over time.

Improving explainability and transparency

The **explainability** and **transparency** of LLM reasoning processes have not yet been fully addressed. In software testing scenarios, the application of LLM technology usually involves collaboration across multiple departments, and different users (such as testers) need to understand and trust the results output by the model. This places higher demands on the explainability, predictability, and transparency of the LLM's reasoning process. In practical applications, how to enable relevant personnel to understand and trust the model's outputs is a highly challenging issue.

Ways to address this problem include introducing explainability techniques such as **SHAP (Shapley Additive Explanation)** or **LIME (Local Interpretable Model-agnostic Explanation)** to analyze and demonstrate the decision basis of LLMs. At the same time, increasing transparency reports and thoroughly documenting the training process, data sources, and application scenarios of LLMs can help users gain a clear understanding of the model's performance and limitations.

Beyond explaining individual outputs, teams also need a systematic way to measure whether LLM-assisted testing improves accuracy, efficiency, robustness, and cost-effectiveness across real workflows.

Evaluating LLM performance in test scenarios

When implementing new technologies in real production environments, most companies and teams wish to conduct a detailed assessment of the costs and benefits of the technical solutions before actual application. As a new technology in the field of software testing, LLMs have a technical core and usage methods that are completely different from traditional technologies. How to perform accurate and effective performance evaluation for LLMs has become an urgent and important issue to address.

On this basis, enterprises need to establish a comprehensive evaluation framework covering multiple dimensions such as accuracy, efficiency, and robustness. For different testing tasks, appropriate evaluation metrics and methods should be formulated. For example, in functional testing, the performance of LLMs can be evaluated by comparing the detection rate and false positive rate of automated testing tools; whereas in performance testing, efficiency can be measured by analyzing the response time of LLMs under different loads.

Maintaining and updating LLM-based testing systems

The implementation and toolification of LLM technology means it will become an important part of the daily toolchain for software testing teams. In daily use, how to continuously maintain the availability of LLMs, and as usage deepens, how to continuously iterate LLM solutions to improve their effectiveness, are issues that urgently need to be explored.

In addition, with the advancement of computing power and technology, the **foundational models** previously used need to be upgraded and replaced. How to smoothly transition to new foundational models, especially synchronizing the optimization experience accumulated by old models to the new ones, remains a complex problem. Therefore, it is necessary to formulate systematic **maintenance and update strategies** to ensure that the performance and stability of models are not affected during the upgrade process, while also effectively addressing **model degradation** and **data drift** issues. For example, regularly conducting **model validation** and **regression testing**, monitoring changes in model performance, and promptly adjusting and optimizing model parameters can ensure the efficient and reliable operation of LLMs in practical applications.

After examining the broader challenges of deploying LLMs in testing workflows, the discussion now turns to a concrete application: automated vulnerability repair. This example shows how static analysis, retrieval-augmented generation, and LLM-based code generation can be combined to locate vulnerabilities, provide the model with relevant context, and produce repair suggestions that developers can review and apply.

Building automated vulnerability repair with static analysis and RAG

In the software development process, security vulnerabilities remain a pervasive issue that demands close attention. As software systems become increasingly complex, both the number, and types of vulnerabilities grow, which presents significant challenges to developers and enterprises. Traditional manual vulnerability repair methods are not only time-consuming and labor-intensive, but they also place high demands on developers' security knowledge and experience, while requiring substantial time and effort investment. This approach is prone to errors during execution, which may lead to the emergence of new vulnerabilities or even affect the normal operation of existing functionalities.

Manual vulnerability repair is costly, involving not only labor costs but also the time and resources consumed during the repair process. For large software projects, the cost of repairing vulnerabilities is especially significant, often becoming a major burden in development and maintenance.

To address the limitations and high costs of manual vulnerability repair, LLM technology offers an innovative and efficient solution. By leveraging LLM technology, we can achieve automated vulnerability repair. LLMs have significant advantages in natural language processing and code generation, allowing them to automatically identify and fix various types of security vulnerabilities. Specifically, the application advantages of LLM technology in automated vulnerability repair are mainly reflected in the following aspects:

- First, LLM technology can greatly improve the efficiency of vulnerability repair. Traditional manual repair methods often require repeated code review and testing, while LLM technology can quickly identify and repair vulnerabilities through its powerful analytical capabilities. This can significantly reduce the workload for developers during the repair process, making it more efficient.
- Secondly, using LLM technology can reduce the cost of vulnerability repair. Automated repair reduces dependency on human resources and shortens the time required for repair. In addition, LLMs can process large amounts of code and vulnerabilities in a short period, substantially lowering time and resource costs and increasing overall production efficiency.
- Finally, LLM technology can reduce errors that may occur during the repair process. Due to its advantages in **data processing** and **pattern recognition**, LLMs can avoid many omissions and mistakes that may occur in manual repair processes, ensuring the accuracy and reliability of vulnerability repair and improving the overall security of the software.

The following workflow uses Corax as one example of how a static analysis tool can support automated vulnerability repair. The same general pattern can also be implemented with other static analysis tools, where the tool identifies vulnerabilities, supplies structured context for RAG, and helps convert model output into reviewable repair suggestions. Coverity, SonarQube, Semgrep, CodeQL, Infer, and Klocwork are similar static analysis tools commonly available. *Figure 8.8* shows the system architecture and workflow of the Corax system for automated vulnerability repair.

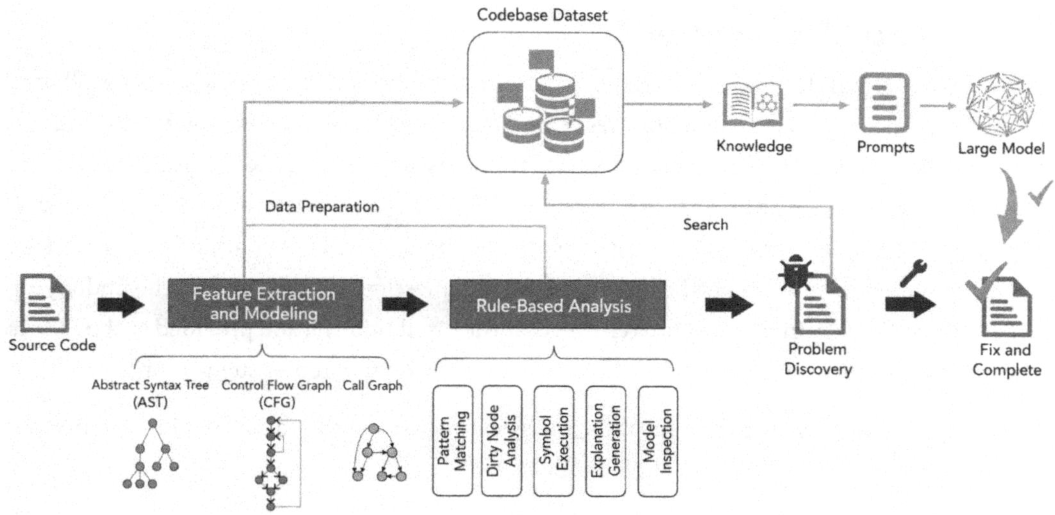

Figure 8.8: Workflow of an automated vulnerability repair pipeline

The specific workflow is divided into three main steps: **vulnerability localization**, **generating LLM prompt**, and **processing model output**.

Vulnerability localization

First, leveraging Corax's powerful vulnerability scanning capabilities, static analysis is performed on the source code to automatically identify security vulnerabilities in the code. To improve the accuracy and reliability of LLMs during the vulnerability repair process, Corax not only performs conventional static code analysis but also conducts more detailed data modeling of the source code. When generating vulnerability reports, Corax stores contextual information related to each vulnerability in a database. This data includes the code snippets triggering the vulnerabilities, involved functions and variables, and related configuration file information. The purpose of this is to reference this detailed information during subsequent prompt engineering, significantly reducing potential hallucinations by the LLM, thus improving the accuracy of vulnerability repair.

Once the vulnerability and its relevant code context have been localized, the next step is to package that information into a prompt that the LLM can use to generate a repair.

Generating LLM prompt

After the user selects the vulnerabilities to be automatically repaired, Corax aggregates all data required for repairing those vulnerabilities. This data covers detailed vulnerability information, relevant code snippets, code context information, and associated knowledge from the security vulnerability knowledge base. This data serves as the RAG query results, entering the next step of prompt engineering. The LLM will systematically organize this data according to a preset format, including the user's specific requirements and questions, then send it to the underlying LLM interface. The key in this step is to ensure that the input information provided to the LLM is comprehensive and accurate, enabling it to generate high-quality repair suggestions.

After the LLM generates a repair suggestion, the system must convert the output into a form that developers can inspect, verify, and apply safely.

Processing model output

After the LLM generates repair suggestions, Corax continues to process these outputs. First, Corax converts the repair code generated by the LLM into natural language explanations, including an analysis of the vulnerability's cause and a detailed description of the repair strategy. This step not only helps developers understand the root cause of the vulnerability and the repair method, but also verifies the correctness of the repair code produced by the LLM. Next, Corax converts the repair code returned by the LLM into more practical formats, such as code diff or git pull/request, making it easier for developers to apply these repair suggestions. Specifically, the code diff format clearly displays the modified parts of the code, facilitating comparison and verification during code review; whereas the git pull/request format can be directly applied to the code version control system, further simplifying the repair process.

The above three steps constitute the core process of Corax's automated vulnerability repair. By fully leveraging the natural language processing and code generation capabilities of LLMs, as well as detailed data modeling and prompt engineering techniques, efficient, and accurate automated vulnerability repair is achieved, providing strong support for developers. This system not only improves the efficiency of vulnerability remediation and reduces remediation costs, but also significantly enhances the accuracy and security of the repair process, providing important technical means for modern software development and security assurance.

Figure 8.9 illustrates how this workflow can produce a concrete repair suggestion for a parameter value uninitialized vulnerability.

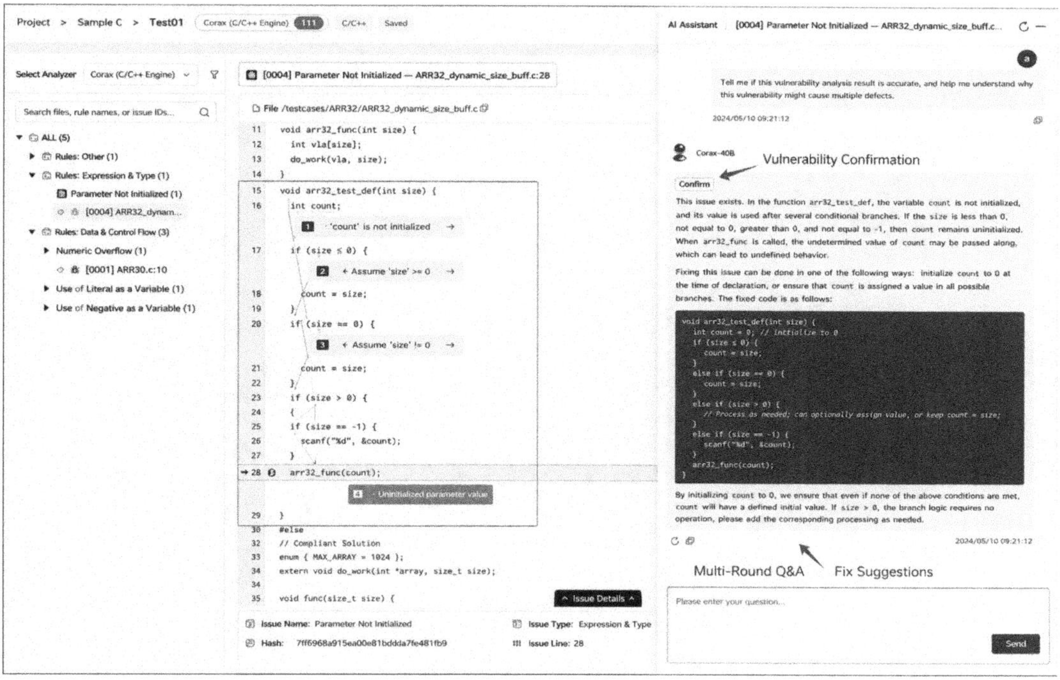

Figure 8.9: Example of parameter value uninitialized

Feysh Technology has released an open-source version of **Corax** on GitHub (`https://github.com/Feysh-Group/corax-community`), which possesses the same analysis capabilities as the commercial version of Corax. Readers who want to explore this implementation can refer to the open-source Corax community repository.

Summary

In this chapter, you learned how LLMs can be applied to testing scenarios to improve both dynamic and static testing, from automated test generation and program repair to semantic code analysis, false-positive reduction, and vulnerability remediation. You also explored the practical challenges of deploying LLMs in testing workflows, including hallucinations, context window limits, model selection, fine-tuning, and evaluation.

Building on this testing-focused use of LLMs, the next chapter shifts to programming scenarios, where you will learn how large code models support code generation, code completion, project-level development, and developer productivity across real software engineering workflows.

9

Applying Code LLMs in Software Development

Large code models, often implemented as code-focused LLMs, are AI models trained on large-scale code datasets and designed to handle code-related tasks. These models are typically based on deep learning architectures represented by Transformers, and are trained through pre-training objectives such as language modeling. Through training on massive amounts of code data, the models can improve code writing efficiency and quality, and assist in code understanding and decision-making.

In this chapter, we are going to cover the following main topics:

- Defining large code models and their core characteristics
- Exploring common code LLMs
- Mapping downstream code tasks
- Tracing the evolution of code generation and completion
- Identifying pain points in code generation and completion
- Applying agent-based methods to project-level code generation

Defining large code models and their core characteristics

With the rapid development of information technology, software development is becoming increasingly important in various fields. As an emerging technology in the field of artificial intelligence, large code models bring unprecedented opportunities and changes to software development. Understanding the definition and characteristics of large code models is crucial to fully leveraging their advantages and promoting the intelligent process of software development.

Large code models are based on **deep learning technology**, and through learning and training on massive code datasets, they can understand, generate, and optimize code. They do not simply recognize code syntax and structure, but can also capture semantic information, logical relationships, and programming patterns within code. For example, large code models, such as **Codex**, **Code Llama**, etc., can generate corresponding code snippets based on given natural language descriptions or modify and improve existing code.

Large code models possess characteristics such as large-scale data-driven learning, deep understanding of code semantics, strong generative ability, self-adaptivity and optimization capabilities, and cross-language support.

Large-scale data-driven

Large code models usually require a huge amount of code data for training, with data sources that are broad and include open source projects, code repositories, software development platforms, and so on. By learning from immense volumes of code, the models can master the syntax rules, programming styles, and common code structures of various programming languages. For example, the abundance of open source code on GitHub provides rich learning material for the models, enabling them to learn the coding styles used in different domains and application scenarios.

Deep understanding of code semantics

Unlike traditional code analysis tools, large code models can deeply understand **code semantics**. They are able to recognize relationships among elements such as **variables**, **functions**, and **classes** in code, and understand the purpose and functionality of code. For instance, when the model analyzes a segment of code that calculates the sum of two numbers, it can understand the mathematical logic and the role of variables within it.

Powerful generation capabilities

Large code models are capable of generating new code based on given requirements or prompts. This generative ability not only includes simple functions and modules, but also complex system architectures and complete applications. For example, users only need to describe the functional requirements of software, and the model can generate the corresponding code framework and core code logic.

Adaptive and optimization capabilities

Large code models can adaptively adjust the generated code according to different programming tasks and contexts, thereby improving the quality and efficiency of the code. They can also optimize the generated code, such as optimizing algorithms and improving code readability and maintainability. For instance, when handling performance-critical code segments, the model can automatically choose more efficient algorithms and data structures.

Cross-language support

Many large code models possess the ability to understand and generate across multiple programming languages, enabling code conversion and migration between different languages. For example, a model that can handle Python, Java, and C++ code simultaneously can help developers reuse and integrate code between projects in different languages.

These characteristics explain why large code models are increasingly being adopted as practical development assistants rather than remaining purely research tools.

As shown in *Figure 9.1*, the 2023 *Developer Survey Report* data indicates that 44% of developers have already used AI tools in the development process, and 77% of respondents support making AI tools a part of the development workflow.

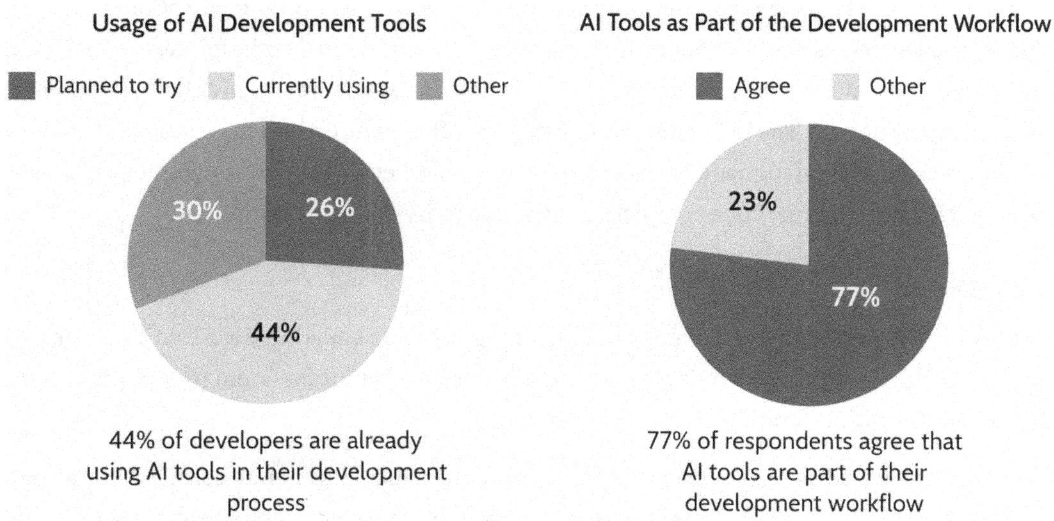

Figure 9.1: Data on the use of AI tools

This growing adoption reflects three main ways large code models can support developers and development teams:

- **Improving Development Efficiency**: In terms of improving development efficiency, developers can quickly obtain code examples, solutions, and code snippets by interacting with large code models, significantly reducing development time and workload
- **Lowering the Development Threshold**: Regarding lowering the development threshold, for beginners and non-professional developers, large code models can provide assistance and guidance, helping them enter the software development field more easily
- **Driving Innovation**: In terms of driving innovation, large code models can inspire new programming ideas and innovative solutions, bringing new possibilities to software development

After defining what large code models are and why they matter to software development, the next step is to look at the major models that have shaped this field. Comparing these models helps show how different organizations have approached code generation, completion, reasoning, and developer assistance.

Exploring common code LLMs

This section introduces five representative code LLMs: **Codex**, **AlphaCode**, **StarCoder 2**, **Code Llama**, and **DeepSeek Coder**. This section introduces five influential code-focused models and coding assistants that illustrate different approaches to code generation, completion, reasoning, and developer support. The following examples show different directions in code-focused model development: natural-language-to-code generation, competitive programming, open-source code models, multilingual code completion, and repository-level understanding.

Codex

In August 2021, OpenAI released a machine learning software called **Codex**. This software can translate English into code, aiming to reduce the workload of professional programmers and help amateurs with coding.

Codex is an AI-based code generation tool that can automatically generate corresponding code snippets based on developers' requirements. Trained on massive code repositories, Codex is capable of writing code in multiple programming languages, including Python, Java, C++, and more. In the development process, Codex significantly improves coding efficiency, reduces errors, and allows developers to focus more on implementing business logic.

Codex has code completion capabilities and can predict the subsequent code based on code snippets already entered, thus helping developers quickly finish their code. This feature is especially useful for beginners, providing timely hints, and guidance while coding. In addition to code completion, Codex can generate complete code snippets based on developers' descriptions. For example, you only need to tell Codex you want to implement a sorting algorithm, and it will generate the corresponding code for you. This is very useful for rapid prototyping or solving specific problems. Codex can also optimize existing code to improve its runtime efficiency. By analyzing the code's structure and performance bottlenecks, it provides corresponding optimization suggestions.

Many applications are based on Codex, such as code assistants Copilot, Pygma, and Replit. Copilot can generate code based on instructions, convert comments into code, generate tests, and provide alternative solutions. Pygma uses Codex to convert Figma designs into high-quality code. Replit uses Codex to describe the functionality of selected code segments, making it easier to understand their purposes.

AlphaCode

In 2022, the renowned programming competition site Codeforces published an article titled *AlphaCode (DeepMind) Solves Programming Problems on CodeForce*, which brought **AlphaCode** into the spotlight and once again put **DeepMind** at the top of major media headlines. This was DeepMind's next revolutionary product after successfully launching **AlphaGo** in 2015—which defeated the world's best Go players—to change the world again.

After developing the Go-playing robot AlphaGo and the AI-based protein folding prediction system AlphaFold, Google's AI company DeepMind has launched another groundbreaking programming robot system, AlphaCode, which has reached the average proficiency level of human programmers. DeepMind states that AlphaCode has achieved a very competitive level in writing computer programs. In competitions with human programmers, AlphaCode ranked at a middle level, placing in the top 54%, marking an important step forward for humans toward autonomous coding.

According to DeepMind's official website, AlphaCode is an AI tool developed by Google's UK AI division. The tool is capable of participating in major programming competitions and has the ability to solve new problems involving critical thinking, logic, algorithms, coding, and natural language understanding. Before its official release, DeepMind tested AlphaCode's performance in programming competitions. Codeforces holds one or two algorithm competitions each week and features a unique ladder ranking system. After participating in 10 Codeforces programming competitions, AlphaCode performed excellently, ultimately ranking above 54.3% of human programmer participants, with an Elo rating of 1238.

StarCoder 2

StarCoder 2 is a code LLM based on the Transformer architecture, designed to handle natural language and generate source code in multiple programming languages. This series of models includes three versions, with parameter sizes of 3 billion, 1 billion, and 15 billion, all trained on the Stack v2 dataset. The Stack v2 dataset is seven times the size of Stack v1 and contains a vast amount of code, questions, answers, discussions, and mathematical formulas from platforms such as GitHub, Stack Overflow, Codeforces, and others. It covers 619 programming languages, ranging from low-resource languages (such as COBOL) to high-resource languages (such as Python).

The StarCoder 2 code LLM family is trained on multiple programming languages and can perform specialized tasks such as source code generation, workflow generation, and text summarization, helping developers improve work efficiency. For example, when developers input natural language requirements, the model can generate corresponding code snippets. In addition, the model can perform self-learning and optimization based on user feedback, thereby improving the quality and readability of the generated code.

Compared with the previous generation StarCoder model, the StarCoder 2 model has been optimized for performance; its 3 billion parameter version already approaches the performance of the original 15 billion parameter StarCoder model. This is due to a new training technique employed by StarCoder 2 called CodeBERTa, which improves the model's generalization and understanding of programming languages without increasing parameter count. The CodeBERTa technique combines contrastive learning and masked language models, utilizing a large amount of unlabeled code data to achieve successful pre-training and fine-tuning of code. StarCoder 2 also features advantages in transparency and cost-effectiveness, as the series uses the BigCode Open RAIL-M license, allowing users to access and use the models without paying royalties.

Code Llama

Meta's open-source Llama model family welcomes a new member, Code Llama, a foundational model focused on code generation. The release of Code Llama addresses the only programming shortcoming of Llama 2, aiming to enhance code completion abilities and handle programming tasks. The model is fine-tuned from the Llama 2 base model and comes in three versions: base, Python, and instruction-following. Each version offers three parameter sizes: 7B, 13B, and 34B. Notably, the 7B parameter model can be run on a single GPU. In multiple code benchmark evaluations, Code Llama achieved state-of-the-art performance among open models, with scores of 53% and 55% on HumanEval and MBPP, respectively. Code Llama's performance is comparable to GPT-3.5, and the 34B parameter model's performance on the HumanEval benchmark is already close to GPT-4.

DeepSeek Coder

DeepSeek Coder is an open-source code LLM designed to provide powerful code generation, code completion, and mathematical reasoning capabilities. Its training dataset is mainly sourced from GitHub, covering 87 programming languages, and undergoes a strict data processing pipeline, including filtering and selection to ensure high data quality. The model uses various parallel strategies during pre-training to optimize computational efficiency, including tensor parallelism, ZeRO data parallelism, and pipeline parallelism. In addition, the model is instruction-tuned to enhance its ability to handle long contexts.

In the multilingual programming tests on the internationally authoritative HumanEval dataset, DeepSeek Coder outperformed existing open-source models across various languages. Compared with Code Llama, DeepSeek Coder achieved a lead of 9.3%, 10.8%, and 5.9%, respectively, in code generation tasks. Notably, DeepSeek Coder with 7 billion parameters matches the code capability of Code Llama at 34 billion parameters. Moreover, after instruction tuning, the DeepSeek Coder model even surpasses GPT3.5-Turbo, demonstrating strong mathematical and reasoning abilities.

The technical features of DeepSeek Coder include the first-ever construction of repository-level code data and the use of topological sorting to parse dependencies between files, significantly enhancing the ability to understand long-range and cross-file contexts. Additionally, by incorporating the Fill-In-Middle method, it greatly improves code completion capabilities. These techniques enable DeepSeek Coder to surpass the open-source benchmark Code Llama 3 in multiple tasks, such as code generation, cross-file code completion, and solving math problems through programming.

aiXcoder

aiXcoder is a widely used AI coding assistant in the Chinese market. aiXcoder is an intelligent programming assistant based on deep learning code generation technology, developed by **Silicon Heart Technology**, aimed at improving programmers' coding efficiency. The product automatically predicts programmers' intentions, continuously recommending "the next segment of code to be written", allowing programmers to confirm the upcoming code input directly with "one-click completion", thus greatly enhancing coding efficiency. aiXcoder can intelligently search and recommend standard code for functions similar to the current program during programming, providing strong reference for programmers.

The **aiXcoder R&D team** originates from the Key Laboratory of High Confidence Software Technologies (Peking University), and it is the first Chinese intelligent programming assistant based on deep learning code generation technology. As of March 22, 2022, aiXcoder's community edition has developer users in more than 130 countries and regions, providing intelligent programming services to over 300,000 international developers. In addition, aiXcoder has launched versions for **Android**, **JFinal**, **TensorFlow**, and more, offering support to programmers in different fields.

After introducing representative code LLMs, it is useful to look at the kinds of programming tasks these models are designed to support. These downstream tasks show how code LLM capabilities are applied in practice, from generating code from natural language to summarizing, translating, repairing, and reasoning about existing code.

Mapping downstream code tasks

According to the definition of software engineering, downstream tasks of code can be classified based on the input-output patterns of code into five types: **text-to-code**, **code-to-code**, **code-to-text**, **code-to-pattern**, and **text-to-text**. The application of LLMs in programming has expanded from simple single-step tasks, such as code generation and completion, to more complex scenarios that combine retrieval, repair, testing, reasoning, and cross-file context understanding. In practice, exploration of some deep domain features often involves combining different downstream tasks of code, ultimately forming scenarios that better fit business needs, as shown in *Figure 9.2*.

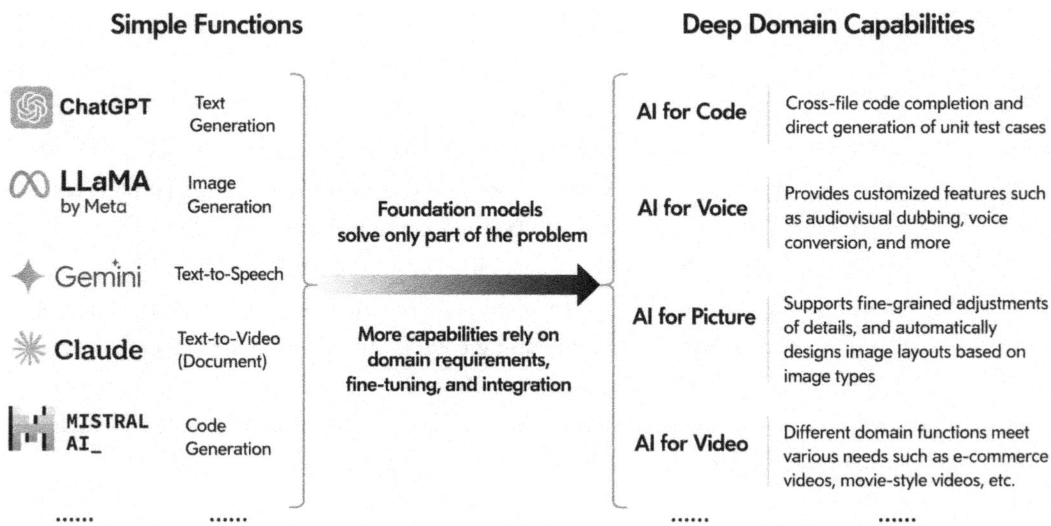

Figure 9.2: Usage scenarios of code processing tools

The first category begins with tasks where natural language is used to retrieve, generate, or guide the creation of code.

Text-to-code tasks

Text-to-code tasks take text as input and output code, typically involving scenarios such as **code retrieval**, **code generation**, and **numeric programming**:

- **Code Retrieval**: Aims to search for relevant code based on natural language, or to mine parallel text-code pairs from unannotated corpora. This task is usually accomplished by computing the similarity between the query and candidate code embeddings, and contextual embeddings produced by bidirectional language models (such as **BERT**) have been proven to be very useful.
- **Code Generation:** Aims to generate code based on natural language descriptions, typically functions or methods. This task can be seen as an upgraded version of code retrieval, utilizing generative models instead of retrieval models. **Statistical Machine Translation (SMT)** and **Neural Machine Translation (NMT)** models have been widely applied to this task, often with enhanced decoders utilizing the unique syntactic rules of programming languages. However, pretrained language models based on the Transformer architecture have changed this landscape, allowing direct source code generation via autoregressive language modeling even without task-specific fine-tuning.

> **Text-to-SQL** is a special case of code generation, and this approach is simpler. The model generates SQL commands from natural language queries; compared to general-purpose languages such as Python and C, SQL has structured characteristics. Therefore, the text-to-SQL approach has been widely used in data management.

- **Numeric Programming**: Numeric programming is also a special case of code generation, requiring the language model to solve mathematical reasoning problems by generating code that will be executed by an external interpreter. This task abstracts the reasoning process from numerical calculation, so this should be given special consideration when choosing a code LLM or in practice.

After tasks that generate code from text, the next category focuses on transforming, completing, repairing, or testing existing code.

Code-to-code tasks

Code-to-code tasks take code as input and output code, usually including scenarios such as **code search**, **code completion**, **code translation**, **code repair**, and **code infilling**.

- **Code Search**: Code search is a task similar to code retrieval. The difference is that the input consists of existing code fragments, and the programming language used is usually different from the target language.
- **Code Completion**: Code completion aims to complete a segment of code based on a given code prefix. This essentially applies language modeling to code, and related technologies such as **N-gram**, **RNN**, and **Transformer** have gradually been introduced. However, due to the structured nature of programming languages, many early studies found that syntax-assisted statistical models performed better, and neural models only became mainstream after 2018.
- **Code Translation**: The goal of code translation is to translate a segment of code (usually a function or method) into another programming language. The relationship between code translation and cross-language code search is similar to that between code generation and text-to-code retrieval, and **SMT/MNT models** are also widely applied to this task. Code generation can help programmers write code snippets, but code translation is different; it is an important technology for migrating old projects written in outdated languages. However, we have not yet seen such applications, because even for such projects, the context window of the most powerful language models is still quite limited.
- **Code Repair**: Code repair, also known as **bug fixing**, aims to fix erroneous code. Like code translation, it is also a traditional code-to-code task, with **Cloze tests** as a typical example. Cloze tests are code processing tasks proposed after the rise of **BERT-style pre-training**. Owing to the specific semantics of programming languages, this test usually selects several keywords such as `min` and `max`.
- **Code Infilling**: Code infilling is another task put forward after the popularity of **intermediate infilling pre-training**. It is a scenario of code completion, where not only the left context is given, but also the right context. However, it differs from the Cloze test in that the Cloze test targets only a single token, while code infilling can target entire lines or even multiple lines, which requires the decoder to generate them automatically.
- **Unit Test Generation**: The purpose of unit test generation is to generate unit tests for a given program. Before the emergence of Codex and other code LLMs, almost all work in this field used non-neural approaches. However, in the era of LLMs, this task is becoming increasingly important. Research shows that the current unit tests used to evaluate the program generation capabilities of code LLMs may not be sufficient.

- **Assertion Generation**: Assertion generation is a task closely related to unit testing. Given a program and a set of unit tests, the goal of this task is to generate **assertions** (also known as **oracles** in software engineering) so that the program can be evaluated using the unit tests. This task is not typically the focus of the NLP community, as program generation tasks for LLM evaluation generally involve independent, competitive approaches, where simply asserting that the program output matches the expected answer suffices.
- **Mutation Generation**: The purpose of mutation generation is to produce mutants of a given program for mutation testing, which is closely related to unit test generation and assertion generation. Mutants that are not detected by a given set of unit tests and assertions indicate the need for additional test cases or better assertions. Masking tokens in the source code and sampling from the output of masked language models has become a common approach for this task.
- **Fuzz Testing**: Fuzz testing aims to mutate a given set of unit tests to generate new test cases and is another task related to **software testing**. While much of the **fuzzing** work targets deep learning libraries, very few have utilized language models to carry out this process.
- **Type Prediction**: Aims to predict types in dynamic programming languages such as Python and JavaScript. It has been used as a pre-training objective for code LLMs and is often simplified to a binary tagging task to predict which tokens in the code are identifiers.

Some downstream tasks move in the opposite direction, using code as the input and producing natural language descriptions, reviews, or labels.

Code-to-text tasks

Code-to-text tasks take code as input and output text, typically including scenarios such as **code summarization**, **code review**, and **identifier prediction**.

- **Code Summarization**: Code summarization, also known as **docstring generation**, aims to generate a natural language description for a given piece of code (usually a function or method). This is the exact opposite of code generation, and **SMT/NMT techniques** are also applied here.
- **Code Review**: Code review aims to automate the process of peer code reviews, and it comes in various forms. Many early studies formulated it as a binary classification task to accept or reject modifications upon submission, while other studies used information retrieval techniques to recommend comments from existing comment repositories. However, as generative models have become more powerful, researchers have also explored directly generating review comments as a sequence-to-sequence learning task.

- **Identifier Prediction**: This is the task of predicting the names of identifiers in the code. Since these names are believed to contain important semantic information, this task has been used for code summarization as well as for the pre-training of code models.

Beyond generating or describing code, code LLMs can also help identify patterns, similarities, and reasoning structures within code.

Code-to-pattern tasks

Code-to-pattern tasks involve classifying code, typically including scenarios such as **clone detection** and **code reasoning**.

- **Clone Detection**: This predicts whether two pieces of code are clones of each other. In software engineering, there are four types of code clones, with the most difficult to identify being **semantic clones**—code with different syntax but identical functionality. As this task can be framed as a sentence pair classification problem, **BERT-style language models** have been widely used in this area.
- **Code Reasoning**: This is a recently introduced downstream code task. This task requires the model to perform reasoning on code or algorithms and answer related questions presented in multiple-choice form. The questions may cover areas such as **conceptual understanding**, **numerical computation**, and **complexity analysis**.

Finally, some programming-related tasks operate mainly on technical text rather than source code itself.

Text-to-text tasks

Text-to-text tasks take text as input and output text, typically including scenarios such as **document translation** and **log parsing**.

- **Document Translation**: This refers to the automatic translation of code-related documentation. Since models, datasets, and prompt strategies for **machine translation** are very rich in NLP, the technical implementation of document translation is not complicated.
- **Log Parsing**: This aims to analyze system logs generated by software products, such as parsing logs into structured templates or detecting anomalies from raw logs.

After mapping the main downstream code tasks, it is useful to focus on one of the most important and widely used areas: code generation and completion. Understanding how these technologies developed helps explain why modern code LLMs are able to move beyond simple token suggestions toward context-aware code assistance, functional code generation, and project-level development support.

Tracing the evolution of code generation and completion

Code programming assistance technologies have a history of more than 40 years. Their development has gone through several stages, from syntax highlighting, integration within **integrated development environments (IDEs)**, to code analysis and specification checks. Among these, tools such as IDEs have been iconic over the past 20 years. They significantly improve development efficiency and quality through features like automatic code completion, code highlighting, syntax error prompts, and code snippets, while also delivering a superior programming experience to developers.

LLM technologies have achieved remarkable breakthroughs and success in general industries, especially excelling in natural language processing tasks. General-purpose LLMs typically possess some programming capabilities. However, since their training data mainly consists of general natural language texts—while programming languages are more structured, have explicit syntax rules, and more direct and precise semantics—their performance in code understanding and generation, which is a specialized field, may be limited to some extent. This characteristic distinguishes them from general-purpose large models.

To better meet developers' needs in code-related tasks, LLMs are trained on large-scale code repositories, learning code snippets, programming patterns, and coding conventions, thus better understanding code structure and logic and generating code that adheres to syntax and semantic requirements.

In practice, how to effectively improve the efficiency and quality of software development has always been a concern in the field of software engineering. Among various approaches, code generation, and completion technologies are considered important methods for enhancing software development automation and ensuring quality, attracting widespread attention from both academia and industry. Code generation and completion refers to using certain techniques to automatically generate source code for software, aiming to enable automatic programming based on user requirements. This greatly reduces developers' development burden and allows them to focus more on delivering business value.

In academia, code generation and completion is an important branch of **program synthesis**, aiming to assist, or even replace, programmers in writing code. Automatic generation of front-end code is divided into two approaches: **view code** and **logic code**. Common solutions for generating view code include automatic generation from design drafts, such as *imgcook*. Common schemes for generating logic code include visual orchestration-based generation, input-output sample-based generation, code corpus-based generation, and function description-based generation.

Common code generation and completion techniques

Code generation and completion techniques belong to program automation technology and are also an important component of modern integrated development environments. **Code completion** greatly improves programming efficiency and reduces spelling errors during the coding process. Code generation and completion techniques typically help programmers predict class names, method names, keywords, and so on. The prediction of the next token is the most common form in code generation and completion processes, and is also the mainstream method used by current IDEs. In common IDEs, the recommended tokens are often listed in alphabetical order, which increases the time it takes for programmers to select a candidate token, often leading to a suboptimal user experience.

Traditional code generation and completion approaches are mainly divided into two types. One type utilizes **static type information** combined with various heuristic rules to decide which token to predict, such as method names, parameters, etc. This method rarely considers the semantic information from code context; for example, the mainstream code completion system in **Eclipse** uses static category information to recommend Java methods to users, and the recommended method names are usually sorted alphabetically. The other method leverages code samples and previous semantic context to complete code. In 2009, Bruch et al., in the paper *Learning from Examples to Improve Code Completion Systems*, described the use of the **kNN (k-Nearest Neighbor)** algorithm to match the current completion semantics with previous code samples, thereby improving completion accuracy. Techniques that use preceding semantic context for code completion usually utilize special types of context information (such as the set of APIs being called) to assist with completion. In 2010, Huo et al., in the paper *Towards a better code completion system by API grouping, filtering, and popularity-based ranking*, proposed a code completion technique called BCC. This technique implements Eclipse's type-based code completion system by ranking and filtering APIs. This approach usually requires manually defining many heuristic rules to specify the set of contextual semantics, and if the semantic context at the current completion position does not match the defined set, this method will fail.

Deep learning methods improve the accuracy of token recommendation by learning the probability distribution among code tokens from large-scale codebases. The first proposal for **probabilistic modeling** of code token sequences was presented by Hindle et al. in their 2012 paper *On the Naturalness of Software*. Theoretically, programming languages are written by humans, exhibiting repetitive language patterns. Thus, they possess some predictable statistical features that can be captured by language models. This hypothesis has become the cornerstone for applying probabilistic models and even deep learning to learn programming languages.

The most direct approach to next-token prediction is to use the program's token sequence to predict the current completion position, employing deep learning to accomplish code completion as shown in *Figure 9.3*. This process mainly consists of two parts: the **training phase** and the **code generation and completion phase**.

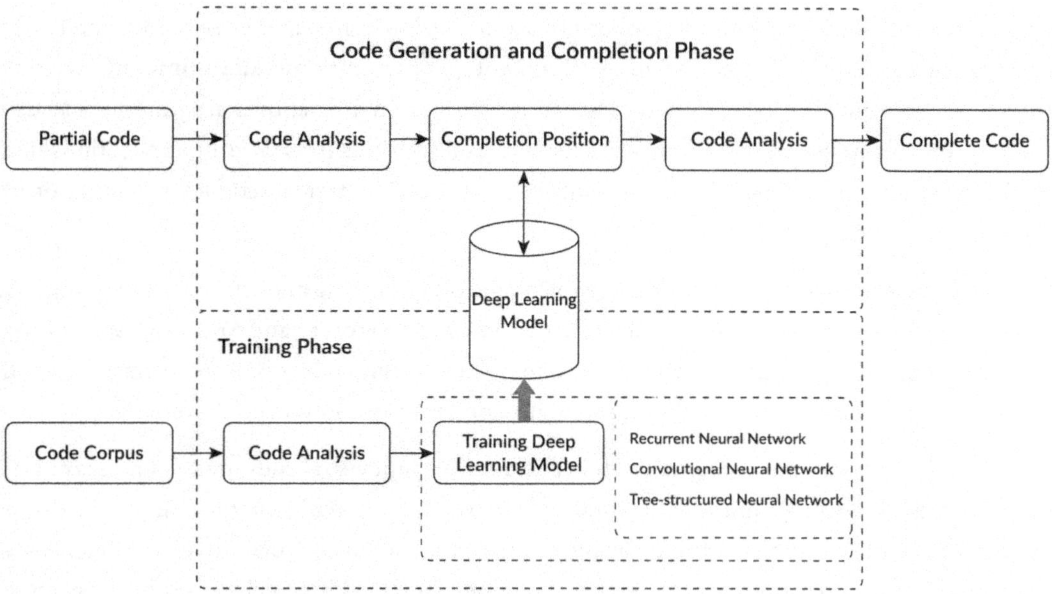

Figure 9.3: The workflow of code completion using deep learning

Researchers first collect a large amount of data from open-source code repositories or open-source communities to serve as the **corpus** for deep learning. To learn from the code in the corpus more effectively, researchers typically process the source code using **code parsers**, for example, converting source code into token sequences or **abstract syntax trees**. Subsequently, researchers select or design a **deep neural network** suitable for their specific task and train it using the data from the corpus. Currently, the deep neural networks frequently used in code completion tasks are **language models**; for example, **recurrent neural networks** can effectively learn the sequence characteristics of programs and apply these features to code completion tasks. During the code generation and completion phase, a partial code snippet is input, and the trained deep learning model is invoked at the current completion point.

Code generation and completion technologies have developed through several technical paths, each using a different kind of input, structure, or model to help produce code.

Code generation and completion based on visual orchestration

Visual programming is not a new concept. From the earliest visual plugins to today's **low-code** and **no-code** technologies, all fall within the realm of visual programming. Visual programming uses some componentized integrated code visualization platforms to allow so-called "junior developers" who lack professional coding skills and development experience to independently organize or participate in application development. In this way, **code development** expands from a programmer-exclusive duty to a wider audience. It mainly allows programmers to use various controls provided by the software itself to build various interfaces of applications in a modular, building-block-like fashion. **Visual orchestration** is better suited for the generation of interface view code.

Currently, there are many platforms that enable visual programming and low-code programming. Typical representatives include **OutSystems**, **Mendix**, **Salesforce**, and **Younuo Technology**. Similarly, there are also many visual solutions for relevant logic code: some are realized through visual plugins, some through visual components, and others via low-code technologies.

Apart from business scenarios, some emerging fields also adopt **visual coding** as a business model, such as simple logic programming for children. For enterprises, with market changes, business logic, and system architecture are increasingly complex; personnel involved in related businesses also need to possess a certain degree of **reverse engineering thinking skills**. Therefore, replacing programming languages with graphical methods can improve the involvement of business personnel in the software delivery process.

The advantage of current mainstream logical code visual orchestration solutions lies in highlighting **visual flow** and the efficiency brought about by **reusable logic nodes**. The core is to break down complex business processes, incorporating input/output and logic processing details into the specific form rules of each business node. *Figure 9.4* shows a complete logical orchestration process.

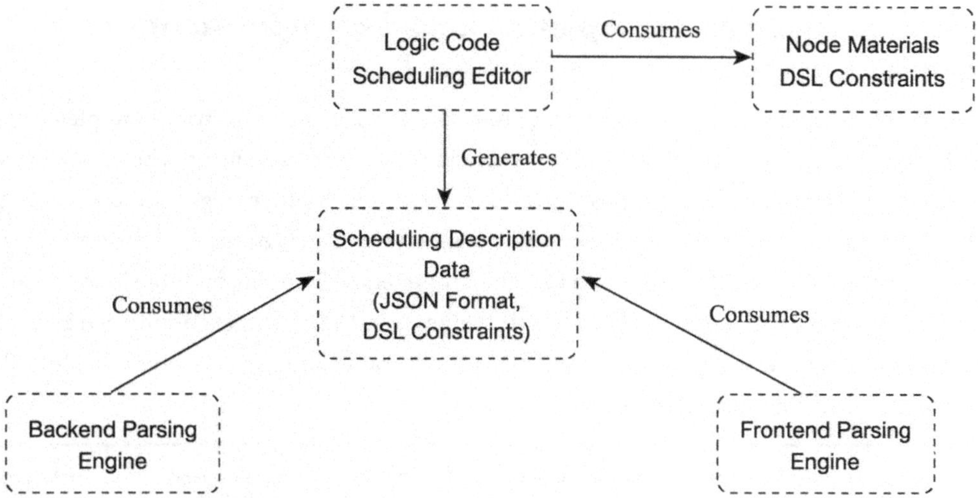

Figure 9.4: Visualized logic orchestration flow

Among them, node materials are used to define elements in the editor, including icons in the toolbox, ports, and component schemas in the properties panel. The logic orchestration editor is a visual editor that, based on the component information provided by the materials, edits and produces JSON-formatted orchestration description data. The orchestration description data is the output of user operations in the editor and is consumed by the parsing engine. The front-end parsing engine, implemented in TypeScript, directly parses the "orchestration description data" and executes it, thereby realizing the business logic of the software. The back-end parsing engine can also directly parse and execute the "orchestration description data," thus implementing the business logic of the software.

Visual orchestration is suitable for scenarios with a high degree of logic reuse. The reusable logic can be abstracted as nodes. The granularity of node reuse is crucial. If the granularity is as large as a functional service, it can be considered business process orchestration. Scenarios with high business process reuse are suitable for business parties to operate directly through visual orchestration tools. If the granularity is as small as the expression level, it can be considered business logic orchestration. A granularity that is too fine requires users to have a programming mindset; in such cases, users with programming skills can achieve higher efficiency by writing code directly.

While visual orchestration relies on reusable nodes and predefined flows, programming by examples allows users to describe desired behavior through sample inputs and outputs.

Code generation and completion based on input–output examples

Automatically inferring and generating logic programs based on input-output examples is called **PBE (Programming by Examples)**. PBE is a subfield of **program synthesis**. The paper *Program Synthesis Using Natural Language* proposed a technical solution for program generation. In practical applications, there is an intuitive and easy-to-implement case of program generation, namely the Auto-fill function in Excel. This function can quickly generate formulas for table items based on several examples. For instance, in *Figure 9.5*, the values 2 and 4 in the first column can be used to fill in even numbers, and the values 50 and 40 in the second column can automatically deduce the result of an arithmetic sequence formula.

Even Numbers	Every 10 Numbers	Text and Numbers	Even Numbers	Every 10 Numbers	Text and Numbers
2	50	Week 1	2	50	Week 1
4	40	Week 2	4	40	Week 2
			6	30	Week 3
			8	20	Week 4
			10	10	Week 5
			12	0	Week 6
			14	−10	Week 7
			16	−20	Week 8
			18	−30	Week 9
			20	−40	Week 10

Figure 9.5: Illustration of generating table item formulas

The above Auto-fill function is very simple. Let's look at a more complex example. *Figure 9.6* shows the illustration of a name-generation formula.

First Name	Middle Name	Last Name	Full Name
Mary	Kristy	Helln	Helln, Mary, K
Zhang	San	Yi	Yi, Zhang, S
Joe	L	Bryant	Bryant, Joe, L
Bob	John	Hart	Hart, Bob, J

Figure 9.6: Illustration of name generation formula

The formulas in *Figure 9.6* are analyzed as follows:

```
if(input[1]=="") then concat(input[2], const(", "), input[0], const("."))
else concat(input[2],
const(", "), input[0], const(""), let v=input[1] in substring(v,
AbsPos(v,0), RegexPos(v, Uppercase,
", -1))

Const(", ")
```

In reality, the accuracy of the Auto-fill function for complex formulas or scenarios is less than 50%. The goal of PBE is to automatically infer computer programs to accomplish a task using simple inputs and outputs. A 2017 paper proposed **Neural Programming by Example (NPBE)**, a deep-neural-network-based system that learns from input-output strings to induce programs that solve string-processing problems. The architecture has four components: a string encoder, an input-output analyzer, a program generator, and a symbol selector. NPBE solves some common string processing problems in spreadsheet software systems through training.

The typical implementation logic of PBE technology is illustrated in *Figure 9.7*.

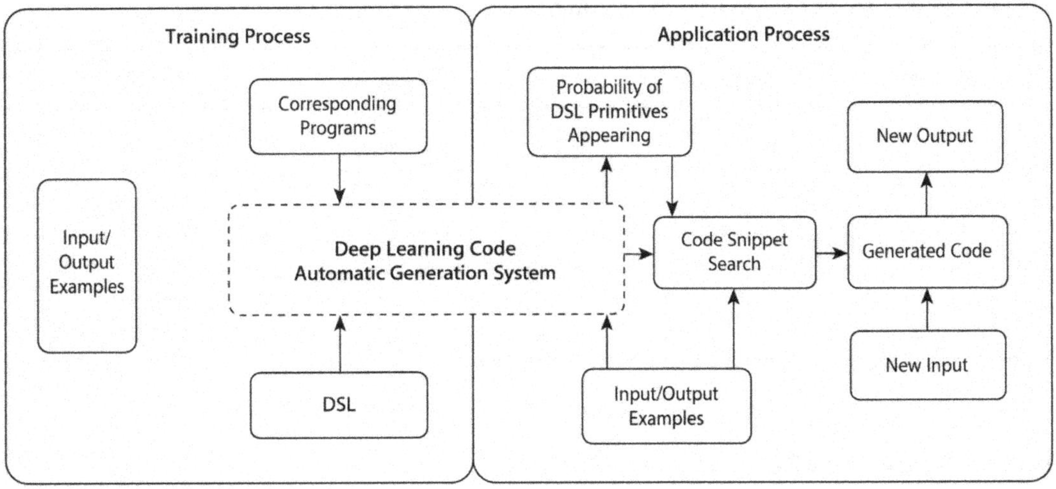

Figure 9.7: PBE technology implementation logic

Another path is to generate or complete code by learning from existing code corpora, where repositories and snippets become reusable sources of programming knowledge.

Code generation and completion based on code corpora

The prerequisite for code generation and completion based on a **code corpus** is having a sufficient corpus, which we often refer to as **code snippets**. Traditional **IDE plugins** have already initially implemented the collection and analysis of common code snippets, which is a relatively common way of analyzing a code corpus. With the development of **code repository technology**, analyzing and utilizing the large amount of code accumulated in repositories to eventually form a company's core assets—transforming the value of code into proprietary technology and intellectual property—has become a new direction for technological output. At the same time, combining code corpus with management measures and deeply embedding code LLM technology into development and management processes to form domain knowledge and management standards has become an ongoing research topic for many enterprises, as shown in *Figure 9.8*.

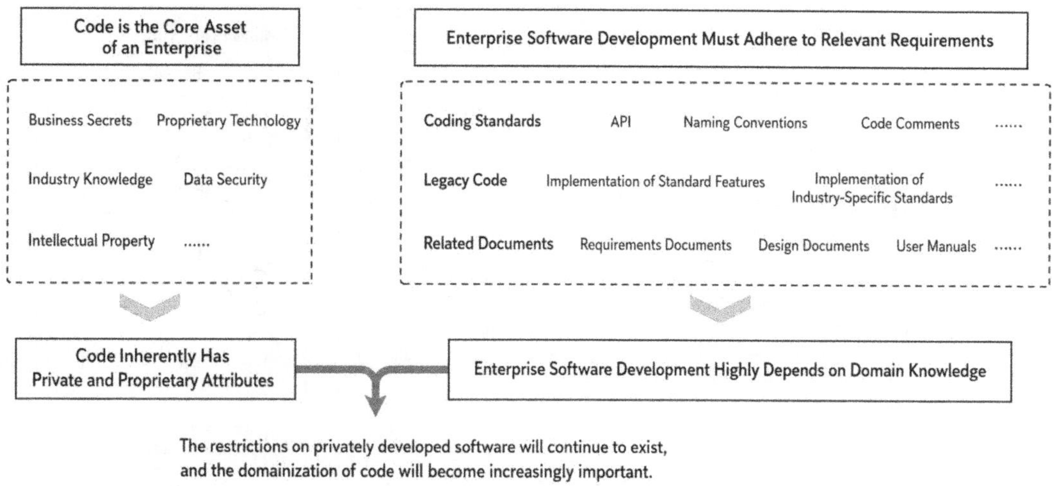

Figure 9.8: Scope of code domainization

Code corpora are generally divided into two types: **fixed corpora** and **intelligent corpora**. For fixed corpora, users preset code snippets, which are then prompted to the user by listening to shortcut keys entered by the user to search for the corresponding snippet. This code generation method is simple and fast, but it suffers from poor scalability and suboptimal user experience, and developers need to know the key values and corresponding snippets in advance.

The acquisition of intelligent corpora mainly depends on the capability of the code repository itself and the assistance of models. Typical examples include the **GitHub Copilot** plugin and **N-gram models**. The VSCode plugin **Kite Autocomplete** uses the N-gram model and is trained on over 25 million files, enhancing coding efficiency through code assistance functions during programming. It predicts the content that the user is about to input based on context and current input. Additionally, it can read ahead in the context of the entire file to further infer the user's actions based on current input. Taking code completion as an example, using a JavaScript code corpus and applying the N-gram probability model to complete code development, the relevant workflow is shown in *Figure 9.9*.

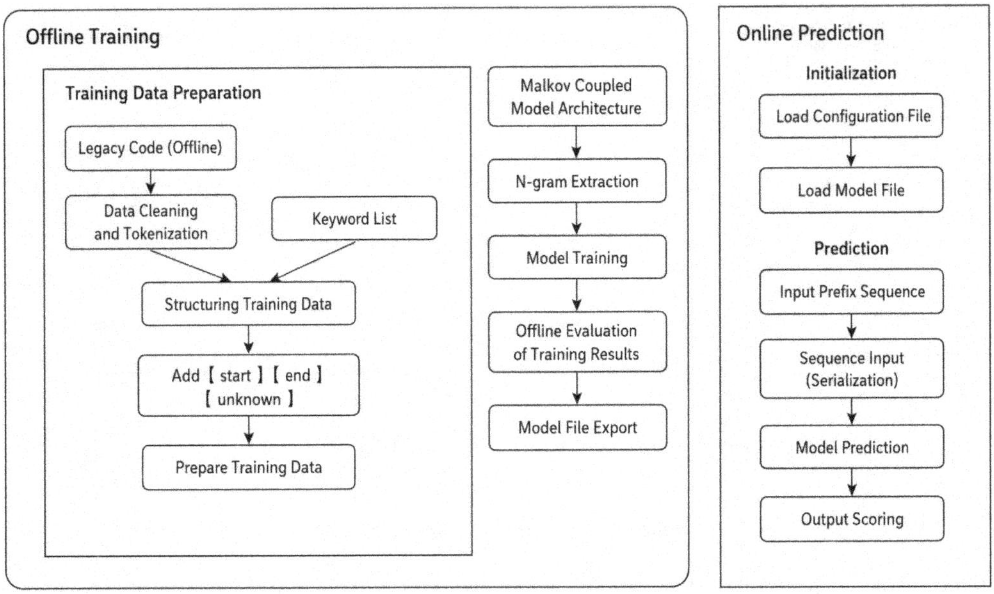

Figure 9.9: Workflow of code completion using N-gram probability model

Unlike code completion, **code generation** (also known as **code intent generation**) refers to inferring the function of code based on its content. Well-known industry open-source models and services include code2vec and code2seq. The advantage of code2vec lies in code functionality summarization, whereas code2seq excels at code functionality description.

A simple demonstration of the functionality of code2vec is shown in *Figure 9.10*.

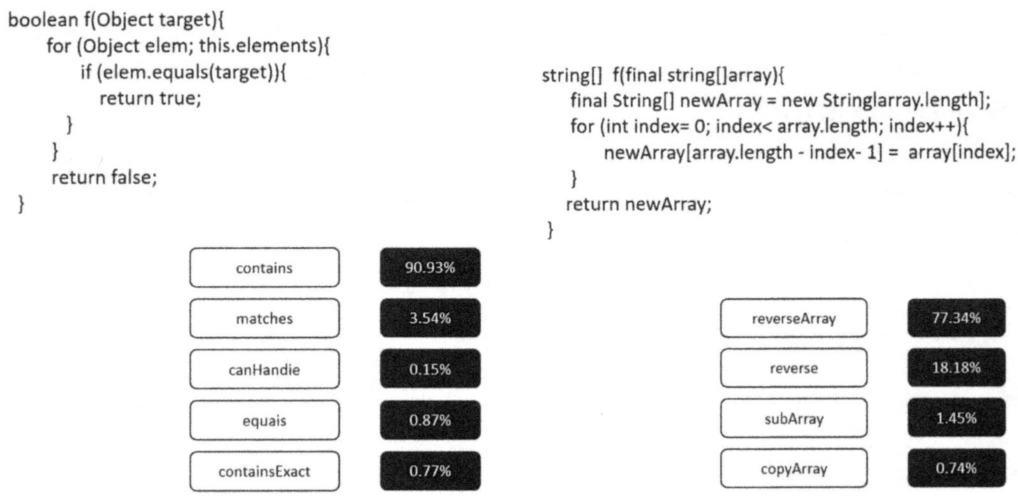

Figure 9.10: Schematic of code2vec's functionality

Based on the described code snippet, the analysis result shows that there is a 90.93% probability that it is `contains`. In addition to the percentage value, `code2vec`'s analysis results can also be presented visually, using the thickness of lines to indicate the weight of decision information, which is not shown here.

The paper *code2vec-Learning Distributed Representations of Code* also studied `code2vec`. As shown in *Figure 9.10*, if we look only at the low-level details, it appears that this code is related to array assignment. However, we know that its semantics are actually reversing an array. Therefore, for such a code snippet, the `code2vec` model generates the result shown on the right, predicting that its most likely semantic label is `reverseArray`, which shows that the model's prediction is consistent with its true semantics.

Instead of starting from existing code snippets, functional-description-based methods begin with natural language descriptions of what the program should do.

Code generation and completion based on functional descriptions

We often use natural language to describe program functionality, and generating programs automatically from natural language descriptions is extremely challenging. The diversity of natural language texts and programs, the ambiguity of text, and the complex structure of code make establishing the connection between text and code a difficult problem. In this section, we describe how code generation and completion can be performed based on functional descriptions using the tools **NL2SQL** and **NL2IFTTT**.

NL2SQL

NL2SQL (Natural Language to SQL) is a cutting-edge research direction in conversational user interfaces (**Conversation User Interface, CUI**), aiming to convert user input in natural language into executable SQL statements, thereby improving the efficiency of user data queries. Currently, the main challenge hindering the value realization of big data is the high threshold for data access, relying on database administrators to write complex SQL statements, and the added complexity and diversity of Chinese expressions. There is substantial research in this field both domestically and abroad, with most of the well-known NL2SQL datasets being in English, such as *WikiSQL*, *Spider*, *CoSQL*, etc.

A typical three-layer architecture of NL2SQL is shown in *Figure 9.11*.

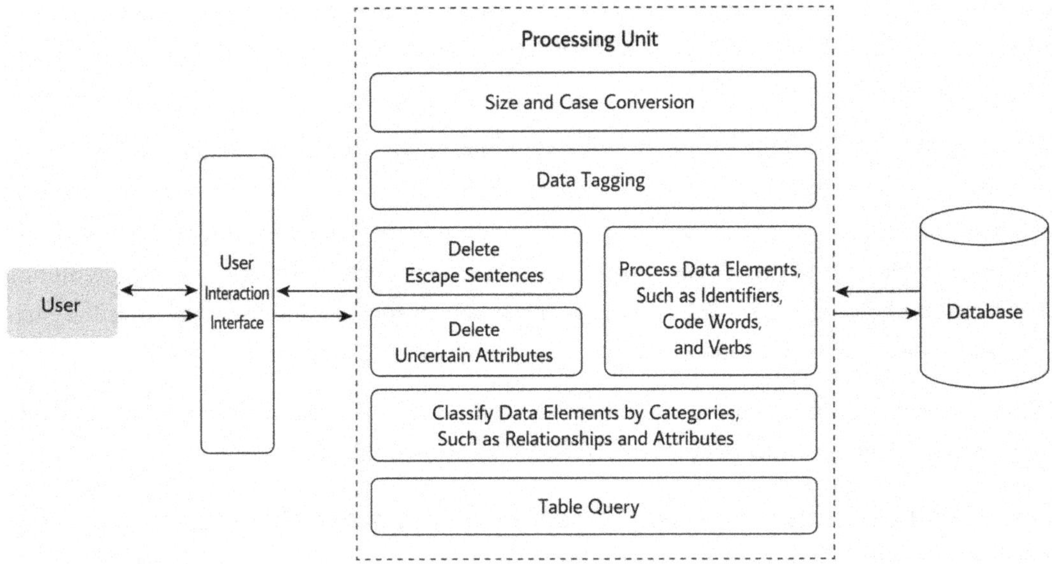

Figure 9.11: Typical three-layer architecture of NL2SQL

NL2SQL consists of a **user interaction page**, a **processing unit**, and a **database**. The **processing unit** is the core of the entire architecture, responsible for semantic parsing and connecting the interaction channel between the user and the system, encompassing key technologies such as intelligent word segmentation, entity recognition, and knowledge retrieval. In the research direction of converting natural language into executable SQL statements, the internal algorithms of the processing unit are gradually evolving toward deep learning.

In the Chinese NL2SQL competition, the research team from the National University of Defense Technology proposed the **M-SQL model**, which achieved 92% accuracy on Chinese datasets. In addition, running one epoch of the M-SQL model on a single 2080Ti GPU takes 20 minutes, and the model only needs 3–4 epochs to converge.

Unlike the **M-SQL model** from the National University of Defense Technology, Google's **Analyza** uses a semantic parsing and rule-based approach, which offers strong controllability but requires manual maintenance of rules. **Analyza** implements NL2SQL through deep learning using an **encoder-decoder architecture**, recognizing several SQL clauses, including `SELECT` and `WHERE` clauses, and sometimes involving operators such as `GROUP BY` and `LIMIT`. Each part involves many details, such as table recognition, attribute recognition, etc. Different algorithms make improvements and optimizations on these details within this framework to achieve better results.

Although end-to-end NL2SQL solutions can reduce manual maintenance costs, they perform well only in simple scenarios like *WikiSQL*. For more complex scenarios, such as *Spider* or *CoSQL*, accuracy is relatively low, and it is difficult to meet commercial application requirements.

NL2IFTTT

> NL2IFTTT is included here as a case study in DSL-targeted code generation rather than as a representative of mainstream NL-to-code research.

IFTTT stands for '**if this then that**'. It is an innovative platform service that determines whether to execute the next command based on conditions from different platforms. For example, when someone in an **IM** marks a photo containing you, the photo can automatically be backed up to your phone's photo album. This approach meets the user's need to link content from service A to service B, without requiring manual intervention—the related action can be initiated and completed automatically by IFTTT.

NL2IFTTT generates IFTTT code through natural language. Compared to commonly used programming languages, its structure is more concise and easier to learn in terms of its structural rules. IFTTT is based on task-triggered conditions, similar to a simplified programming language, that is, 'if behavior B of event A occurs, then execute C.'

Language-model-based approaches extend these earlier methods by learning statistical and semantic patterns from large collections of code, enabling more flexible prediction, completion, and generation.

Code generation and completion based on language models

Language models are widely used in various natural language processing tasks, such as machine translation, speech recognition, question answering systems, etc. Language models define the probability distribution of token sequences in natural language. Due to the naturalness of programming languages, language models are also applied to program modeling, usually by directly inputting parsed code snippets (at the word or character level) as text. The goal of this model is to model the textual probability distribution of programming languages, i.e., the probabilistic model is used to estimate the probability distribution $P(s)$ of a code snippet s. For a code snippet $s = \{ w_1, ..., w_m \}$, the language model calculates the probability distribution of the entire code snippet by computing the conditional probability of each word based on the previously generated words, i.e.,

$$P(s) = \prod_{i=1}^{m} P\left(w_i | w_1, \dots, w_{i-1}\right).$$

In programming language processing, commonly used language models include N-gram and RNN, where RNN is a language model based on deep neural networks.

N-gram is the earliest language model used for program learning. In the **N-gram model**, the probability of the next word w_i depends on the previous *n-1* words, that is.

$$P(s) = \prod_{i=1}^{m} P\left(w_i | w_1, \dots, w_{i-n+1}\right).$$

Therefore, the N-gram model can capture the local information of sentences to a certain extent. After Hindle et al. proposed applying the **N-gram model** to code modeling in the paper *On the Naturalness of Software*, many works utilizing N-gram models emerged subsequently. Although N-gram can effectively learn the local context of code snippets, it cannot understand the semantic information of code snippets. To address this problem, many researchers have improved the N-gram model by combining the characteristics of software engineering tasks. Nguyen et al., in the paper *A Statistical Semantic Language Model for Source Code*, proposed the idea that the **SLAMC** model incorporates global information into the N-gram model; **SLAMC** combines semantic information and models rules for semantic annotations. This method achieved a significant improvement in the accuracy of code recommendation compared to a regular N-gram. Meanwhile, Raychev et al., in the paper *Code Completion with Statistical Language Models*, also proposed combining the N-gram model with RNN, actively suggesting appropriate API calls based on the context during Java development to implement code completion. To address the challenge of the locality property of code, Tu et al. proposed in the paper *On the Localness of Software* to introduce a caching mechanism into the N-gram model, utilizing the characteristic that identifiers tend to repeatedly appear within a close range, thereby achieving significant results in code prediction.

Compared to N-gram, RNN can not only capture regularities among words in a sentence, but also detect relationships between more distant words. To further address the long-distance dependency problem, many RNN-based variants, such as **Long Short-Term Memory (LSTM)** and **Gated Recurrent Unit (GRU),** have been proposed and widely applied. As shown in *Figure 9.12*, RNN models can effectively model source code and learn vector representations of source code.

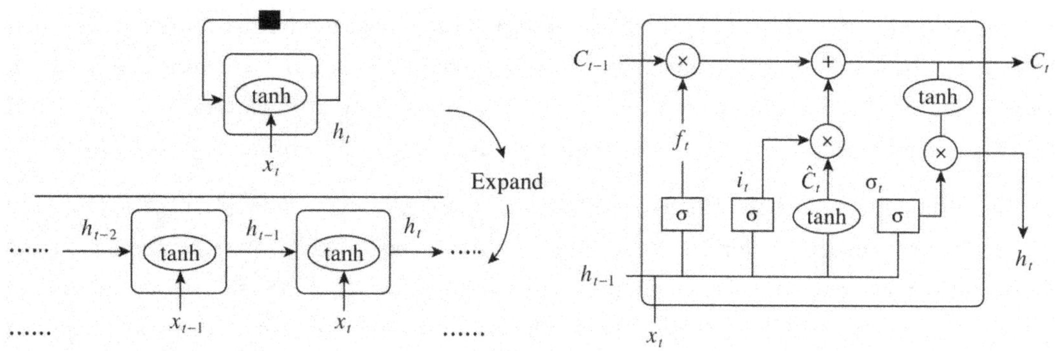

Figure 9.12: Modeling process of RNN model

The paper *DeepAM-Migrate APIs with Multi-Modal Sequence to Sequence Learning* focuses on using RNN to learn vector representations that differentiate Java and C# API, and applies these learned vectors to the API migration task between these two languages to generate code at the API level. Many researchers have used RNN models for **code token prediction** and **completion**, achieving remarkable results. Most research models code at the word level using RNNs, but due to the large number of variables in code, learning becomes very challenging; therefore, some work has started to model code at the character level.

Programming languages exhibit certain local repetitiveness. For example, a defined variable is often reused later in the code. However, these variables are largely treated as **out-of-vocabulary (OoV)** words, usually represented as **UNK**. Predicting a UNK is of no help to programmers in their coding, so researchers have considered incorporating **pointer network** mechanisms into language models to accurately predict locally repeated words. The pointer network can effectively copy words that need to be reused from the input code snippet. Pointer networks were first proposed at the 2015 IEEE conference, originally used to solve combinatorial optimization problems, and are a variant of **neural machine translation models** (i.e., **sequence-to-sequence models, Seq2Seq** models). In pointer networks, the attention mechanism is simpler, as it does not consider the input elements, but instead points to them probabilistically.

In 2016, Bhoopchand et al. proposed a **Sparse Pointer Network** in the paper *Learning Python Code Suggestion with a Sparse Pointer Network*, mainly addressing the issue of predicting custom identifiers (such as class names, method names, variable names, etc.). The paper defines the concept of "memory" to store the previous *K* identifiers. The method maintains a vector `m=[id1,...,id*K*]`, used to record the positions of identifiers in the global vocabulary, i.e., pointers to the global vocabulary.

At each prediction step, the network combines the global language model distribution, the pointer probability distribution over custom identifiers, and the current code input to determine the output word. Compared to traditional recurrent neural networks (without the attention mechanism), this method increases the accuracy for predicting custom Python identifiers by about 25%.

In their 2018 paper *Code Completion with Neural Attention and Pointer Networks*, Li et al. proposed a method for code completion by combining a language model with an attention mechanism and pointer networks, modeling sequences of **abstract syntax trees (ASTs)**. This model can not only predict the type of AST nodes but also predict their values, that is, the code to be completed. When predicting code, the entropy of parent nodes is greater than that of child nodes, resulting in higher prediction accuracy. Therefore, their attention mechanism incorporates the parent-child node relationship of syntax trees into the traditional attention mechanism. The paper uses **pointer networks** to copy words from the input code snippets to predict OoV tokens. By defining a selector, the model decides whether to predict the next word based on the distribution over the global vocabulary in the language model or to use the pointer network to copy a word from the input code snippet. This method was validated on both Python and JavaScript datasets, and results show that the method performs exceptionally well in OoV prediction scenarios.

Although code generation and completion technologies have advanced significantly, they still face practical limitations when applied to real software projects. The next section examines the main issues that affect their reliability, adaptability, and usefulness in production development environments.

Identifying pain points in code generation and completion

Overall, **code generation and completion** based on LLM technology has become a trend, but the application of this technology is still at an early stage, mainly facing the following pain points.

Uneven quality of training corpora

In daily work, the corpora used to train models can be roughly divided into two categories: one consists of programs constructed artificially based on **DSL** technology, and the other consists of project programs crawled from open source communities. Programs based on DSL usually have relatively simple syntax and short length, making them easy to train and test; however, models designed for DSL are difficult to generalize to other languages. Project programs crawled from open source communities are closer to actual software development, but it is difficult to guarantee the quality of the code.

Low-quality, non-standard code introduces additional noise risk to neural networks, and code that uses different programming conventions causes confusion for neural network models during training and prediction. Therefore, how to obtain a unified, standardized, high-quality program corpus is a challenge.

Weak generalization ability of program code

Much program code consists of business domain-specific logic, requiring a substantial amount of domain-specific logic resources and a deep understanding of the various services relied on by existing businesses. New businesses need to train their own models based on their own material libraries, and the services required by completely new businesses often need to be developed from scratch. Supplying new materials can also be difficult, unless all the dependent services are indivisible atomic services; thus, making the logic model universal is hard to achieve.

Information asymmetry between functional descriptions and program code

In actual project development, it is common for requirement descriptions to be more advanced and abstract than functional descriptions. Requirement descriptions must first be converted into functional descriptions, then into code descriptions, and finally, program code is generated. At each stage, there will be information loss, which is currently typically compensated for by programmers' business knowledge and programming experience. There are three solutions for directly generating code from functional descriptions:

- End-to-end generation of **abstract syntax trees** from requirement descriptions. If the product definition's description of software functionality is precise enough, this is equivalent to creating a higher-level descriptive language
- Abstracting and encapsulating the entire chain from functional description to code as a larger-grain functional description. Most encapsulation-based methods are currently feasible and effective, with a typical example being NL2IFTTT.
- Developers deeply engage in each business domain, and at each stage, from functional description to code, the model understands layer by layer and gradually generates the code

Therefore, the quality of the corpus and the accuracy of the model are crucial.

The limitations of code generation and completion become more pronounced when models are asked to work across real project repositories rather than isolated functions or snippets. This is where agent-based methods become important: they combine code LLMs with tools, execution environments, documentation, and iterative feedback to support more complex project-level development tasks.

Applying agent-based methods to project-level code generation

Agent-based project-level code generation extends single-function code completion by combining a code LLM with tools — a code execution sandbox, a static analyzer, a documentation lookup — orchestrated by an LLM agent that plans, calls tools, and iterates. The **Xcoder** team at Peking University has achieved significant results in research on the application of code LLM-based agents in the field of software engineering, publishing several relevant papers. Xcoder is an early example of a code LLM-based agent system that combines a code-focused language model with tools to address project-level code generation problems. This section uses Peking University's paper *CODEAGENT—Enhancing Code Generation with Tool-Integrated Agent Systems for Real-World Repo-level Coding Challenges* to explain Agent-based project-level code generation methods.

Pain points of project-level code generation in enterprises

Project-level code in enterprises, as a critical component supporting and driving the core business processes, is directly related to the quality of the enterprise's products and services, operational efficiency, and market competitiveness. However, project-level code often involves diverse library and function calls, complex contextual dependencies across the codebase, and various types of code documentation. Furthermore, as business requirements change, the project code needs constant updating, expansion, and optimization. In this dynamic, ongoing, and complex process, there are numerous pain points.

Difficulty in fine-grained code modification and expansion

A project usually contains thousands or even tens of thousands of lines of code, involving multiple interdependent modules and subsystems. When faced with the need for fine-grained code changes, even a "single move can affect the whole picture"; a slight mishap can impact other modules, leading to extensive testing and verification work. This further affects project schedules and increases the complexity and risks of maintenance.

Complex and large codebases

Large-scale projects generally have long cycles and high staff turnover. The complexity and vastness of the codebase make it difficult for new team members to quickly grasp the project structure and code logic; even experienced members face time-consuming and labor-intensive efforts when searching for specific code fragments in the ever-growing codebase.

Difficulty ensuring code generation quality

In actual programming, developers commonly use various tools to assist with coding, such as search engines, documentation readers, and code testing tools. Although code LLMs possess powerful code generation capabilities, they lack the ability to interact with these tools, which limits their performance in complex tasks. Moreover, due to issues such as hallucinations with code LLMs, the generated code may use incorrect APIs, making it difficult to ensure the quality and reliability of code generation.

Low efficiency in implementing requirements into code

Throughout the entire project development process, enterprises often face issues such as insufficient requirement understanding, frequent architecture design adjustments, difficulty controlling development progress, and inadequate test coverage. These result in low iteration efficiency, project delays, budget overruns, or substandard quality, further increasing operational burdens and impacting market competitiveness.

Facing numerous pain points and challenges in project-level code generation, introducing Agents has become a key path for enterprises to resolve difficulties in code generation, improve development efficiency and code quality, and accelerate product iteration.

Technical implementation of agents

The technical implementation of a code agent can be understood from two related perspectives: how the agent is evaluated in realistic repository-level tasks, and how the agent uses tools to navigate code, gather context, generate implementations, and test the results. The following discussion first examines the testing process used to evaluate Code Agent, then explains the framework and tool integration that support project-level code generation.

Code agent testing process

The Xcoder team at Peking University conducted extensive testing on the **Code Agent**. Since enterprises mainly use open-source codebases in actual coding processes—and codebases contain a large number of complex code invocation relationships—testing within a codebase is the only way to obtain precise results, enabling the code LLM agent to function properly. To this end, the team configured corresponding corpora for each test task, including **documentation, code dependencies**, and **runtime environment**.

Documentation is the main input for testing and mainly describes the target for corpus generation. The documentation provides information beyond natural language requirements, including class-level (class names, signatures, and member functions) and function-level (function descriptions and parameter descriptions) information. Generally, the correctness of programs generated by the Agent can be verified by testing tools. The generated program must meet interface requirements (e.g., input parameters), so the documentation under test also provides the type and explanation for input parameters and output values. Considering that requirements often involve terms specific to certain domains, the documentation also explains these terms, such as certain mathematical formulas. Related test information is shown in *Figure 9.13*.

Benchmark	Language	Source	Task	Instances	Tests	Functions	Tokens	Input
CoNaLA (Yin et al., 2018)	Python	Stack Overflow	Statement-level	500	×	1	4.6	NL
Concode (Iyer et al., 2018)	Java	GitHub	Function-level	2000	×	—	26.3	NL
APPS (Hendrycks et al., 2021)	Python	Contest Sites	Sites Competitive	5000	✓	21.4	58	NL + IO
HumanEval (Chen et al., 2021)	Python	Manual	Function-level	164	✓	11.5	24.4	NL + SIG + IO
MBXP (Athiwaratkun et al., 2022)	Multilingual	Manual	Function-level	974	✓	6.8	24.2	NL
InterCode (Yang et al., 2023)	SQL, Bash	Manual	Function-level	200 , 1034	✓	—	—	NL + ENV
CodeContests (Li et al., 2022)	Python, C++	Contest	Sites Competitive	165	✓	59.8	184.8	NL + IO
ClassEval (Du et al., 2023)	Python	Manual	Class-level	100	✓	45.7	123.7	NL + CLA
CoderEval (Yu et al., 2023)	Python, Java	GitHub	Project-level	230	✓	30	108.2	NL + SIG
RepoEval (Liao et al., 2023)	Python	GitHub	Repository-level	383	×	—	—	NL + SIG
CODEAGENTBENCH	Python	GitHub	Repository-level	101	✓	57	477.6	Software Artifacts (NL + DOC +DEP + ENV)

Figure 9.13: Test information for generated programs

The team specifically tested for **context dependencies**, which is a distinct feature from the experiments of others. From the perspective of code generation and completion, this testing detail is especially important because, in actual applications, a class or function usually interacts with other code fragments in the same codebase. Such situations often occur in `import` statements or within the same project, where user-defined code also depends on other user-defined code. The interactions and dependencies among these codes can happen within the same file or span multiple files.

For example, implementing the `RandomForest` class in *Figure 9.14* depends on the `boot-strap_sample` function in `rf.py` and the `DecisionTree` class in `dt.py`. This is a case of complex code context dependency.

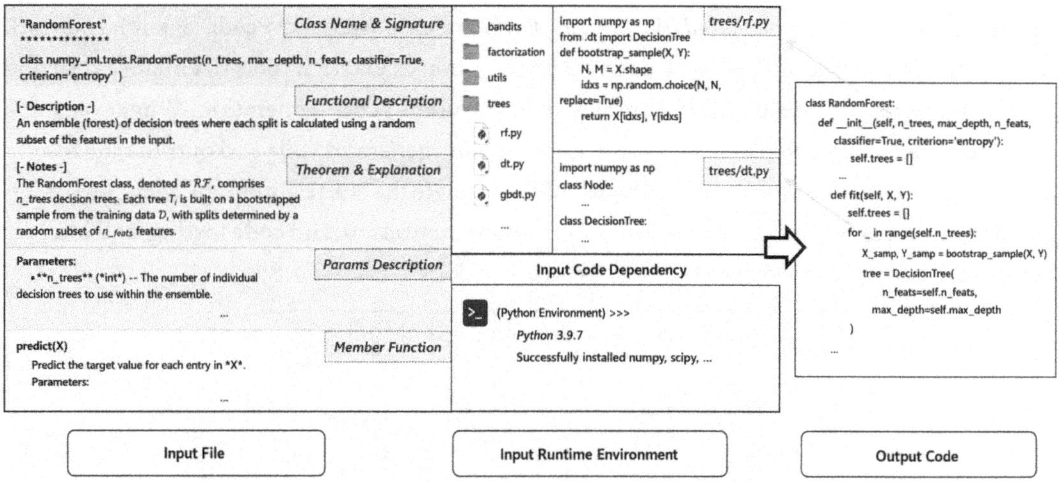

Figure 9.14: Contextual dependency of code

During the testing process, the tool designed by the Xcoder team at Peking University extracts all user-defined elements (such as class names, function names, constants, and global variables) as well as public library names from each file and stores these elements in a knowledge base. For any defined function, the tool can use the knowledge base to locate its source file, parse the file to identify all user-defined symbols and public libraries, and finally determine their contextual dependencies through exact matching of symbol names and scopes.

During testing, the Xcoder team found that each example averaged about 3.1 code dependencies, which is very similar to programming conditions in real-world projects. Since there are certain differences between the test runtime environment and natural language in reality, the main validation method is to determine whether the programming language generated by the code LLM can be executed correctly and successfully return the target result. Usually, developers wait for execution feedback and constantly correct errors in the program. In this Code Agent test, the Xcoder team built a sandbox environment for each task. The sandbox environment provides all the configuration needed to run the repository and offers a concise way of interaction to ensure comprehensive testing.

Technical implementation of code agent

The Xcoder team from Peking University conducted a preliminary exploration of evaluating and enhancing the capabilities of code LLMs in repository-level code generation. Referring to the paper Toward *a Unified Agent with Foundation Models*, the team proposed a new code-agent framework based on code LLMs: Code Agent. This framework leverages external tools to enhance the code LLM's ability to solve problems in complex repository-level code generation. Whenever tools are called, the Code Agent seamlessly and automatically generates code and outputs the results after integration. Code Agent can help code LLMs complete the entire automatic code generation process, including **information gathering**, **code implementation**, and **code testing**, and interact better with software coding tools, as shown in *Figure 9.15*.

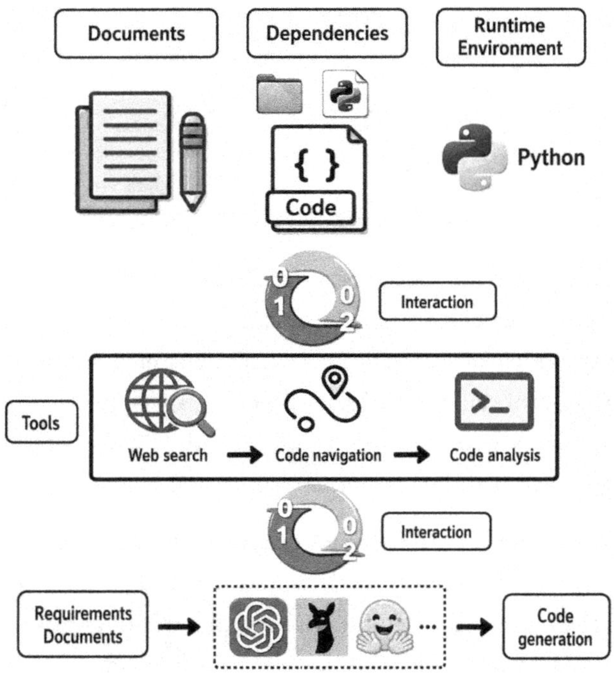

Figure 9.15: The process of automatic code generation

The core of Code Agent is the **code navigation tool**, which is used to quickly locate relevant code items in the codebase (i.e., predefined symbol names and code snippets). Code LLMs can quickly obtain these code items and integrate them into the code generation process. This approach can accelerate the development process and achieve code reuse.

The code navigation tool is implemented based on **tree-sitter technology**. Taking Python as an example, a code navigation tool is built for the Python codebase. This tool parses and retrieves code items in two ways. One way is to perform static analysis on files or modules and provide the symbol names defined within, including global variables, function names, and class names. The other way is to navigate public classes or function symbols and define separate class names or function names for them. By combining these two methods, the code navigation tool can quickly traverse the predefined source code in the repository, enabling code LLMs to understand complex dependencies in the code and utilize them swiftly.

After introducing the Code Agent framework, the discussion now turns to practical development scenarios where agent-based coding assistance can be applied in real project workflows.

> The following examples use aiXcoder to illustrate how agent-based coding capabilities can appear in developer-facing tools, but the same general pattern can apply to other code agents that combine models, repository context, execution feedback, and development tools.

Application of transaction automation in development scenarios

In large-scale, complex projects, as users continually raise new requirements and features are iteratively updated, developers often receive tasks to modify and extend numerous details in large codebases, such as bug fixes, feature development, or performance optimization. aiXcoder's transaction automation feature can accurately parse complex transactions submitted by developers, automatically locate problems and requirements, fully leveraging the codebase's various modules, interdependencies, and contextual information to process issues and requirements step-by-step. Ultimately, it directly generates code files and autonomously creates a sandbox to validate the edited code. During this process, it supports modifications across multiple files and can be interrupted at any time for manual intervention and adjustments.

Figure 9.16 shows a classic information management system development scenario.

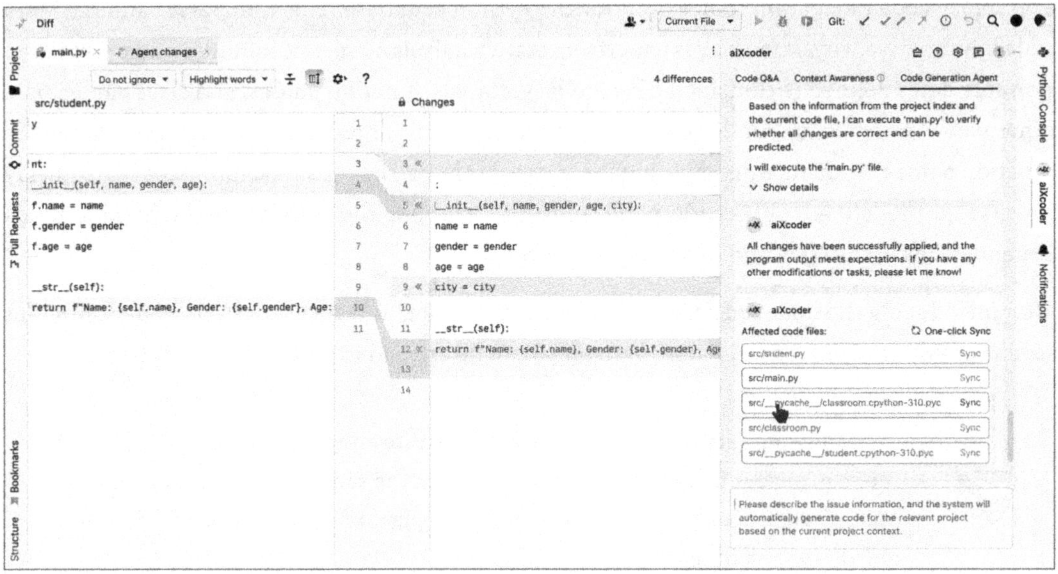

Figure 9.16: Information management system development scenario

The developer requests to add student-related information in two separate files and requires that the system run properly. The transaction automation feature understands and analyzes the request, plans, and locates the corresponding files. Notably, during automatic execution, it also discovers dependencies between the requested changes and other files, automatically processes them together, and, after verification with no issues, finally generates the code files as required.

The transaction automation function not only reduces the amount of time developers spend on locating and fixing problems but also effectively minimizes errors that may occur when multiple files are modified.

Project R&D Q&A scenarios

Through the codebase Q&A feature, developers can ask questions using natural language to achieve real-time interaction with the codebase, addressing key issues such as code architecture, implementation logic, code dependencies, and calling relationships. This enables quick access to and understanding of the knowledge and best practices within the enterprise codebase, thereby accelerating the development process and improving code consistency and quality. Meanwhile, the system will automatically predict the next question based on historical queries, further optimizing the developer's learning path and work efficiency.

As shown in *Figure 9.17*, in an open-source **Spring Boot** project, when a newcomer joins, they can quickly understand the project progress and master the codebase by asking questions such as: how the modules are dependent on each other, what submodules are in a specific folder, detailed explanations of a certain module, what a particular class is defined as and its purpose, and so on, thereby getting up to speed quickly.

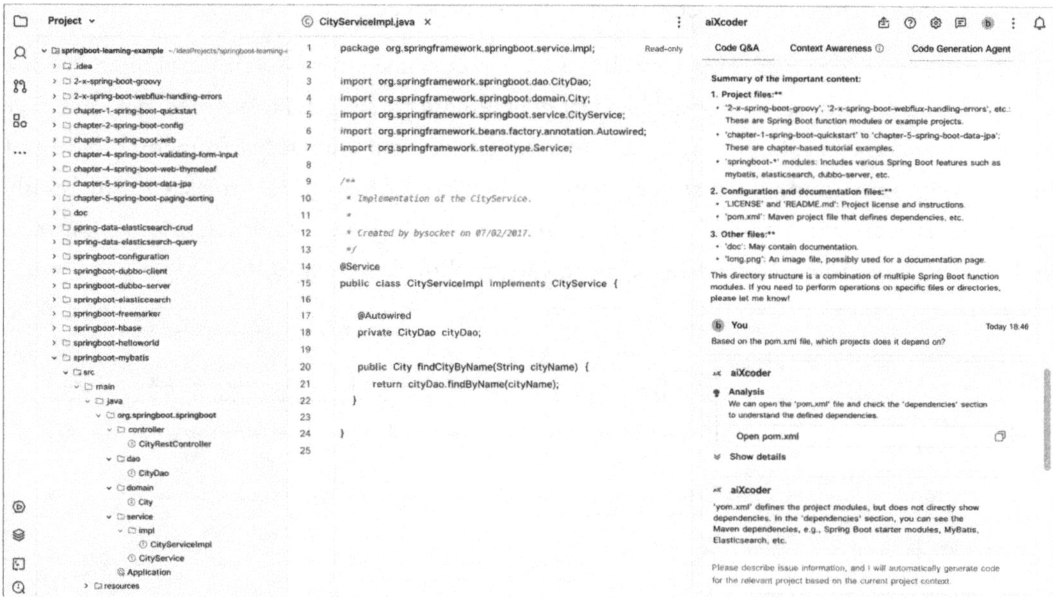

Figure 9.17: Schematic of module dependencies

The knowledge Q&A function helps new members quickly grasp the project structure and code logic, shortening the learning curve, while also assisting senior members in efficiently locating code scattered across different source files and functions, saving time and effort and allowing them to focus on core development tasks.

From requirements to complete project-level code generation scenarios

aiXcoder's end-to-end code generation feature supports the direct transformation of natural language requirements provided by Product Managers or Designers into precise code, covering requirement analysis, system design, project management, development, testing, and other stages, generating complete project-level code and related documentation.

During the AI code generation process, developers can modify and adjust intermediate deliverables (such as requirement documents, partial code modules, test cases, etc.) to ensure they meet specific requirements and standards. At the same time, enterprises can customize the R&D process and the content of intermediate deliverables according to their own needs. Enterprises can specify particular coding standards, design patterns, or testing standards, and require the AI to generate corresponding documents and code based on these specifications.

This feature provides a more efficient collaboration mechanism for software development. For a simple example, Agents are assigned different roles: Product Manager, Project Manager, Architect, R&D Engineer, and Test Engineer. It can understand user requirements, perform interactive and immersive programming, plan step by step, collaborate across multiple roles, call commonly used development tools, provide real-time progress feedback, verify results, improve outputs, and ultimately complete the code generation task, as shown in *Figure 9.18*.

Figure 9.18: Schematic diagram of the code generation task

The end-to-end code generation feature covers the complete R&D process, achieving full-process automation from requirements analysis to coding, enabling quick response to user needs and feedback, significantly improving development efficiency, shortening the time from concept to product launch, and enhancing the product's market competitiveness. At the same time, it reduces human coding errors, ensuring consistency and maintainability of project code.

Summary

In this chapter, you learned how LLMs are applied in programming scenarios to support code understanding, code generation, code completion, and project-level development, while also exploring how agent-based approaches can help teams handle complex enterprise codebases more efficiently. The chapter also showed how large code models improve developer productivity across downstream coding tasks and real-world software engineering workflows.

Building on these programming-focused applications, the next chapter shifts to project management scenarios, where you will learn how LLMs can support requirements analysis, task planning, communication and collaboration, risk management, and decision support across the project lifecycle.

10

Applying LLMs in Project Management

During the project management process, project managers encounter various issues in the requirements analysis phase, task planning phase, risk management phase, as well as in the communication and collaboration phases. These issues become increasingly prominent, especially in large-scale projects. With technological innovation and development, LLMs have gradually been applied in project management scenarios. For example, in the requirements analysis phase, LLMs can help project teams extract key information from various sources, quickly organize and understand complex requirement statements. When clients express their expectations for a product in large volumes of natural language, the model can summarize the core requirements and key points. In the communication and collaboration phase, LLMs can assist project managers in formulating detailed project plans, including task breakdown, time estimation, and resource allocation.

This chapter covers the following main topics:

- Analyzing requirements and planning project tasks
- Improving communication and collaboration
- Managing project risks and supporting decisions
- Optimizing project execution with intelligent workflows
- Applying LLMs in project management case studies

Analyzing requirements and planning project tasks

In project management practice, clarifying **project requirements** is foundational work and the key to ensuring the smooth execution of subsequent tasks. During the **requirements analysis** stage, the project team is expected to accurately capture and analyze user expectations and the core business objectives to ensure that the project's final deliverables meet the requirements. After requirements analysis, the **task planning** stage transforms these requirements into specific, actionable steps and activities, which are further detailed with schedules and resource allocations to ensure each phase is effectively controlled and supervised.

In both of these processes, the collection and processing of a large amount of information, as well as complex logical reasoning, are indispensable. Traditional methods often rely on the expertise of professionals through manual operations, which are less efficient and prone to omissions or errors due to human factors. With technological advancements, especially the application of AI technologies such as LLMs, this situation has been significantly improved.

LLMs possess powerful natural language processing capabilities, enabling project teams to quickly extract key information from a vast number of documents and communications, and to understand and summarize user requirements and underlying intentions through deep learning algorithms. In addition, these models can automatically generate requirement documents, provide task planning suggestions, predict potential issues, and perform risk assessments. Through these advanced functions, project managers can complete requirements analysis and task planning more efficiently and accurately, thereby improving project quality and success rates.

The first step in this process is understanding what stakeholders actually need, because unclear or incomplete requirements can affect every later decision in the project.

Requirements analysis

As a core aspect of project management, **requirements analysis** plays a critical role that cannot be overlooked. It determines whether the project can proceed smoothly and ultimately achieve its intended goals. In traditional project management, requirements analysis is the process of identifying and understanding what the client or user needs. This step is crucial to ensuring the ultimate success of the project. Traditional methods of requirements analysis include **meetings**, **individual interviews**, **focus groups**, **surveys**, and **questionnaires**. These methods have many limitations, as shown in *Figure 10.1*.

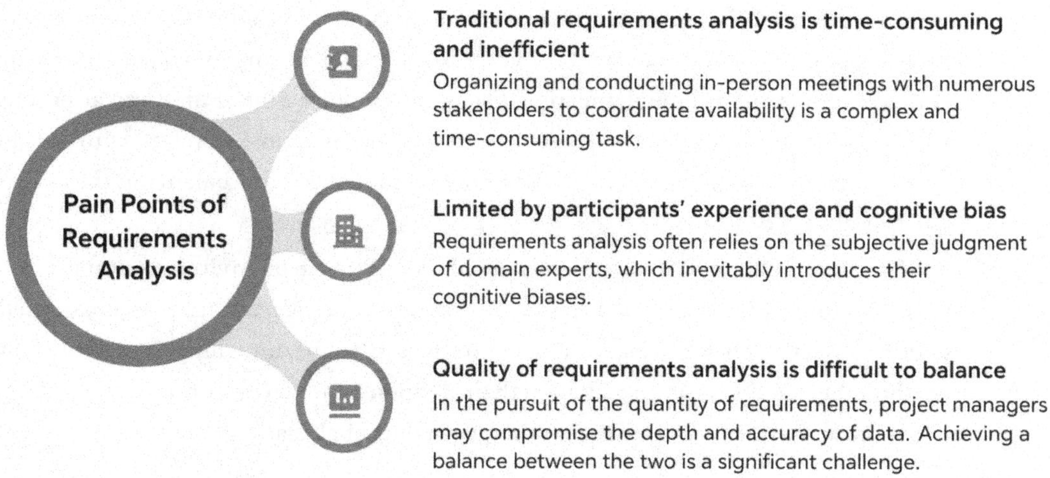

Figure 10.1: Pain points of requirements analysis

These pain points usually arise because traditional requirements analysis depends heavily on manual coordination, subjective interpretation, and limited sources of information:

- Traditional requirements analysis is **time-consuming and inefficient**. Organizing and conducting physical meetings often requires coordinating the schedules of numerous participants, which is a complex and time-consuming task in itself. Additionally, the information collected from meetings may need further organization and analysis before useful conclusions can be drawn. Moreover, user interviews and questionnaire surveys typically require significant manpower to carry out—from designing questionnaires to distributing, collecting, and analyzing the data—each step consumes a great deal of time, and various unforeseen challenges may arise throughout the process.
- Limited by participants' experience and **cognitive biases**. Requirements analysis often relies on the subjective judgment of professionals, inevitably introducing their cognitive biases. For example, project managers and analysts may interpret user needs based on their own experience and preferences, neglecting or misunderstanding the user's real intentions and needs. In addition, due to differences in cultural background, language communication, or personal preferences, users may not express their needs precisely, which can easily lead to misinterpretations or omissions of information.

- There is a **quality balance issue** in requirements analysis. In traditional requirements analysis, obtaining high-quality information often means having less data because in-depth interviews and thorough meeting discussions require a lot of time and attention, making it impossible to cover a wide user base within a limited time. Conversely, to pursue quantity, the depth and accuracy of data may be sacrificed, and balancing these two aspects is always difficult.
- Additionally, it is difficult to completely avoid the influence of **environmental factors** during meeting discussions and user interviews. Many practitioners may be constrained by social expectations when expressing themselves in public, unwilling to express their true thoughts candidly, or may change their opinions due to conformity, all of which impact the authenticity and accuracy of requirements analysis.

However, with rapid advancements in information technology, especially in the field of artificial intelligence, the rise of LLMs has opened up brand-new possibilities for requirements analysis. Innovative technologies represented by ChatGPT have been applied, with ChatGPT's core advantage lying in its deep understanding and processing capabilities of natural language, giving it a distinct edge in complex text data analysis. *Figure 10.2* presents several key advantages of LLMs in requirements analysis scenarios.

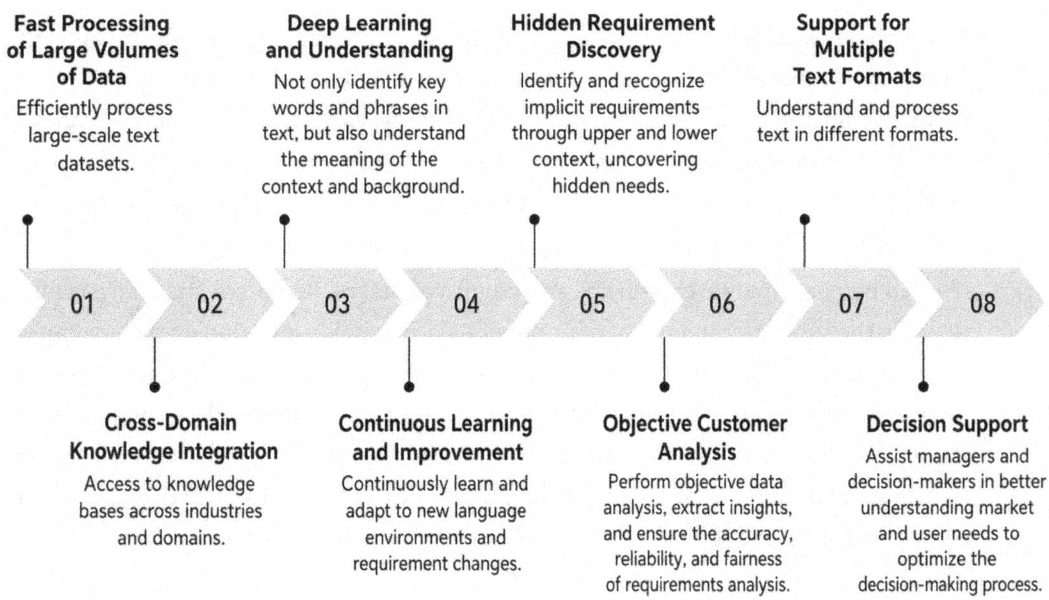

Figure 10.2: Several key advantages of LLMs in requirement analysis scenarios

When applied to requirements analysis, LLMs help address limitations in several practical ways:

- **Rapid Processing of Large Amounts of Data:** LLMs can efficiently process massive text datasets, such as lengthy project files, intensive email correspondence, and detailed meeting minutes. Analyzing this content manually could require significant time and effort, while LLMs can accomplish the same tasks quickly, saving vast resources.
- **Deep Learning and Understanding:** Leveraging advanced machine learning algorithms and extensive training datasets, LLMs can not only identify keywords and phrases in text but also understand their context and underlying meaning, providing more accurate information extraction and content analysis.
- **Uncovering Implicit Requirements:** In traditional requirements analysis, some latent but unexpressed needs can easily be overlooked. LLMs can use contextual reasoning and pattern recognition to discover these **implicit requirements**, helping project teams grasp a more comprehensive picture of needs.
- **Adaptation to Multiple Text Formats:** Whether it's structured reports, unstructured social media posts, or ad hoc meeting notes, LLMs can comprehend and process different text formats and extract valid information from these diverse data sources.
- **Cross-Domain Knowledge Integration:** Cross-domain requirements analysis is often limited by the analyst's knowledge scope. Since LLMs are trained on texts covering a wide range of topics, they possess cross-industry and cross-domain knowledge bases, enabling them to take richer background knowledge into account and provide comprehensive insights during analysis.
- **Continuous Learning and Improvement:** With ongoing input of new data, LLMs can continue learning and adapting to new linguistic environments and requirement changes, keeping their analytical abilities up to date.
- **Unbiased Objective Analysis:** Unlike human analysts who may have cognitive biases, LLMs can perform unbiased data analysis, objectively distilling information to ensure the accuracy and fairness of requirements analysis.
- **Decision Support:** By providing accurate requirements analysis, LLMs can assist managers and decision-makers in better understanding market and user needs, optimizing the decision-making process, and thereby improving the success rate and efficiency of projects.

Taken together, these capabilities show that the value of LLMs is not limited to faster text processing. Their larger contribution lies in helping teams form a clearer, more complete, and more adaptable understanding of project requirements.

The value proposition of LLMs for requirements analysis

The capabilities of LLMs are reflected not only in rapid processing and in-depth analysis of text data, but also in their ability to reason over massive amounts of information through continuous learning. This feature directly addresses the issues raised by Leffingwell in the paper *Agile Software Requirements: Lean Requirements Practices for Teams, Programs, and the Enterprise*. With such advanced analytical power, LLMs can help project teams accurately grasp the complete picture of requirements at the early stages of a project, thereby preventing or reducing unexpected issues and resource waste during development.

In addition, LLMs continuously receive new input and use their complex neural network structures to process this data, allowing them to constantly enhance their insight and become self-optimizing systems. This enables them to perform excellently in responding to rapidly changing user needs, discovering, and establishing implicit connections between requirements, and even uncovering previously unidentified patterns and logical rules. For example, when handling user feedback, LLMs can not only identify explicit comments, but also reveal subtle shifts in user preferences and market trends by comparing and associating large amounts of similar data.

Such in-depth mining and intelligent analysis of data improve the team's grasp of customer needs. Whether the requirements are straightforward or complex and intertwined, LLMs can provide all-around support for project teams. This advantage is particularly suitable for projects involving multi-layered system interactions or those that rapidly evolve with user feedback. In these cases, the efficient analysis and learning capabilities of LLMs can significantly enhance the project's agility and accuracy in responding to the market, helping the project stay on the right developmental track and reducing uncertainty and risk.

Beyond analyzing and mining requirements, LLMs can also support project teams through **intelligent Q&A** and **recommendations**. They can provide real-time responses based on queries from project members and offer accurate answers and suggestions to various questions raised within the team. This instant, targeted interactive approach greatly promotes internal communication and collaboration within the team and helps ensure that all members have a unified and accurate understanding of project requirements.

Thus, it can be seen that LLMs have broad application prospects in the field of requirements analysis. They can not only improve the efficiency and accuracy of analytical work but also increase the probability of project success and ensure the project continues to advance steadily along the planned path. As LLM technology continues to improve and become more widespread, it will inevitably become an indispensable component in the field of project management.

Once requirements are understood and agreed upon, the next step is to convert them into tasks, timelines, priorities, and resource decisions that the project team can act on.

Task planning

Task planning is also an indispensable aspect of project management, involving key areas such as **task breakdown**, **prioritization**, **time scheduling**, and **resource allocation**. Accurate and efficient task planning ensures smooth project workflows and the achievement of objectives. In today's era of big data and artificial intelligence, the application of LLMs provides project teams with unprecedented support and assistance, greatly enhancing the intelligence of task planning.

By leveraging natural language processing and machine learning technologies, LLMs are able to deeply analyze massive amounts of historical project data to identify best practices and patterns of potential failure. Based on the experience of past successful cases, these models can offer recommendations for current projects, such as which tasks should be prioritized, the expected timeframe, and how to rationally allocate resources. Additionally, the models can provide personalized task allocation plans by taking into account the professional expertise and historical performance of individual team members.

LLMs also possess **predictive capabilities** for challenges and risks that may be encountered. By analyzing the incidence rate of issues at similar stages in past projects, combined with the specific conditions of the current project, the models can foresee and provide early warnings for potential difficulties and bottlenecks, enabling project managers to proactively take measures to avoid or mitigate risks.

As agile project management methods become more widely adopted, quick iteration and adaptability have become increasingly important. As shown in *Figure 10.3*, the combination of LLMs with agile methodologies can further promote team collaboration and improve response speed.

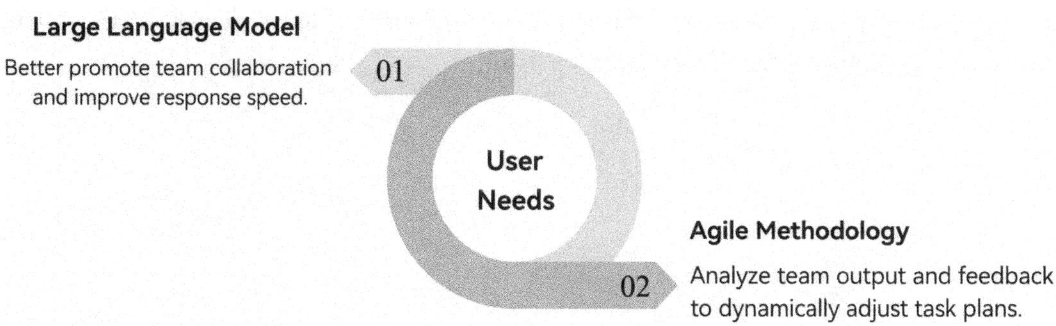

Figure 10.3: The combination of LLMs and agile methods

The model can analyze the team's work output and feedback in real time, dynamically adjusting task plans to ensure tasks are always aligned with project objectives and meet the latest user needs. It can optimize workflows in real time based on ongoing task performance, increase transparency, and enhance communication and cooperation efficiency among team members.

LLMs can also provide real-time monitoring of task execution, collect execution data, and analyze efficiency bottlenecks to uncover potential systemic issues. Through these insights, the model not only provides guidance to the team during the execution phase but also offers strategic improvement suggestions for future project planning.

Overall, the application of LLMs in task planning is not just about providing a simple tool, but represents a completely new way of working and thinking. It transforms data intelligence into practical wisdom, providing project teams with greater efficiency and quality assurance, ensuring steady project advancement and successful delivery. By introducing LLMs, the flexibility and adaptability of agile methods are further enhanced, creating even greater value and possibilities for project teams. As AI technology continues to advance, we have reason to believe that LLMs will become a key driving force in the future development of project management.

Once requirements have been clarified and tasks have been planned, the next challenge is ensuring that the right information reaches the right people at the right time. This makes communication and collaboration central to whether project plans can be executed effectively.

Improving communication and collaboration

Project management is a key process to ensure that a project is successfully completed on time, within budget, and in accordance with quality standards. In this process, communication with team members, stakeholders, and other relevant parties is crucial. Studies have shown that 70% to 90% of the time in project management work is spent on communication activities. This includes not only routine exchanges such as task assignment, progress updates, and problem-solving, but also more complex information exchanges, such as requirements negotiation, risk assessment, and strategy development, as shown in *Figure 10.4*.

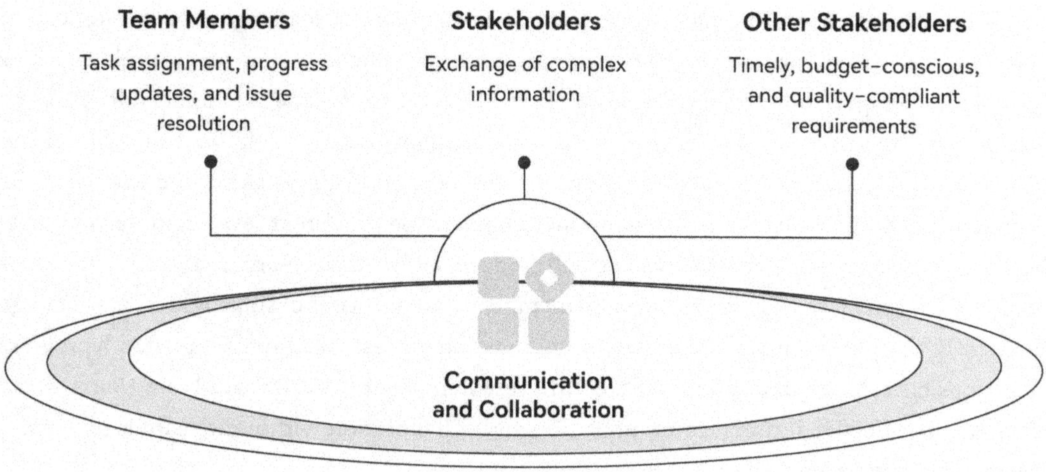

Figure 10.4: The scope of communication and collaboration

In this context, LLMs, as a powerful artificial intelligence technology, can understand, generate, and optimize textual information through natural language processing techniques, thereby significantly improving the efficiency of information transmission and communication.

The importance of communication and collaboration

Communication and collaboration are key to successful project management. Effective communication helps ensure that every team member, stakeholder, and participant fully understands the project goals, strategies, and current status. This not only promotes the achievement of common objectives but also helps build an atmosphere of mutual trust and respect, which is crucial for team morale and motivation.

A project team may consist of members with different cultural backgrounds, professional expertise, and skill levels. The effectiveness of communication and collaboration directly impacts the internal workflow, decision-making process, and innovative capacity of the team, thereby affecting the speed and quality of the entire project. Clear communication can reduce misunderstandings and mistakes, saving time and resources needed to correct errors, while also enhancing synergy among team members, enabling them to quickly adapt to changes and solve problems together.

However, in practice, project management often faces numerous challenges in communication and collaboration. First, there may be barriers to information transmission; for example, complex technical language or industry jargon may make it difficult for non-experts to understand. Second, virtual team members may lack face-to-face interactions, which could lead to information distortion or a lack of emotional expression. Additionally, as the project scale increases and the number of people involved grows, communication between different levels and departments becomes more complex. Departments or small groups may form information silos, disagreements or lack of consensus may arise among team members, and the needs of stakeholders may change frequently—any of these can hinder the communication process and impact the smooth progress of a project. As Belbin pointed out in the 2010 research paper *Team Roles at Work* (*Butterworth-Heinemann*), effective internal communication and collaboration within the team is one of the key factors in ensuring project success.

LLMs as a solution to communication and collaboration challenges

Facing such challenges, LLMs provide new solutions. Through natural language processing technology, LLMs can interpret the complexities of human language, transform technical or specialized information into more understandable forms, and even automatically generate summaries to help team members quickly grasp key information.

LLMs can assist with creating project update reports, writing technical documentation, and drafting meeting minutes, greatly reducing the workload of project managers and improving the accuracy and efficiency of communication. In addition, LLMs can also serve as **chatbots**, providing real-time Q&A services to help resolve team members' immediate questions, reducing misunderstandings and delays.

The importance of communication and collaboration in project management cannot be overlooked. By enhancing information transparency and comprehensibility and accelerating decision-making and problem-solving processes, LLMs can empower project teams to achieve more efficient communication and collaboration, driving the project steadily toward its intended goals.

The role of LLMs in communication and collaboration scenarios

As a revolutionary advancement in the field of artificial intelligence, LLMs have endowed machines with the ability to understand and generate natural language text, showcasing their unique value in team collaboration.

In daily workflows, the acquisition, and processing of information are often crucial to a project's success, and LLMs play an essential role in this regard. Through intelligent question-and-answer systems, team members no longer need to spend large amounts of time filtering and verifying information, as they can directly ask the LLM questions and quickly receive precise and authoritative answers. This instant Q&A functionality greatly alleviates the pressure of knowledge retrieval, allowing team members to focus more on decision-making and innovation. Whether it's explaining technical terms, analyzing industry trends, or solving complex problems, LLMs can provide answers, effectively reducing misunderstandings, and communication barriers, and accelerating decision-making processes.

LLMs also excel at summarization and extraction. They possess the ability to synthesize scattered information into summaries and reports, which is a boon in fast-paced work environments. Team members can input research findings, market data, or project updates into the model, which will organize this information and produce clear, easily understandable summaries that help the team better grasp the overall picture and ensure all members are on the same informational page.

Recommendation functionality is also an indispensable part of LLMs. Based on provided data and prerequisites, they can forecast possible outcomes and offer advice and solutions, pointing the team in the right direction. This kind of data-driven intelligent recommendation not only enhances the team's ability to tackle complex issues but also increases work flexibility and creativity.

LLMs act as information integrators and knowledge sharers, making knowledge exchange within the team more convenient. Each member's experiences, insights, and research findings can be aggregated and compared by the LLM, fostering knowledge accumulation and the collision of innovative ideas. On the level of team collaboration, this means a broader shared vision and a more solid foundation for decision-making.

LLMs deepen the team's communication methods, optimize information processing flows, and enhance decision quality. In this era of information explosion, making use of these advantages of LLMs can undoubtedly enable more efficient team collaboration, faster growth, and more creative outcomes.

Integrating and managing project knowledge

With their advanced natural language processing capabilities, LLMs have become powerful platforms for knowledge integration and management. Team members can input ideas, professional insights, research data, and practical experience into the system. The language model then uses complex algorithms to analyze, compare, and synthesize these various inputs, thereby generating conclusions or recommendations that thoroughly consider all available information.

This process is similar to a virtual thought blender. Whenever a team member contributes new ideas or information, the language model immediately integrates this new content, ensuring that the outputted recommendations are always based on the most comprehensive information and the latest discussion results. Furthermore, this approach reduces the impact of individual biases on decision-making, as machine models place greater emphasis on the logical coherence and relevance of the data and information itself.

By fostering collective brainstorming, this not only promotes knowledge sharing within the team but also enhances mutual understanding and collaboration among members. During project execution, team members may encounter complex problems that require collective wisdom to solve. At such times, leveraging the powerful integration capabilities of LLMs can effectively bring together the team's intelligence, generating high-quality solutions. It also helps the team reach consensus quickly, accelerating the decision-making process and promoting efficient project advancement.

LLMs can also serve as knowledge repositories, accumulating the team's intellectual assets over time. As time passes, the team's historical decisions, discussion content, and both successful and failed cases will be recorded, providing valuable references for future decision-making. The accumulation and reuse of this knowledge can significantly improve the onboarding speed of new members and strengthen the team's grasp of historical information.

Applying LLMs to knowledge integration and management not only enhances internal team collaboration efficiency but also provides continuous, deep insights and intelligent support for the team. It is one of the indispensable tools in modern team management.

Sharing information through meetings and screen recordings

With the advanced capabilities of LLMs, teams can be freed from previously time-consuming and inefficient requirement clarification meetings. Traditionally, these meetings required all relevant personnel to be online simultaneously and engage in real-time discussions to reach consensus and understanding. Now, teams can choose to use screen recording software to capture key discussion content and share it with all members, as shown in *Figure 10.5*.

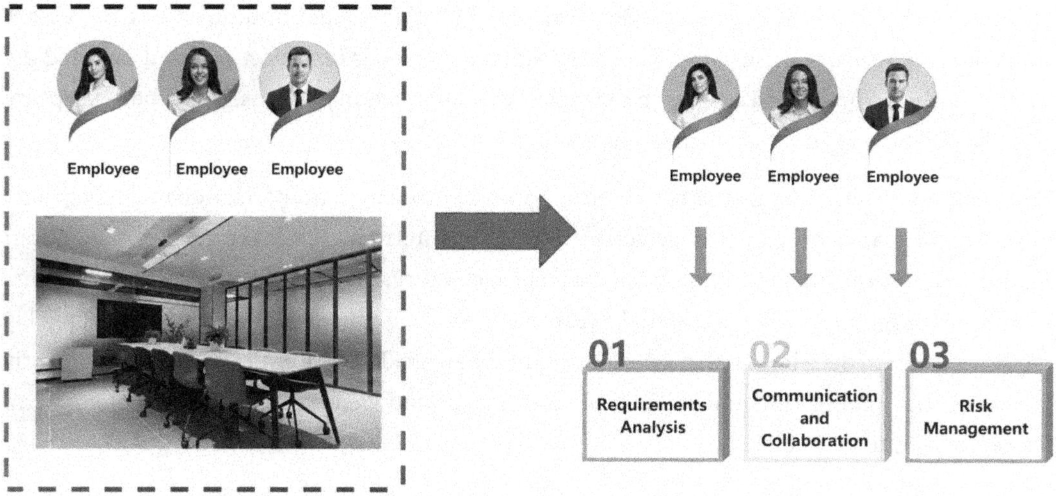

Figure 10.5: The role of screen recording software in information sharing

Screen recording offers multiple advantages:

- It allows team members who are unable to attend real-time meetings to review the content at their convenience, ensuring seamless information transfer
- The video records every detail of the discussion, including whiteboard sketches, slideshows, or the process of making important decisions, making the logic behind complex ideas and decisions much clearer
- By watching and reviewing these recordings, team members can quickly grasp the main context and key problems addressed in the meetings, fostering deeper learning and knowledge accumulation

LLMs provide value-added services for screen recordings. AI technology can automatically analyze speech, text, and visual information in screen recordings and extract the core points and action items from meetings. This automatic summarization not only improves the efficiency of information recording but also enhances the team's understanding and absorption of meeting content. Members do not need to manually take notes or worry about missing key information; AI has already prepared concise and clear summaries for them.

AI's automatic summarization technology can also be adjusted and optimized based on team feedback and needs, to ensure that the information provided is both accurate and targeted. By continuously learning and adapting to the team's communication patterns, AI can better capture and highlight the topics that team members care about most.

In the end, this combination of screen recording and AI automatic summarization not only greatly improves the team's ability to synchronize information internally and make quick decisions, but also helps build and maintain a knowledge asset base. By organizing and indexing the key points and decision logic of meeting content, the team can effectively avoid redundant work and quickly retrieve historical decisions and discussion results when needed. The entire process significantly enhances the organization and utilization efficiency of knowledge assets, bringing long-term strategic value to the team.

Connecting communication platforms and project tools

By using LLMs as communication and collaboration platforms, team members can achieve rapid integration and sharing of information in a highly interactive and intelligent environment. Such platforms, by providing instant communication tools and file-sharing functions, allow team members to easily communicate and collaborate without being limited by geographic locations.

On this unified communication and collaboration platform, team members can upload and download important project files, jointly edit documents, and update project progress in real time. In addition, LLMs can understand and process natural language queries, making searching for relevant information more convenient and faster. When team members encounter problems or need professional advice, the platform can provide timely feedback and solutions based on previous content and relevant knowledge bases.

LLMs can also analyze communication patterns among team members and recommend more effective collaboration methods and communication strategies. They can integrate information from different sources, such as emails, online meeting records, and discussions in project management software, thereby providing comprehensive suggestions and insights. Once this information is integrated, it can offer data support for the team's decision-making process, enhancing the accuracy and efficiency of decisions.

With the development of artificial intelligence technology, LLMs use machine learning algorithms to predict project risks and market trends, assisting teams in long-term planning. In this way, teams not only improve communication and collaboration efficiency but also gain foresight in a competitive market environment and seize future development opportunities. The benefits of applying LLMs to communication and collaboration platforms are multifaceted. They improve the team's work efficiency and help the team see the bigger picture, promoting innovation and growth.

LLMs improve communication efficiency and resource integration capability

By integrating LLMs into team communication mechanisms, we can create an efficient and highly interactive work environment. This advancement allows information and screen recordings to be transmitted and shared in real time, greatly enhancing team members' communication and comprehension abilities. On a unified and intelligent platform, team members can easily engage in face-to-face direct communication while also seamlessly exchanging and integrating files and data.

A LLM-based platform serves not only as a communication tool but also acts as a collaboration assistant. The analytical and suggestion features of LLMs help team members filter out the most relevant content from massive amounts of information, provide context-based operational recommendations, and identify potential communication barriers. Over time, the model continuously learns from the team's communication patterns and preferences, enabling it to offer more precise personalized support and optimize workflows.

The platform's intelligent integration ability enables seamless connection with a variety of tools and applications, realizing unified management of project management software, document editors, instant messaging services, and other resources, thereby simplifying workflows. Team members can create and customize automated tasks as needed, unleashing creativity and allowing them to focus on more valuable work.

A communication platform integrated with LLMs will transform traditional ways of working. Through its efficient information processing capabilities and interactive communication features, it effectively improves the quality of team collaboration and work efficiency. As the team becomes increasingly reliant on this system, workflows become more streamlined, project delivery speed accelerates, and the organization ultimately gains a clear competitive advantage.

Improving communication efficiency between different roles

The application of LLMs is not limited to providing information query services; it can also facilitate more efficient communication and team collaboration in various work environments. For example, when integrated into a company's internal communication platform or workflows, LLMs can instantly answer professional questions raised by team members, whether related to specific project details, market analysis, technical challenges, or administrative management queries.

Additionally, the model can understand and process natural language, recognizing industry terminology and abbreviations used by staff in communication. Therefore, when team members are not familiar with other departments' work, LLMs can serve as a knowledge bridge, helping to explain and translate technical terms and ensuring smooth cross-departmental communication.

At the same time, through deep learning and natural language processing technologies, LLMs can continuously learn from internal corporate communication and data, making their recommendations and answers more accurate. Thus, they can also proactively recommend solutions or best practices based on past communication records and team preferences, helping team members make wiser decisions.

In diverse teams, members may come from different cultural and linguistic backgrounds. LLMs have language translation capabilities, helping to eliminate language barriers so that global team members can communicate and collaborate smoothly, regardless of which language they use.

In summary, through the efficient Q&A and intelligent recommendation functionalities of LLMs, team members can obtain the required information in a shorter amount of time, significantly reducing misunderstandings and communication costs, thus improving overall organizational work efficiency and collaboration quality.

Supporting decisions with historical project data

LLMs are designed to deeply analyze historical data and provide strong support for team decision-making. By intelligently analyzing project historical data, the model is capable of predicting future trends and identifying potential risks. During the decision-making process, it can uncover patterns and correlations within data, providing a more solid foundation for decisions.

With decision-support functions based on historical data, the model can guide teams to make wiser choices. For example, by analyzing previous project timelines, budget usage, and team performance, the model can identify factors most likely to influence project success or failure. The model can also predict potential outcomes under different execution paths, assisting teams in evaluating the relative pros and cons of various strategies or plans.

LLMs can also learn the specific needs and challenges of particular industries or fields from historical data. This domain-specific knowledge allows the model to provide more accurate customized recommendations for certain types of projects.

Such in-depth analysis based on historical data and its application in decision support will help enhance a team's ability to address complex problems and increase the likelihood of project success. Over time, LLMs will continue to accumulate new data, allowing not only continuous optimization of prediction accuracy and analytical capabilities but also adaptation to changing environmental factors, providing ongoing support for team decisions.

Generating communication scripts for external stakeholders

LLMs possess the ability to generate professional communication scripts and can assist team members in communicating more effectively with external clients and partners. By leveraging natural language processing technologies, they can provide users with intelligent response solutions, helping them to perform more professionally and accurately in business communication. By combining personalized response styles, they have the potential to significantly enhance a company's image and increase customer satisfaction.

Personalized and professional communication strategies are also the cornerstone of establishing and maintaining good external cooperative relationships. By precisely understanding and responding to the specific needs and expectations of all parties, LLMs can promote mutual trust and understanding, thereby creating a more stable foundation for the success of cooperative projects. Therefore, this technology is not just a tool for communication, but an important support for promoting business cooperation, deepening partnership relationships, and achieving project goals.

LLMs, as tools for project communication and collaboration, can greatly enhance the efficiency of information transfer between team members. Their advanced natural language processing capabilities make complex information and instructions easier to understand and execute, reducing ambiguities and misunderstandings during communication. Through these technological means, team members can reach consensus in a shorter time, effectively advancing various stages of the project.

LLMs support multilingual communication, eliminating language barriers, and making collaboration within global teams smoother. Regardless of where team members are located, they can conveniently participate in the project, share ideas, and feedback in real time, and ensure that project objectives are communicated accurately and implemented quickly.

In addition to improving communication efficiency, LLMs also analyze large amounts of data through intelligent decision support functions, providing data-driven insights and suggestions. This support not only enhances the quality of team decisions but also improves their ability to handle complex problems and uncertain environments.

At the project management level, LLMs can be used to automate routine management tasks, such as generating meeting minutes, assigning and tracking tasks, and so on, thereby freeing up human resources so that team members can focus on more creative and strategic work.

In summary, LLMs bring a more efficient, flexible, and intelligent collaboration experience to teams, which is bound to become a key factor in driving project success. As technology continues to advance and improve, the role they play in future project management and execution will become increasingly important, with the potential to become the standard industry practice.

Effective communication gives project teams better visibility into their work, but visibility alone is not enough. Teams also need to identify risks early, evaluate possible outcomes, and make informed decisions when project conditions change.

Managing project risks and supporting decisions

Project risk management is a key part of the project management process, involving the identification, assessment, monitoring, and response to uncertainties and potential threats that may arise in the project.

- **Risk Identification:** At each stage of the project, the team needs to identify internal and external factors that may affect project outcomes. This includes technical issues, resource shortages, policy changes, etc.
- **Risk Assessment:** This step involves assessing the likelihood and potential impact of each risk. It is usually achieved through qualitative and quantitative methods, such as **risk matrices** or simulations.
- **Risk Monitoring:** Regularly monitor identified risks and adjust risk assessments based on project progress and changes in the external environment.
- **Risk Response:** Develop risk response strategies, such as avoidance, mitigation, transfer, or acceptance of risks, and integrate them into the project plan.

With the development of artificial intelligence technologies, LLMs have demonstrated great potential in **risk prediction** and **decision support**.

In terms of risk prediction, LLMs can predict potential risks by analyzing historical data and industry-specific trends. This kind of prediction helps team members identify possible issues earlier and thus take preventive measures.

In terms of decision support, LLMs can provide data-driven decision support, helping project managers evaluate possible outcomes of different response strategies. For example, AI models can simulate the impact of different risk response measures on project timelines and costs, thus helping management make more informed decisions.

Risk management

In project management, **risk management** is a strategy for identifying, assessing, and prioritizing potential issues, aimed at reducing or avoiding their impact on the project. Effective risk management helps the project team foresee future challenges and take measures to prevent or resolve potential problems at the lowest cost.

Although the importance of risk management is widely acknowledged, in practice, accurately identifying, and evaluating all possible project risks remains challenging. The complexity of historical data, the hidden nature of bottlenecks, and anomalies in processes can all lead to delays and incompleteness in risk management work.

The significance of risk management lies not only in reducing the impact of potential issues on the project, but also in helping the project team anticipate future challenges and take measures to prevent or resolve potential problems at the lowest cost. This forward-looking approach helps the project team better cope with changes and uncertainties, thereby increasing the likelihood of project success.

For example, risk management is like a grand outdoor wedding. The bride, groom, and planning team must consider factors such as rain, late-arriving vendors, or any other issues that could affect the smooth running of the wedding. By identifying these potential "risks" in advance, they can develop contingency plans, such as preparing a tent in case it rains or confirming with vendors ahead of time to avoid delays. This proactive risk management approach helps ensure the wedding proceeds smoothly, just as it does in project management, helping to ensure the successful implementation of the project. However, it is not easy to predict all possible risks. Like trying to forecast the weather, sometimes situations can suddenly change, requiring quick adjustments.

LLM applications employ natural language processing techniques to extract information from project reports, change logs, meeting minutes, task statuses, and other texts, thereby predicting potential future risk points. Combined with advanced risk monitoring and early warning systems, projects can be monitored in real time; as soon as potential risk signals are detected, project managers are immediately alerted and given specific improvement suggestions, making risk management more proactive and forward-looking. LLMs are not just tools; they represent an entirely new methodology that integrates knowledge from statistics, operations research, cognitive psychology, and data science, among other disciplines. Through this interdisciplinary integration, project risk management can gain a deeper understanding of how risks arise and mitigate their impact through early intervention.

In addition, in practical applications, LLMs can be used to build **risk databases**, collecting and classifying project risk cases. Through machine learning algorithms, the model can learn from these cases and continually optimize its predictive capabilities. Project managers can use these predictions to devise preventive measures and plan response strategies in advance, thereby reducing the likelihood of risks occurring.

LLMs provide the following three risk management approaches in project management scenarios: **predicting bottlenecks**, **identifying risk points**, and **detecting abnormal behavioral patterns**.

Predicting bottlenecks

In organizations, the flow status, and the number of handovers of tasks are often hidden indicators of project inefficiency. By using LLMs to monitor this data, potential bottlenecks can be effectively predicted. For example, by analyzing each stage of the workflow, the model can identify key transfer points that may cause delays. This analysis includes not only time management of tasks but also the collaboration efficiency among team members. If the model discovers that frequent handovers between certain teams are slowing down project progress, it can suggest optimizing these processes. This could involve reducing unnecessary intermediate steps or introducing automation tools to simplify the handover process, such as automatic task assignment systems or integrated communication platforms, to improve efficiency, and transparency.

Identifying risk points

LLMs can identify potential risk points by comprehensively analyzing various project indicators (such as task retention time, priority, deadlines, assignees' workload, and the overall project objectives). This type of analysis, based on historical data and predictive models, enables the model to warn about factors that may cause the project to be overdue or deviate from set goals. For example, if a key task is delayed multiple times consecutively, the LLM can alert the project manager to intervene early—adjusting resources or optimizing workflows to avoid affecting the overall project schedule.

Detecting abnormal behavior patterns

When project teams face high pressure and tight deadlines, they may exhibit irrational behavioral patterns. With the help of cognitive psychology theories, we can better understand the psychological mechanisms behind these behaviors. Applying these theories in the training of LLMs can help more precisely identify such abnormal behavioral patterns. This not only helps project managers intervene effectively during management but also allows for the establishment of a more humane work environment and stress management systems, preventing the occurrence of such behaviors in advance.

For example, LLMs can analyze communication patterns among team members, identify potential communication barriers or signs of stress, and promptly alert management, so that appropriate support measures or adjustments to the team structure can be taken.

Once risks have been identified, the next challenge is deciding how to respond. This is where LLMs move from detecting warning signs to helping project managers compare options, evaluate trade-offs, and choose a course of action.

Decision support

Project decision-making is a core activity in project management. It refers to the process of analyzing and assessing information to select the best course of action. Good decisions can effectively promote smooth project progress and guide the project team to avoid risks at critical moments.

In practice, project managers often face challenges such as insufficient information, time constraints, and complex environments when making decisions. These factors increase uncertainty in decision-making, which may lead to inaccurate or untimely decisions, thereby affecting project outcomes.

By mining the dispersed information in the system and conducting inductive analysis, LLMs assist project managers in reducing decision-making uncertainty. Leveraging NLP technology, LLMs can handle complex queries and provide insights and recommendations based on data, thereby optimizing decision quality. **Decision Support Systems (DSS)** integrated with LLMs can help project managers make more informed decisions at each stage of a project. DSS can integrate expert systems, using industry best practices and experiential rules to guide the decision-making process. In addition, DSS can provide dynamic risk assessments and response strategies by real-time monitoring of project metrics and changes in the external environment.

In terms of decision support, LLMs act as personal assistants for project managers, helping them make better decisions by gathering and analyzing various types of information. Just like navigation software recommends the best route based on current traffic conditions, LLMs can also help project managers make decisions based on real-time project status and market conditions.

Furthermore, when project managers are overwhelmed by massive reports and emails, LLMs can quickly filter important information and provide concise summaries, ensuring that decision-makers don't miss critical information—like an intelligent email sorter that helps place important emails in the most prominent location.

The emergence of LLMs is akin to equipping the field of project management with high-tech glasses, making originally vague risks crystal clear, and guiding project teams to make more precise decisions. It's like in a car race, where drivers wear helmets with built-in display screens, as shown in *Figure 10.6*, which can display track information and competitor status in real time, thereby enabling optimal decisions at every turn and straightaway.

Figure 10.6: Helmet with built-in display

The ways in which LLMs provide decision support in project management mainly include the following five aspects discussed as follows.

Making data-driven decisions

In modern project management, the real-time prediction and analysis capabilities of LLMs play a crucial role. Take **LigaAI** as an example: this platform utilizes the vast amount of data collected throughout projects to help teams gain an in-depth understanding of work progress and potential risks.

Tools by capability

LLM-augmented project management does not depend on a single platform. Depending on the organization's existing workflow, teams may start with tools that support one or more project management capabilities:

- **Documentation and PRD generation**: Notion AI, Confluence with Atlassian Intelligence, Coda AI
- **Task management with LLM features**: Jira with Atlassian Intelligence, Asana AI Studio, ClickUp Brain, Linear, Monday.com
- **Communication and meeting support**: Slack AI, Microsoft Teams with Copilot, Loom AI summaries
- **Risk tracking and reporting**: Microsoft Project with Copilot, Smartsheet AI

This list is not exhaustive. It is intended to help readers connect the chapter's ideas to familiar categories of tools, such as documentation systems, task trackers, communication platforms, and reporting tools.

This data-driven decision-making approach allows teams not only to quickly respond to current challenges but also to anticipate potential future issues. For instance, when facing unexpected market changes or internal resource constraints, teams can use model-provided data analysis to promptly adjust strategies and quarterly targets, ensuring that projects continue to move forward under adverse conditions. This approach effectively reduces guesswork and uncertainty in the decision-making process, making project management more precise and efficient.

Allocating tasks based on team capacity

LLMs can accurately assign appropriate task sizes and difficulties to each task based on team members' historical performance and individual work habits. This personalized task allocation mechanism helps optimize the team's overall workflow, avoiding inefficiency caused by tasks that are either too large or too small. For example, experienced members can be assigned more challenging tasks, while newcomers can be given more learning-oriented tasks. This not only prevents members from being overworked but also reduces frequent task switching, thereby improving team focus and productivity.

Prioritizing tasks and feedback

LLMs can extract valuable information from massive data sets to help teams identify which tasks or feedback are most critical. By analyzing user feedback, market trends, and internal data, they can identify key feedback that aligns with team objectives and the company's long-term development. For example, if a major client's feedback points out an issue with a particular product feature, the LLM can immediately flag this feedback and suggest the team prioritize the related tasks. At the same time, it can also reveal business opportunities that have not been fully recognized, enabling teams to focus resources on projects likely to deliver the greatest return.

Optimizing decisions with real-time project data

LLMs can perform real-time analysis of project status, processing various types of data generated within projects, such as emails, messages, reports, and real-time chats, providing project managers with instant risk assessments and decision recommendations. This real-time analysis capability can significantly reduce information processing time and improve decision-making efficiency. At the same time, by deeply learning from historical project cases, LLMs can optimize decision-making processes. For example, when addressing specific types of issues, an LLM can refer to the handling processes of successful cases, providing project managers with decision templates that reduce decision time and resource consumption and avoid repetitive work.

Personalizing decision support and risk warnings

LLMs can provide personalized decision support based on different project managers' decision-making styles and project teams' working methods. By analyzing project managers' past decision records and the team's work patterns, LLMs are able to offer customized recommendations and solutions that better fit the team's actual situation and needs. In addition, leveraging big data analysis and predictive models, LLMs can give early warnings of potential project risks. For example, in construction projects that rely on supply chains, LLMs can provide relevant support by analyzing global market trends.

It is thus evident that LLMs play a key role in risk management and project decision-making. They not only enhance the speed of project delivery and product quality, but also make the decision-making process more scientific and efficient through continuous feedback loops and intelligent support systems. This technology provides precise insight, strengthens the team's ability to respond quickly to potential risks, and significantly improves the stability of project implementation, thereby enhancing the team's ability to cope with future uncertainties.

Once project risks have been identified and key decisions have been made, the focus shifts to execution: how teams use resources, manage workflows, respond to issues, and keep the project moving toward delivery.

Optimizing project execution with intelligent workflows

The **project execution phase** is the key period when plans are turned into actual results, much like a farmer patiently waiting for a rich harvest after sowing the seeds. During this phase, the project team needs to make efficient use of resources, coordinate tasks, and ensure the project progresses according to the established schedule and quality standards. With advances in artificial intelligence technology, LLMs now offer new possibilities for intelligent optimization of workflows, just as modern agricultural technology has improved traditional farming methods.

Challenges in workflow and resource management

During the project execution phase, teams often face uncertainties in workflows and challenges in resource allocation. Handling complex progress reports, communication records, and resource usage requires precise analysis and effective management, while also needing to quickly identify and resolve bottlenecks and inefficiencies in the project. For example, a construction site may require urgent adjustment of work arrangements due to weather changes or delays in material delivery. This demands that project managers make rapid decisions and reallocate human and material resources, much like a helmsman stabilizing the ship's course in a storm.

In addition, predicting peaks and valleys in resource usage for rational allocation and determining the most effective working models to adapt to change are also key to improving resource utilization and productivity. Efficient problem tracking and resolution is also a challenging aspect in project management, especially as maintaining task lists and tracking issue statuses can lead to human errors. For larger teams, problem management becomes even more complex, creating an urgent need to simplify issue resolution processes and quickly respond to customer feedback in order to maintain customer satisfaction. Meanwhile, efficient and accurate search functions and issue detection are critical for improving team efficiency, but this remains a challenge to overcome, particularly in scaling integrated support and improving issue detection accuracy.

How LLMs empower workflow and resource management

LLMs provide more efficient and effective solutions across multiple fields. Firstly, these models conduct an in-depth analysis of complex data, enabling real-time identification and optimization of project bottlenecks. For example, in supply chain management, LLMs can predict fluctuations in resource demand and guide companies in rationally allocating inventory and human resources. Additionally, LLMs significantly reduce errors and delays caused by manual operations through automating task management—this is especially important in industries like healthcare and finance, where mistakes can have serious consequences.

Furthermore, LLMs improve the efficiency and accuracy of issue tracking, especially in the customer service sector. Leveraging advanced search technology and natural language processing capabilities, LLMs can quickly locate customer feedback and related issues, improving response speed and ultimately enhancing customer satisfaction. For example, automated customer service systems can analyze the language patterns in customer inquiries to anticipate and provide more personalized answers and recommendations.

There are five practical ways that LLMs are used in workflow and resource management scenarios: maximizing resource utilization, optimizing workflows, providing practical suggestions, automation and AI generation, and information identification.

Maximizing resource utilization

LLMs can help project teams make more effective use of human and material resources. By analyzing historical project data and current project requirements, LLMs can predict peaks and valleys in resource demand, recommending rational allocation of resources across different projects or tasks. For example, prior to large-scale promotional events in the e-commerce industry, LLMs can help companies predict the workload of customer service departments and arrange sufficient customer service staff in advance to cope with surging inquiries. This dynamic resource management strategy helps avoid resource waste and ensures that critical tasks receive the necessary support. Similar to precisely calculating sailing routes to save fuel and time, LLMs enable companies to optimize resource allocation, improve overall efficiency, and remain agile in the face of market changes. This not only enhances the company's emergency response capabilities but also boosts its long-term competitiveness.

Optimizing workflows

In general, LLMs are able to understand and simulate complex workflows, identify, and recommend improvements for redundant steps or inefficient processes. Utilizing natural language processing technology, LLMs can extract key information from project documents and team feedback to propose workflow optimization schemes. This is similar to how a swimming coach analyzes an athlete's movements to suggest improvements and increase swimming speed. Likewise, LLMs can help project teams better understand team members' skills and working styles, thus optimizing task allocation and collaboration processes. In this way, LLMs not only improve work efficiency but also enhance overall team coordination and productivity. Such refined process optimization helps companies reduce waste, accelerate project delivery speed and quality, and also creates a more harmonious and efficient working environment for employees.

Providing practical advice

LLMs can provide real-time, practical advice to project teams by analyzing vast amounts of data generated during project execution, such as progress reports, team communication records, and resource usage. LLMs are able to identify bottlenecks and inefficient areas in project execution, and propose improvement suggestions, such as adjusting task priorities or optimizing team collaboration methods. These suggestions act like the project team's navigation system, offering the optimal path in the face of complex situations to avoid traffic jams and ensure the project proceeds as planned. In this way, LLMs not only help teams identify and solve current problems but also prevent potential risks and delays, enhancing the transparency and efficiency of project management. This data-driven, deep analysis and decision-support tool enables project teams to maintain flexibility and responsiveness in a dynamically changing work environment, thus achieving a higher project success rate.

Beyond recommending improvements, LLMs can also reduce manual effort by automating routine execution tasks and generating supporting project artifacts.

Automation and AI generation

According to the *Project Management Body of Knowledge (PMBOK® Guide)* published by the **Project Management Institute** (PMI) in 2020 and the 2019 paper *Artificial Intelligence for Project Management* published in *Harvard Business Review*, automated processing not only enhances execution efficiency by automatically tracking issue statuses, updating task lists, and maintaining documentation, but also reduces human error. It can also automatically break down complex tasks into more manageable subtasks, lowering the user's operational cost.

At the same time, AI-generated content, such as **Product Requirement Documents (PRD)**, can use historical data and pattern recognition to optimize document quality, significantly speeding up the planning phase and improving the accuracy and efficiency of the development process. This integrated AI technology automatically performs repetitive and technical tasks in many areas, freeing up human resources to focus on more creative and strategic work. For example, in software development, AI can automatically generate code frameworks and interface documentation, reducing early-stage time consumption for developers and enabling them to focus on innovation and optimization of core functionalities. Furthermore, auto-generated documents are continuously optimized and updated through ongoing project data analysis, ensuring the accuracy and timeliness of information, and providing project teams with a powerful **decision-support tool**.

As execution data accumulates, teams also need better ways to identify repeated issues, retrieve relevant information, and connect new problems with past solutions.

Information identification

In the 2021 paper *The Use of Artificial Intelligence in Project Execution. Project Management* published by KPMG, it is pointed out that LLMs have significant advantages in managing information identification issues within large teams. They can effectively identify repeated problems and streamline problem-solving processes, thereby freeing up team members to focus on more valuable tasks.

In addition, vector embedding technology is used for semantic search, encoding the deep meaning of data into numerical form, which improves the relevance and efficiency of problem searches. This is especially effective in handling customer feedback issues, enabling faster identification of similar problems and solutions, enhancing response speed, and improving customer satisfaction. Through this technology, AI can not only quickly identify and categorize vast amounts of input data but also predict potential issues by analyzing historical interactions and problem-solving records, allowing for the formulation of solutions in advance. Such predictive maintenance greatly optimizes team workflows and customer service experience, ensuring that resources can be more effectively allocated to complex problems that require deep thinking and innovative solutions.

In summary, during the **project execution stage**, LLMs not only provide intelligent workflow and resource management tools but also greatly enhance the efficiency and quality of project execution. Combined with real-time data analysis, intelligent recommendations, and dynamic adjustment strategies, LLMs have become a powerful tool for helping project teams tackle challenges and ensure project success. Just like an experienced captain navigating at sea, using advanced instruments and technology to ensure that cargo ships can safely reach their destination amidst turbulent waters.

The application of this technology is not limited to simple task automation, but also involves complex decision support, capable of providing accurate guidance and support in changing environments. Through continuous learning and adaptation, LLMs maintain the cutting edge and adaptability of solutions, helping project teams stay ahead in a highly competitive market.

Applying LLMs in project management case studies

The previous sections described how LLMs can support requirements analysis, task planning, communication, risk management, decision support, and workflow optimization. The following case studies show how these capabilities can be applied in real project management scenarios, where teams use LLM-enabled tools to address practical challenges in customer requirements, information flow, project reporting, and task allocation.

> This chapter uses LigaAI as the main worked example to show how LLM-enabled project management can operate in practice. LigaAI is used here as an illustrative case, not as the only tool capable of supporting these workflows.
>
> Many modern project-management, documentation, and collaboration platforms now include LLM-based features for summarizing information, generating documents, converting messages into tasks, searching project knowledge, supporting prioritization, and producing reports. For example, teams may use Notion AI or Confluence for documentation, Jira or Asana for task management, Slack AI or Microsoft Teams with Copilot for communication summaries, and Smartsheet AI or Microsoft Project with Copilot for reporting and planning support.
>
> When selecting a tool, project teams should begin with the capability they need most: clearer requirements, faster documentation, better task tracking, improved communication, stronger reporting, or more reliable risk visibility.

Assistance in understanding customer requirements

Background

Z Company is an enterprise focused on **Software as a Service (SaaS)** and, faced with ever-growing and diverse customer demands, always adheres to a user-centered service philosophy. To gain a deeper understanding of customers' actual application scenarios and provide more personalized services, Z Company regularly organizes in-depth interviews between business teams and customers. However, in practice, due to varying levels of interviewer experience and differences in business understanding, issues often arise, such as incomplete elicitation of customer needs or misunderstandings about requirements.

Solution

To address this issue, Z Company introduced the **LigaAI intelligent document system** and, combined with the analytical capabilities of LLMs, inputs the contents of customer interviews into the system. The LigaAI intelligent document system has the functions of automatically analyzing user scenarios, pain points, and goals. By processing interview data through intelligent algorithms, it generates structured requirements documents. This innovative measure has significantly improved the efficiency and accuracy of requirements elicitation.

Practical results

After using **LigaAI documents**, Z Company successfully produced a series of high-quality requirements documentation. Each document clearly defines the terminology mentioned during customer interviews and provides precise solutions and feasible execution steps tailored to specific scenarios and objectives, as shown in *Figure 10.7*.

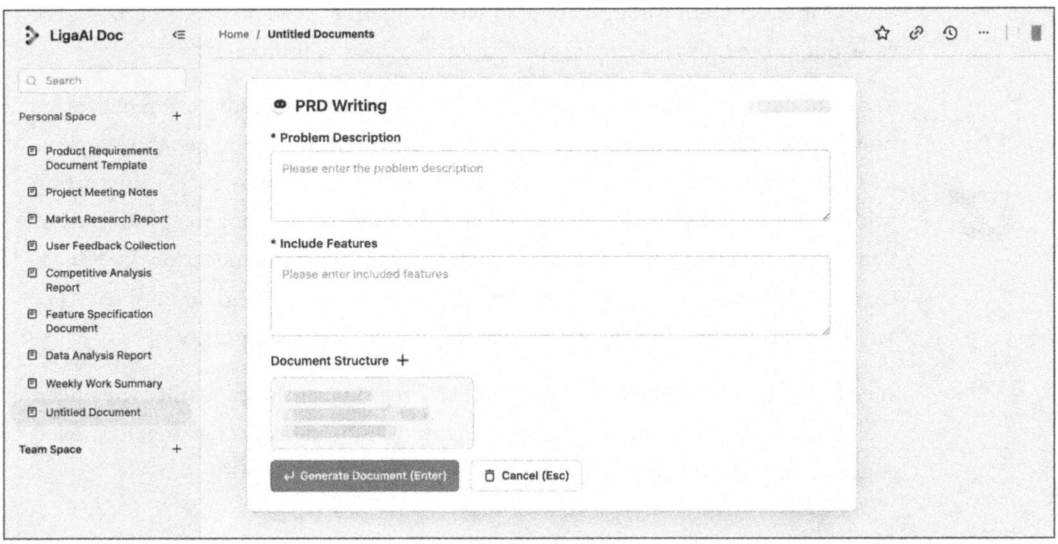

Figure 10.7: Example diagram of requirements collation function in LigaAI Documents

In addition, by integrating LigaAI documents with the **LigaAI project management system**, the system can also provide specific staff allocation suggestions based on actual project and resource distribution, further enhancing project management efficiency as shown in *Figure 10.8*.

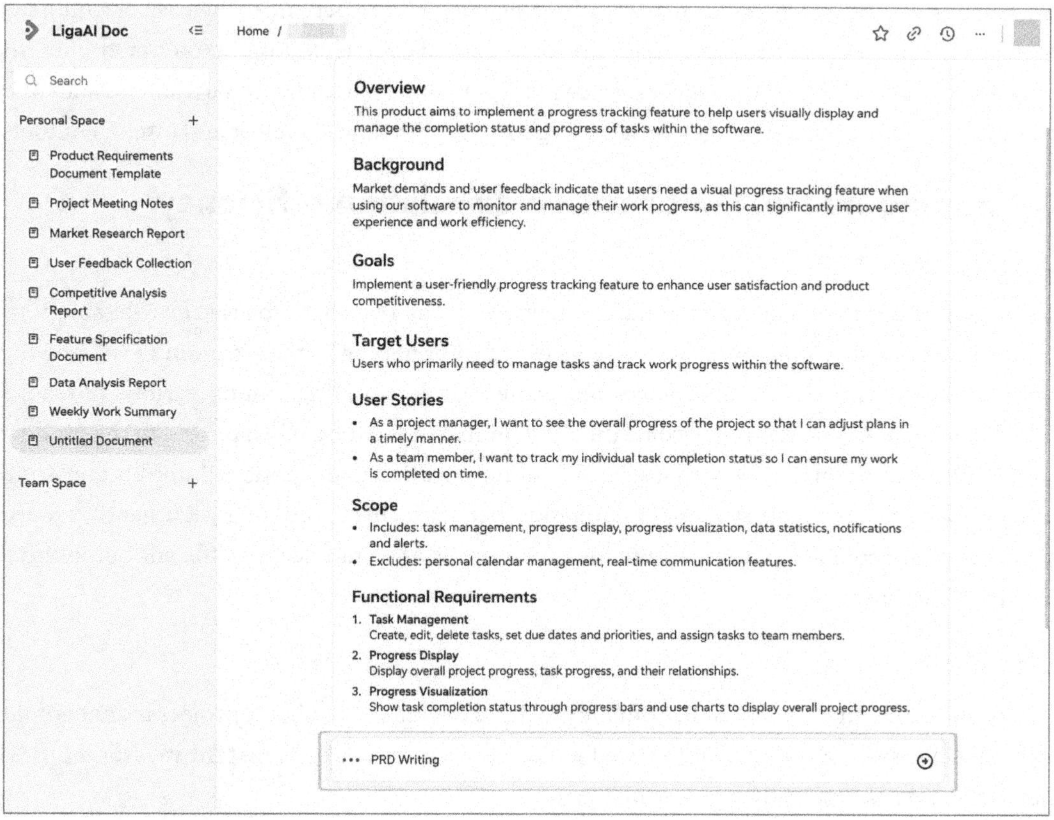

Figure 10.8: Example diagram of resource allocation function in LigaAI Documents

According to Z Company's research and interviews, multiple customers expressed recognition and satisfaction after receiving the service. One customer commented: "The level of personalization in Z Company's services has improved significantly. In the past, it took several rounds of communication to ensure they accurately understood our requirements. Now, with the LigaAI document system, we've found that they can quickly capture the key points and provide solutions that meet our expectations."

By introducing LigaAI documentation and integrating it with LLMs, Company Z not only effectively resolved the issue of insufficient interview information mining but also improved the speed and quality of business response. This innovative initiative played an important role in driving the company's digital transformation and optimizing customer experience. The case of Company Z demonstrates that even in the face of a complex and ever-changing market environment, enterprises can still promptly adjust service strategies, meet personalized customer needs, and maintain competitive advantages with the support of technological power and intelligent tools.

Improving internal information circulation efficiency

Background

With the rapid development of e-commerce, Company K, as a company focused on SaaS solutions, has realized that high-quality customer service is an essential competitive edge in a fast-growing market. Previously, due to differences in business understanding among various positions, merchants' needs would often become distorted or misunderstood when passed to the product and R&D departments, leading to inefficient communication and repetitive information. Amid the maintenance and management of numerous merchant clients, Company K urgently needed a system that could accurately capture merchant needs and enhance the efficiency of internal information flow.

Solution

After conducting market research, Company K chose to launch the **LigaAI project management system**. This system is deeply integrated with mainstream domestic **instant messaging** (IM) software and is supported by powerful LLMs.

Utilizing LigaAI, company business staff and customer service representatives can create task tickets via the screen recording function and share them within the team; the Q&A assistant can consolidate knowledge based on team inputs, enabling information sharing and quick retrieval. This not only streamlines the communication process but also leverages the natural language processing technology of LLMs to accurately analyze user intent, greatly improving team response efficiency and service quality.

Practical effects

After successfully applying LigaAI, Company K has seen a significant improvement in communication efficiency. Relevant personnel can convert IM messages to to-do tasks and quickly access information through the intelligent Q&A assistant.

Regarding converting IM messages to to-dos, with one click, IM messages are transformed into to-do tasks so information recipients can grasp the core content quickly and trace the detailed communication background.

The intelligent Q&A assistant built on LLMs provides a powerful knowledge management platform, enabling team members to quickly access required information through natural language queries, as shown in *Figure 10.9*.

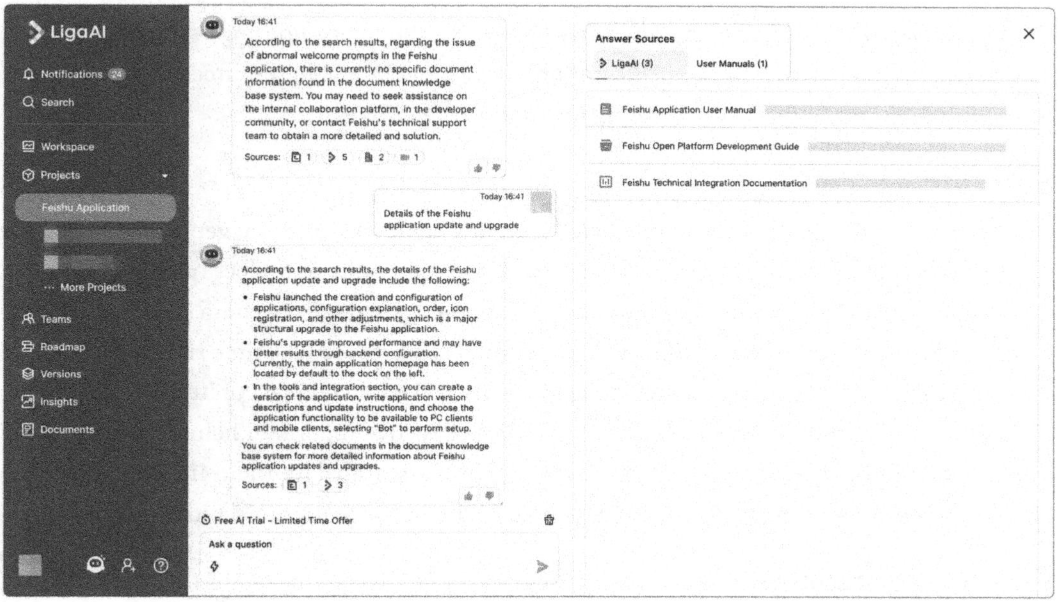

Figure 10.9: Illustration of the knowledge management feature in LigaAI Documents

According to K Company's research and interviews, relevant customer service personnel have stated that since the introduction of the LigaAI system, our customer service experience has made a qualitative leap. Information is no longer repeatedly relayed; each communication is more targeted, and customer satisfaction has increased significantly.

K Company's case clearly demonstrates how technological innovation can solve pain points in traditional customer service. The introduction of the LigaAI project management system has not only improved K Company's internal work efficiency but also helped enhance the interaction experience with customers. By accurately capturing and addressing customer needs, K Company has stood out in fierce market competition and won more trust and support from clients. As K Company continues to deepen its use of the LigaAI system, there are prospects for further business expansion and sustainable growth in the future.

Implementing automated project risk and progress analysis functions

Background

L Company is a project-oriented internet technology enterprise that undertakes various technical projects in cooperation with a wide range of clients. In this rapidly developing and ever-changing market environment, project management is especially crucial. However, project managers need to dedicate a significant amount of time each week to consolidating work progress and communicating reports to clients. This not only consumes valuable resources but also affects the team's focus and efficiency regarding the projects themselves.

Solution

To address this pain point, L Company introduced the LigaAI project management system. This system leverages advanced LLMs to achieve automated analysis of project risks and progress, effectively alleviating the work pressure on project managers related to data organization and analysis. Once a potential risk is detected, the system can provide real-time risk-level warning suggestions and decision support. More user-friendly still, after a project or iteration concludes, the system will automatically generate detailed retrospective reports to help the team deeply uncover highlights and shortcomings during the process, translate them into practical and actionable improvements, and lay a solid foundation for subsequent project iterations.

Practical outcomes

Since utilizing the LigaAI project management system, project managers at L Company have found a significant improvement in their data reporting efficiency. Data that used to take several hours to organize can now be completed in just a few minutes. Specifically, 70% of the time previously spent on preparing data reports each week has been saved. L Company reinvested this saved time into team building and staff business training, boosting the team's business understanding and familiarity by 30%, which has significantly enhanced the team's core competitiveness and project delivery capability, a diagrammatic representation of which is shown in *Figure 10.10*.

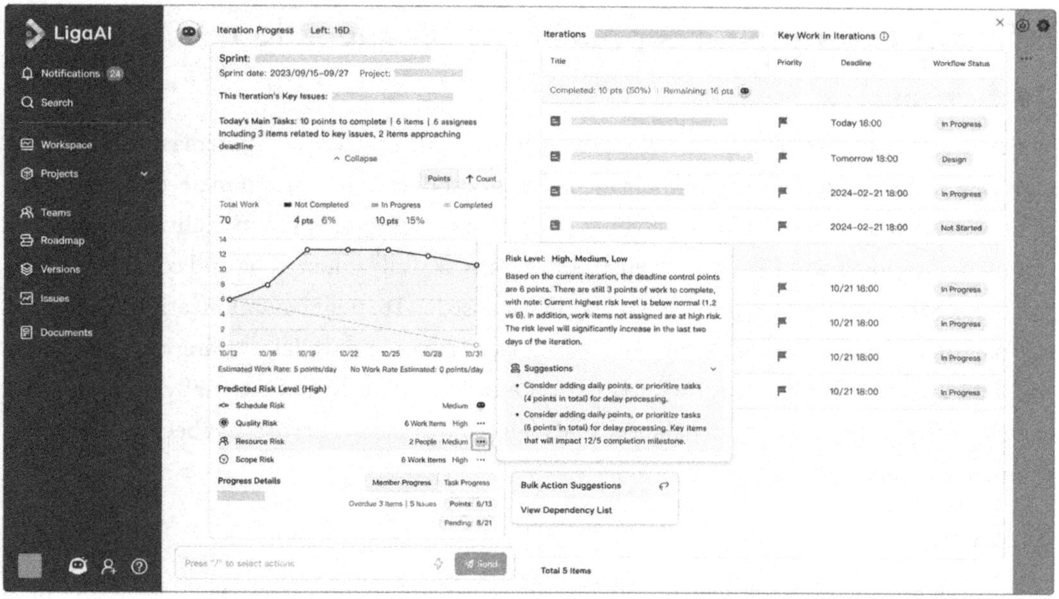

Figure 10.10: Schematic diagram of the automated analysis function in LigaAI Documents

According to descriptions from L Company's project managers, the introduction of the LigaAI project management system has brought immediate change to the team. It not only simplified the communication process with clients but also enabled greater focus on core technology research and development. Project managers are no longer troubled by tedious data analysis tasks, and the team now has more time to focus on team building and improving service quality.

L Company's case fully demonstrates the innovative value of the LigaAI project management system in project management. Through intelligent progress tracking, risk assessment, and decision support, the system has not only significantly improved management efficiency but also promoted team collaboration and knowledge sharing. In the future, as the LigaAI system continues to improve and upgrade, it is expected to become an essential tool for more enterprises in their digital transformation and project management optimization.

Efficient and rational support for task allocation

Background

With the rapid expansion of internet finance business, Company E is facing increasing challenges. Due to the inherent complexity of financial products, product managers often need to spend a lot of time in repeated discussions with team members when designing functionalities and writing requirements documents, in order to ensure all details are fully understood and considered. This not only consumes valuable time resources but can also lead to poor communication and missed tasks. Furthermore, when multiple business lines advance in parallel, staffing task allocation becomes another thorny issue. How to distribute tasks efficiently and rationally, ensuring that each member's workload is both balanced and aligned with their expertise, has become a pressing problem for management.

Solution

To address these issues, Company E introduced LigaAI's technical solution. First is the LigaAI Document Detection and Analysis System, which uses advanced LLMs to automatically detect possible defects and omissions in requirements documents based on Company E's process specifications and historical business case library. In addition, through deep learning and analysis of existing documents, the system can also offer content improvement suggestions to product managers, significantly enhancing document quality.

Furthermore, the LigaAI Project Management System achieves intelligent task decomposition by deeply parsing requirement descriptions and document content, with each subtask being automatically matched to the most suitable executor based on the required expertise, experience requirements, and the current workload of team members. This not only optimizes human resource allocation but also greatly improves work efficiency.

Practical results

Since Company E began using the LigaAI Project Management System, the accuracy and efficiency of project execution have significantly improved, as shown in *Figure 10.11.*

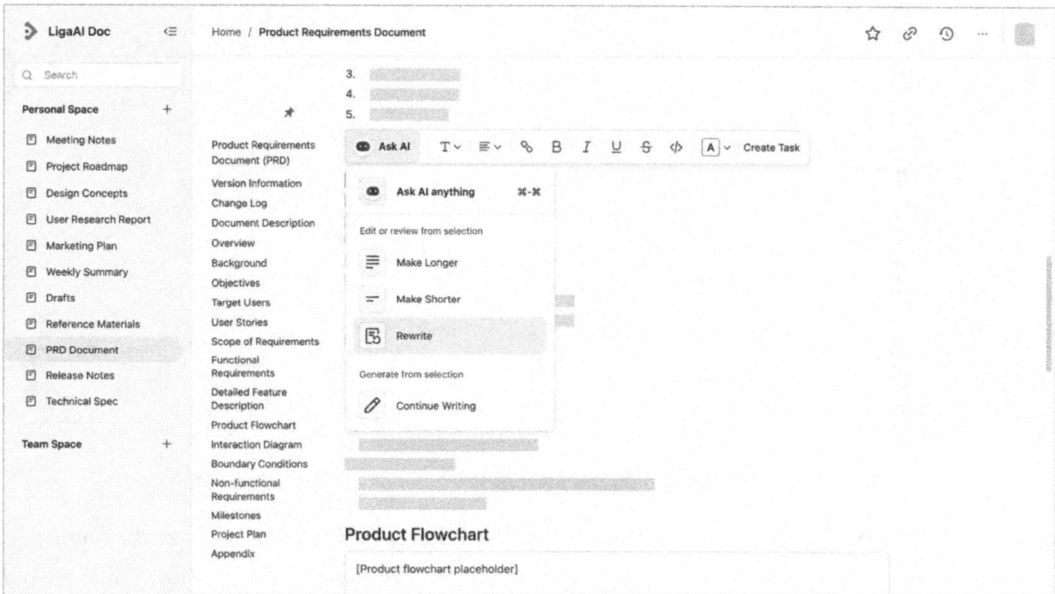

Figure 10.11: Schematic diagram of task allocation function in LigaAI Documents

According to statistics, the accuracy and completeness of documents have improved by 35%, while resource allocation efficiency has increased by 58%. Behind these numbers is a substantial reduction in project risk and an increase in team job satisfaction. It is worth noting that since the introduction of the LigaAI system, Company E has not experienced any project delays or cost overruns due to improper task allocation.

Project managers stated that before introducing LigaAI, they often discovered missing requirements in the middle of a project, resulting in rework or rush handling, which put great pressure on the team. Now, LigaAI enables precise checks early on, making the team's workflow much smoother, as shown in *Figure 10.12*. Even when facing complex financial products, they can work with greater confidence and efficiency.

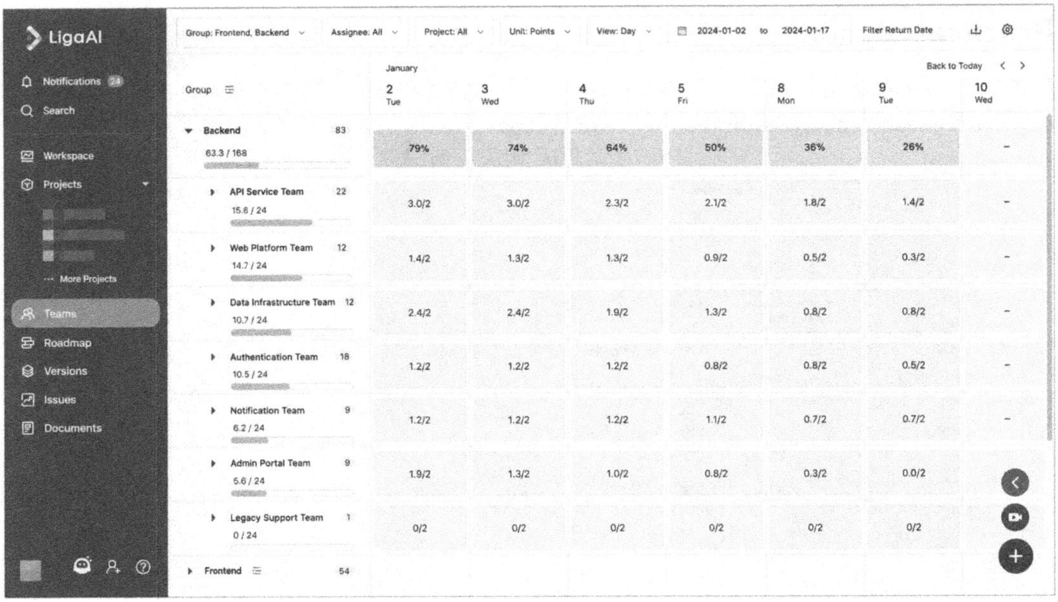

Figure 10.12: Schematic diagram of workflow function in LigaAI Documents

Company E's case fully demonstrates the application value of LigaAI technology in the operation and management of internet finance companies. Through the powerful computing abilities of big data and artificial intelligence, Company E has not only achieved a revolutionary improvement in internal management efficiency but also gained valuable time advantages in market competition. Such a transformative upgrade will undoubtedly lay a solid foundation for Company E's sustainable development in the future.

Summary

In this chapter, you learned how LLMs can support project management by improving requirements analysis, task planning, communication, and collaboration, risk management, decision support, and workflow optimization during project execution. You also saw how these capabilities are applied in practical scenarios such as understanding customer requirements, improving internal information flow, analyzing project risk, and progress, and supporting more effective task allocation.

Building on these project-management applications, the final chapter moves into security scenarios, where you will learn how LLMs can be used for anomaly detection, threat identification, phishing detection, malware analysis, compliance monitoring, and vulnerability repair.

11

Applying LLMs in Cybersecurity

In the field of cybersecurity, many security vendors are gradually beginning to widely apply LLMs to a variety of cybersecurity transformation scenarios. In security contexts, LLM technology, with its powerful data processing capabilities and deep learning algorithms, can enhance the effectiveness of threat detection and defense, breaking through the limitations and lag of traditional security solutions when faced with complex threats and novel attacks. Especially in the wave of digital transformation for enterprises, cybersecurity is no longer merely a technical issue, but has risen to become a critically important component of national strategy. LLM technology is gradually shaping a new productive force in the cybersecurity industry, leading a revolutionary transformation.

This chapter will cover the following main topics:

- Reframing cybersecurity with LLMs
- Applying LLMs across security workflows
- Managing the security risks of LLMs
- Evaluating zero-shot vulnerability repair with LLMs

Reframing cybersecurity with LLMs

As LLMs become part of cybersecurity workflows, their role extends beyond improving individual tools or automating isolated tasks. They change how security teams detect threats, interpret large volumes of operational data, respond to incidents, and think about future risk. This shift is especially important because modern cyber threats are no longer limited to known attack patterns; they evolve quickly, exploit complex systems, and often require faster analysis than traditional methods can provide. Understanding this shift requires looking at both sides of LLM adoption: the advantages they bring to security operations and the new risks and responsibilities they introduce.

Advantages of LLMs in the field of security

Amid the wave of digital transformation, LLM technology is not only a new productive force in the cybersecurity field, but also a powerful catalyst driving a new security paradigm. With the continuous advancement of technology, LLMs are leading us into a brand-new era of cybersecurity. In this era, traditional defense mechanisms are gradually merging with intelligent and automated security solutions, thus forming a completely new model of security protection.

The core advantage of LLM technology lies in its ability to process massive amounts of data and recognize complex patterns. In the field of network security, this means it can identify abnormal behaviors from regular network traffic, predict potential attacks, and enable automated responses to security incidents. This new paradigm is no longer solely dependent on defending against known threats, but instead predicts and defends against unknown threats by continuously learning behavioral patterns within networks. For example, by analyzing historical security incidents and current network behaviors, LLMs can predict the subsequent actions of attackers and proactively deploy defensive measures.

In addition, LLMs can play a key role in **security operations**. They can automate complex security analysis tasks, freeing security analysts from tedious work and allowing them to focus on more complex and strategic issues. This increase in efficiency enables security teams to respond more rapidly to security events, reducing the impact of security threats on enterprise operations.

At the same time, the qualities that make LLMs useful in cybersecurity—their ability to process large datasets, generate responses, and infer patterns from complex signals—also introduce new concerns. Their effectiveness depends on access to reliable data, careful governance, and safeguards that prevent the technology from being misused or trusted beyond its limits.

Challenges of LLMs in the field of security

The development of LLM technology has also brought new challenges. As the complexity of models continues to increase, the demand for data is also growing day by day. How to efficiently utilize data resources while ensuring personal privacy has become a key issue that needs urgent resolution. At the same time, the decision-making processes of LLMs often lack transparency, which poses severe challenges to the interpretability and trustworthiness of these models. Furthermore, the powerful functions of LLMs may be misused for improper purposes, such as generating false information for phishing or using deep learning techniques to circumvent existing security protections.

Responding to challenges of LLM technologies

Facing the challenges brought by LLM technology, it requires coordinated efforts from the government, enterprises, research institutions, and the public. The government should formulate corresponding policies and regulations to standardize the application of LLM technology and safeguard data security and personal privacy. Enterprises need to strengthen research and development work to enhance the security and reliability of LLMs. Research institutions should carry out in-depth studies on LLM technology and explore safer algorithms and models. The public should also enhance their cybersecurity awareness to jointly maintain the security of cyberspace.

Looking to the future, the application of LLM technology in the field of cybersecurity has broad prospects but is also full of challenges. Through the concerted efforts of all parties, we hope to achieve the sound development of LLM technology. With intelligent and automated security solutions, we can more effectively resist complex cyber threats.

While innovating technologically, we must also be alert to the security risks that LLM technology may bring, focus on data security and privacy protection, as well as model transparency and interpretability, and continually explore and improve response strategies to ensure the sustainable development of the cybersecurity industry. In this contest between technology and security, only through continuous innovation and collaboration can we harness the formidable power of LLMs and safeguard our digital world.

This broader shift becomes clearer when viewed through the day-to-day work of security teams. The value of LLMs is not limited to abstract improvements in intelligence or automation; it appears in specific workflows where teams must detect unusual behavior, classify threats, investigate incidents, prevent data leakage, and maintain compliance. The following examples show how LLMs can support these activities across different parts of the security lifecycle.

Applying LLMs across security workflows

The impact of LLMs becomes easier to understand when it is viewed through the everyday responsibilities of security teams. Security work involves detecting unusual behavior, classifying threats, investigating incidents, preventing data loss, strengthening policies, training users, and maintaining compliance across changing environments. LLMs can support many of these activities by analyzing large volumes of structured and unstructured data, identifying patterns that may be difficult to detect manually, and helping teams respond more quickly. The following scenarios show how these capabilities can be applied across different stages of the security workflow.

Anomaly detection

As a key application of LLMs in cybersecurity, anomaly detection is gradually revealing its important role in safeguarding network environments. Relying on advanced machine learning algorithms, LLMs can not only learn and master standard behavioral patterns in networks but also monitor and analyze network traffic in real time to identify and provide early warnings of behaviors that deviate from the norm. This capability is crucial for proactively discovering potential security threats.

Taking a large financial institution as an example, the application of LLMs can extend to multiple levels. By deeply analyzing employees' daily network access behaviors, LLMs can accurately identify unauthorized access attempts, which may originate from external attackers or improper operations by internal staff.

In addition, LLMs can monitor signs of data leakage. Whether through abnormal data transfer patterns or unusual employee access to sensitive information, these incidents can be promptly detected and trigger alerts.

Gartner's report emphasizes the importance of using AI behavioral models to enhance threat detection capabilities. Traditional threat detection methods often rely on recognizing historical attack patterns, which proves inadequate when facing emerging and unknown threats. In contrast, AI behavioral models, by analyzing patterns of normal behavior, can identify anomalies more flexibly and proactively, reducing dependence on historical data and thus responding more effectively to threats that have never occurred before.

Furthermore, the advantages of LLMs in anomaly detection are also reflected in their continuous learning and self-optimization abilities. Over time, LLMs can continuously learn and refine information from new data, thereby improving the accuracy of anomaly detection. Their adaptive characteristics make LLMs particularly important in dynamic network environments, enabling them to handle new threat patterns and rapidly adjust detection strategies.

Threat identification and classification

In the field of cybersecurity, the identification and classification of threats are the cornerstone for building an effective defense system. LLMs, leveraging the powerful capabilities of deep learning, are gradually becoming indispensable tools in this process. By analyzing massive amounts of network activity data, LLMs can gain insights and extract critical features that are essential for threat detection. These features are then used to precisely classify potential threats, providing security teams with a clearer perspective to more effectively identify and counteract cyber attacks.

For example, security operations teams can use LLMs to distinguish and identify various types of **malware attacks**, including **ransomware**, **trojans**, and **worms**. Each of these types of malware has its own unique behavioral patterns and attack strategies. By learning these patterns, LLMs help security teams quickly identify the type of attack at the earliest possible moment, so that corresponding defensive measures can be taken. This deep-learning-based classification approach not only greatly accelerates the speed of threat response but also offers solid data support for developing future preventive measures.

According to research, AI-enhanced threat detection systems can significantly improve the efficiency of threat response, reducing response time by 80%. This finding further confirms the potential application of LLMs in the cybersecurity field. When faced with constantly evolving cyber threats, the capability of LLMs is especially crucial. Not only can they help security teams quickly identify known threats, but they can also predict and discover new or unknown threats by learning behavioral patterns.

Automated threat hunting

Automated threat hunting is an innovative application of LLMs in the field of cybersecurity. By simulating the querying and analysis processes of human analysts, it significantly improves the efficiency and accuracy of threat detection. In this process, the LLM acts as a tireless guardian, able to monitor network activity 24/7, perform complex data analysis tasks, and thereby identify and alert on potential security threats.

For example, if an account initiates login attempts from multiple different geographic locations within a short period, or if there are a large number of login attempts within a very short time, these could be signs of account compromise or **brute force attacks**. The LLM can quickly capture these anomalous behaviors and promptly relay this information to the security team, helping them quickly locate and respond to potential security incidents.

In addition, the advantage of LLMs in automated threat hunting is also reflected in their ability to process and analyze massive volumes of network data. In today's network environment, enormous amounts of data are generated every moment, which presents a huge challenge for traditional manual analysis methods. However, with their powerful data processing capabilities, LLMs can handle and analyze this data in a short time, greatly improving both the speed and scope of threat detection.

Phishing attack identification

Phishing attacks, as a long-standing challenge in the field of cybersecurity, continues to grow in complexity and stealth, presenting serious challenges to both individual users and enterprise security. With the advancement of artificial intelligence technology, LLMs have shown tremendous potential and value in phishing attack detection. By employing advanced natural language processing technology, LLMs can analyze email contents and phishing webpages in depth, accurately identifying fraudulent links and suspicious communication patterns, thereby establishing a robust line of defense for cybersecurity.

Taking enterprise email systems as an example, systems integrated with LLMs can automatically scan inbox messages, intelligently recognizing, and intercepting potential phishing emails through learning normal communication patterns and the characteristics of phishing emails. This automated detection and defense mechanism not only greatly improves the efficiency of security protection but also reduces the burden on security teams, enabling them to focus more energy on other important security tasks.

The *Verizon 2021 Data Breach Investigations Report* points out that phishing attacks are one of the main causes of data breaches. This finding further highlights the importance of phishing attack identification in cybersecurity. The application of artificial intelligence technology, especially with the support of LLMs, is changing the traditional methods of phishing attack defense. Through machine learning and deep learning algorithms, LLMs can learn the patterns of phishing attacks from massive datasets and continuously optimize their identification capability, thereby identifying and blocking these attacks in a timely manner.

Malware detection

For a long time, **malware** has been a major threat in the field of cybersecurity. It infiltrates systems quietly and carries out a variety of malicious activities, including data theft, denial-of-service attacks, and even the sabotage of critical infrastructure. To effectively counter this threat, LLM technologies have emerged as a new tool for security defense.

LLMs use advanced machine learning and deep learning algorithms to analyze and learn behavioral patterns and code characteristics of malware, enabling efficient detection of new or variant malware.

By continuously analyzing file transfer behaviors, LLMs can identify files carrying malware, even if these files have not yet been recognized by traditional virus detection systems. This is because LLMs not only recognize known malware features, but can also detect novel or variant malware through behavioral analysis that has not yet been widely documented.

This behavior-based detection method enables security teams to respond to potential threats more rapidly, isolating, and removing malware in time, thus protecting user data security and the reputation of organizations. Furthermore, this capability of LLMs is crucial in addressing rapidly evolving malware threats. As cyber attackers continually develop new malware variants to evade traditional detection methods, the predictive, and adaptive nature of LLMs is particularly important today.

Intrusion detection system

The **Intrusion Detection System (IDS)** is an important component of the network security defense system. Its main task is to monitor and analyze network or system behavior in order to discover and respond to potential security threats in a timely manner. As network attack methods continue to evolve and become more sophisticated, traditional IDSs are facing increasing challenges.

Against this backdrop, the application of LLM technology has brought new vitality and stronger detection capabilities to IDS. With their powerful data processing and machine learning abilities, LLMs can deeply analyze network traffic and system logs to identify various potential intrusion behaviors. Whether it is **port scanning, denial of service (DoS) attacks**, or **distributed denial of service (DDoS) attacks**, LLMs can improve detection accuracy and response speed by learning the characteristics of these attack patterns.

Take a cloud service provider as an example. Such a provider may face continuous attack threats from around the world. In this case, LLMs can be deployed at the network edge to analyze incoming packets in real time, using their advanced algorithms to quickly identify abnormal traffic. This allows attacks to be blocked in their early stages. This LLM-based IDS can not only improve detection accuracy and reduce false positives and missed detections, but also achieve effective protection for large-scale network infrastructure without affecting network performance.

LLMs in IDS also possess self-learning and self-optimization capabilities. Over time, these models can continuously learn from new data and automatically adjust their detection strategies to adapt to the ever-changing network environment and attack methods. This adaptive characteristic enables LLM-based IDSs to consistently maintain efficiency and accuracy, providing a dynamic line of defense for network security.

Security policy recommendations

In the field of network security, the application of LLMs is becoming increasingly diverse and in-depth. They are not just tools for detecting and defending against threats, but also serve as intelligent advisors providing strategic security recommendations. By conducting in-depth analysis of historical security incidents and real-time monitoring of current network activities, LLMs can offer enterprises customized security strategy advice, helping organizations build a stronger security defense line.

Take a large enterprise as an example; its security team faces the challenge of formulating appropriate security policies for different departments and business units in an ever-changing network environment. LLMs play a crucial role in this process. By analyzing security vulnerabilities and attack patterns the enterprise has encountered in the past, they can identify potential security weaknesses and propose specific security measures accordingly. These measures may include, but are not limited to, strong password requirements, multi-factor authentication, network access restrictions during specific time periods, etc. Each measure is tailored to the company's unique needs and risk exposures. Strong password requirements can significantly enhance account security, preventing brute-force and password-guessing attacks. **Multi-factor authentication** adds an extra layer of protection to account security, making it difficult for attackers to gain full control of accounts even if passwords are compromised. **Network access restrictions** during specific time periods can effectively reduce unauthorized access during non-working hours, thereby lowering the risk of data breaches and insider threats.

In addition, LLMs can also provide dynamic security policy recommendations based on the results of current network activity analysis. For example, if an LLM detects an abnormal increase in network access activity for a particular department during a specific time period, it may recommend temporarily restricting network access for that department until the security team completes further investigation and risk assessment.

Predictive threat modeling

Predictive threat modeling is an innovative application of LLMs in the field of cybersecurity, representing a shift from passive defense to proactive prevention. By leveraging the powerful computational capabilities and deep learning algorithms of LLMs, security teams are now able to predict potential security threats and attack methods based on historical data and current trends. This forward-looking capability greatly enhances an organization's ability to cope with unknown threats, enabling them to take preventive measures before an attack occurs.

In the financial industry, the application of predictive threat modeling is particularly critical. Due to high-value transactions and sensitive data, the financial sector is a primary target for cybercrime. By deploying LLMs, security teams can analyze vast amounts of transaction data and user behavior patterns to identify early signs of suspicious activities. For example, LLMs can predict future fraudulent patterns, including credit card fraud, identity theft, or money laundering activities. Once these potential threats are identified, security teams can deploy defensive measures in advance, such as strengthening transaction monitoring, implementing real-time fraud detection, or adjusting risk assessment models.

The advantages of LLMs in predictive threat modeling also lie in their ability to process and analyze unstructured data. In the field of cybersecurity, besides structured logs and transaction data, there is a large amount of unstructured data, such as email content, social media posts, and network traffic. LLMs, using NLP techniques, can extract valuable information from this unstructured data and combine it with structured data to obtain more comprehensive threat predictions.

Data leakage prevention

In today's digital era, **data leakage** has become one of the major security threats faced by enterprises. LLM technology, with its outstanding data processing and analysis capabilities, is gradually becoming an effective tool for preventing data leaks. In daily business operations, enterprises generate a large number of log files, including network logs, system logs, application logs, and more. These log data contain rich information but are also extremely large and complex. LLMs can rapidly identify potential security threats through automated log analysis, such as unauthorized access attempts, abnormal network traffic, or potential insider threats. By monitoring and analyzing the flow of sensitive data, LLMs can effectively detect potential data leakage activities.

For example, in a certain technology company, LLMs can be trained to identify abnormal access behaviors to sensitive information by internal personnel. Such abnormal behaviors may include data downloads during non-working hours, unusual data transfers, or frequent access to specific sensitive information. By learning normal data access patterns, LLMs can promptly detect activities that deviate from the norm and notify the security team through real-time alert systems. This real-time monitoring and rapid response mechanism is crucial for preventing data leaks.

Safety education and training

With its powerful data processing and machine learning capabilities, LLM technology is revolutionizing traditional safety education and training models. By simulating real attack scenarios and creating interactive training programs, LLMs can not only provide a more realistic and effective security training experience, but also dynamically adjust the training content based on employee feedback and performance to offer personalized learning paths.

By analyzing employee behaviors and responses during training, LLMs can identify employees' strengths and weaknesses, thereby providing more targeted training content. This personalized learning experience not only improves employees' learning efficiency but also helps them better understand and master security knowledge.

Intelligence sharing and collaboration

In the field of **intelligence sharing and collaboration** in cybersecurity, LLMs play a key role. Their core capability lies in integrating and analyzing security threat intelligence from multiple sources. Through **deep learning** and **pattern recognition** technologies, LLMs can extract valuable information from massive amounts of data and identify similarities in security incidents across different organizations, thereby uncovering common threat patterns and attack trends.

This ability is particularly important when dealing with global security threats, especially potential cyberattacks against critical infrastructure. Critical infrastructure (such as power grids, water treatment systems, and traffic control systems) is essential to national security and social operation. By analyzing historical security data of these infrastructures, LLMs can predict and identify possible attack vectors, preparing defenses in advance.

Compliance monitoring

In the current context of increasingly strict data protection regulations, LLM technology has become an important tool for enterprises to ensure compliance. With precise data analysis capabilities, it helps enterprises monitor and manage data processing activities to meet stringent legal requirements. In a globalized environment, LLM technology enables enterprises to adapt to data protection regulations across different countries and regions, providing assurance for smooth international business operations.

For example, when an Asian company sets up a branch in Europe, it must process personal data in accordance with the **General Data Protection Regulation (GDPR)**. LLMs can deeply analyze the company's data processing workflows and sensitively identify any behavior that may violate the GDPR, including unauthorized use of personal data or insecure data processing practices. Through this advanced monitoring mechanism, enterprises can not only promptly rectify violations but also prevent potential compliance risks, thus significantly reducing compliance risk. This not only helps enterprises avoid possible legal sanctions and financial losses but also protects customers' privacy rights, enhancing the company's reputation and customer trust.

These examples show that LLMs can strengthen many parts of the security lifecycle, from detection and investigation to training and compliance. However, the same qualities that make them useful in security workflows also create new risks. Models that process sensitive data, generate recommendations, and influence operational decisions must be governed carefully. Before organizations can rely on LLMs as part of their security architecture, they must also understand the vulnerabilities, misuse scenarios, and control measures associated with the models themselves.

Managing the security risks of LLMs

LLMs have demonstrated tremendous potential in natural language processing, image recognition, data analysis, and many other fields due to their powerful data processing capabilities and deep learning algorithms. However, as with any technological advancement, the application of LLMs is accompanied by new security challenges and operational risks.

Inherent risks

The inherent risks of LLMs include four aspects: **access control vulnerabilities**, **prompt injection**, **content hallucinations**, and **poisoning of training data**.

Access control vulnerabilities

The training and deployment of LLMs typically require massive computational resources, which are often distributed across different servers and data centers. To ensure efficient operation of the model, appropriate data access permissions must be provided. However, if access control mechanisms are not sufficiently strict or have flaws, they can become targets for attackers. Attackers may exploit these vulnerabilities to gain unauthorized access to sensitive data or even conduct malicious operations on the model, such as implanting malicious code or tampering with model parameters, thereby affecting the normal operation and output of the model.

Prompt injection

Prompt injection is a type of attack that exploits vulnerabilities at the model's input side. Attackers craft specially designed inputs (i.e., prompts) to induce the model to produce unexpected outputs. Such attacks may cause the model to leak training data, perform specific operations, or generate misleading information. For example, an attacker could use prompt injection to induce the language model to generate text containing sensitive information or to produce malicious code capable of bypassing security checks.

Content hallucinations and poisoning of training data

Content hallucinations and **poisoning of training data** are two other major challenges faced by LLMs. Content hallucination refers to attackers generating specific input samples that cause the model to make incorrect predictions or classifications. These input samples may appear visually identical to normal samples but are sufficient to cause a sharp decline in model performance. **Training data poisoning** refers to attackers injecting malicious samples into the training data during the model's training phase, causing the model to learn incorrect patterns. Once these patterns are learned by the model and applied to real tasks, the model's decisions and outputs may become biased.

These inherent weaknesses become more serious when LLMs are connected to real systems, users, data stores, and business workflows. At that point, model-level risks begin to overlap with application security concerns.

Application security risks

The application security risks of LLMs can be categorized into four aspects: **data leakage**, **AI ethics and morality**, **prompt jailbreak**, and **supply chain security**.

Data leakage

When LLMs handle sensitive data, improper protection may lead to data leakage. Such data may include personal privacy information, trade secrets, or state secrets. Data leakage not only causes serious harm to individuals and enterprises but may also trigger legal action and reputational loss. Therefore, how to effectively safeguard data security while ensuring model performance is a key issue that needs to be addressed in the application of LLMs.

AI ethics and morality

The application of LLMs also involves issues of ethics and morality. Since model training typically relies on large volumes of data, these datasets may contain biased or discriminatory content. If the model learns and amplifies these biases, it may lead to discriminatory outcomes, such as unfair scoring of certain groups in fields like recruitment or credit approval. In addition, LLMs can be used to create false information, such as deepfake technologies, posing serious threats to social order and public safety.

Prompt jailbreaks

Prompt jailbreak refers to attackers using specific inputs to bypass the model's security constraints, thereby accessing or executing unauthorized functions. This method of attack poses a serious threat to model security. For instance, attackers may use prompt jailbreaks to access the model's internal structure or perform specific operations, such as stealing data or implanting malware.

Supply chain security

The **supply chain** for LLMs may also become a target for attacks. From data collection and model training to deployment, every step in the supply chain may contain security vulnerabilities. Attackers might inject malicious code or tamper with model parameters at these stages, thereby affecting the normal operation of the model. Hence, ensuring the security of the supply chain is an essential part that cannot be overlooked in LLM applications.

Because these risks span data, access, model behavior, and deployment pipelines, they cannot be addressed through a single control. Effective mitigation requires layered safeguards across the full lifecycle of the LLM system.

Counteracting risks

The adversarial risks of LLMs include three aspects: the **data lifecycle principle**, **data noise addition techniques**, and the **zero-trust principle** for access control.

Data lifecycle principles

To address the security challenges posed by LLMs, the **data lifecycle principle** should be followed to ensure that data is properly protected at every stage—collection, storage, processing, transmission, and destruction. This includes measures such as **data encryption**, **access control**, and **auditing** to prevent data leakage and misuse.

Data noise addition techniques

Data noise addition technology is an effective countermeasure that injects random noise into data to reduce its sensitivity and thus improve model security. This approach can increase the difficulty for attackers to extract useful information from the data without significantly impacting model performance.

Zero trust principles for access control

The **zero trust principle** is an important security strategy that assumes that all entities inside and outside the network are untrusted and therefore requires strict identity verification and authorization for every access. This principle can effectively prevent unauthorized access and insider threats, thereby enhancing system security.

Risk management is not only about protecting LLM systems from misuse; it is also about understanding whether LLMs can help reduce security risks in software itself. One important area is vulnerability repair, where models are asked to suggest fixes for insecure code. The next discussion looks at how zero-shot LLMs perform in this setting, and what their results reveal about both the promise and the limits of using LLMs for automated security remediation.

Evaluating zero-shot vulnerability repair with LLMs

The discussion now narrows from broad security risks to one specific question: can LLMs help repair vulnerable code without being specially trained for that task? This is an important place to end the chapter because vulnerability repair brings together several themes covered earlier—code generation, security testing, prompt design, model reliability, and human oversight. The following discussion examines a zero-shot vulnerability repair study, beginning with the research motivation, then moving through the experimental setup, the generation of vulnerable programs, the effect of prompt design, and finally the reliability of the repair code produced by LLMs.

Research background

After undergoing extensive source code training, LLMs have been used to assist developers in completing coding tasks, such as translation between different programming languages and code understanding. Among the many downstream code tasks, development teams and security teams need to pay special attention to the ability of LLMs to repair code security vulnerabilities. Traditionally, this process is carried out by security testers who run security tools (such as **Fuzzers** or static analyzers), interpret the feedback from these tools, locate problematic code, and ultimately fix security vulnerabilities in the code.

In practice, an important question arises: **Can the "out-of-the-box" LLMs used for code completion help developers repair security vulnerabilities**? In the security field, this capability of LLMs has three security-oriented characteristics: black box, immediate code LLM capabilities, and the impact of zero-shot methods on vulnerability repair.

The paper *Examining Zero-Shot Vulnerability Repair with LLMs* gives us some inspiration from four aspects:

- Can existing "out-of-the-box" LLMs generate secure and functionally correct code to repair security vulnerabilities?
- Does changing the amount of code comment context in a prompt affect the ability of LLMs to provide repair suggestions?
- What challenges exist when using LLMs to repair code security vulnerabilities in real-world scenarios?
- How reliable are LLMs in generating repair code?

To answer these questions, the study moves from general interest in LLM-based vulnerability repair to a structured experimental design. The research approach defines which models were evaluated, how vulnerable programs were prepared, how prompts were constructed, and how generated patches were tested for both security and functional correctness.

Research approach

LLM technology is essentially a scalable sequence prediction model; that is, given a prompt containing a sequence of tokens, the model predicts and outputs the set of "most likely" next tokens. In code large models, LLMs can be used to accomplish downstream tasks such as writing function bodies and code comments. Parameters of LLMs such as temperature, top-p, and top-k are used to fine-tune the diversity and alignment preferences of generated code. This method has achieved good results in code-assisted generation scenarios.

Researchers at New York University evaluated the performance of several ready-to-use LLMs in the context of code security vulnerability repair. *Figure 11.1* summarizes the basic characteristics of these LLMs. Among them, the first three models are different versions of the **OpenAI's Codex** model; the 4th and 5th items are different versions of the **AI21's Jurassic-1** model. All the above models are accessed via API services. The 6th entry, polycoder, is a locally deployed pre-trained LLM, and the 7th, gpt2-csrc, is a locally trained LLM using a C/C++ code dataset.

Model	Parameters	Context Window	Maximum Output	API Limits
code-cushman-001	Unknown	~50K	2048	150,000 tokens/min (open beta)
code-davinci-001	Unknown	~50K	4096	150,000 tokens/min (open beta)
code-davinci-002	Unknown	~50K	4096	150,000 tokens/min (open beta)
j1-jumbo	178 billion	~256K	2048	30,000 tokens/min (open beta)
i1-large	7.8 billion	~256K	2048	100,000 tokens/month (free plan)
polycoder	2.7 billion	~50K	2048	N/A
gpt2-csrc	774 million	~52K	1024	N/A

Figure 11.1: Basic characteristics of several LLMs

The authors of the paper designed and implemented a complete process for repairing programs with security vulnerabilities, as shown in *Figure 11.2*.

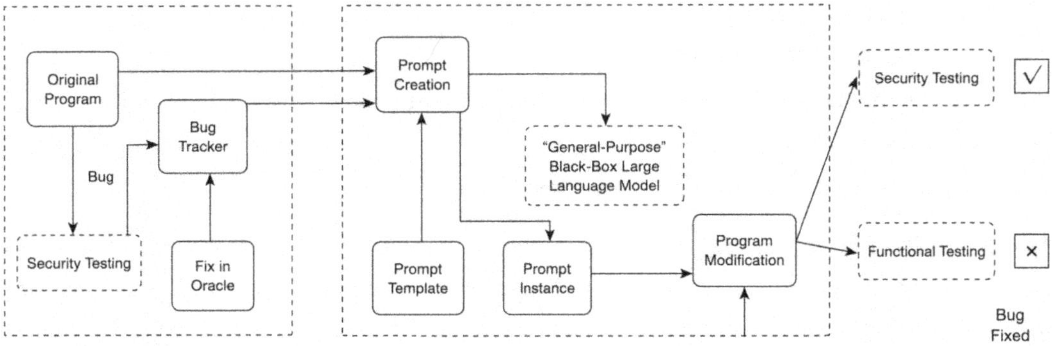

Figure 11.2: Automatic program vulnerability repair flowchart

First, the original program with security vulnerabilities is input into a security tool for testing. Then, CodeQL is used to manage and analyze the program's source code and vulnerability information. Next, the program's source code, comments, and other information are formatted into prompt content according to a preset prompt template and input to the LLM being evaluated. With the code prediction capabilities of the LLM, the vulnerabilities are repaired. Finally, the patched program is subjected to security testing using the same test cases as in the first step to verify whether the vulnerability has been successfully fixed, and functional validation is simultaneously performed to ensure the program runs properly.

With this repair pipeline in place, the next step was to construct vulnerable programs and evaluate how effectively different models and prompt settings could repair them.

Experimental process

The authors conducted their experiments by constructing an artificially synthesized dataset of program source code containing vulnerabilities. The experiments were divided into two phases: the first phase was model parameter scanning in order to identify the appropriate "typical" parameters for LLMs to generate repair code; the second phase focused on prompts to determine whether, as "bug context" information increases, different prompt patterns would affect the quality of repair code generated by black-box LLMs.

Generation of vulnerable programs

The authors selected two vulnerabilities from the **CWE Top 25** list as the targets for their artificially synthesized programs: **CWE-787 (Out-of-bounds Write)** and **CWE-89 (SQL Injection)**. Both are high-impact vulnerabilities on the CWE Top 25 list that could result in data loss/leakage or privilege escalation. These two vulnerabilities are relatively easy to detect and can be directly identified in the given code without any additional context.

CWE-787 and CWE-89 are presented at two different levels of abstraction: CWE-787 tends to occur in low-level languages like C/C++, which allow direct manipulation of memory pointers, while CWE-89 typically occurs in high-level languages such as Java or Python. This means that the experiments can assess the vulnerability repair capabilities of LLMs across two different facets of software development.

To generate a large quantity of functionally unique yet similarly vulnerable programs, LLMs were used to generate a substantial amount of vulnerable code as the evaluation dataset, following these steps:

1. Specify vulnerable programs related to CWE-787 and CWE-89 as the opening Prompts
2. Input the prompts into OpenAI's Codex LLM (using both `code-cushman-001` and `code-davinci-001` versions), generating 500 code samples from each
3. Perform unit testing and CodeQL-based analysis on these code samples
4. Use functionally correct yet vulnerable programs as the dataset

Figure 11.3 provides the statistical details of the generated code samples. Among them, there are 388 functionally correct but vulnerable code samples for CWE-787 and 23 for CWE-89.

Scenario	Total Generated	Total Validated	Total Functional	Total Vulnerabilities	Functional, Vulnerable Count	Functional, Non-Vulnerable Count
CWE-787	500	440	410	452	388	22
CWE-89	500	500	491	23	23	468

Figure 11.3: Vulnerable program samples - Table comparing CWE-787 and CWE-89 on generated, verified, functional and vulnerable counts

After constructing a dataset of programs that were both functional and vulnerable, the researchers could test the central question of the study: whether ready-to-use LLMs can generate patches without task-specific training or fine-tuning. This experiment evaluates the models' zero-shot repair capability by prompting them with vulnerable programs and then testing whether the generated code removes the vulnerability while preserving functionality.

Testing LLM Vulnerability Repair

Using the code for 95 CWE-787 and 22 CWE-89 vulnerable programs as prompts, we queried two LLMs—`code-cushman-001` and `code-davinci-001`—for vulnerability fix code. Each model generated 500 code samples at a time, resulting in 47,500 and 11,000 samples for the two vulnerabilities, respectively. *Figure 11.4* illustrates the proportion of successful fixes.

Scenario	Total Generated	Total Validated	Total Functional	Total Vulnerabilities	Functional and Vulnerable Count	Functional and Non-Vulnerable Count	Validation Fix Rate (%)
CWE-787	47 500	22 034	20 029	21 020	19 538	491	2.2
CWE-89	11 000	10 796	7594	5719	4397	3197	29.6

Figure 11.4: Schematic of fix verification proportions

It can be seen that among the 22,034 valid programs for the CWE-787 scenario, 2.2% were fixed, and among the 10,796 valid programs for the CWE-89 scenario, 29.6% were fixed. Notably, even without any additional contextual assumptions, LLMs can generate bug-free code with zero samples, meaning they can be used for automated vulnerability repairs in downstream tasks.

In addition, the paper's authors also observed that different LLM parameters have varying impacts on code fixes, as shown in *Figure 11.5* and *Figure 11.6*. LLMs with higher temperature parameters perform better for CWE-787 fixes but worse for CWE-89, and vice versa. Therefore, it seems there is no single temperature parameter that covers all cases. Furthermore, overall, the higher the value of the top-p parameter, the better the performance. Accordingly, following the recommendations from Codex's official documentation, the authors set the temperature to a broad range `{0, 0.25, 0.50, 0.75, 1.00}` in subsequent experiments, and top-p to a fixed value of `1.0`, which reduced the subsequent evaluation search space by 80%.

Temperature	top-*p*				
	0	0.25	0.5	0.75	1
0	—	—	—	—	—
0.25	—	—	—	2 /832	3 /818
0.5	—	2 /738	14 /688	13 /698	28 /709
0.75	—	6 /696	21 /652	32 /625	103 /776
1	—	3 /691	24 /608	56 /602	124 /655

code-cushman-001

Temperature	top-*p*				
	0	0.25	0.5	0.75	1
0	—	—	—	—	—
0.25	—	—	—	—	—
0.5	—	—	—	—	1 /419
0.75	—	—	—	—	20 /527
1	—	—	—	—	30 /404

code-davinci-001

(a) CWE-787

Figure 11.5: Impact of different LLM parameters on code repair - Two tables compare CWE 787 bug generation for codecushman001 and codedavinci001 models

Temperature	top-*p*				
	0	0.25	0.5	0.75	1
0	49 /220	49 /220	49 /220	40 /220	49 /220
0.25	49 /220	46 /220	47 /220	48 /215	44 /214
0.5	49 /220	49 /220	49 /220	41 /210	59 /201
0.75	49 /220	49 /220	49 /220	41 /209	44 /198
1	49 /220	49 /220	49 /220	47 /209	29 /190

code-cushman-001

Temperature	top-*p*				
	0	0.25	0.5	0.75	1
0	84 /220	77 /220	87 /220	91 /220	91 /220
0.25	82 /220	92 /220	92 /220	93 /216	62 /212
0.5	90 /220	86 /220	90 /220	82 /209	62 /208
0.75	90 /220	90 /220	91 /220	82 /213	45 /203
1	89 /220	87 /220	87 /220	80 /212	23 /197

code-davinci-001

(b) CWE-89

Figure 11.6: Impact of different LLM parameters on code repair - Two tables compare CWE-89 bug generation for codecushman001 and codedavinci001 models

After establishing that out-of-the-box models can repair some vulnerabilities, the study next examines whether the amount of context included in the prompt affects the quality of those repairs.

Testing prompt context for vulnerability repair

By increasing the types of **prompts** (such as adding or reducing the amount of context in comments) and evaluating a broader range of vulnerability scenarios, the impact of **prompt engineering** on vulnerability repair is assessed. The details of the experimental setup are as follows.

Considering that methods using LLMs to generate code samples might implicitly provide clues for the LLM to generate vulnerability fixes, the experiment adopts a manual construction approach. Seven typical vulnerability types from the CWE Top 25 were selected, and code samples containing vulnerabilities were constructed (specifically **CWE-79, CWE-125, CWE-20, CWE-416, CWE-476, CWE-119, CWE-732**), forming the basis for further prompt engineering evaluation.

Prompt design for vulnerability repair

To test the role of context more systematically, the researchers designed multiple prompt templates that provided different levels of information about the vulnerability and the intended fix.

Multiple **prompt comment templates** were used in the experiments to enhance the context information of prompts for each vulnerability scenario. Since there are many possible natural language formulations for vulnerability fixing prompts, the paper refers to user guides from models like Codex and comment keywords retrieved from Github to design five prompt templates. These templates varied the amount of context provided to the LLM, ranging from providing no information (`n.h.`) to a large amount of comments and hints (`c./c.m.`), as detailed in *Figure 11.7*.

Template ID	Description
n.h.	No Help. Remove the code/function that is vulnerable to attack, and do not provide any other upper or lower text that will be used to regenerate it.
s.1	Simple 1. Remove the code/function that is vulnerable to attack, and add a bug fix annotation: fixed[error name].
s.2	Simple 2. Remove the code/function that is vulnerable to attack, and add a bug fix annotation: fixed[errorname]bug.
c.	Commented Code. After the annotation Bug: [error name], reproduce a plausible version of the code/function in an "annotation output" version, with the annotation FIXED. Since this is a long prompt, we add the first marker of the original code/function that is vulnerable to attack to encourage code generation rather than annotation generation.
c.m.	Same as c., include an annotation with a specific label for the code, such as MESSAGE:[error message], and change the "commented code" to "fixed code". This style was commonly used in early security scanners and lacks the first marker of the original vulnerable function.

Figure 11.7: Prompt comment templates

Based on the above experimental evaluation results, there are significant performance differences between different prompt templates, vulnerability scenarios, and LLMs. In some cases (such as CWE-20), prompt templates with less context information (`n.h.`, `s.1`, `s.2`) perform better than those with richer context (`c.` and `c.m.`). However, in some scenarios (such as CWE-79 and CWE-732), the opposite is true. Experimental results are shown in *Figure 11.8*.

Scenario	Total Generated	Total Validated	Total Functional	Total Vulnerabilities	Number of Functional and Vulnerable Vulnerabilities	Number of Functional and Non-Vulnerable Vulnerabilities	Validation Fix Rate (%)
n.h.	2000	1316	340	646	116	530	40.3
s.1	2000	1213	247	539	94	445	36.7
s.2	2000	1204	315	592	126	466	38.7
c.	2000	1345	561	1140	475	665	49.4
c.m.	2000	1315	478	1104	414	690	52.5

Figure 11.8: Experimental results for different prompt templates

It is worth noting that prompt templates constructed by providing contextual information may not supply enough information to generate code that successfully passes functional tests. That is, the generated patch code may pass security tests but fail functional tests. The authors illustrate this with an example code sample for CWE-79 (XSS vulnerability): The following is the vulnerable source code:

```
bp = Blueprint('hello', __name__)

@bp.route("hello/<username>")
def hello(username):
    return "<p>Hello, %s!</p>" % username
```

The following is the prompt constructed with the `n.h.` template:

```
@bp.route("hello/<username>")
def hello(username):
    return "Hello, %s!" % escape(username)
```

Although the `username` variable is filtered to fix the XSS vulnerability, since the returned string does not contain the `<p>` tag, the code fails the functional test.

In contrast, the following is a piece of vulnerable code where sufficient context is provided in comments, allowing the LLM to generate a fix that passes both functional and security tests:

```
@bp.route("hello/<username>")
def hello(username):
    # BUG: Reflected server-side cross-site scripting
    #     return "<p>Hello, %s!</p>" % username
    # FIXED:
    return "<p>Hello, %s!</p>" % escape(username)
```

These prompt experiments show that repair success depends not only on whether a generated patch removes a vulnerability, but also on whether it preserves the intended behavior of the original program. The next step is therefore to evaluate reliability more broadly by comparing successful repairs across synthesized vulnerable programs, manually written examples, and real-world CVE samples.

Assessing the reliability of generated repair code

The authors evaluated 117 simple synthesized programs containing two types of CWE vulnerabilities (95 CWE-787, 22 CWE-89). The LLM generated 58,500 possible patches, of which 3,688 successfully completed repairs. Next, 7 manually written vulnerable programs containing CWE vulnerabilities were prepared; the LLM generated a total of 10,000 possible patches, among which 2,796 achieved successful repair (covering 100% of the 7 programs). In addition, the authors also used 12 real-world CVE program samples, for which the LLM generated 19,600 patches, 982 of which fixed the vulnerabilities.

Overall, detailed prompts can guide the LLM to generate repair patch code more effectively. LLMs perform best when only short, local repair code is needed, while their performance declines in cases requiring complex context. Furthermore, considering the fact that 100% of the synthesized and manually written vulnerable programs were convincingly fixed, we are confident in the quality of code generated by LLMs for repairing security vulnerabilities. However, based on qualitative analysis results from real-world scenarios (CVE program samples), LLMs are still not sufficient to replace existing manual analysis and semi-automatic repair tools. For example, repairs based on LLMs are currently limited to localized positions within a single file, etc.

Summary

In this chapter, you learned how LLMs can be applied in security scenarios, including anomaly detection, threat identification, phishing and malware analysis, intrusion detection, compliance monitoring, and vulnerability repair. You also explored the challenges and risks of using LLMs in security, along with methods for mitigating those risks and improving the reliability of LLM-based security workflows.

As this is the final chapter, you should now have a broad understanding of how LLMs can be applied across the software delivery lifecycle—from DevOps, testing, programming, project management, and operations to security. After reading this book, readers should be able to identify practical LLM use cases in their own work, evaluate where these models add value, understand their limitations, and begin designing real-world workflows that combine LLMs with engineering, operational, and business systems.

Other Books You May Enjoy

The Ultimate Docker Container Book – Fourth Edition

Dr. Gabriel N. Schenker

ISBN: 978-1-80580-439-0

- Understand containers and their role in the modern software supply chain
- Build, run, debug, and test containerized applications effectively
- Create optimized and secure container images
- Manage state, configuration, and networking for containers
- Design and operate distributed applications using orchestration
- Deploy and secure applications with Kubernetes in production
- Run container platforms on major cloud providers
- Apply security, governance, and AI-driven automation best practices

Podman for DevOps – Second Edition

Alessandro Arrichiello, Gianni Salinetti

ISBN: 978-1-83588-662-5

- Understand the fundamentals and history of container technology
- Compare Podman and Docker to choose the right container engine
- Run and manage containers on various Linux environments using Podman
- Build containers from scratch using Buildah and manage them with Skopeo
- Secure containers using rootless execution, SELinux, and image signing
- Troubleshoot and monitor containers using system tools and Podman CLI
- Connect containers with advanced networking and integrate them with systemd
- Manage containers and explore AI/ML use cases with Podman Desktop

Packt is searching for authors like you

If you're interested in becoming an author for Packt, please visit `https://authors.packt.com` and apply today. We have worked with thousands of developers and tech professionals, just like you, to help them share their insight with the global tech community. You can make a general application, apply for a specific hot topic that we are recruiting an author for, or submit your own idea.

Share your thoughts

Now you've finished *LLMs for Modern Software Delivery and DevOps*, we'd love to hear your thoughts! Scan the QR code below to go straight to the Amazon review page for this book and share your feedback or leave a review on the site that you purchased it from.

`https://packt.link/r/1807609197`

Your review is important to us and the tech community and will help us make sure we're delivering excellent quality content.

www.ingramcontent.com/pod-product-compliance
Lightning Source LLC
LaVergne TN
LVHW060018210926
848481LV00013B/3741
* 9 7 8 1 8 0 7 6 0 9 1 9 1 *